W9-ASO-934

CITY GOVERNMENTS AND URBAN PROBLEMS

a new introduction to urban politics

City Governments and Urban Problems

a new introduction to urban politics

Demetrios Caraley

Barnard College
Columbia University

PRENTICE-HALL, INC., *Englewood Cliffs, New Jersey 07632*

Library of Congress Cataloging in Publication Data

CARALEY, DEMETRIOS.
City government and urban problems.

Includes bibliographical references and index.
1. Municipal government—United States.
2. Cities and towns—United States. I. Title.
JS331.C33 352'.008'0973 76-28327
ISBN 0-13-134973-2

Printed in the United States of America

10 9 8 7 6 5 4 3 2 1

Prentice-Hall International, Inc., *London*
Prentice-Hall of Australia Pty. Limited, *Sydney*
Prentice-Hall of Canada, Ltd., *Toronto*
Prentice-Hall of India Private Limited, *New Delhi*
Prentice-Hall of Japan, Inc., *Tokyo*
Prentice-Hall of Southeast Asia Pte. Ltd., *Singapore*
Whitehall Books Limited, *Wellington, New Zealand*

For My Mother
and to the Memory
of My Father

Contents

Preface

There are innumerable ways of writing about city governments and urban problems. In this book, the focus will be on two interrelated processes: how politics shapes city governmental decision-making and how shortcomings in city governmental performance are turning many large cities into underserviced, crime-ridden, bankruptcy-skirting slum ghettoes.

The book assumes that the core part of governing any city consists of making decisions about the content of its policies and programs. It further assumes that such decision-making is a political process, normally taking place in a context of conflict. The conflict typically involves rival coalitions of city officials and private activists who are supporting different positions and trying to impress their respective preferences on particular decisions. Once a conflict develops, the content of the eventual decisions is determined by the relative amounts of influence by the conflict's various participants.

The analysis of how "politics," that is, the competitive exertion of influence, shapes city governmental decisions has a fascination all its own for many students of city government. For this is the "game" aspect of politics that controls in the most immediate sense "who gets what, when, how?" But the outcomes of this play of influence also constitute the substantive programs and policies that have a heavy impact on how millions of people live.

With respect to city governmental performance, the book assumes that if present programs, policies, and trends continue, many cities, especially the larger and older ones of the East and Middle West, will experience a worsening of five key pathological conditions—the declining quality of city housekeeping services and amenities, the persistence of concentrated poverty and slum neighborhoods, high levels of crime, the erosion of city tax bases, and "white flight" and the drift of large cities toward becoming black ghettoes. Unchecked, these trends will make large cities steadily less desirable locales in which to live, work, play, or, for that matter, govern.

Chapters 2-16 examine various facets of how politics shapes city governmental decision-making. Chapter 2 analyzes the general nature of political decision-making. Chapters 3-7 examine the constitutional, legal, and structural setting within which city decision-making takes place with special attention being given to the increasingly more crucial role of the federal government. Chapters 8-16 explain how the leading categories of participants in a city's political process try to influence its governmental decisions. Separate attention is given to the characteristic resources, strategies, and tactics of city party leaders, mayors, city managers, councilmen, heads of city departments, city career bureaucrats, city trial judges, social and economic notables, interest group leaders, mass media elites, and city mass publics. The policy implications of the patterns described and the extent to which such patterns conform to a "democratic" governing of cities are examined throughout the analysis.

Chapter 1 and chapters 17-20 deal with the substantive conditions of large cities. Chapter 1 describes the large variety of city governmental programs that deliver services to, regulate the behavior of, and extract taxes from city populations. It also explores the nature of the urban problems with which city governments are trying to cope. Chapters 17-20 describe the kind of "slum ghetto" future toward which, I contend, many large cities are drifting and also the various obstacles—epistemological, fiscal, and especially political—that are preventing city governments from shifting adverse trends toward more benign directions. In these chapters there is a description of a more desirable future that I believe is possible for large cities and an explanation of the strategies and conditions that must prevail both at the city and national level if such an alternative future is to have any chance of coming about. I call this alternative for large cities the "healthy, multiracial" future.

Whether multiracial central cities and suburbs are more desirable than heavily black central cities surrounded by almost exclusively white suburbs is clearly a value-laden question. My own values include a strong commitment to the nation having cities viable enough to be one realistic choice for residence, employment, or recreation for substantial parts of the metropolitan population, whether white or black, or of upper, middle, or lower income. These values also include an equally strong commitment to families of whatever skin color having real choices open to them for living in cities or in suburbs without regard to their color. Such choices would, for example, permit black families to live either in heavily black areas where they will be culturally dominant or in multiracial neighborhoods where race will eventually be deemed an irrelevant characteristic.

This book has a "large" city emphasis, with "large" meaning a 1970 population exceeding 250,000. First, it is this size city that has been most written about in the political science literature, is most covered by the mass media, and for which census data is most complete in readily available form. Second, the combined population of the fifty-six cities of this size in 1970 was 42,226,000—or about twice the roughly 200 other central cities of metropolitan areas put together. It is also these fifty-six large cities with their surrounding suburbs that form the metropolitan areas containing over half the nation's entire population. Third, it is this size city that is experiencing most acutely the so-called urban crisis and about whose ultimate "governability" the most questions have been raised.

Acknowledgments

The first debt I wish to acknowledge is to the late Wallace S. Sayre. "Wally" was instrumental both to my becoming interested in the field of urban government and politics and to my deciding to write this book. He also read an early version of the complete manuscript and provided me with his usual helpful comments. Other friends and colleagues who were generous enough to read and offer constructive criticism on part or all of the manuscript are Bernard Barber, Flora S. Davidson, Mary Ann Epstein, Bruce Feld, Gerald Finch, Ira Katznelson, Louis Maisel, Astrid E. Merget, Frances Penn, Jeffrey L. Pressman, Inez S. Reid, Robert D. Reischauer, Wilbur C. Rich, Phillip A. Singerman, and Kathryn B. Yatrakis. Frances Penn, in addition, used her editorial skills to improve the style of many of the book's chapters. The Urban Center of Columbia University and the Barnard Faculty Research Fund awarded me various grants for release from teaching, research assistance, and typing. Mary Lou Maisel, Susan Escoffery, and Martha Bashford succeeded in deciphering my handwriting and typed different drafts of the manuscript. David Caraley, Flora Davidson, Francine Dobranski, Bruce Feld, and Susan Ogulnick helped me with various kinds of research. Susan Ogulnick also performed innumerable other chores for getting the manuscript into final form for the printer and through production. Stan Wakefield and Natalie Krivanek, my editors at Prentice-Hall, were helpful and supportive throughout. My wife, Jeanne, and my children, Christopher, David, and Anne, suffered patiently with the writing of this book and without an excessive amount of complaining, and for that and many other things, they have my appreciation and love.

D.C.

I

THE NATURE OF CITY GOVERNMENT AND POLITICS

1

The Roles and Problems of City Governments

Every day the governments of America's large cities carry out an extraordinarily wide array of programs and policies that have vital impacts on the lives of their citizenry. These governments provide various desired services, goods, cash, and available facilities. They promulgate and enforce restrictions and requirements on various kinds of behavior. They take away various valued objects: money in the form of taxes, charges, fees, fines, and penalties; property under powers of condemnation or "eminent domain"; and occasionally liberty, as when city governments imprison violators of their restrictions and requirements. Thus city governments act in their governing role as "benefactors," "regulators," and "extractors."[1] This chapter will first describe the variety of benefactory, regulative, and extractive programs currently pursued by large city governments and then proceed to analyze the major unresolved problems being faced by these governments in the 1970s.

WHAT CITY GOVERNMENTS DO

City Governments as Benefactors

Throughout this century, city governments have been benefactors by delivering the basic housekeeping services necessary to insure the survival as organized communities of densely concentrated populations rivaling in size

[1]This differentiation was suggested by Gabriel Almond's "A Developmental Approach to Political Systems," *World Politics,* 17 (1965): 183–214.

those of entire foreign nations. These services include fire protection; water supply; collection and disposal of garbage and sewerage; maintenance of streets and highways including the provision of street lighting; and public health measures for the prevention and detection of infectious and other serious diseases.

City governments have gradually come to provide various services and facilities that go beyond merely guaranteeing survival. These can be considered "amenities" which are intended, as Aristotle put it, to allow people in cities not only to "live," but to "live well." In this century, city governments have provided free primary and secondary schooling and libraries to permit and encourage personal development and a minimum of literacy. Lately some large city governments have also been making available free college and even graduate school education. And over the years city governments have increasingly taken on the operation of recreational and cultural facilities like museums, concert halls, municipal parks and playgrounds, swimming pools, skating rinks, and even ski slopes in an attempt to provide enjoyment and thus enhance the quality of urban life.

At the same time that city governments are delivering housekeeping services and offering various measures of amenities, they have had to deal more and more with a variety of intensifying and infectious social problems that have become disproportionately concentrated in spreading slum areas within their boundaries. The most serious of these problems include the interrelated ones of poverty, unemployment, blighted and dilapidated housing, racial discrimination, drug addiction, juvenile delinquency, and crime. To cope with this "tangle of pathology" found in their slums, city governments have been providing welfare payments and food-stuffs for the needy, day care centers, free or low-cost medical and hospital care and mental health clinics, slum clearance projects, low rental, and otherwise subsidized housing, "enrichment" programs to help disadvantaged children in primary and secondary school grades, job training programs to improve employment skills, and other services to improve job opportunities, such as incentives to encourage new businesses to locate in the city and old businesses to stay and expand.

Finally, city governments have always distributed less tangible, but at times no less important, "benefactions" in the form of honors, awards, prizes, the declaration of commemorative days, and other "recognitions" for a multiplicity of individuals and groups.

City Governments as Regulators

In the course of providing necessities and amenities and coping with social problems, large city governments make and enforce a wide variety of regulations prohibiting or requiring certain kinds of behavior. The most elemental form of regulation is their enforcement of state criminal laws and local ordinances that declare illegal certain kinds of conduct—like homicide, assault, theft, etc.—that are intrinsically injurious to life, person, and property. This "regulatory" role of city governments is necessary to protect their citizens against the increasing risk of harm from illegal violence, whether it be of the street crime variety or, more sporadically, from disruptions, riots, and guerilla type warfare. Protection of life and property is, of course, a basic function of all governments. For if any community is to escape self-destruction from that "war . . . of every man, against every man," that the sixteenth century British political philosopher Thomas Hobbes forcefully described, where men live in "continual fear, and danger of violent death; and the life of man [is] solitary, poor, nasty, brutish, and short,"[2] violence must be ruled out as a means for settling the disputes that inevitably arise when people with sharply diverse life-styles, beliefs, and values live in close proximity.

In the large complex communities represented by our big cities, a great many types of behavior in addition to the "standard crimes" against persons and property have become regarded as harmful to human health, safety, welfare, or morals. They too, therefore, have become objects of regulation. Large city governments thus currently prohibit, require certain standards to be met, or otherwise regulate such activities as:

Selling in restaurants and markets of unsanitary, spoiled, adulterated, or misbranded food;

Business frauds like misleading or false advertising;

Maintenance of tenement (i.e., apartment) buildings or factories in unheated, unsanitary, infested, or hazardous conditions;

The methods of building construction;

The methods of daily business or hours of operation of employment services, private nursing homes, dance halls, coffee houses, parking lots, taxi cabs, private garbage collection services;

Parking and traffic patterns;

Emission into the air of smoke, and other chemicals and pollutants;

Pollution of waterways;

Discrimination because of race, religion, ethnic descent, or sex in job hiring or renting or selling property;

Types of businesses and hours of operation to be allowed on Sundays;

The physical and aesthetic development of the city and of its different neighborhoods by means of master plans, zoning codes, and other land use restrictions.

[2]*Leviathan,* pt. 1, chap. 13.

City Governments as Extractors

One of the great tragedies of human existence is that "nothing," as Shakespeare's King Lear explained to his daughter Cordelia, "comes of nothing." This is true for city governments as much as it is for individuals. The operational consequence of this dictum is that city governments must extract the massive money cost of providing services and other benefactions and of regulating the behavior of the citizenry from that self-same citizenry. (Or, if possible, as will be explained later, monies may be extracted from some obliging other level of government.) The amount of money that must be extracted, furthermore, grows larger every year as the cost of delivering even a constant level of services spirals because of constant increases in the salaries of employees, in costs of supplies, in maintaining and rebuilding deteriorating physical plants, and as city governments take on a seemingly ever-expanding range of functions.

City governments' most visible and widespread form of extraction is, of course, taxation (see Figure 1–1). The single largest chunk of revenue raised by the largest city governments is from taxes on property. The next most important source of revenue is typically the general sales tax or some kind of city income, earnings or payroll tax. Although not even approaching the magnitude of revenues collected by these so-called broad based taxes—i.e., property, sales, or income taxes—the typical large city governments also raise substantial amounts by imposing "nuisance taxes" on many or all of the following:

Utility company, bank, or general business gross receipts
Cigarettes
Theater tickets
Gasoline and other motor fuel sales
Stock transfers (for cities lucky enough to have stock exchanges)
Transient hotel room occupancies
Automobile use
Conveyances of real estate
Renting of commercial property.

City governments also extract money by imposing "user charges" for the provision of certain of its services and the "use" of some of its facilities. Examples of such user charges are the price of admission to zoos, recreational facilities or museums; bridge or tunnel tolls; bus or subway fares; rentals from public housing; sewer "rentals"; charges for water supply; and charges for hospital care. City governments also raise money through the "fees" they require for various franchises, licenses, and permits. These franchises, licenses, and special permits are essentially permissions—

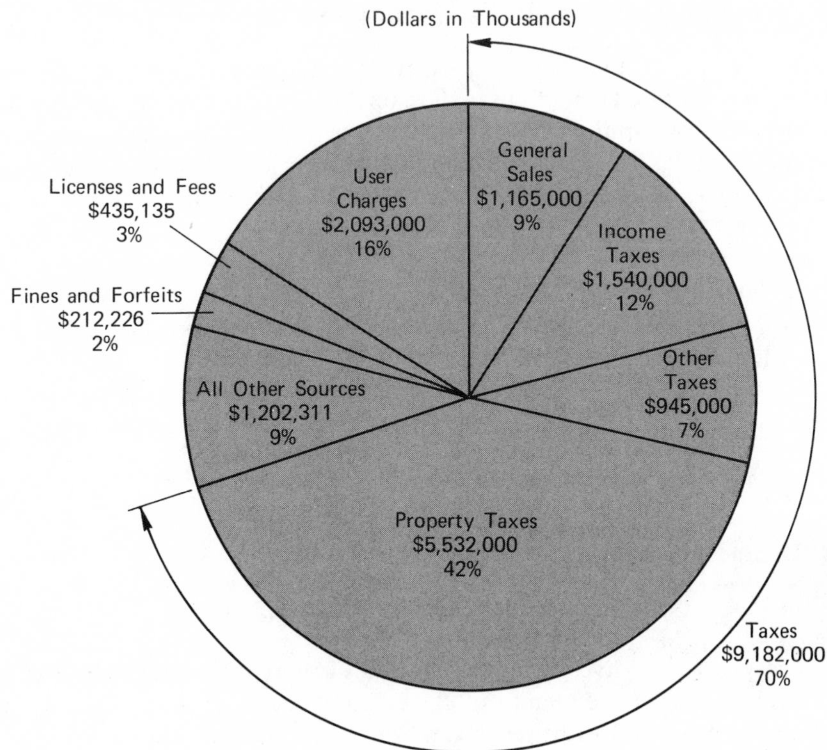

Figure 1-1 Revenue from own sources by type for large-city governments, fiscal 1973-74 (cities of over 300,000 in population, excluding Washington, D.C).

Source: Calculated from U.S. Bureau of the Census, *City Government Finances in 1973-74.*

sometimes exclusive permissions as in the case of some franchises—to engage in an activity that would otherwise be prohibited. Examples of activities that are licensed or for which a franchise or special permit is required include operating taxi-cabs or bus lines, constructing or demolishing buildings, and engaging in various kinds of businesses or trades.

Still another form of money extraction is the fines and penalties big city governments collect for the violations of their regulations, ordinances, and statutes. And in the case of the more serious violations, city governments also extract people's liberty through the incarceration of offenders. Finally, city governments forcefully extract private property from its owners through the power of "eminent domain," when that property is declared necessary for a public purpose and the owner is compensated for its monetary value.

MAJOR PROBLEMS FOR CITY GOVERNMENTS

Serious shortcomings in the performance of these roles of city governments have allowed conditions to develop that are referred to as the "urban crisis" and have spurred questions about whether the large city has become "ungovernable." The urban conditions or problems that are most commonly regarded as the major indicators of the "ungovernability" of large cities are:

The decline in the quality of their housekeeping services and amenities
The persistence in them of concentrated poverty and slum neighborhoods
The high levels of crime taking place
The erosion of their tax bases
White flight and their drift toward becoming black ghettoes.

Decline in the Quality of Housekeeping Services and Amenities

Few people who live, work, or visit large cities deny that there has been a general decline in the quality of their housekeeping services. This is the result of these services being chronically underfinanced and understaffed and, increasingly in recent years, being interrupted by strikes. Traffic congestion seems to be getting worse; the streets appear dirtier and more cluttered with abandoned cars; mass transit facilities like subways, buses, and commuter railroads are also dirtier as well as being less reliable and subject to more accidents and delays; abandoned housing is left undemolished; parts of the city's own physical plant like hospitals, prisons, school buildings, and garages are deteriorating and overcrowded; city equipment, such as garbage trucks, is insufficient and often in disrepair.

There is some argument about whether this decline in housekeeping services is a decline in some absolute sense or whether it is simply perceived as such because of a steady rise in expectations about acceptable levels of service. In most of the older cities of the East and Midwest, the decline seems to be real enough. But whether the decline is absolute or only apparent in the light of rising expectations is irrelevant with respect to the city's being perceived as a less attractive place. It is how people see the city that will determine whether they will want to live, work, or play there if they have other choices or whether they will make demands for new governmental policies to change the situation.

It may seem paradoxical to claim that city housekeeping services are

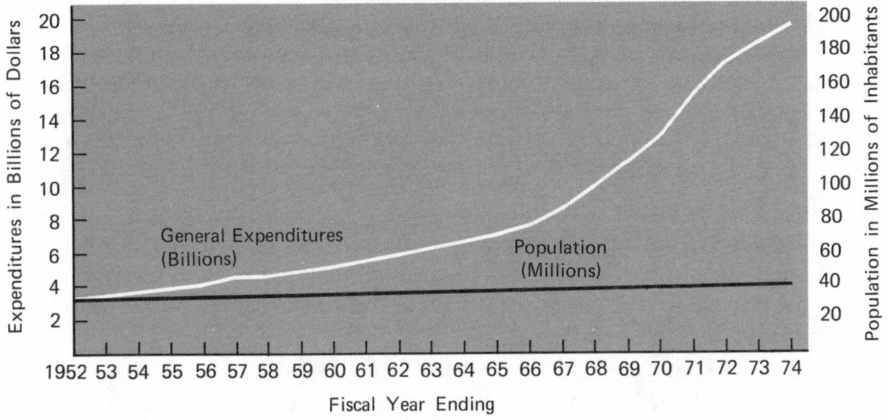

Figure 1-2 City government general expenditures and population for large cities, 1952-74 (Cities of over 300,000 in population excluding Washington, D.C.).

Source: Calculated from U.S. Bureau of the Census, City Government Finances, 1951-52 to 1973-74.

declining in quality, since city expenditures have been steadily climbing[3] while the size of the populations of most large cities has remained relatively stable or declined (see Figure 1–2). But the answer is that employees' salaries (including pension benefits) have also been rising rapidly as a result of both the greater bargaining power of civil service unions and inflation. The work output of each employee has remained steady or even been decreasing due to shorter hours, improved vacations, and other fringe benefits. Plant and equipment have been getting older while being subjected by the changed population in large cities to more intensive and harder use, thus requiring larger sums just for maintenance, repair, and replacement of existing capacity. The price of standard products keeps rising. Accordingly, the cost of delivering a particular unit or level of service has been getting more expensive all the time. The extra funds that can be spent each year by city governments, therefore, seldom cause any visible improvement in the quality of performance. At most they simply allow the city to conduct holding actions against any rapid worsening of services or deterioration of facilities.

[3]Throughout this book, unless stated otherwise, financial statistics will be given for cities exceeding 300,000 in population, but excluding Washington, D.C. The U.S. Bureau of the Census series *City Government Finances* restricts its detailed financial reporting to this population size of cities, while Washington, D.C., is excluded because of its unique status: it is not part of any state and as the nation's capital, it has a special relationship to the federal government.

With respect to the quality of upkeep of "amenities" like parks, zoos, museums, libraries, and botanical gardens, cities have been even less successful than in housekeeping matters. Because such amenities are commonly defined as "less essential" or of "lower priority" than standard housekeeping services, slum- and poverty-related programs, or law enforcement efforts, amenities are the most vulnerable targets in competition for scarce dollars during budgetary crunches. As a result, not only is sufficient additional money not made available to improve their quality, but recreational and cultural facilities have had such small increases in many cities or even been made to absorb cuts that the result has been sharply curtailed hours and days of operation.

Strikes of city civil service workers are, as will be explained, almost everywhere illegal. And up to ten years ago strikes were in fact infrequent or nonexistent, especially by uniformed forces like police or firemen. But during the last decade strikes by municipal workers stopped the operation of public schools, garbage collections, transit facilities, welfare services and municipal hospitals in various cities, and not even police and fire departments have been free of brief "job actions," threats of more serious strikes, feigned mass illnesses, and slowdowns.

Persistence of Concentrated Poverty and Slum Neighborhoods

Another sign of ungovernability is the failure of large city governments to eliminate, improve, or even stop the expansion of slum neighborhoods in which large numbers of poor are concentrated. These slum poor are primarily black, but in certain cities they include sizable numbers of Puerto Ricans (e.g., New York), Mexican-Americans (e.g., Denver, El Paso, Houston, Los Angeles, San Antonio, San Diego), and Appalachian whites (e.g., Chicago). Many of the buildings they live in are overcrowded, dilapidated, and unsafe. Foul-smelling, garbage-strewn alleys, yards, and hallways and infestations of rodents are common sights. The buildings may lack heat or operating plumbing. Large proportions of the men living in these slum neighborhoods are without jobs or with jobs that do not pay enough to support a family. As long ago as 1968, the Kerner Commission found that in the worst neighborhoods up to 91 percent of the housing units were dilapidated, up to 9.3 percent of the working force was unemployed, and up to an additional 23 percent of the work force was underemployed.[4] There are many families headed by women who, with their children, are completely dependent for sustenance on welfare payments. Large numbers

[4]United States National Advisory Commission on Civil Disorders, *Report* (New York: Bantam, 1968), pp. 257, 469 (hereinafter cited as *Kerner Commission Report*).

of children in these neighborhoods find it difficult to acquire the most fundamental skills of literacy in school and eventually "drop out"; thus they remain unskilled and largely unemployable. The use of hard drugs is rampant and there is an extremely high rate of juvenile delinquency and crime. The Kerner Commission described the social atmosphere that pervades these slum neighborhoods as that of a "jungle":

> With the father absent and the mother working, many ghetto children spend the bulk of their time on the streets—the streets of a crime-ridden, violence-prone, and poverty-stricken world. The image of success in this world is not that of the "solid citizen," the responsible husband and father, but rather that of the "hustler" who takes care of himself by exploiting others. The dope sellers and the numbers runners are the "successful" men because their earnings far outstrip those men who try to climb the economic ladder in honest ways.
> . . . Under these circumstances, many adopt exploitation and "hustle" as a way of life, . . .
> [This] unemployment and family disorganization generates a system of ruthless, exploitative relationships within the ghetto. Prostitution, dope addiction, casual sexual affairs, and crime create an environmental jungle characterized by personal insecurity and tension.[5]

In recent years, an additional problem in such slums has been created by numbers of buildings being "abandoned" by their owners. Some of these buildings have families continuing to live there without paying rent or receiving services while other structures have become completely vacated, vandalized, and stripped of fixtures like water heaters, plumbing, and wiring. These gutted buildings become loci of criminal activity and are often set fire to. Abandonment has in the past decade contributed significantly to the shrinkage of available, low-rental housing in ghetto areas and has stimulated the flight to safer, less unattractive neighborhoods by black working- and middle-class families. Abandonment has increased the speed by which neighborhoods are turning into slums, for even a single abandoned building in a particular block can render it threatening enough to cause anyone who can afford rent the rent to flee to safer neighborhoods. Winston Moore, Charles P. Livermore, and George F. Galland, Jr., have described how in a short span of years, the Woodlawn section of Chicago's black ghetto saw a population decline of almost half. "Between 1965 and 1971," they reported, "the city demolished over 400 Woodlawn [abandoned] buildings. Lately the city has been demolishing at a rate of 500

[5]*Ibid.*, p. 262.

dwelling units a year in Woodlawn, and currently has a demolition backlog there of over 1500.'' The authors warn that:

> It is taking less and less time for neighborhoods to collapse . . . [The] black lower-class may wear out one neighborhood after another at a pace unimaginable a few years ago.[6]

There are those who argue that large cities have always contained slums and poor people living in them and that therefore the present situation is in no sense very serious.[7] Whether or not large numbers of human beings living in slum poverty is considered a serious problem depends, of course, on an individual's personal values. There are, however, factual distinctions between the slum poverty of past decades and that of the present. First, life in slum neighborhoods used to be a temporary situation for much of its population, restricted usually to a single generation of the newest immigrant wave. Opportunities were available for moving out of the slum to better neighborhoods as a family improved its economic position. Now, because many slum families are black, they become trapped in slum neighborhoods. This results from two factors: One is a shortage of black neighborhoods that are slum-free and to which black families can move who modestly improve their incomes and raise their living standards and cultural levels but do not yet achieve solid middle-class status. Another factor is discriminatory renting and selling practices that keep such black families out of better neighborhoods far from the slum if those neighborhoods are white.

Current slum poverty is also self-perpetuating because many of the black families lack stable male wage earners, and thus, instead of being able to improve their economic position, they pass on from one generation to the next the pattern of living in a female-headed household dependent on welfare payments. This cycle of dependency becomes a permanent way of life and as these low income black women without husbands tend to have numerous children, this part of the poor population is increasing rather than contracting or being self-limiting. Government statistics indicate that contrary to general trends showing a decrease in poverty over the years 1957–1972, the number of poor persons in households headed by black women actually increased by 53 percent, from 2.8 million to 4.3 million.[8]

Another way of explaining why this part of the poverty population is not decreasing is that a substantial proportion not only has low income, but also

[6]"Woodlawn: The Zone of Destruction," *The Public Interest,* Winter 1973, pp. 45, 54.

[7]See Edward C. Banfield, *The Unheavenly City* (Boston: Little, Brown, 1970); and Banfield, *The Unheavenly City Revisited* (Boston: Little, Brown, 1974).

[8]U.S. Bureau of the Census, *Statistical Abstract of the United States, 1974* (Washington, D.C.: U.S. Government Printing Office, 1974), Table 635, p. 392. In 1972 a nonfarm family of four was considered poor if its annual income fell below $4275. Ibid., Table 632, p. 390.

lives in what has been called a "culture of poverty." Not having a father with a steady, well-paying job to model themselves after, the children fail to learn the habits of mind and action that would enable them to become self-sustaining members of society. Instead, they develop attitudes of hopelessness and despair and engage in the same practices—juvenile delinquency and crime for boys, precocious sexual activity and illegitimate births for girls—that led to their parents' generation becoming trapped in poverty. As a result both the condition of poverty itself and the attitudes that interfere with being able to escape from it become self-perpetuating:

> Low wages, chronic unemployment and underemployment lead to low income, lack of property ownership, absence of savings, absence of food reserves in the home, and a chronic shortage of cash . . . [We] find in the culture of poverty a high incidence of pawning of personal goods, borrowing from local money lenders at usurious rates of interest, spontaneous informal credit devices organized by neighbors, the use of second-hand clothing and furniture, and the pattern of frequent buying of small quantities of food many times a day as the need arises.
>
> People with a culture of poverty produce very little wealth and receive very little in return. They have a low level of literacy and education, usually do not belong to labor unions, are not members of political parties, generally do not participate in the national welfare agencies and make very little use of banks, hospitals, department stores, museums or art galleries . . .[9]

And the self-perpetuating nature of the condition extends over generations:

> Once it comes into existence it tends to perpetuate itself because of its effects on the children. By the time slum children are six or seven they have usually absorbed the basic values and attitudes of their subculture and are not psychologically geared to take full advantage of changing conditions or increased opportunities which may occur in their lifetime.[10]

This culture of poverty is highly infectious and there are always large numbers of potential new victims close at hand. As a 1973 census analysis of "low income areas" in fifty large cities shows, although only 27 percent of the black population in those cities was below the poverty level, fully 63 percent of the entire black population lived in census tracts with a poverty rate

[9]Oscar Lewis, *La Vida* (New York: Random House, 1965), p. xlvi.
[10]*Ibid.*, p. xlv.

exceeding 20 percent and thus was subject to being influenced by its culture.[11]

The second major difference between past and present slums is that the presence of a sizable slum population in a big city was not in earlier times a major economic burden for a city government. At the present time, the cost of welfare payments and other poverty-oriented enrichment services and programs plus the cost of providing the extra intensity of housekeeping services necessary under slum conditions to maintain the level of quality now demanded in the slums—a level that earlier generations of slumdwellers neither expected nor received—this cost is astronomical and constantly increasing. One consequence is that even the current programs and housekeeping services, which do little to eliminate slum conditions, place a drain on the city's budget that prevents adequate financing of housekeeping services and amenities and more adequate police protection in nonslum areas of the city.

High Levels of Crime

Opinion surveys suggest that what many people consider to be the most critical evidence of the ungovernability of large cities is the high levels of crime that exist in them.[12] Over the past decade the kind of crime that has been of major concern includes both those acts committed by individuals, such as various forms of street robberies and assaults, and mass violence like riots, lootings, and large forcible demonstrations.

Just as with the question of deterioration of housekeeping services, there is some disagreement about whether the greatly increased fear of crime is justified by the amount of crime that actually takes place. The optimists tell us that our time perspective is too short and that the safety in today's large cities compares favorably with that of a hundred or even fifty years ago. What affects people's satisfaction with city living, however, is what they see as the trend of conditions within their own lifetime, and especially in the recent past. And this satisfaction is also affected by whether they see "live" alternative locales that are much safer. Since 1933 the Federal Bureau of Investigation has been collecting and publishing statistics yearly about the incidence of major crimes reported to the police. These have included homicide, forcible rape, aggravated assault, robbery, burglary, larceny of goods valued at fifty dollars and more, and automobile theft. The first four crimes are referred to as "crimes against the person" or "violent crimes"

[11]U.S. Bureau of the Census, Census of Population: 1970 Subject Reports, Final Report PC(2)-9B, *Low-Income Areas in Large Cities* (Washington, D.C.: U.S. Government Printing Office, 1973), Table 1, p. 10.

[12]See, e.g., Peter H. Rossi, Richard A. Berk, and Bettye K. Eidson, *The Roots of Urban Discontent* (New York: Wiley, 1974), chap. 4; and Floyd J. Fowler, Jr., *Citizen Attitudes Toward Local Government Services and Taxes* (Cambridge, Mass.: Ballinger Publishing Co., 1974), chap. 8.

since they all involve using or threatening to use force to injure or kill another person. The last three crimes are classified as "crimes against property" or "property crimes" since violence is not directly involved in their commission. (It should be noted, however, that burglaries pose the risk of a physical confrontation if the resident is at home or returns while the burglary is in progress, and so fear about burglaries generates fear not only about loss of possessions but also about the possibility of physical attack.)

The Uniform Crime Reports (UCR) for 1974 show that in that year both the absolute number of violent crimes and burglaries and the "incidence" of such crimes (meaning the number committed for each 100,000 persons in the population) was the highest since 1933—the year when the FBI began to publish its statistics and after which a majority of all Americans now living have been born. Furthermore, in the last decade, when the FBI statistics have been conceded to be more reliable than in the past, the rate of increase in violent crimes and burglaries has been the sharpest yet. In large cities, from 1963 to 1974, the incidence of willful homicides[13] almost tripled (272 percent increase), that of forcible rape more than tripled (324 percent), the incidence of robbery went up 406 percent, the incidence of aggravated assaults rose 218 percent, and that of burglaries climbed 261 percent.[14] And still further, since the FBI statistics include only crimes reported or otherwise known to local police forces, they sharply *under*state the actual amount of crime taking place. This is because many victims choose not to report their victimization; because police records may not be accurately kept; and because certain police forces systematically underreport known crimes in order to make their performance records look better. In 1967 the President's Commission on Law Enforcement and the Administration of Justice (the Crime Commission) had the National Opinion Research Center (NORC) of the University of Chicago survey 10,000 households to ask whether anyone in that household had been a victim of a crime in the previous year. Additional surveys were conducted by other opinion-seeking organizations in a number of high and medium crime rate precincts of Washington, D.C., Chicago, and Boston. All of these surveys showed that the actual crime rate was several times that reported in the UCR. The amount of personal injury crime reported to the NORC was almost twice the UCR rate, and the amount of burglary more than three times.[15] The Crime Commission's other surveys presented evidence indicating that even the NORC rates probably under-

[13]Defined as murder and nonnegligent homicide.

[14]U.S. Department of Justice, Federal Bureau of Investigation, *Uniform Crime Reports for the United States,* 1962–1974.

[15]U.S. President's Commission on Law Enforcement and the Administration of Justice, *The Challenge of Crime in a Free Society* (Washington, D.C.: U.S. Government Printing Office, 1967), pp. 20–22.

estimated the actual amount of crime. In 1974 the Justice Department's Law Enforcement Assistance Administration released studies based on census surveys showing that in thirteen large cities the ratio of unreported crimes to reported crimes ranged from 1.4 in Newark to 5.1 in Philadelphia; the unweighted average of unreported to reported crimes for all thirteen cities was 2.6.[16]

Despite the imperfection of the UCR data with respect to reflecting exact numbers, there can be no doubt about the trend. Not only is the risk of becoming a victim of a violent crime or of a burglary higher in recent years than at any time in the past two generations, but the upward trend since 1963 —the more recent past—has been sharper than the upward trend over the longer run.

The reason that crime is considered to be evidence of ungovernability of large cities in particular is that these cities have a disproportionately larger share of crime than their population justifies, making the risk of victimization there much higher than the national average (Figure 1–3). In 1974, for example, while the fifty-eight cities with 250,000 or more residents contained about 24 percent of the population of all governmental units reporting to the F.B.I., they accounted for 53 percent of all reported violent crimes, 50 percent of all the willful homicides, 47 percent of all the forcible rapes, 66 percent of the robberies, 40 percent of the aggravated assaults, and 35 percent of the burglaries. The six largest cities with 1,000,000 residents or more contained only 10 percent of the population yet they accounted for 28 percent of all violent crimes (24 percent of all homicides, 21 percent of all rapes, 37 percent of all robberies, 20 percent of all aggravated assaults) and 14 percent of all burglaries. Put differently, the risk of becoming a victim of a violent crime in the fifty-eight cities of 250,000 or more residents was over twice (221 percent) as great as in the nation generally; and in the six largest cities, it was almost three times (272 percent) as great.[17]

Furthermore, the levels of violence in large cities no doubt appear unacceptably high because of the awareness of much lower rates in the surrounding suburbs. In 1974, the crime rates in the nation's suburban areas compared to those of the fifty-eight cities of over 250,000 residents were less than one-fourth for homicide, about one-third for forcible rape, slightly over one-seventh for robbery, about two-fifths for aggravated assault, and slightly over one-half for burglaries. As compared with the nation's six cities of 1,000,000 or more residents, the crime rates in the suburbs were slightly under one-quarter for homicides, one-third for rape, one-tenth for robberies, somewhat over one-third for aggravated assault, and slightly more than three-fifths for burglaries.[18]

[16]*New York Times,* April 15, 1974; U.S. Department of Justice, Law Enforcement Assistance Administration, *Crime in Eight American Cities* and *Crime in the Nation's Five Largest Cities* (Washington, D.C.: U.S. Government Printing Office, 1974).

[17]Calculated from *Uniform Crime Reports,* 1974, Table 14.

[18]*Ibid.*

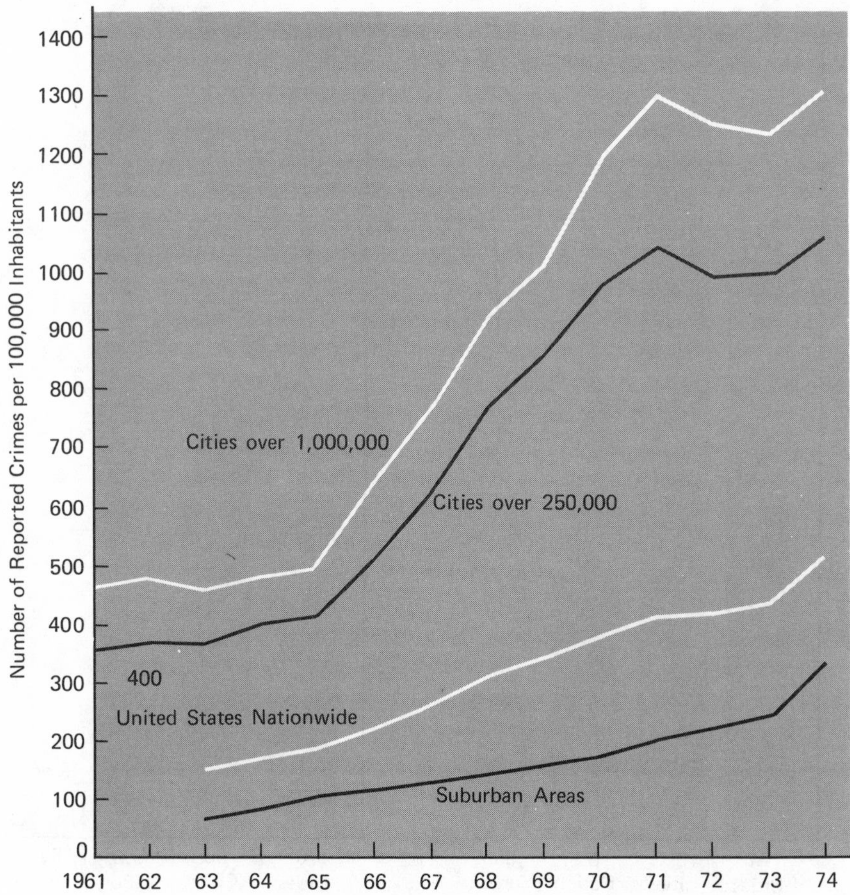

Figure 1–3 Violent crime rate according to type of local jurisdiction and nationwide, 1963–1974.

Source: Calculated from U.S. Department of Justice, Federal Bureau of Investigation, *Uniform Crime Reports for the United States,* 1961-1974.

Placing these statistics in still another framework, in 1974 the chance of being a victim of a violent crime was 1 in 199 in the nation generally, 1 in 361 in the suburbs, 1 in 90 in the fifty-eight largest cities, and 1 in 73 in the six largest cities. With respect to robberies, which probably engender the greatest anxiety about using the streets and other public places, the chance of being a victim was 1 in 425 in the nation generally, 1 in 1126 in the suburbs, but 1 in 154 in the fifty-eight largest cities, and 1 in 119 in the six largest cities (Figure 1-4).[19] And the 77,940 robberies that took place in New York City (with a population of some 7,895,000) represented almost one-

[19]*Ibid.*

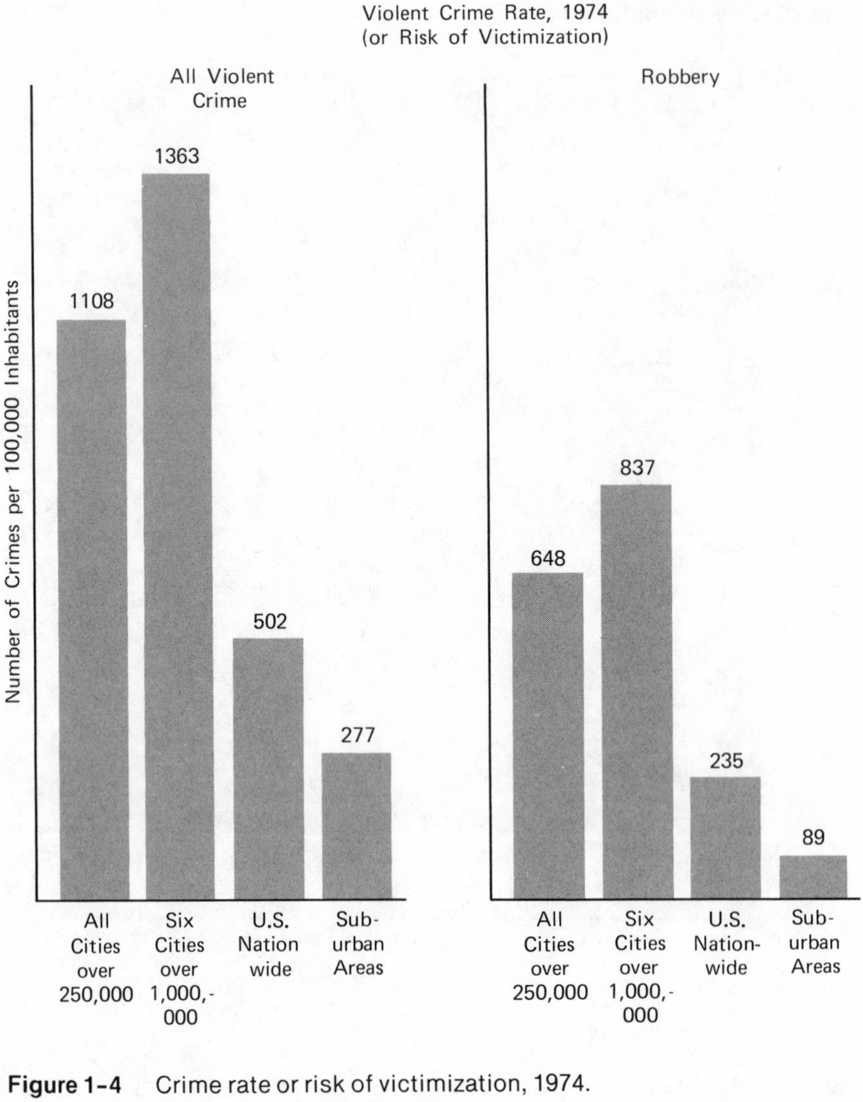

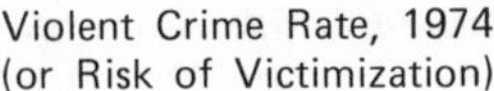

Figure 1-4 Crime rate or risk of victimization, 1974.

Source: Calculated from U.S. Department of Justice, Federal Bureau of Investigation, *Uniform Crime Reports for the United States, 1974.*

and-one-half as many as the 54,672 that took place in all of the jurisdictions in the nation's suburban areas that were reporting (which had a combined population of 58,643,000).

The incidence of violent crime in large cities is not evenly spread throughout their boundaries. The chief victims are people living in the lowest-income, slum neighborhoods. A study for the Kerner Commission found that the rate in a very low-income, heavily black neighborhood in Chicago was thirty-five times what it was in an upper-income, white neighborhood.[20]

[20] Kerner Commission Report, p. 267.

A 1973 study conducted by the New York City Police Department and the Rand Institute found that the robbery rate in the most crime-ridden residential precinct (one in central Harlem) was sixty-seven times that in the least crime-ridden (a precinct covering part of semi-rural Staten Island). Even within the island of Manhattan, the chance of becoming the victim of a robbery in the central Harlem precinct was eight times that in an upper-income, almost exclusively white neighborhood on the east side of Central Park, not more than thirty blocks away.[21]

These same studies also show that with the general spread of low-income neighborhoods in different parts of the city, with the mobility afforded by the automobile, and with greatly increased pressures on the police not to stop and question people who appear to be strangers in a neighborhood, middle-class neighborhoods, the downtown, and other smaller shopping and residential areas have also experienced sharp increases in serious crime.

Another aspect of the high level of crime in large cities is the riots that took place between 1964 and 1968. In those years there were large scale riots with associated looting, rock-throwing, arson and fire bombing, and some sniping with firearms that lasted two days or more in New York City (Harlem and Brooklyn), Philadelphia, Los Angeles (Watts), Chicago, Cleveland, Atlanta, San Francisco, Newark, Detroit, Cincinnati, Buffalo, and New Haven. These riots resulted in over one hundred deaths, thousands of injuries, and the destruction of hundreds of millions of dollars of property. The acts of violence during the riots were almost exclusively directed against the police and stores in the ghetto areas themselves, though there was talk and apparently some preparation by extremist black militants of starting citywide "urban guerrilla warfare." This presumably would have involved indiscriminate terrorist acts against white persons and property anywhere in the city.

There have not been any large-scale, multi-day ghetto riots since the summer of 1968. However, there have been occasional limited, "flash-fire" lootings and vandalism as well as sniping at firemen and police officers in ghetto neighborhoods. The increased propensity to use violence against police is demonstrated by the rising trend in the number of police killed from ambush without warning.

The high crime rate in large cities and the recollection of the mass violence of recent years have major consequences. First, city governments are pressed to continually expand force levels and expenditures for police in an effort to contain, if not reduce, the crime rate. And since police forces are labor-intensive, the cost of trying to strengthen the law enforcement efforts consumes funds that could otherwise go to improve housekeeping services and amenities or upgrade slum- and poverty-oriented programs.

The most serious consequence of the high levels of violence in cities is

[21]Computed from *New York Times,* July 30, 1973.

the fear they engender among vast segments of the urban population—a fear that erodes the basic quality of urban life. As the National Commission on the Causes and Prevention of Violence reported, national surveys have found that:

> half of the women and one-fifth of the men said they were afraid to walk outdoors at night, even near their homes. One-third of American householders keep guns in the hope that they will provide protection against intruders. In some urban neighborhoods, nearly one-third of the residents wish to move because of high rates of crime, and very large numbers have moved for that reason. In fear of crime, bus drivers in many cities do not carry change, and drivers in some areas are in scarce supply, and some merchants are closing their businesses.[22]

An earlier study, commissioned by the President's Commission on Law Enforcement and the Administration of Justice, found that in certain high crime districts surveyed in Boston and Chicago, 43 percent of the respondents said they stayed off the streets at night because of their fear of crime, another 21 percent said that they always used cars or taxis at night, thirty-five percent answered that they would not speak to strangers anymore, and 20 percent wanted to move out of their neighborhood because of their fear of crime.[23] A 1975 Gallup poll of residents of cities exceeding 500,000 in population similarly found that 45 percent of the entire sample and 77 percent of the women were afraid to walk in their neighborhoods at night and that 19 percent did not even feel safe at night inside their own homes. As could be expected from the differential distribution of crime among different neighborhoods, a larger proportion of nonwhites than whites were fearful. Indeed, during what was a period of large-scale unemployment and inflation, nonwhites and low-income persons asserted that crime was a bigger problem in their cities than either unemployment or inflation.[24]

Fear of becoming a victim of a crime encourages changes in behavior. Because people are afraid, most especially alone and after dark, of being in public places like streets, subways, parks, and parking lots, they cannot take full advantage of the specialty shopping or cultural and recreational facilities that a big city offers. They may stop visiting friends. They may stay away from events like PTA meetings. In short, more and more people sit behind locked doors and feel besieged rather than risk victimization by using the streets at night. And this fear provides strong incentive for those who can afford to do so, to move out of the city altogether and into the safer suburbs.

[22]U.S. National Commission on the Causes and Prevention of Violence, *To Establish Justice, To Insure Domestic Tranquility: Final Report* (New York: Bantam, 1968), p. 16.

[23]*The Challenge of Crime in a Free Society,* pp. 50–51.

[24]*New York Times,* July 28, 1975.

Eroding Tax Bases

Another problem for large city governments is their eroding tax bases. In their heyday, large cities had strong and vigorously expanding tax bases. This advantageous position was derived from the fact that expensive manufacturing, commercial, and residential properties, high volume retail sales, new construction, and holders of well-paying jobs were all disproportionately concentrated in such cities. And these are the primary sources from which local taxes are generated. Thus, as these sources of revenue were growing rapidly, large additional amounts of revenues became available automatically each year without tax rates having to be raised. And even if rates did have to be raised to provide for increased expenditures, the growing economies of large cities could easily afford the new extractions.

In recent decades, however, the tax bases of most large cities have either been growing very slowly relative to increased needs for expenditures or have declined even in absolute terms. For new construction, retail sales, jobs, and middle- and higher-income families have all been decentralizing to the suburbs. This decentralization of jobs has taken place in retailing, manufacturing, warehousing and wholesaling, and service occupations. A 1974 Bureau of Labor Statistics study shows that in ten of fourteen large cities, the decline in the total number of jobs between 1967 and 1973 ranged from .9 percent for the twin cities of Minneapolis and St. Paul to 19.4 percent for Detroit. (See Figure 1–5.) A 1975 study by the Congressional Budget Office found that in the five year period of 1970 to 1975, New York City lost some 369,000 jobs or about 10 percent of its 1970 total.[25]

The reasons for loss of jobs in most large cities are complex and interrelated. Jobs normally accompany the movement of population, and increasingly since World War II the movement of population has been out of the older central cities to private houses with yards in lower-density suburban areas. In the suburbs there has been greater availability of large, vacant sites for the spread-out, single story buildings preferred for modern production and warehousing activities. The widespread use of truck transportation, the availability of electric power, the telephone, and automobile-driving employees have for most businesses obviated past needs for a central city location near seaports, freight terminals, rail lines, steam power generating plants, and mass transit facilities.[26]

This weakening or erosion of their tax bases has forced city governments to constantly raise tax rates, increase their borrowing, and seek additional

[25]Congressional Budget Office, "The Causes of New York City's Fiscal Crisis," *Political Science Quarterly*, 90 (1975), 668, Table 4.

[26]Central cities have retained certain advantages for major financial institutions, corporate offices, advertising and law firms and similar business activities requiring close physical proximity to each other to facilitate frequent conferences and personal contacts; for small enterprises that require to be performed for them a variety of specialized services not easily found in the suburbs; and for very specialized services and one-of-a-kind shops that cannot survive without the customer density of a large city's central business district.

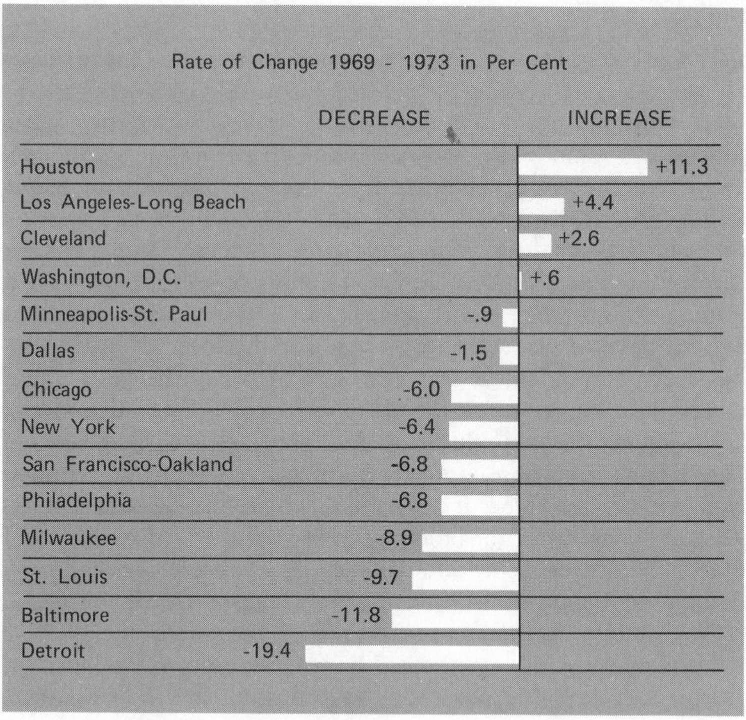

Rate of Change 1969 - 1973 in Per Cent

City	DECREASE	INCREASE
Houston		+11.3
Los Angeles-Long Beach		+4.4
Cleveland		+2.6
Washington, D.C.		+.6
Minneapolis-St. Paul	-.9	
Dallas	-1.5	
Chicago	-6.0	
New York	-6.4	
San Francisco-Oakland	-6.8	
Philadelphia	-6.8	
Milwaukee	-8.9	
St. Louis	-9.7	
Baltimore	-11.8	
Detroit	-19.4	

FIGURE 1-5 Employment in 14 selected central cities (rate of change 1969-1973, in percent).

Source: Bureau of Labor Statistics.

state and federal aid in order to meet the steadily increasing costs of providing services, amenities, antislum and crime protection programs that are only holding steady or declining in quality. And in a vicious circle, the inability to raise sufficient funds because of this erosion of the tax base has caused large cities to become steadily less attractive to middle- and higher-income families and to businesses who see themselves paying constantly higher taxes for what they perceive to be a deteriorating physical, social, and economic environment. Thus, the stimulus is continuously strengthened for even more of this "low service-demanding" and "higher taxpaying" part of the population and economy to relocate to the suburbs, thus constantly causing a further weakening of the city's tax base, which in turn makes necessary still higher tax rates just to pay for the declining quality of services being received, and which provides still stronger stimulus for exodus to the suburbs, etc., etc.

White Flight and the Drift Toward Black Ghettoes

The families who have had the economic ability to move to the suburbs have been disproportionately white. Those families left behind because of relative economic inability and of discriminatory barriers against their buying or renting housing in suburbia have, on the other hand, been heavily black.

In specific numbers, between 1950 and 1960 some 5.8 million whites (12.7 percent of the total 1950 central city white population) left central cities of all sizes for the suburbs. Between 1960 and 1970 some 6.5 million whites (13 percent of the cities' 1960 white population) also migrated to the suburbs from central cities.[27] These aggregate figures for central cities of all sizes mask the even greater white exodus or "flight" from some cities of the largest size.[28] For example, among large cities that by 1970 had experienced the most dramatic-sized proportionate exoduses to the suburbs of their 1960 white population are: Washington, D.C. (40 percent), Newark (40 percent), St. Louis (34 percent), Cleveland (33 percent), Detroit (33 percent), Dayton (29 percent), Atlanta (27 percent), Cincinnati (27 percent), Birmingham (25 percent), Chicago (24 percent), Buffalo (24 percent), Louisville (24 percent), New Orleans (23 percent), and Rochester (23 percent). New York City had one of the smallest *rates* of white exodus for large cities—only 14.4 percent; the 956,255 people that percentage represents, however, exceeded *in absolute numbers* the white exodus of any other city.[29]

In the 1950s the massive white exodus from central cities to the suburbs was stimulated primarily by the "pull" of the availability in suburbia of roomier housing, yards with trees, and newer schools. Furthermore, the rising affluence levels of working class as well as of middle- and upper-

[27]The 1950 to 1960 figures for the white exodus are from the Kerner Commission Report, pp. 246, 250; and the 1960 to 1970 figures for the white exodus have been calculated from U.S. Bureau of the Census, Census of Population and Housing: 1970, *General Demographic Trends for Metropolitan Areas, 1960-1970,* Final Report PHC(2)-1 (Washington, D.C.: U.S. Government Printing Office, 1971) (hereinafter cited as PHC(2)-1, Table 1, p. 1-23, using the same assumptions as the Kerner Report. The terms "suburbs" or "suburban ring" are used interchangeably in this book with the "outside central city" (OCC) portion of "standard metropolitan statistical areas" (SMSAs). The Census Bureau defines SMSA as "a county or group of contiguous counties which contains at least one city of 50,000 inhabitants or more, or 'twin cities' with a combined population of at least 50,000. In addition to the county or counties, containing such a city or cities, contiguous counties are included in an SMSA if . . . they are socially and economically integrated with the central city." PHC(2)-1, p. 116.

[28]This is because they include the small increases in the white populations that took place in central cities of intermediate size and the fairly large increases in the smallest cities. PHC(2)-1, p. 12.

[29]*Ibid.,* Table 12.

income families coupled with the availability of government guaranteed long-term mortgages plus the almost universal ownership of private automobiles and the construction of new express highways made surburbanization feasible for large numbers. In the 1960s these "pulls" were supplemented by "pushes" from a central city experiencing deteriorating services with rising taxes, accelerated blight, mounting crime rates, and the steady expansion of black neighborhoods into previously all-white areas. An additional stimulus for white exodus in recent years has been the prospect, or reality in some cities, of long-distance busing of school children among different school zones in order to achieve "racial balance." Racial balance essentially consists of having in each school the same proportion of white children to black children as exists in the entire city-wide, school-going population.

As a result of this massive white flight to suburbia, large cities have been shifting steadily to a larger black proportion in their populations. The magnitude of this shift has been augmented by two other trends: heavy black immigration to large central cities from nonmetropolitan areas, particularly rural areas in the south, and a higher growth rate among blacks already living in large cities than among whites. This higher growth rate is a result of black women giving birth to more children than white women and of the black population living in large cities being considerably younger than the white.[30] The younger black population contains a greater number of women of child-bearing age and thus compounds the increase in the black population caused by higher black birth rates.

The combination of white flight and of black immigration and high growth rate has caused the black proportion in central cities of all sizes to increase from 12 percent in 1950 to 17 percent in 1960 to 21 percent in 1970. This compares to a nationwide black population that between 1950 and 1970 only increased from 10 to 11 percent. In terms of absolute numbers the growth of the black population in central cities of all sizes amounted to some 3,342,000 in the 1950 to 1960 decade and to some 3,190,000 in the decade from 1960 to 1970.[31] Table 1-1 shows the proportionate and absolute growth between 1950 and 1970 of the black population for the thirty cities having the largest black populations in 1970. In ten of the cities with over 250,000 in population—Baltimore, Chicago, Cleveland, Detroit, Memphis, New Orleans, Philadelphia, St. Louis, Birmingham, and Oakland—blacks constituted in 1970 between 30 percent and 50 percent of the population, and in three—Washington, D.C., Newark, and Atlanta—they were already in the majority. Although the overall proportion of New York City's black population in 1970 was only 21 percent, that proportion was higher in the city's

[30] See *Kerner Commission Report,* pp. 237–239; U.S. Bureau of the Census, *The Social and Economic Status of the Black Population in the United States, 1973* (Washington, D.C.: U.S. Government Printing Office, 1974).

[31] *Statistical Abstract of the United States,* 1974, Table 16, p. 17.

TABLE 1-1 Black Population, 1970, 1960, and 1950, for 30 Cities With the Largest Black Population

(Rank according to 1970 Black proportion of population. Numbers in thousands)

Rank	City and State	% Black			Number Black		
		1970	*1960*	*1950*	*1970*	*1960*	*1950*
1	Washington, D.C.	71	54	35	538	412	280
2	Newark, N.J.	54	34	17	207	138	75
3	Gary, Ind.	53	39	29	93	69	39
4	Atlanta, Ga.	51	38	37	255	186	121
5	Baltimore, Md.	46	35	24	420	326	224
6	New Orleans, La.	45	37	32	267	234	181
7	Detroit, Mich.	44	29	16	660	482	299
8	Birmingham, Ala.	42	40	40	126	135	130
9	Richmond, Va.	42	42	32	105	92	73
10	St. Louis, Mo.	41	29	18	254	214	153
11	Memphis, Tenn.	39	37	37	243	184	147
12	Cleveland, Ohio	38	29	16	288	251	148
13	Oakland, Calif.	35	23	12	125	84	48
14	Philadelphia, Pa.	34	26	18	654	529	376
15	Chicago, Ill.	33	23	14	1,103	813	493
16	Cincinnati, Ohio	28	22	16	125	109	78
17	Houston, Tex.	26	23	21	317	215	125
18	Dallas, Tex.	25	19	13	210	129	58
19	Kansas City, Mo.	22	18	12	112	83	56
19	Jacksonville, Fla.	22	23*	27*	118	106*	82*
21	New York, N.Y.	21	14	10	1,667	1,088	749
22	Pittsburgh, Pa.	20	17	12	105	101	82
22	Buffalo, N.Y.	20	13	6	94	71	37
22	Nashville-Davidson, Tenn.	20	19*	20*	88	76*	64*
25	Columbus, Ohio	19	16	12	100	77	45
26	Indianapolis, Ind.	18	21	15	134	98	64
27	Los Angeles, Calif.	18	14	9	504	335	171
28	Boston, Mass.	16	9	5	105	63	40
29	Milwaukee, Wis.	15	8	3	105	62	22
30	San Francisco, Calif.	13	10	6	96	74	43
	30 selected cities, average	32	25	19			
	United States, total	11	11	10			

*1960 and 1950 populations revised in accordance with 1970 boundaries.

Source: Adapted from U.S. Bureau of the Census, Current Population Reports, Series P-3, No. 38, *The Social and Economic Status of Negroes in the United States, 1970* (Washington, D.C.: U.S. Government Printing Office, 1971), Table 11, p. 17.

central core of Manhattan, the South Bronx, and Brooklyn; in fact the absolute size of the 1970 black population in New York—1,667,000—was larger than that of any other city.[32]

[32]U.S. Bureau of the Census, Current Population Reports, Series P–23, No. 38 *The Social and Economic Status of Negroes in the United States, 1970* (Washington, D.C.: U.S. Government Printing Office, 1971), Table 11, p. 17.

In addition, blacks constitute even larger proportions of public school enrollments than of the population generally. In 1970 the black proportion of public school enrollments ranged between 30 percent and 50 percent in ten large cities, and they were already in the majority in fourteen others. (See Table 1–2.)

The very great bulk of this expanding black population in large cities lives in all-black, ghetto neighborhoods.[33] This is because discrimination in the renting and selling of housing keeps black families out of white neighborhoods at some distance from the ghetto. Also if black families do succeed in occupying vacancies in white neighborhoods on the ghetto's periphery, when additional vacancies occur, whites typically refuse to move into them.

TABLE 1–2 Large Cities with More Than 30 Percent Black Enrollment in Public Schools, 1970

City	Percent Black Enrollment
Washington, D.C.	94.6
Newark	72.2
New Orleans	69.5
Atlanta	68.7
Baltimore	67.1
St. Louis	65.6
Detroit	63.8
Philadelphia	60.5
Cleveland	57.6
Oakland	56.9
Chicago	54.8
Birmingham	54.6
Memphis	51.5
Kansas City	50.2
Cincinnati	45.0
Norfolk	44.9
Jersey City	44.4
Pittsburgh	40.3
Buffalo	38.5
Indianapolis	35.8
Houston	35.6
New York	34.5
Dallas	33.8
Rochester	33.1

Source: U.S. Department of Health, Education and Welfare, Office for Civil Rights, "Fall 1970, Racial and Ethnic Enrollment in Public Elementary and Secondary Schools," (Washington, D.C.: U.S. Government Printing Office, 1971).

[33]Karl E. Tauber and Alma F. Tauber, *Negroes in Cities: Residential Segregation and Neighborhood Change* (New York: Atheneum, 1969).

Since almost all new vacancies thus become filled by black families, the neighborhood, and especially the public elementary school district, inexorably shifts toward increasingly heavier black occupancy. Then as a "tipping point" is reached, the remaining whites leave *en masse* and the neighborhood turns all black, thus still keeping the would-be mobile families trapped in the expanding ghetto.

The growth of the black population in large cities would not in itself pose any very great problems of governance if it had the same economic and social characteristics and life-style as the white population that it was replacing. If such were the case, the shift from heavily white cities to heavily black large cities surrounded by almost exclusively white suburbs (in 1970 the suburban population was 94 percent white) could be seen simply as an expression of preference for living in different kinds of locales, but this is not the case. The black population in large cities contains disproportionately fewer middle-and upper-middle class families and larger numbers of low-income, female-headed, multi-problem lower-class families than the white population it replaces. And it is this change in the socio-economic characteristics of the population of large cities that creates such massive demands for governmental expenditures. Such expenditures are necessary to provide income, social services, and intensified housekeeping to arrest physical deterioration of neighborhoods and to contain crime. The expansion of the black population in large cities also indicates that black families are not enjoying the same choices for securing housing in the suburbs as do white families with similar incomes and life-styles.

Because many whites incorrectly attribute to all blacks the life-style of lower-class slum-dwellers and also because whites, in Anthony Downs' term, wish to live in areas where they feel "culturally dominant,"[34] the perceived shifting of large central cities into black ghettoes works as an independent force to stimulate the exodus of white families out of the central city. This feeds back on the economic base, hastening its erosion, and also makes it extremely difficult to establish and maintain integrated neighborhoods and public schools.

DIFFERENCES IN CITY HARDSHIP

There are, of course, differences among large cities in the severity of their urban problems. Richard Nathan of the Brookings Institution has constructed a "hardship" index, based on the extent to which fifty-eight cities in 1970 were experiencing selected undesirable characteristics relative

[34]By "culturally dominant" is meant to have one's own "social, cultural, and economic milieu and values . . . dominate [one's] own residential environment and the educational environment of one's children." Anthony Downs, *Urban Problems and Prospects* (Chicago: Markham, 1970), p. 34.

to their surrounding suburban rings.[35] The index shows that most of the large cities (36 of 46) do suffer "hardship" or "disadvantage" and with varying degrees of severity. The cities experiencing the most severe hardship are located primarily in the eastern and midwestern part of the nation. The hardship index also shows, however, that a small minority of large cities (10 of 46) were either on a par with their suburbs or enjoyed degrees of relative advantage. These cities are almost exclusively in the "sunbelt" area of the nation's southern and western rim. The cities of over 250,000 population that according to Nathan's index were most seriously experiencing hardship are (in descending order of hardship with an index of 100 indicating parity between central city and suburban ring):

City	Index	City	Index
Newark	422	Boston	198
Cleveland	331	Milwaukee	195
Baltimore	317	Buffalo	189
Chicago	256	San Jose	181
St. Louis	245	Columbus	173
Atlanta	226	Miami	172
San Antonio	220	New Orleans	168
Rochester	215	Louisville	165
New York	211	Akron	152
Detroit	210	Kansas City	152
Philadelphia	205		

Those large cities that were experiencing the least hardship or were even enjoying advantages relative to their suburban rings were:

City	Index	City	Index
Tampa	107	Houston	93
Los Angeles	105	Phoenix	85
San Francisco	105	Norfolk	82
Portland	100	Nashville	77
Omaha	98	Seattle	67
Dallas	97	Memphis	55

[35]See Richard P. Nathan and Charles Adams, "Understanding Central City Hardship," *Political Science Quarterly*, 90 (1976), 55–56, Table 1. The indicators used in Nathan's index were unemployment, "dependency" (percentage of the population less than eighteen or older than sixty-four years of age), low education (percentage of population twenty-five years of age or more with less than a twelfth grade education), low per capita income, "crowded housing" (percentage of occupied housing units with more than one person per room), and "poverty" (percentage of families below 125 percent of the low-income level).

2

Political Decision-Making in Cities

The core part of governing any large city is the making and implementing of decisions about what its benefactory, regulative, and extractive policies and programs are to be. And the making of these decisions is largely a political process.

This kind of city governmental decision-making is political because it takes place in a context of disagreement and conflict, where various coalitions of individuals and groups support different, and frequently contradictory, positions about what the city government should do on the matter that is at issue. These coalitions normally include both city officials and employees with decision-making powers and private activists. City govermental decision-making is also political in the sense that once disagreement develops, the eventual decision is determined by the relative amount of influence that can be exerted by the opposing participants. Only one aspect of that influence is any technical or logical arguments demonstrating the superiority of either side's preferred position for furthering some mutually acknowledged, agreed-upon public interest. The term "politics" will be used in this book to refer to the competitive exertion of influence on city governmental decision-making.

Not all large city governmental operations involve political decision-making. Much of the activity of any large city government is the routine carrying out of previously established policies and programs. If conditions never changed; if everyone was already satisfied; and if people's expectations of what the city government should be doing remained the same, the "governing" of large cities could consist entirely of this kind of "administrative" activity. The job of even the highest city officials would then be to supervise the administration of ongoing programs to insure that they were executed at a satisfactory high level of efficiency.

But conditions and expectations do change constantly, and there are grave dissatisfactions in large cities. In response to these changes and dissatisfactions, decisions have to be made at various levels of city governments about whether existing programs should be continued or altered and what their level of funding should be. Decisions also have to be made about whether new programs should be established and, if so, about how they should be designed and implemented. Decisions are required about whether new facilities should be built and where they should be located as well as which existing ones should be closed down. Decisions must also be made about filling vacancies to appointive positions and, less frequently, about dismissing the incumbents of such positions or forcing their resignations. At intervals decisions have to be made about instituting changes in the structure of the city government itself—in the rules by which decision-making takes place and by which individuals are elected or appointed to office. The analysis in this book will concentrate on the politics of decision-making as the core process in city government. The politics of elections, appointments, and "restructuring" will be referred to only insofar as it becomes a means for influencing the outcome of such policy and program decision-making.

DECISION-MAKING STAGES

Formulation of Demands

The process of political decision-making begins when a "demand," "claim," or "proposal" is asserted for adding, eliminating, or changing in any way some ongoing city government distribution, regulation, or extraction.[1] Such demands normally arise when some individual or group experiences a "problem" and also perceives a "solution" through some kind of governmental action. One kind of problem consists of people feeling thwarted from their goals: Parents, for example, who want their children to get a good education but the schools they attend are not succeeding in teaching them; people who want to be able to walk the streets safely at night to go to stores or to theaters or to visit friends, but the risk of being assaulted or robbed prevents them from doing so; or "successful" black people with rising incomes who want to move out of lower-class ghettos to middle-class

[1]The following discussion draws on analysis in Robert Agger, Daniel Goldrich and Bert Swanson, *The Rulers and the Ruled* (New York: Wiley, 1964), chap. 2; and David Easton, *A Systems Analysis of Political Life* (New York: Wiley, 1965).

neighborhoods in a city, but discriminatory rent practices by landlords prevent them from doing so.

Another kind of problem involves a threatened interruption of a satisfactory state of affairs. Examples include people living in a house and neighborhood that they enjoy who are confronted with a proposal to build a superhighway through it; parents who are basically satisfied with their neighborhood schools being told that their children must in the future be bused long distances; or people experiencing a sudden drop in the level of any city government service—e.g., a fall-off in the frequency of garbage collections.

Problems are experienced not only when *conditions* change, but also when *expectations* change about what goals or state of affairs people are entitled to have. For example, two or three decades ago, most black people did not expect that they would receive completely equal treatment with white people with respect to deference, income, public facilities, housing, education, etc. Consequently, except for persons like the leaders of black civil rights groups, the discrimination and lower levels of service that most black people experienced were not perceived as a "problem" but only as a "given," fixed part of their reality. In the last three decades, except possibly in the hard core slum areas, conditions for blacks in large cities have improved, both in the great reduction of discrimination and in the improvement of their physical, social, and economic environment. But, although conditions have in some absolute sense improved, many more blacks consider them to be unsatisfactory and as problems demanding further remedial action. This is because black people's "expectations" of what they are entitled to have risen faster than the city government's performance.

Most demands for policy or program changes grow out of the desire to relieve *problems*. Occasionally, however, policy demands are generated by perception of *opportunities* to achieve new or additional goals or satisfactions. For example, a pond or a lake which exists in a neighborhood is already giving aesthetic satisfaction. At some point it is also seen as a "chance" or "opportunity" to provide a recreational service like ice-skating or canoeing and such a policy demand is made.

Policy or program demands vary both in the degree of their explicitness and in their specificity. Demands may be implied in general complaints about poverty or traffic congestion. On the other hand, the demand may include both an exact, explicit articulation of the problem or grievance and a specific proposed solution, such as the installation of a traffic light on a particular, dangerous corner or the replacement of an obsolete school.

Recognizing a problem, perceiving a government remedy, and asserting the relevant policy demand need not all be performed by the same person. That is, one set of individuals or groups may experience a problem. Different individuals or groups may have the knowledge and capacity to perceive or design a remedy for that problem. And still others may be in the best position to assert and press for the remedy's adoption. The individuals involved in recognizing a problem, developing a remedy, or pressing for its adoption may have positions inside the city's formal governmental institutions, like city officials and employees, or they may be private persons or groups.

Limits on Problems Generating Political Demands

Not every felt problem leads to a *political* demand. At any point in time, most people in a city share a dominant set of politically relevant cognitions, attitudes, and beliefs—a "political culture"—about what kinds of situations are appropriate or even possible to be dealt with by city governmental action. For example, a person may be severely frustrated by the length of women's skirts, feeling that they are too short or too long. Or he or she may be bothered that neighbors play Mozart and Bach instead of hard rock, or vice versa. But in no city is such a person likely to formulate a political demand that the city regulate skirt lengths or "zone out" a particular kind of music in a particular neighborhood. In the 1970s such problems would be considered "private" and not "public" and hence inappropriate for action by the city government.

The line between what is and is not appropriate political action is, of course, not a clear or unchanging one. Conceptions of what constitutes a "public" as opposed to a "private" problem change, in response to new ideas, new events, and new scientific discoveries. And because there are always some people who do not share the dominant conception, these changes in conditions and technologies provide opportunities to introduce policy demands that were previously construed to be outside the limits of what is appropriate. A half to three-quarters of a century ago, for example, welfare payments, low-cost public housing, mental health facilities, or other special services for the poor were thought not to be a city government responsibility. The dominant cultural values of the time considered poverty to be a private problem that had to be dealt with through self-help and extended families and by private charity organizations. Currently, the "tangle of pathology" associated with slum poverty is perhaps the city problem that places the greatest demands on its resources. Similarly, the cultural values of even less than half a century ago favoring "rugged individualism" precluded taking seriously proposals for the regulation of business operations except in the most exceptional circumstances. Those values have, of course, given way to new ones that accept massive intervention by the city government to protect the economy or the health or welfare of consumers, employees, or other members of the public.

How city governments have responded to the problem of air pollution is a good example of scientific and technological advances leading to changes in political demands. Fifty years ago, many people were already concerned with smoke pollution, especially in cities having factories with steel mills, like Pittsburgh. But because there was no technological means available then for controlling such pollution, political demands for dealing with the problem were not forthcoming. Once it became known that devices could be developed and installed to help control smoke pollution, the demands for regulation came. Progress in the various medical fields also brought demands for public health programs to protect against various kinds of epidemics. The effect of the state of technical knowledge on political demands has been summed up by Lasswell as follows:

> Although political movements begin in unrest, all social unrest does not find expression in political movements. Under some conditions, a community which is visited by plague may pray; under other conditions, the community will demand the resignation of the health commissioner.[2]

Official Consideration

The next stage in the political decision-making process begins when a policy demand or the existence of a problem likely to lead to a policy demand penetrates the city governmental structure by coming to the attention of some elected or appointed city decision-maker with the legal power to act. In large cities, key decision-making officials include mayors, city councilmen, city managers, commissioners who head the various administrative departments, bureau chiefs, and judges. Different policy demands can be directed to one of these various decision-makers or to their staffs. Consideration of policy demands can range from informal and even unconscious thinking about the advantages and disadvantages of a particular proposal, including at times an evaluation of various alternatives, to explicit discussions of the matter among a number of officials. At its most serious stage, consideration involves placing the proposal on a decision-making body's formal agenda for dispositive action.

Decisional Outcome: Adoption, Rejection, or Amendment

The clearest-cut decisional action on a policy demand is formal adoption or rejection. Formal adoption can take the form of city officials promulgating relevant charter amendments, legislation, executive orders, administrative rules or resolutions, or judicial decrees. Formal rejection can take

[2]Harold D. Lasswell, "The Measurement of Public Opinion," *American Political Science Review*, 25 (1931): 312.

place by voting down legislation or by promulgating orders, rules, regulations, or decrees that explicitly disapprove the policy change being demanded. Adoption or rejection of a proposal need not be complete, as proposals may be acted upon at the final stage in a modified, amended, or otherwise compromised form. And not all decisions are made in this explicit, formal way involving some discrete act. Negative decisions, especially, may involve the relevant city decision-makers simply never giving adequate thought and attention to a policy demand. Indeed, most policy demands are probably rejected in this implicit way, by failing to come under active and sustained consideration. Or even if a policy demand has been explicitly considered, a negative decision can take the form of city officials stopping further consideration and failing to take the additional steps that would be necessary for formal adoption without any announcement of that fact.

Less frequently, city governments also make positive decisions inexplicitly: For example, a highly placed city decision-maker may be aware that, unless he takes formal action to stop them, certain decisions will be announced or changes will be instituted, or objected-to practices will be continued by officials or employees legally subject to his control. Failure to act in this kind of situation constitutes tacit acceptance of the policy changes being made.

The distinctions among the first three stages of decision-making are primarily analytical ones. Admittedly, much of the time these stages also proceed separately in time and remain distinct operationally. But there are also occasions—the most notable being under conditions of crisis or emergency—where the stages involving perception of a problem and articulation of a demand or remedy, official consideration, and the actual making of the decision can all be so compressed in time as to appear to be taking place simultaneously.

Decisional Implementation

Most political decisions on the adoption of new policies or changes in existing policies and programs are future-oriented. That is, it is only the rare case where the policy change that is being demanded can take place coincidentally with the making and announcement of the decision itself. Typically, a promulgated policy decision is essentially a commitment that the city government will perform the future sequence of regulative, distributive, or extractive activity necessary for having that decision make an actual impact on the public. But for reasons that will be explained in detail in later chapters, these necessary implementary actions are not always automatically forthcoming. Broadly speaking, this is because subordinate city officials and employees that are responsible for performing these actions have means for undoing or reshaping a policy decision in the process of implementation. When we speak in this book of political decision-making, consequently, it should be noted that the term refers not only to that part of the process culminating in the promulgation of a decision, but also to the implementing actions that must be taken for it to have its intended impact on the future state of affairs.

THE INESCAPABILITY OF CONFLICT

At times particular policies being demanded of city governments are perceived by everyone as so clearly beneficial that they generate a consensus in their favor. They then go through the various decision-making stages and get adopted fairly automatically. And at times, policy demands are considered so generally injurious or unfeasible that these generate a "negative" consensus that causes them to be dropped without much or any cross-discussion. But most of the time, demands for major new policies or programs or for important changes in existing policies and programs are not evaluated in the same way by everyone and therefore generate not consensus, but conflict. Such conflict involves different proponents and opponents engaging in mutually obstructive action, one set trying to exert influence to bring about the adoption by the city government of the controversial policy demand and the other set trying to exert influence to bring about its defeat. These sets of proponents and opponents usually include both city officials and employees with decision-making powers and private activists.

It should be understood that conflict in city decision-making is not pathological. Political decision-making about the adoption of demands for remedying complex urban problems is not akin to some purely analytical exercise like geometry where to any stated problem there is always a single correct answer or solution on which all persons of good will and intelligence must eventually agree. Obviously there are individuals and groups in a city who have different occupations and businesses. They have different religious, ethnic, and racial backgrounds. They hold different social positions and have different sources and sizes of income. They live in different types of neighborhoods. They pursue different life-styles and adhere to different ideological convictions. And, even when they are city officials and employees, each may have different responsibilities and functions to perform. All these combinations of differences in position and outlook inevitably cause at least some of the myriad of people living in a particular large city to have different goals, beliefs, and priorities. Obviously those who, given their goals, beliefs, and priorities, anticipate that they could gain from a policy become its supporters, just as those who given their goals, beliefs, and priorities anticipate losing become its opponents, and conflict ensues.

Although all decision-making conflicts in large cities are fundamentally the same in that they involve opposed participants, there are three different underlying kinds of cleavage on which such conflicts can be based. These are disagreement over goals, disagreement over means, and disagreement over priorities.

Disagreement over Goals

Every policy demand in city politics contains explicitly or implicitly one or more goals or purposes that its proponents seek to achieve. The commitment to the goal or purpose can be because of direct personal attachment or, as will be explained, "by proxy." Decision-making conflict is based on goal-disagreement when the goals of the proponents of a measure and the goals of their opponents are intrinsically contradictory.

The goal, for example, of a policy demand for an "antidiscrimination housing ordinance" or for "scattered-site housing" is in the immediate sense "the promotion of racially integrated housing and neighborhoods." If individuals exist—and they do in every city—who are opposed to racially integrated housing and neighborhoods and are committed to the goal of "racial segregation," the foundation exists for a conflict based on pure disagreement over end goals. What one side wants is exactly what the other side does not. The goal of the proponents of rent control, to take another example, is to "keep rents low for tenants." The landlords who usually fight rent control measures want to keep rents as high as possible in order to maximize their income. Once again, this is a situation of pure goal conflict where the opposed sides are directly committed to maintaining opposite states of affairs.

Conflicts based on contradictory goals are seldom resolved by "more discussions," "getting the parties together," and "talking things out." For the implicit assumption in such an outlook is that "better understanding" will always reduce or eliminate the incentives for mutual opposition. But the fact is that there are in city politics many conflicts based on deep-seated, correctly-seen goal conflicts which no amount of discussion can eliminate. Indeed, under such conditions, face-to-face discussion between the parties may even exacerbate the conflict by demonstrating how well founded were the original calculations of gains and losses that led to the mutual opposition.

Disagreement over Means

Decision-making conflicts can take place in city politics even when the participants share the goal or goals to be furthered by a particular policy demand. For people can share a goal, yet still disagree about whether a proposed measure is either the best or an acceptable means for accomplishing it. This disagreement can exist because they don't have the same beliefs about the efficacy of the means—i.e., about whether the proposed means will actually bring about the goal that both sides want. And even if they agree that the proposed measure will work, they can still disagree about whether it will do so at as low or lower a cost as other alternatives. Similarly, they may disagree because they don't have the same views about who should enjoy the "side benefits" or bear the "side costs" that will almost inevitably be produced by any particular means.

Efficacy and Efficiency of Means. An example of this first kind of "mean disagreement" is the conflict over proposals for "guaranteed minimum annual wage" or "negative income tax" as a substitute for the traditional welfare system. The goal of the proponents of these new measures can be stated as "ending welfare dependency," that is, ending the vicious circle of families learning to live on welfare payments generation after generation and not being able to break out of the pattern to become self-sufficient members of society. The proponents claim that these new means of subsidizing the poor will remove the "stigma" of being welfare recipients and will therefore increase morale and the incentive to seek job training and actual work. It will reduce disincentives to gain employment by not subtracting total earnings from the size of the money subsidy provided by "guaranteed annual wage," as has essentially been done under the traditional welfare program. Some opponents of these substitutes for the welfare system do not oppose the goal of "ending welfare dependency." These opponents simply disagree that establishment of the new programs will have the benign results predicted. The opponents claim that if a minimum income is guaranteed to everyone without the necessity of applying for welfare payments, etc., even more people will stop working. The prediction of the opponents is, in other words, that the guaranteed income, rather than increasing incentive to work, will decrease such incentive, especially for those people holding jobs involving dirty, unsatisfactory work at a wage only slightly above what would be the guaranteed income. As long as these welfare substitutes are not tried and their actual results monitored and evaluated, there will be uncertainty and therefore continued disagreement over what would be the consequences of their establishment.

A decision-making conflict based on disagreement over efficiency can be seen in the example of a police commissioner of a large city who is given certain additional millions of dollars for the objective of "reducing street crime." This is a goal that almost everybody shares (except, of course, street criminals themselves) and certainly everybody shares at the planning level of the police department (again, except for corrupt police officials). But various police officials and units put forth different proposals for spending the additional money, based on differences in their beliefs and predictions of what the consequences will be. Some believe that the greatest impact from a given amount of additional expenditure will be made by putting out more uniformed police on walking beats. Others claim that uniformed police are not as effective as saturating high-risk areas with plainclothesmen who will catch perpetrators in the act. Still others argue that whether in uniform or not, foot police are wasteful of manpower since they can cover only limited territory and that the greater impact will be made by increasing the number of patrol cars, each of which can cover large areas. Since there is usually some evidence available to support each of these contentions and no conclusive evidence on the superiority of any, different factions can retain their different estimates, and the decision-making conflict over the most efficient use of manpower goes on endlessly in most big city police departments.

Distribution of "Side" Costs and Benefits. Aside from certain "direct" or "primary" benefits and costs that are an intrinsic part of a policy or program, any means also produces "side benefits" and "side costs" that are in some sense an undesigned or secondary by-product. Consequently, although the opponents of a policy demand can share the goal of the proposals and also agree on the efficacy of the means in question, they may want a means that will impose fewer side costs on themselves (or those with whom they identify) or confer greater side benefits or both.

For example, a new six-lane expressway is proposed to improve traffic flow and relieve congestion in a particular part of the city and some people oppose the expressway plan being offered. These opponents agree that relief of traffic congestion is absolutely necessary and they also agree that a new six-lane expressway is the most efficacious means of accomplishing the objective, as improving existing streets or mass transit seems unfeasible. What they disagree about is the exact location of the route—"in whose backyard" the highway will go. Both sides want a route that will give them the benefit of the greatest convenience and access but one that will be far enough from their homes so that they will not have to bear the side costs of the added noise, air pollution, and aesthetic unsightliness. Similar conflicts take place over the location of a whole array of new city facilities: Even though everyone concerned may agree with the need for a new facility, and in that sense share the same ultimate goal, conflict takes place as a result of spokesmen for different parts of the city trying to locate in their neighborhoods what are commonly defined as "good" projects like new schools or parks and trying to keep out of their neighborhoods "bad" projects like new prisons or incinerator plans or low-cost housing complexes.

Proposals for new city tax packages to raise needed additional revenues often produce classic cases of political conflicts based on disagreements over the allocation of side costs and benefits. Such conflicts take place among participants who all agree that raising more money is absolutely necessary and increased taxes provide the most efficacious means. However, they back different tax packages because of divergent beliefs about which people or businesses should bear more or less of the added tax burden.

Disagreement Over Priorities

Conflicts can occur even when all the participants share the goals of the policy and do not disagree about the means proposed, either on the basis of efficiency or allocation of side costs and benefits. This is because most participants in a city's political decision-making and the city government itself as an institution are committed not only to a single goal but to a whole array of goals. City officials, other activists, and members of the public may simultaneously want a reduction in street crime, an improvement in standard housekeeping services, and amelioration of slum conditions. But city governments all have a chronic shortage of funds, manpower, and facilities relative to all the program goals they are committed to promoting and are being asked to expand. This means that the establishment or expansion of any program will result in foregoing opportunities for establishing or expanding some other ones. Accordingly, an individual or group can oppose a policy proposal both whose objective and means are completely acceptable per se for the reason that its implementation will draw resources away from another program area to which these opponents assign a higher priority. Given limited "new" money in every city's "next year's" budget, should more of it go to improve slum conditions and relieve the desperate plight of those who live there? Or should services be improved in middle-class areas to try to slow down the exodus from the city of this segment of the population with high tax-paying capacity? If limited funds are available for improving transportation, should more or less go to express streets, or off-street parking, or to subways, or buses? These are the kinds of questions that arise in large cities to generate political conflicts based on differences in priorities.

Furthermore, political conflicts arise not only as a result of different priorities being assigned to different city governmental programs but also from different priorities being assigned to money being spent in the "public" as opposed to the "private" sector. Should more funds be extracted from the citizenry through taxes or should it be left in the private sector so that individuals, families, and businesses will have more to spend for self-defined purposes? Much of this conflict below the surface is between spokesmen for the low-income, low-taxpaying, and heavy service-demanding segments of the population and those who speak for the higher-income, lower-service demanding parts who would have to foot the tax bill. The latter, although perhaps not opposed in principle to expansion of services for the low-income part of the population, are opposed to having their higher income redistributed to others by means of the city's budget and tax mechanisms. But even on those programs which are not inherently redistributive—the expansion of universally used services or facilities like water supply, or sewers, or fire protection—the extra margin of benefit anticipated by such expansion may simply not be deemed worth the cost in increased taxes. Similarly, regulations admittedly effective for the promotion of common goals in the protection of safety or health—as in standards of cleanliness in restaurants or exhaust emission standards for automobiles or standards for discharge of wastes into waterways—may be opposed on the basis that the additional increment of protection to the public is not worth the extra financial cost needed to comply with the standards.

Conflicts over priorities do not involve simply money costs. It is sometimes a case of nonmonetary "private" goals that would have to be sacrificed in implementing the proposal. Thus increasingly in recent years, proposals for new superhighways are fought not on the basis of their opponents trying to change the location so as to reduce the side cost/benefit ratio to themselves but these expressways are fought with the claim of "misapplied priorities." It is argued that whatever the specific route proposed, the value of not further destroying important parts of a city, including its housing and parks, historic sites, aesthetics, character, etc., exceeds that of reducing traffic congestion.

A Mixture of Cleavages

Many political conflicts in large cities do not conform to any of the three types just discussed. Often particular proposals are fought because there are varying combinations of disagreement about the stated policy goals, disagreement about means because of uncertainty over whether a particular means will work or disquietude over the side costs being produced, and disagreement over how much sacrifice of other, higher-priority goals is being contemplated. And many conflicts involve much more highly specific issues than the examples given in the general discussion.

"STAKES" OF LARGE CITY DECISION-MAKING CONFLICTS

It was mentioned earlier that different individuals and groups engaging in political conflicts within large cities are motivated by different perceptions of what they stand to gain or lose by the adoption or rejection of a contested proposal. It is these perceived gains or losses that represent their "stakes" in the conflict. Most political conflicts in large cities take place over the following stakes: direct use of city governmental services or facilities; money; "ideological principles"; social, aesthetic, or psychological rewards or deprivations including power; public office; and "proxy" stakes.

Governmental Services and Facilities

The direct use of city services and facilities is obviously a key stake in urban political conflict. For the kinds, level, and quality of the particular services and facilities that the city makes available have a direct impact on the physical nature of people's surroundings, on the amenities they enjoy, and in the relief they obtain from oppressive social problems and conditions. As Sayre and Kaufman have explained:

> Groups and individuals strive to influence the city to institute new services in the welfare, mental health, and public housing fields. They seek help for the aging, centers for the care of children of working mothers, and assistance to more limited clienteles (such as the hay fever sufferers, by the destruction of ragweed). . . . There are campaigns to expand existing services—efforts to get new schools, new playgrounds, traffic signals and police crossing-guards at dangerous intersections, heavier police protection, more subway trains—and to prevent the contraction of familiar operations. . . .
>
> The quality of services is sometimes a bone of contention, too. How often will the sanitation trucks visit a given neighborhood? How often will a police officer patrol a particular street? How frequently will buses or subway trains operate over a route? Will a neighborhood have a full branch library with twenty or thirty thousand volumes and day and evening service, or a sub-branch open only twenty-five or thirty hours a week to administer a collection of four or five thousand books?[3]

The services or facilities may be valued because they would not be available from any institution but the city government or because the money cost of securing them elsewhere would be prohibitive.

Money

Money is obviously a vital stake that people fight about in city political conflicts. For almost every city governmental decision either directly or indirectly takes money out of somebody's personal or official pocketbook and puts it into someone else's.

[3]Wallace S. Sayre and Herbert Kaufman, *Governing New York City* (New York: Norton, 1965), p. 63.

One major set of decisions where money is the central stake concerns who will get the money a city government spends. In the first and most immediate sense, this involves decisions about the size of the budget to be approved for carrying on the operations of all the different departments, divisions, and other units that make up the city government. Both absolute size and the proportionate share of the budgetary pie that each agency gets often become the focus of conflict between the backers of a particular agency and those responsible for making the overall budget. The officials who draft the budget must balance the claims of all agencies against one another and against the resources that are available under the existing revenue structure (or a new one that they are willing to turn to and adopt). In the ultimate sense, conflict over spending involves decisions about the kinds and size of cash money payments that the city government will distribute to various individuals and groups in its population. Examples include the eligibility criteria for, and size of, welfare payments; salaries and other monetary benefits for present or retired city employees; the firms to use for purchase of goods and services the city government needs for its operation; what building contractors or landlords to favor when constructing buildings or leasing space for the use of different city departments.

The other major set of decision-making conflicts where money is the central stake is over how and from whom the city government will extract the money that it needs to finance its operations. Whether and at what rates property or income or sales will be taxed are of vital importance to everyone who is a potential target. Since each type of tax will bear most heavily on different parts of the population, each segment will normally try to shift the overall revenue-raising structure to taxes that will burden it the least.

Decisions about what business activities to regulate, what standards to require, and levels of enforcement affect the monetary well-being of many industries indirectly. For such things as minimum standards governing the cleanliness of restaurants or markets, or the method of construction of buildings, almost always raise the cost of operation and reduce the profit of those engaged in the particular business. Also, decisions to change traffic patterns by establishing one-way streets or no parking areas may redistribute business away from those firms that previously enjoyed easier access and transfer it to others in a more advantageous location. Businesses may profit from some kinds of regulations, such as when restricting parking on streets forces cars into parking lots and garages or the requiring of smoke-abatement and other air-pollution devices increases the volume of business for firms manufacturing that kind of expensive apparatus.

Finally, it should be noted that to the extent to which the services a city government provides are available for purchase privately, the services confer an indirect monetary benefit on their recipients. Conversely, if an individual either does not benefit from a particular new service or is content with the existing level of a service as opposed to an expansion, an addition or expansion of that service will confer an indirect monetary loss by redistributing part of his income to those who will be the direct beneficiaries of the service but not be contributing their full share of its cost.

Ideological Principles

Not all the anticipated gains and losses that motivate people to participate in decision-making conflicts concern tangibles like city governmental services and facilities or money. Both city officials and private individuals and groups can support or oppose proposals without perceiving any personal tangible stake involved in them at all and sometimes, even to the detriment of their economic well-being. That is, participants in decision-making conflicts often hold ideological principles about what is intrinsically desirable or undesirable or "right" or "wrong" politically. Their overall reaction may thus be controlled by whether a particular proposal coincides or conflicts with personal ideological principles. These principles may be general and thus relevant to evaluating a wide array of policy and program decisions, or the standards may be highly specific, and thus be applicable only to a particular subject.

For example, people in an upper-income group may support low-rent public housing or welfare programs—services they would never themselves receive but for which they would be taxed. Another example is homeowners whose children are past school age or who are in private schools and who support increased expenditures for public schools. In both these cases, persons are supporting a position damaging to their economic stakes because they think that "as a matter of principle, it's the right thing to do." Similarly, persons oppose policies such as birth control clinics, legal abortion, city-owned liquor stores, municipal lotteries, or off-track betting facilities not because they expect to profit financially or in any other tangible way by their opposition. These policies are simply offensive to their ideological beliefs about what kinds of activities it is "right" or "proper" for a city government to undertake.

Aesthetic, Social, and Psychological Rewards or Deprivations

There are other intangible stakes besides the "principled" or "ideological" ones. A proposal may be perceived as conferring rewards or deprivations that are aesthetic, social or psychological. Thus, a decision to construct a city facility in an area may be opposed because it will offend a person's aesthetic sensibilities by increasing noise, or eliminating trees, or changing the overall attractive appearance of a neighborhood. A similar decision may be opposed because it will force the relocation of families to other neighborhoods, thus possibly destroying lifetime friendships and other social relationships. Or, a particular city policy may be supported not only, or even primarily, because of the tangible benefits it will confer, but because it symbolizes social recognition of the importance of the members of the group benefiting, thus raising their self-esteem. Thus the grant programs adopted during the Johnson Administration for helping the black poor not only delivered some tangible goods and services but also—and more immediately—symbolically demonstrated that the federal government and cooperating city governments deemed black people deserving of attention and help.

Conversely, a particular regulation may be opposed not only because it is especially burdensome in a tangible way, but also because its targets feel they are being socially ostracized and degraded. A number of law enforcement agencies were importuned to stop using the word "Mafia" as an equivalent for organized crime since the practice was casting a smear on all Italian-Americans. Finally, persons may support or oppose a decision simply because of the psychological feeling of fun, excitement, glamor, prestige, or indulgence of a sense of civic duty they receive from being associated with the formation of policy on an important matter. Some people also get involved in political conflicts just for the pleasure of the fight or of having the opportunity to exercise political influence or power successfully, a pleasure that is healthy enough for some but for others serves as a means of compensating for deep-seated and painful feelings of personal inadequacy.[4]

Public Office

Who gets what public office is the central stake in electoral politics or in conflicts having to do with the politics of appointment. Public office is considered by those seeking it and by their allies both as an end in itself and as a means for achieving or protecting still other stakes. That is, public office can bring direct psychological satisfaction and economic rewards to the person holding it. And it can also convey the influence that comes from official city positions for the purpose of increasing the office-gainer's ability to shape policy decisions.

Since this book is about the politics of decision-making, public office per se is not the central issue here. But it is involved in the sense that elective officials and would-be officials may anticipate that a particular decisional outcome will either enhance or damage their chances for election or reelection. And for appointive officials or career bureaucrats, particular decisions may bring a rise or drop in popularity or prestige and thus make them more or less vulnerable to attempts at their removal by higher officials. Or a

[4]Harold D. Lasswell, *Psychopathology and Politics* (Chicago: University of Chicago Press, 1930) and *Power and Personality* (New York: Norton, 1948).

particular decision may increase or decrease their chances of furthering their careers by being appointed to a higher, more important post or it may allow them to expand the jurisdiction and budget of their agencies.

"Proxy" Stakes

Persons can also become participants in decision-making conflicts when they perceive proposals as harmful to individuals or groups for whom they have positive feelings or as beneficial to individuals or groups for whom they have negative feelings. The stake for these participants who are not directly affected by a conflict is thus there only, so to speak, "by proxy."

Regular activists in city politics frequently take positions on the simple basis of "If he's for it, I'm against it" or "If he's for it, I want to support it." And not only regular political activists but also members of the general public support policy decisions without knowing much or anything about their merits because "it's good for . . . (some favored, popular, or considered deserving, group)" or oppose a decision because "they (some disliked or considered undeserving group that is anticipated to benefit) are getting too much already."

The Intertwining of Stakes

Obviously, a person may have more than a single stake in a particular decision-making conflict. Indeed, there may be such a complicated, intertwined combination of anticipated gains and losses in services, money, intangibles and ideological satisfaction as well as proxy stakes motivating involvement in a conflict that it may be nearly impossible for a person to consciously and explicitly spell them all out. Furthermore a person's stakes in a proposal may be "mixed," or cross-pressuring, in the sense of having some feelings that motivate him to go one way in the conflict and some that motivate him to go the other way. Under the latter circumstances, unless the cross-pressuring makes it so painful that he withdraws from the conflict completely, the stakes that are the most valued and most intensely-held will be the ones to determine the participant's position in the conflict.

GENERAL STRATEGIES OF EXERTING INFLUENCE

As has been explained, policy demands get adopted or rejected in the city decision-making process when certain formal acts are performed by city officials as specified in city charters, laws, and other standing regulations. These acts can be an oral declaration, the placement of a signature on an executive order or administrative regulation, the issuance of a judicial decree by a city trial judge, or the casting of votes by a specified number or proportion of members of a city legislative body or by a constituency electorate. The term "political influence" is used in this book to refer to the ability to affect any of these acts, either directly or through intermediaries, in an intended way.

On those rare policy demands that immediately generate spontaneous and complete agreement on their merits, no influence need be exercised. Everyone simply is predisposed to act in concert from the very beginning, either to adopt or defeat the proposal. But the more typical case is where initially there is disagreement. Supporters of the original demands then must try to exert influence in order to get the city officials who control the formal governmental machinery for promulgating decisions to exercise their powers in the desired way. Opponents of the policy demand also must exert influence in order to defeat the original proposal, possibly by stopping its consideration, by watering it down as much as possible, or by getting a more acceptable alternative adopted. The "politics" of city government involves the attempt to exert influence on city governmental decisions in this kind of competitive fashion.

Part III of this book will explain in detail the resources and characteristic ways that different participants use to influence city decisions and therefore engage in its politics. The purpose of the discussion here is simply to alert the reader that all the specific tactics and strategies are essentially examples of the following general strategies of influence: invoking authority; persuasion; bargaining; and coercion.

Invoking Authority

Those who have the "authority" or legal power to perform the acts that formally constitute adoption or rejection of a policy demand can obviously influence how it is disposed of. Similarly, having and invoking the authority to direct the behavior of those subordinate city officials or employees who need to perform the acts necessary for a decision's implementation is also a way of influencing the decision-making process. Indeed, authority is a key and unique base of influence. Would-be influentials who possess no formal authority must influence those who do in order to achieve their objectives. On the other hand, those who do possess authority need only keep themselves from being influenced away from the decision they wish to promulgate in order to achieve their objective.

This is not to say that city officials with formal authority can always promulgate and have implemented the decision that coincides most closely with their own personal goals and preferences, beliefs about the best means, or priorities. For as this book will attempt to make clear, city officials are not invulnerable to the "nonauthoritative" kinds of influence that can be brought to bear on them. And as, hopefully, will also be made clear in later parts of the book, the mere assertion of authority in an attempt to direct the performances of subordinates who are under a legal obligation to obey does not guarantee that their compliance will actually be forthcoming.

Persuasion

Persuasion as a general strategy of influence in city politics assumes that although there is initial disagreement about a proposal, exchanges of information and discussions can lead to eventual agreement "on the merits." If the officials involved admittedly share the policy goal of the proposal in question, the persuasive effort of the proponents need be only to give information to show that the measure being proposed will in fact accomplish the shared goal. If it is the measure's opponents that are trying to exert influence, their persuasive effort will concentrate on providing information to show that it will not in fact do so, or even that it will promote goals that the officials are known to be against.

A persuasive effort can also be based on trying to prove a linkage between the policy demands and the enhancement or injury of some non-policy goal of the city official—i.e., the desire to be reelected or to be praised as an effective official. For the effort to be "persuasion" rather than "bargaining" or "coercion," the persuader must not control and thus be able to confer these other advantages or disadvantages. He must merely report on the effects that would follow from taking or refraining from taking a particular position.

Bargaining

Persuasion as a strategy assumes that goals are or will be shared so that an exchange of information and discussion will lead to eventual agreement. Bargaining takes for granted that the relevant city official or officials cannot be persuaded to agree on the merits of a particular proposition or proposal. The objective of the bargainer is therefore to offer, explicitly or implicitly, new advantages, rewards, or inducements that are in his control in exchange for the decision-maker's compliance with the bargainer's point of view. The crassest form of inducement, and one that is illegal in all large cities, is the promise of an unmarked envelope full of large denomination bills if a decision is made a certain way. A legal inducement is the promise to support a measure desired by the decision-maker in exchange for his cooperation on the policy that the decision-maker is opposing. If the policy demand in dispute is a complex one with many different features, there can be "trade-offs" of one side ceasing their opposition to some features they dislike in exchange for similar concessions from the opponents. Still other bargaining measures involve exchanging such inducements as appointments to office, budgetary additions for certain programs, campaign funds, the expression of gratifying feelings like respect, approval, gratitude, love, etc. The proposed inducement for the bargain need not be explicit. It can also be indefinite and payable at some indefinite future date, such as the assurance that if the city official "goes along" with a particular policy position, its proponent will "owe" the decision-maker a "favor."

Coercion

Like bargaining, coercion takes for granted that the city decision-maker cannot be persuaded to agree on the merits of a particular position because he cannot be convinced that it is to his overall advantage given the then-existing situation. But unlike bargaining, the strategy of coercion does not consist of offering some new advantage or reward that the decision-maker wants in exchange for compliance. The strategy of coercion threatens to impose, if compliance is not forthcoming, something new that the decision-maker does not want and considers injurious. These unwanted impositions are often referred to as "sanctions." Examples of sanctions include non-cooperation on policy and other matters of importance to the city decision-maker, withdrawal of campaign contributions, retaliation at the polls, budgetary cuts or dismissals, engaging in disruptions or other illegal violence, or simply expression of negative feelings like disapproval, scorn, contempt, ridicule, etc. Once again, as in the case of bargaining, the sanctions threatened can be indefinite and not be operative until some future date. The message here is that if compliance is not forthcoming, what will be owed is a grudge rather than a favor. If the sanctions threatened are heavy enough, coercion approaches "compulsion," with the decision-maker not really being left any choice but to comply.

Table 2–1 summarizes the four forms of influence in terms of the base of their potential impact on city political decision-makers.

It should be understood that in any real-world attempt to influence a particular city governmental decision, all these strategies can be used in mutually supportive combination. Thus a particular memorandum or conversation may invoke authority, make attempts at persuasion, reinforce them with proffered inducements, and perhaps even vaguely allude to the existence of sanctions that might be brought to bear if compliance is not forthcoming.

FEEDBACKS FROM DECISION-MAKING OUTCOMES

What motivates the immediate participants in, and how the play of influence shapes the outcome of, decision-making conflicts in large cities has a fascinating intrinsic interest to students of city political systems. For

TABLE 2-1 Bases for Overcoming Disagreement

AUTHORITY	Control of decision-making machinery and the legal right to demand compliance
PERSUASION	Changing decision-maker's beliefs or goals so that disagreement ends and he comes to agree with the proposal. The message here is: "If you understand, you will see it is to your advantage to comply."
BARGAINING	Changing decision-maker's situation so that despite continued disagreement, new advantages offered will provide incentive for compliance. The message here is: "It can be *made* to your advantage if you comply."
COERCION	Changing decision-maker's situation so that despite continued disagreement, the wish to avoid new disadvantages will provide incentive for compliance. The message here is: "It can be made to your disadvantage if you don't comply."

this is the "game" aspect of city politics, controlling in the most immediate sense "who gets what, when, how?" But from the point of view of city politics as a core part of the governing process in large cities, there is a vital additional question to be asked: How does the fact that one decision and its set of implementing actions is produced, instead of some other, affect the people living in a city? From this point of view the two most important "feedbacks" are the impacts that decisions have on the "problems" being experienced by different people and on the level of "support" forthcoming for a city's government and official decision-makers.

Impact on Problems

City governmental decisions have been treated in this chapter as the outcomes of the processing of demands for solutions to problems that are felt by some parts of a city's people. These outcomes should therefore presumably have some beneficial impact on the problems that originally generated the demands. The impact of a city governmental decision, however, can range from partial or complete elimination of the conditions that were originally defined as the problem to the production of no change in, or even to the aggravation of, the undesired situation. Therefore, one crucial question in the analysis of city politics is the extent to which a city government's decisions are or are not improving conditions and otherwise successfully coping with what people consider to be problems.

Later chapters will indicate the varying degree of commitment that different city officials have to the actual alleviation of problems within their jurisdictions because of their own internally felt conceptions of their proper role. But an additional incentive to improve conditions and alleviate problems comes from the realization that many of the most basic problems currently found in large cities will eventually have to be attended to because they only grow worse by being neglected. Thus, the demands for coping with them will only expand and become even more difficult to satisfy as time goes by. And still another incentive comes from the recognition that the success by city officials in coping with problems and satisfying demands is inextricably tied up with the ability to maintain political support.

Impact on Support

The term "political support" refers to people's willingness to engage in activity that promotes, complies with, or at least does not actively oppose their city government's decisions and implementing actions. The opposite of support would involve feelings of resentment and hostility and actions constituting refusal to voluntarily obey governmental regulations, yield governmental extractions, and cooperate with the delivery of governmental benefactions. At the extreme, it would include terrorism and guerrilla warfare tactics against city officials and employees and even active efforts to overthrow the government itself by revolution, or *coup d'etat*. Almost as a matter of definition, no government can survive without minimal support or at least passive acceptance from its broad citizenry and active support from those of its employees that directly control the instruments of violence —i.e., the police on the city level and, on a higher level of government, the military. Also, in elective political systems such as those that operate in our large cities, top city officials cannot continue in office without the voting support of majorities or pluralities of their electorates.

Combinations of habit, widespread feelings of the legitimacy of government and attachment to the society of which the city government is a part, agreement with the substance of specific policies and programs, loyalty to the person or party of particular city officials, and even apathy, assure a high enough level of support in our large cities to preclude the possibility of such radical instances of nonsupport as a *coup d'etat* or revolution. Fluctuations in the level of support do, however, have a vital impact on the election and reelection prospects of incumbent city officials or new candidates, on the success or failure of specific city policies and programs depending on extensive voluntary compliance, and on the occurrence in large cities of such indications of nonsupport as disruptive mass demonstrations, strikes, and protests including sporadic outbreaks of mass violence like riots, lootings, burnings, etc.

Maintaining Support via Performance

City governments and officials can normally maintain or increase existing levels of support among particular individuals, groups, or publics if they satisfy their demands and alleviate their problems. They can also nourish support if they confer "windfall" or "free" benefits—that is, benefits that no one has yet made a demand for. City governments and officials normally lose support when they fail to alleviate problems or when they themselves inflict new, unwanted costs or dissatisfactions.

In a utopian city political system, maintenance of support would not be problematical. City decision-makers could automatically maintain or increase support by satisfying all demands, alleviating all problems, and always producing undemanded or windfall benefits and satisfactions for everyone. But in any real contemporary large city this kind of action is obviously impossible. First, city decision-makers do not have available, nor can they create, all the resources of implementation—i.e., time, money, manpower, skill, knowledge, or intelligence—necessary to satisfy all demands and solve all problems, let alone provide free, windfall benefits. This is the "there aren't enough goodies to go around" problem of governing. Second, apart from the limits on the availability of resources, there are inevitable conflicts and incompatibilities in goals, values, interests, beliefs, outlooks and priorities held by different people in large cities. The satisfaction of some people's demands and the solution of some people's problems by city governments will therefore almost always involve the rejection of other people's demands, the imposition on them of costs, and the creation for them of new problems or the aggravation of existing ones. These new or aggravated problems then generate new "demands" by the adversely affected people for new "solutions" which in turn create still new problems, and so on, *ad infinitum.* This is the "you can't please everybody" problem of governing.

Maintaining Support via Symbolic Substitutes

For the reasons just indicated, city governments and officials cannot count on maintaining sufficient support exclusively through performance that actually satisfies demands and alleviates problems. City governments and officials consequently try to counter the erosion of support by also providing various valued (but in terms of scarce resources, relatively uncostly) symbolic substitutes. Thus, city decision-makers often grant opportunities for the venting of grievances and the sympathetic consideration of demands. Because such a willingness to listen symbolizes concern and goodwill, it can sometimes serve as a catharsis and drain off part or all of the intensity behind the original demands even without taking further action. Similarly, city officials attempt to stave off loss of support by verbal declarations that 1) indicate acceptance of demands (even if without any intent to perform the necessary implementing actions); or 2) express agreement with the validity of the demands but explain the necessity for postponement of action (because, for example, of the unavailability of resources or the unavoidable need for "further studies"); or 3) explain the need for sacrifice because of the conflicting needs of some overriding "common interests" or "general good." Finally, city officials can bolster their support by displaying and celebrating symbols such as city charters, constitutions, political theories, etc., that justify obedience to government. They can also use symbols such as flags, monuments, national heroes, and traditions that are widely admired and thus provoke enthusiasm, love and loyalty for the political system. These are the two kinds of symbols that Charles Merriam has termed credenda" and "miranda" (symbols believed in and symbols admired) and they can stimulate or reintensify warm feelings constituting "diffuse," or general, support and thus counter or prevent any overall erosion because of the failure to satisfy specific demands by actual performance.[5]

Exactly how long city governments can use cathartic opportunities, verbal declarations, and symbolic displays and celebrations to prevent loss of support in the face of repeated rejection of demands and the nonalleviation of problems will vary with different circumstances. The many instances in history of revolutions, *coups d'etat,* mass outbreaks of violence, and electoral defeats demonstrate, however, that there are definite limits to what this kind of symbolic substitution can accomplish. For, after a point, a credibility gap develops: thus grievance sessions can cease to have any cathartic effect, verbal declarations can cease being believed, and, as Gabriel Almond has explained, other symbols of belief or admiration

> . . . may cease to be edifying, menacing, stirring, credible, or even observed, listened to, or read. Royalty or high officials may be spat upon, pelted with rotten vegetables, statues thrown down from high places, pamphlets cast aside, television and radio sets can be turned off . . . Symbolic messages may be transmitted but not received.[6]

Or as John Locke, the seventeenth-century English philosopher, more pithily put it, "Whatever flatterers may talk to amuse people's understandings, it hinders not men from feeling."[7]

[5]Charles E. Merriam, *Political Power* (New York: Macmillan, 1964),chap. 4 .

[6]Gabriel A. Almond, "A Developmental Approach to Political Systems," *World Politics,* 17 (1965): 201.

[7]John Locke, *The Second Treatise of Civil Government,* chap.7, sec. 94.

Maintaining "Support" via Coercive Power

Most persons in large cities have sufficiently high levels of "specific" or "diffuse" support to comply voluntarily with their government's decisions most of the time. Nevertheless, occasions arise on which even the most generally supportive person wants to oppose some specific decision or policy. This can be because that person rejects the legitimacy or authority of the city government on that matter, e.g., "they've gone too far, I don't concede them the right to bus my children ten miles away from their neighborhood." Or, even while conceding its authority and legitimacy, a person can be motivated to disobey because of the immediate benefit to be gained by that disobedience—such as by cheating on a tax return or parking by a fire hydrant when late for the theater.

In order to maintain themselves as the city's government, city officials must, therefore, be able at times to stimulate support—or at least curb noncompliance—through the use of coercive power. By "coercive power" is meant the capacity to compel compliance or inflict punishment even though resort to physical force and even against physical resistance.[8]

The question arises whether it would not be easier for city governments not to bother with trying to maintain support through performance or symbolic substitutes and simply rely on securing compliance by the threat or use of force. This might especially be a temptation with respect to lower-class slum-dwellers, whose demands are highly expensive to satisfy through programs designed to improve their conditions and who also constitute permanent minorities of the electorate and so cannot by themselves vote out of office incumbent city officials. With large-size, well-equipped police forces plus aid from their state's national guard and even the federal government's regular army, large city governments can deploy enough coercive power to overwhelm and force compliance from any would-be challengers presently on the city scene.

Attempting to govern with exclusive or primary reliance on coercive power does, however, have some major disadvantages. First of all, if a city government was not receiving voluntary support from a sufficiently high proportion of its citizenry and therefore had to overcome the resistance of massive numbers all at the same time, it might find it difficult or impossible to do so. Or it might have to use such a high level of organized violence and fire-power that the results would be carnage among the population it had an obligation to protect. Force, in short, works best when it only has to be used at a particular time against isolated, particular noncomplying individuals or relatively small groups. Second, if a city government is faced with resistance from numbers that are sizable—even if they are far smaller than majorities

[8]See Harold D. Lasswell and Abraham Kaplan, *Power and Society: A Framework for Political Inquiry* (New Haven: Yale University Press, 1950), p. 220.

of the entire population—the deployment of the large numbers of police necessary to contain those resisters is extremely costly financially if it has to be done over an extended period of time. And the calling for the national guard or regular army with any degree of frequency will probably be extremely costly politically to high city officials since the dominant expectations in large cities are still that city officials should be adroit enough to keep things "cool" and avoid frequent outbreaks of massive resistance or violence. Third, force as the ultimate basis for support is inherently unreliable. For as guerrilla warfare, episodes of hit-and-run looting, sniping, and sabotage show, when there is no internally generated incentive for compliance with city decisions, people can indulge their noncompliant feelings as soon as the police or soldiers turn the corner and are not in a position to catch the perpetrators in the act. Fourth, any city government (or for that matter any government) that relied heavily on maintaining support through the use of force would cause a fundamental change in the basic atmosphere of city living. Gone would be the atmosphere of openness, tolerance, respect for differences, and the low-to-moderate temperature politics that is still to be found in almost all large American cities. What would inevitably develop as a substitute would be a "police-state" or "garrison-state" atmosphere laden with suspicion, bitterness, and fear in which a gradual or rapid erosion of civil liberties and procedural due process rules-of-the-game would take place.

In short, the answer to the original question is that coercive power is not a better, easier, or stronger basis of governing than that of voluntary support stimulated by effective and responsive city governmental performance. Obviously, every city government must rely on force to deal with criminals and at periodic intervals may have to resort to force to suppress individual disobedience or mass disorders among those who are ordinarily compliant. A city government that had no capacity or willingness to use force at all would be weak indeed—so weak that it would be problematical whether it could survive. But equally ineffective would be a city government whose only or primary means of securing support and compliance was the threat or use of force. For as Charles Merriam so aptly put it:

> Power is not strongest when it uses violence, but weakest. It is strongest when it employs the instruments of substitution and counter attraction, of allurement, of participation rather than of annihilation. Rape is not evidence of irresistible power in politics or in sex.[9]

[9]Charles E. Merriam, *Political Power* (New York: Macmillan, 1964), p. 179.

II

CONSTITUTIONAL, LEGAL, AND STRUCTURAL SETTING

Part II attempts to explain the constitutional, legal, and structural setting within which city governments operate. Because legally, cities are only creatures of their respective states, Chapter 3 gives explicit attention to how state governments are helping or hindering city governments in the performance of their governmental tasks. And because the play of influence in a city's decision-making process does not take the form of a chaotic free-for-all but proceeds within formal governmental structures according to a variety of preexisting rules, Chapter 4 discusses the different kinds of structural forms and procedural rules found in large cities, the impact such differences have on the actual operation of city governments, and the advantages and disadvantages different structures and rules confer on participants in a city's politics. Chapter 5 explains the variety of local governments besides the "general" city government—special districts, county governments, metropolitan councils—that overlie and directly exercise governmental functions within the boundaries of large cities and how the operation of these other local governmental entities affects the capacity of the general city government to govern. Chapter 6 analyzes how the federal government has become increasingly involved in urban affairs and how the nature of its actual and potential involvement has a very strong impact on city governmental performance. Chapter 7 briefly summarizes the case for the proposition that city governments have not become mere administrative agents for higher levels of government but are still important loci of independent decision-making.

3

The City in the State Political System

Neither cities nor any other kinds of localities enjoy any inherent rights of self-government. Indeed, local governments are not even mentioned in the federal constitution. According to our constitutional scheme, all governmental authority is divided between the federal government and the states, with certain kinds of authority, for example over speech, religion, etc., being denied to all governments because of prohibitions in the Bill of Rights.

THE CONSTITUTIONAL AND LEGAL INFERIORITY OF CITIES

Legally, cities are merely municipal corporations, created by their states and assigned the right to perform certain governmental functions within specified, relatively densely-populated, geographic areas. As creatures of their states, cities can exercise only those governmental powers expressly granted to them, and such powers can be contracted or taken away by the state without the city's consent at any time. As the U.S. Supreme Court stated in *Trenton v. New Jersey.*

> The City is a political subdivision of the State, created as a convenient agency for the exercise of such of the governmental powers of the State as may be entrusted to it. . . . The State, therefore, at its pleasure may modify or withdraw all such powers, . . . expand or contract the territorial area, unite the whole or a part of it with

> another municipality, repeal the charter and destroy the corporation. All this may be done, conditionally or unconditionally, with or without the consent of the citizens, or even against their protest. In all these respects the State is supreme, and its legislative body, conforming its action to the state constitution, may do as it will, unrestrained by any provision of the Constitution of the United States. . . .[1]

As a further indication of the legally inferior position of cities, under long-standing judicial doctrine, whatever grants of power are made to cities by their states must be "narrowly" or "strictly" construed. This means that if some attempted exercise of city governmental authority is challenged and if the state court system, which settles the question, finds there can be a reasonable doubt as to whether the language of the applicable statutory or charter provision supports the challenged power, the doubt is resolved against the city. The classic statement of this rule of interpretation was written by John F. Dillon, himself a state judge, who in 1872 published a leading treatise on municipal law:

> It is a general and undisputed proposition of law that a *municipal corporation possesses and can exercise the following powers, and no others:* First, those granted in *express words;* second, *those necessarily or fairly implied* in or *incident* to the powers expressly granted; third, those *essential* to the accomplishment of the declared objects and purposes of the corporation—not simply convenient, but indispensable. Any fair, reasonable, substantial doubt concerning the existence of power is resolved by the courts against the corporation, and the power is denied.[2]

The impact of "Dillon's Rule" can be seen in the following court rulings, all of which took place in Chicago: A general grant of power in the Chicago charter "to pass and enforce all necessary police ordinances" was interpreted by the courts not to support regulation of hotels or lodging houses; a grant of statutory authority to regulate dealers in "junk and second-hand articles" was held not to authorize licensing and regulating of used-car dealers or second-hand bookshops; and a statutory grant to regulate "machine shops" was similarly held not to apply to incidental machine-shop operations of factories.[3]

By contrast, from the time of Chief Justice John Marshall who served

[1] *Trenton v. New Jersey,* 262 U.S.182, 185-186 (1923).

[2] John F. Dillon, *Commentaries on the Law of Municipal Corporations,* 5th ed. (Boston: Little, Brown,1911), I: 448.

[3] Cited in *Modernizing a City Government,* Report of the Chicago Home Rule Commission (Chicago: University of Chicago Press, 1954), chap. 13.

from 1801 to 1835, the U.S. Supreme Court, in adjudicating whether Congress or the federal government generally has exceeded its authority under the Constitution, has followed the rule of liberal interpretation of delegated powers. Thus when there is ambiguity about the language of the U.S. Constitution, the Court resolves reasonable doubts in favor of the constitutionality of the act being challenged.[4] State courts normally follow a similar rule when passing on state legislation.

The City Charter

The basic source of a city's governmental authority is its charter. The city's charter serves as organic law, specifying in varying degrees of detail, depending on the city, the form, composition, and specific powers and duties of, as well as at times the procedures to be followed by, its various decision-making officials and bodies. It also normally indicates the method of selection of the different city decision-makers, the kinds of matters to which the city's authority extends and various limits on that authority, the city's geographic boundaries, and, particularly in "home-rule" cities (to be explained), the methods for changing the charter itself.

In defining the powers of a particular city, the charter does not stand by itself: The authority granted and the limits imposed by the charter are supplemented by relevant state constitutional provisions as well as by state statutes applicable to all cities, to that particular city, or to cities of the population class to which it belongs. Indeed, a very few cities do not even have a single document to serve as a charter, with all of their authority resting on state legislative or constitutional provisions.

Originally, in colonial times, cities were incorporated and their charters granted by the colonial governors, acting in the name of the King or the colony's proprietor. The charter was regarded as a contract between the governor and the municipality and thus not subject to change without the consent of both parties. After independence,[5] charters were granted by state legislatures and came to be regarded as acts of ordinary legislation, capable of amendment and even repeal by the legislature alone.

The usual practice of granting charters, at least to the middle of the nineteenth century, was by a special legislative act defining the form of government, scope of authority, etc., of the specific city to which the charter applied. These were the so-called special act charters. Largely in

[4]See *McCulloch v. Maryland,* 4 Wheaton 316 (1819): ". . . we must never forget that it is a constitution we are expounding. . . . Let the end be legitimate, let it be within the scope of the Constitution, and all means which are appropriate, which are plainly adapted to that end, which are not prohibited, but consist with the letter and spirit of the Constitution, are constitutional. . . ."

[5]Actually, at the time of independence there were only twenty-four incorporated municipalities. In 1790, when the first census was taken, the largest city, New York, had a population of 33,131.

response to the movement against special legislation for cities (i.e., legislation applying only to a single city rather than generally throughout the state), an increasingly large number of states enacted standing general legislation which provided for the granting of charters with specific provisions upon petition by a required number of inhabitants and compliance with various other requirements such as a referendum. These are known as "general act charters." At first only one charter was available to all would-be cities applying, but later general legislation in some states made available different "optional charters" for cities of different size. A few states even permitted choice for cities of a particular size from among more than a single basic charter (up to five in Massachusetts and fourteen in New Jersey).

Home Rule

Over three-quarters of our large cities presently have "home-rule" charters—charters that are framed and adopted by a city through local action without reference to the state legislature.[6]

After an abortive beginning in Iowa in 1851 and a later successful adoption of home rule by the Missouri constitutional convention of 1875, slightly over half of all the states have come to allow home-rule charters for their cities. The authority for framing a home-rule charter is specified in self-executing constitutional provisions, in simple legislation, or in enabling legislation passed in pursuance of state constitutional authority. Either type of authority invariably specifies what are the limits of discretion that cities have with respect to provisions they can adopt. The procedure for adopting a charter normally involves the election of a charter commission at the call of the city council or in response to initiative petitions (signed by a requisite percentage of the electorate) to draw up a proposed charter and its subsequent submission to the electorate in a referendum. In most states approval of the proposed charter by a majority of those voting is sufficient for adoption, though in a few states (e.g., California, Arizona, Oklahoma) approving action by specified state administrative authorities is also required.

Charters can usually be amended the same way they were originally issued or adopted. Thus special or general act charters can be amended by further special or general legislation, while home-rule charters provide for their own self-amendment locally. The process for amendment may be the same as that for framing the home-rule charter or a change can be proposed by initiative petition or the city's legislative body and then ratified by the

[6]Notable exceptions include Chicago, Boston, Indianapolis, Milwaukee, Pittsburgh, and Honolulu. *The Municipal Year Book, 1972* (Washington, D.C.: International City Management Association 1972), Table 3/20.

electorate. In a few cases, when changes of a minor nature are involved, home-rule charters can be amended by the city's normal legislative process. Many home-rule states now also permit amendment to all charters, however originally received, through these home-rule processes.

Home-Rule Charters and Substantive Powers

The greatest amount of autonomy that state home-rule provisions and home-rule charters give cities is the power to decide upon and make changes in the form of their government. Home-rule charters do not give complete autonomy (or even necessarily more autonomy than nonhome-rule charters) to city governments or city electorates for adopting substantive policies and programs, and cities cannot use home-rule procedures to enlarge the scope of their overall substantive powers. Either in lieu of or in addition to grants of authority over specific matters, many home-rule charters contain language apparently granting broad substantive powers to enact ordinances covering "local and municipal affairs" (Colorado), "municipal affairs" (California), "municipal concerns" (Michigan), "[the city's] property, affairs, or government" (New York), "local affairs and government" (Wisconsin), "powers of local self-government" (Pennsylvania), or "all powers of local self-government" (Ohio).[7] Nevertheless, state constitutional or statutory provisions, the home-rule charters themselves, and court decisions all make it clear that even home-rule cities can adopt no ordinances that conflict explicitly or implicity with provisions of the state constitution or state law or that affect matters of "general state interest." Only in California, Colorado, and perhaps one or two other states, are local ordinances concerning "municipal affairs" allowed to take precedence over general state laws attempting to deal with municipal affairs. However, even in these states local ordinances cannot take precedence over state laws dealing with "state affairs." And whether there exists such a conflict between a city ordinance and state law or state constitutional provisions or whether a matter is a municipal affair as opposed to a state affair is a subject for judicial determination, with the state courts deciding and Dillon's Rule applying.

Thus, in recent decades, decisions in California, New York, and other states with large cities have held that attempted city regulation of city school teachers and other aspects of education were invalid because they concerned state as opposed to municipal affairs. Attempted regulations of public utilities (even when wholly within city borders), of wages, hours, and pensions of city police and firemen, of the care of neglected or delinquent

[7]Note that nonhome-rule charters sometimes also contain grants of authority in general language.

children have all been held to be invalid as being by definition not concerned with municipal affairs. Similarly, the following concerns have been held to be permeated with "state" rather than "municipal" or "local" interest: closing hours for taverns, speed limits within a city, opening and closing hours of barbershops, a city retirement annuity law for police and firemen, regulation of plumbers, attempts to prohibit manufacture of ice cream under certain conditions, regulation of taxicab service performed on city streets, and the requirement that the date be stamped on milk containers. Ordinances affecting them have thus been declared invalid as being in conflict implicitly with general state laws or exceeding the scope of the city's authority.[8] Furthermore, except in California and to a limited extent in Ohio and Colorado, taxation even within a city's borders is considered to be a state concern and thus not to flow from any general grant of power in a city's home-rule charter, as well as everywhere being subject to various explicit state restrictions and limitations. Finally, some states assign only charter-making powers and no substantive authority at all through home-rule provisions. Their cities are thus dependent, as are all nonhome-rule cities, on specific state legislative action for all their substantive programs.

VEHICLES OF STATE INFLUENCE ON CITY GOVERNMENTS

The bedrock of the relationship between the states and their cities is that the city is completely the state's legal creature. As a result, various elements of the state government—the legislature, the governor, the courts, administrative officials—can exert influence on the city's decision-making process and performance by drawing in various manners on their superior legal authority. Increasingly in recent decades, state governments have also been able to influence city governments through the awarding of various kinds and sizes of cash grants-in-aid.

Constitutional or Statutory Authorizations and Restrictions

Since cities can perform only those functions for which they have a clear charter, state constitutional, or statutory base, state governments can influence decisions by withholding certain kinds of new authority or by placing restrictions or requirements on the exercise of whatever authority is granted. Consequently, unless some proposed city benefaction, regulation, or extraction is beyond a reasonable doubt within the scope of the city's general grant of substantive powers (or unless it constitutes a relatively minor change in policies or programs already specifically authorized), the city will not be able to perform it if the state legislature refuses to pass new

[8]Many of these examples are from *Modernizing a City Government,* chaps. 13–15.

authorizing legislation. Even applying for grants under various federal aid programs normally requires prior state legislative authorization. Furthermore, apart from the existence of positive authority, a proposed new regulation, benefaction, or extraction cannot be adopted if it conflicts with some specific restriction or with some general state law dealing with the same subject, unless the legislature lifts the restriction or grants express exempting permission.

Clearly the most onerous specific restrictions on city decision-making concern financial matters. Almost every state maintains constitutional or statutory limits or both on various tax rates, particularly with respect to property taxes that city governments can impose and on debt they can incur.[9] With the rising expenditures in almost every city pressing it to exceed existing limits and look for new sources, the willingness of state governments to lift these limits and authorize new kinds of taxes has a great impact on the level of operations and quality of performance a city can maintain. When the limits or restrictions are constitutional rather than statutory, not even the legislature can modify them except through the process of proposing a constitutional amendment (usually requiring approval by two successive legislatures) to be ratified by the state-wide electorate. There are a few cities that enjoy an exceptional degree of freedom from restrictions on their taxing powers—Philadelphia, Denver, and all California home-rule cities can essentially impose taxes on their residents without limit. (Philadelphia, however, is restricted to sources not taxed by the state of Pennsylvania.)

Occasionally, the state government restricts city decision-making by withdrawing authority over particular local functions and transfering it to newly-created governmental bodies (boards, commissions, etc.) that are relatively or completely independent of the city government. This precludes the city government from making decisions on those functions although the costs of their operations, when they are not self-financing, are made a charge on the city government.

Constitutional and Legislative Mandates

State governments can influence city decision-making not only through constitutional and statutory provisions that grant or restrict scopes of authority. Through constitutional or statutory provisions, the states can also "mandate" or command that certain specific things be done. These mandates can involve both the procedures and substance of city policies and programs.

[9]See Advisory Commission on Intergovernmental Relations, *State Constitutional and Statutory Restrictions on Local Government Debt* (Washington, D.C.: U.S. Government Printing Office, 1961); Advisory Commission on Intergovernmental Relations, *State Constitutional and Statutory Restrictions Upon the Structural, Functional, and Personnel Powers of Local Government* (Washington, D.C.: U.S. Government Printing Office, 1962).

Thus states normally mandate for their large cities many or all of the following procedural and housekeeping practices: suffrage requirements and election procedures including qualifications of voters, registration methods, details for the operation of the polls, timing of elections, allowable methods of nomination, etc.; personnel regulations, including provisions for merit systems in hiring and promotions, veterans' preference and credits, pension and retirement plans, vacation provisions, and minimum salaries for certain categories of local employees like schoolteachers, police and firemen; the structure of the municipal court system and methods of selection and tenure of city judges (to the extent that the municipal system is not already fully integrated with the state judicial system); the details of city fiscal operations, including required practices in assessment of local property, collections of taxes, custody of funds, budgeting, borrowing, and debt management, purchasing, property management, disbursement, accounting, auditing, and financial reporting; and the details of public school operations including teacher certification, minimum length of school sessions, rules of student attendance, required courses, etc.

In addition to these and a host of other procedural and housekeeping details for cities, the states also mandate the substance of many city policies and programs. Especially through state "penal" or criminal laws, state prison laws, state welfare laws, state education laws, and state public health laws, or their equivalents, the states fix much of the substantive content of the regulations being enforced, and benefactions being offered, by such city departments or boards as police, fire, buildings inspection, correction (i.e., prisons), education, and health. The officers and employees of these departments and boards draw their pay from and nominally work for the city. But they function in large part as agents of the state, being engaged primarily in carrying out state-mandated duties rather than programs formulated locally.

Cash Grants-in-Aid

Another vehicle of state influence on city decision-making is the "cash grant-in-aid," which can be defined as state appropriation of funds paid to a city to help finance its governmental operations. In fiscal 1973–74, approximately 31 percent of the total general expenditures of large cities came from their states in the form of grants (or, to a much lesser extent, as shared taxes).[10] The percentage of their general expenditures received by individual cities from their states varies greatly, ranging in 1973-74 from

[10]U.S. Bureau of the Census, *City Government Finances in 1973-1974* (Washington, D.C.: U.S. Government Printing Office, 1975). Table 7, pp. 90-103. Shared taxes, which are specified portions of the yields of certain state taxes that are automatically returned to local governments, are not, technically speaking, the same as grants, the latter being appropriated funds; but since the available financial data in Census Bureau publications lumps the two together and since shared taxes are known to constitute a very small part of the total, the analysis here will treat the whole amount of state transfers of funds to cities as grants.

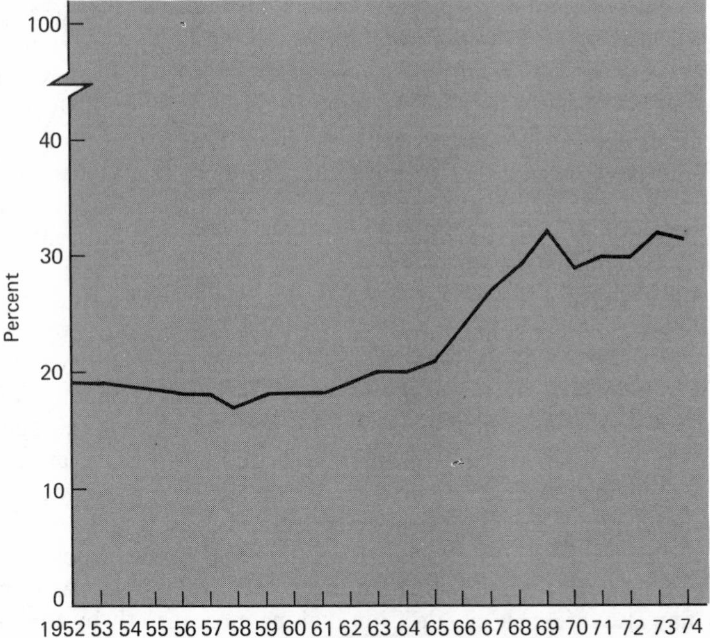

FIGURE 3-1 State Aid as Percentage of Large-City Government General Expenditures, 1952–74 (Cities of Over 300,000 in Population, Excluding Washington, D.C.).

Source: Calculated from U.S. Bureau of the Census, *City Government Finances,* 1951–52 to 1973–74.

highs of 53 percent, 45 percent, and 43 percent for Baltimore, Newark and New York, to lows of 1 percent, 1 percent, and 2 percent for Houston, San Antonio, and El Paso.[11] Both in absolute amounts and as proportions of total city expenditures, state grants have been increasing this century and particularly since the 1930s.

By far the largest proportion of state grants is allocated to support specific functions. In terms of the aggregate amount of grants going to all large cities in fiscal 1973-74, 23 percent was for education; 40 percent for welfare; 7 percent for highways; and 14 percent was for various other specific purposes such as health and hospitals, and housing and urban renewal. Only 16 percent was not earmarked for any particular function, but went for general support of city governments.[12]

It should be noted that there may be some distortion of the amount of state aid shown as given to cities due to the way these aggregate financial statistics are collected and reported by the Census Bureau. On the one hand,

[11] *City Government Finances in 1973-74,* Table 7, pp. 90-103.
[12] *Ibid.*

because over half of all large cities do not directly operate or finance public schools or welfare programs for their residents, the amounts of state grants subsidizing the operation of these programs—which are both heavily state-aided—are not included in the totals reported as being made to cities. These payments are listed elsewhere as state grants to local school districts or to the county governments that operate the programs. If all cities operated their schools and welfare programs directly, both the absolute amount of state aid going to large cities and the percentage that such aid bears to city expenditures would show as being higher than the figures cited earlier.

On the other hand, the amounts reported as state grants include not only moneys raised by the states through their own revenue systems, but also moneys received as federal grants, like aid to dependent children and aid to primary and secondary schools. These funds are simply channeled through the states for redistribution to local governments. But since the amounts are included in the totals for state grants, the actual effort that state governments are making to help cities out of their own funds is exaggerated.

In general, grants-in-aid influence city decision-making and performance by permitting levels of operations that would not otherwise be possible at all or that would not be possible without increases in local taxes. At times the grants may also influence city decision-making more directly by stimulating the channeling of more city funds to functions for which state aid is available in order to avoid losing such aid. Such channeling by city officials results from the fact that state grants programs often require some "matching" funds to be provided by the city as a prerequisite for receiving the grant.

Many grants to cities are conditional on the observance by the city of certain procedural or substantive criteria or both in the administration of the aided program. Thus, in New York, which is not atypical in these matters, grants for public welfare are conditional on the compliance of the City Department of Social Services with the requirements of the State Board and Department of Social Welfare, both with respect to organization, administrative procedures, and facilities and with respect to substantive aspects of the program. In addition:

> Library grants are conditioned upon the requirement that all residents of the city be allowed to use the libraries free, that librarians meet the training specifications set by the state Commissioner of Education, and that library standards be at or above a stated minimum. State funds for tuberculosis control may be withheld if the city constructs a tuberculosis hospital having more than 500 beds, if it has the space but refuses to accept a patient recommended by the state Commissioner of Health, if an approved patient is requested or required to pay for treatment, or if the hospital fails to comply with

> the rules prescribed by the state Commissioner of Health. In the case of education, administrative practices as well as substantive educational policy are so tightly regulated by the provisions of state legislation and the rules of the [State] Board of Regents and the [State] Department of Education that additional qualifications are rarely necessary in connection with grants-in-aid; nevertheless, administrative refinement and interpretation of the definitions of the activities eligible for state assistance sometimes add to the stringency of the requirements.[13]

Administrative Supervision

State influence on city decision-making can also be exercised through various kinds of administrative supervision involving review of past city decisions and clearance or consultation about proposals. These devices serve as means of enforcing compliance with state requirements, restrictions, and grant conditions.

The requirements for submission of a prospective decision for approval before its taking effect, i.e., "clearance," or for informing of and soliciting advice about a prospective decision, i.e., "consultation," are particularly widespread in those programs enjoying state financial assistance: Thus, city welfare agencies are almost always required to clear welfare plans specifying organizational structure, criteria for size of payments and eligibility. City road and highway departments must clear their proposals for "arterial highways," i.e., highways within the city that form part of the state highway network, in order to be assured of a state contribution for their construction. City health agencies must submit proposals for new public health programs or facilities or major expansion of ongoing ones to state boards or departments of health if they wish to receive assistance from state public health grants. Even in such nonaided functions as personnel and finance administration, changes in rules or procedures very often require clearance by state civil service commissions or by state tax commissioners or comptrollers.[14]

"Review" by state administrative officials of past city decisions obviously cannot affect those particular decisions. Such review does, however, provide information to state officials for spotting past instances of noncompliance and for stopping them in the future. The most usual review devices employed by state officials include requiring submission of annual and other periodic reports, hearing appeals concerning city decisions in

[13]Wallace S. Sayre and Herbert Kaufman, *Governing New York City* (New York: W. W. Norton, 1965), p. 573.

[14]W. Brooke Graves, *American Intergovernmental Relations; Their Origins, Historical Development, and Current Status* (New York: Charles Scribner's Sons, 1964), pp. 717-734.

certain areas, and conducting routine or other self-initiated inspections, examinations, and audits of various city activities.

Most state-city administrative supervision takes place along functional lines, with the activities of particular city administrative departments being the objects of concern of state administrative agencies with similar substantive responsibilities. Thus, state education departments will supervise local education boards, state welfare departments will supervise local welfare programs, state highway departments will supervise city highways and roads departments, etc. About one-half of all state governments—e.g., California, New Jersey, New York, Massachusetts, Connecticut, Illinois, Pennsylvania, Rhode Island—have also established state administrative offices or divisions of "local government" or "municipal affairs" or "community affairs" whose titles imply responsibilities for general supervision of local and municipal activities. However, these state agencies for local affairs have for the most part concentrated on supervising financial matters and to a lesser extent on collecting statistical data, publishing reports and studies, providing consulting services, and serving as clearinghouses of information and general facilitators of contacts between the state and local governments. None of them has become any kind of general supervisory organ of city governments.[15]

Special Investigations, Removals, and Substitute Administration

Probably the most drastic set of vehicles of state influence over city decision-making is conducting special investigations, removing city officials, and establishing "substitute administration." Special investigations are conducted by investigative officers or bodies specially appointed by the governor or the legislature or by the state's regular law enforcement officials such as the attorney general. As opposed to routine inspections and examinations of ongoing programs, investigations are concerned with the conduct of particular officials or various problem situations. Such investigations almost always imply suspicion of illegal or inadequate performance by the city officials being investigated so that the possibility or threat of investigations may be enough to stimulate a change of behavior. Investigations can also uncover actual evidence of corruption or gross inefficiency and thus lead to forced resignations, electoral defeats, and to new legislative restrictions, mandates, or rescinding of authority. State-initiated investigation into the Newark city government led to the indictment and trial in 1970 of, among others, its mayor, Hugh Addonizio. Addonizio ran for reelection

[15]See *ibid.*, pp. 712-16; Advisory Commission on Intergovernmental Relations, *Fiscal Balance in the American Federal System* (Washington, D.C.: U.S. Government Printing Office, 1967), I: 255–56, 306–11.

as mayor during his trial and was defeated. He was later found guilty and sentenced to imprisonment.

Under many state constitutions and laws, state finance, health, and education officers have the authority to remove their city counterparts from office for various serious forms of malfeasance. In a few states, the governor, after the filing of formal charges and the holding of a hearing at which the officials concerned can testify in their own behalf, can remove from office not only such appointed officers as police commissioners, sheriffs, etc., but also top elected officials, including mayors. For example, as a result of the scandals uncovered by the famous Seabury investigations of the New York City government in 1932, Governor Franklin D. Roosevelt removed from office the Sheriff of New York County (Manhattan) and filed charges against, and was apparently considering also removing, Mayor James J. Walker, when the mayor obligingly submitted his resignation.

Many state constitutions and laws also give state officials authority under certain emergency conditions to actually take over temporarily the direct administration of a particular city program, with the city, of course, continuing to bear its cost. In 1968, for example, after continuous strikes, boycotts, and disruptions plagued the Ocean Hill-Brownsville experimental school district in New York City, the New York State Department of Education assumed direct control of the schools there until a normal situation was restored. The use of this kind of "substitute administration" has extended to the field of public health activities, as when the state health agency decides that a local health board or department is not enforcing the state health law properly or cannot cope with an emergency such as an epidemic. It has been employed in financial affairs, as when the state takes over in whole or part the administration of the finances of a city in danger of defaulting on its bonds until the city attains an improved financial situation. During New York City's 1975 fiscal crisis, the New York State legislature created a State Municipal Assistance Corporation (Big Mac), which would borrow money on behalf of New York City, but also have a large say on that city's budgetary and accounting procedures and receive automatically a share of the city's sales and stock transfer taxes for the purpose of paying off its borrowing. When, after a few months, Big Mac itself found it impossible to borrow the funds needed by New York City, the state legislature in special session created an Emergency Financial Control Board. This board was given the power to take all city revenues into its own bank accounts and to disburse those revenues only in accordance with a city financial plan it approved. Members of the board were the governor, the state controller, New York's mayor, the city controller, and three other members appointed by the governor.

Substitute administration has also been used lately in criminal law enforcement, as when a governor orders the state police or the national guard to restore order to a riot-torn city whose police are not sufficiently numerous or efficient for the task.

POLICY ORIENTATION OF STATE GOVERNMENTS

It should be understood that the exercise of state influence on large city governments is not all competitive, denying, limiting, or otherwise unhelpful. State governments have over the years allowed their cities to undertake increasingly broader ranges of service and regulatory functions. They have authorized the tapping of new sources for taxes and sometimes raised the limits on traditional ones, like the property tax. And state governments have been increasing grants-in-aid to city governments in recent decades, both in terms of absolute dollars and in terms of the proportion of total city expenditures financed by such grants.

The State Governments' Basic Negativism

Nevertheless, the overall orientation of state governments toward their large cities has traditionally been a negative one. Extra grants of authority have normally been given out grudgingly and with a "what's the least possible we can do for you" attitude, frequently after initial resistance, and some have in fact been denied. A 1967 survey of city officials found, for example, that among those from large cities, 60 percent reported that their states were either "seldom" or "only occasionally" helpful or sympathetic.[16] Only 12 percent reported that their state government was "nearly always" helpful or sympathetic:

TABLE 3-1 Helpfulness of State Governments Toward Cities As Seen by Large City Officials

Population Group	Number of cities reporting	Seldom	Occasionally	Usually	Nearly always
over 500,000	20	35%	20%	30%	15%
250,000–500,000	23	9%	57%	26%	9%
Total	43	21%	39%	28%	12%

Source: Adapted from B. Douglas Harman, "The Block Grant: Readings from a First Experiment," *Public Administration Review,* 30 (1970): 147.

[16]B. Douglas Harman, "The Block Grant: Readings from a First Experiment," *Public Administration Review,* 30 (1970):147. On the other hand, of officials from the smallest sized cities reporting—25,000 to 100,000 population—fully 59 percent felt their states were "usually" or "nearly always" helpful and sympathetic.

With respect to grants-in-aid, the amounts that go to large cities have been low relative to the taxes paid by city residents and businesses, to the perceived needs of city officials for improving the level of performance of their governments, or to what political jurisdictions in the state's rural or suburban areas receive. This results from allocation formulas for grants or shared taxes being skewed so that large-city areas receive less—sometimes far less—per capita than non large-city areas and from the unwillingness of all but a tiny handful of states like New York, California, Massachusetts, and Pennsylvania, to establish grant programs relevant to the specially burdensome and expensive conditions that local governments must cope with in large cities.[17] Even in recent years during which it has become apparent that large-city school systems must spend more money per child than schools in other areas because of their large population of disadvantaged, lower-class black children needing "enriched" schools, in over half of all states with large cities, state educational aid actually gave larger amounts per student to school systems in generally wealthier and more educable suburbs.[18]

Causes of State Negativism

Up to a decade ago, the state governments' low level of responsiveness to the needs of large cities was primarily the result of at least one house of every state legislature being malapportioned and thus dominated by members from rural areas. Many rural legislators commonly shared with their constituents an anti-big city mentality, regarding the cities as sources of corruption, low morals and boss rule, and populated by alien peoples like Irish-Catholics, later, Italian and Eastern European Catholics and Jews, and still later, slum blacks. Furthermore, cities were perceived as the homes of intellectuals, free-thinkers, and radical types of all sorts.[19] Finally, diverting tax moneys collected in cities to the running of local governments in rural areas was inherently attractive to country folk, quite apart from any biases they might feel against city people.

This domination of state legislatures by rural legislators was possible essentially because they at one time did represent a majority of the people in

[17]See Alan K. Campbell and Donna E. Shalala, "Problems Unsolved, Solutions Untried: The Urban Crisis," in Alan K. Campbell, ed., *The States and the Urban Crisis* (Englewood Cliffs, N.J.: Prentice-Hall, 1970), pp. 9–11; Advisory Commission on Intergovernmental Relations, *Urban America and the Federal System* (Washington, D.C.: U.S. Government Printing Office, 1969), esp. chap. 2.

[18]Advisory Commission on Intergovernmental Relations, *Urban America and the Federal System,* pp. 14, 19-20; Advisory Commission on Intergovernmental Relations, *City Financial Emergencies: The Intergovernmental Dimension* (Washington, D.C.: U.S. Government Printing Office, 1973), Table B-29, pp. 149-50.

[19]See Gordon E. Baker, *The Reapportionment Revolution* (New York: Random House, 1966), chap. 4; Roscoe C. Martin, *The Cities and the Federal System* (New York: Atherton, 1965), chap. 1.

their states. With the burgeoning growth of cities in the late nineteenth and early twentieth century, and the realization that the majority was about to be lost, rural-oriented state officials inserted provisions in their state constitutions and enacted reapportionment legislation that normally guaranteed them permanent control of at least one house regardless of further population shifts.

A number of devices were used to achieve that objective: Seats in one house of the legislature were allocated equally to geographic subdivisions like counties or townships despite their differences in population (some states already had this pattern in imitation of the national Senate). Even when population was considered in apportionment of seats, progressively less representation was allowed to the more populous areas. Often a minimum representation was granted to each county regardless of population, and since maximum limits were placed on the number of legislators from any county regardless of the size of its population, the most populous areas received only marginally more representation than the least populous. Even in the legislative houses legally required to be based in whole or part on population, state legislatures simply failed to redistrict after every decennial census so as not to reflect the loss of population in rural areas.

As a result of these devices, rural areas as recently as the early 1960s enjoyed in a large majority of the states fantastic overrepresentation relative to their populations. In Connecticut, New Jersey, and California, for example:

> Hartford's 162,178 residents sent two representatives [to the lower house], as did the town of Union, with a population of only 383. In fact, in 1962 Connecticut's four most populous cities (Hartford, Bridgeport, New Haven, and Waterbury), with a combined population of 578,104, elected only eight members to a lower house of 294. The same share of legislative strength at the small town end of the scale represented only 3,312 persons. . . .
>
> Rural Sussex County's 49,255 inhabitants, and Metropolitan Essex [including the city of Newark] County's 923,545 each sent one senator to the New Jersey legislature.
>
> Los Angeles County's 6,038,771 people received the same senate representation as 14,196 in the state senate district composed of Mono, Inyo, and Alpine counties in the Sierra Nevada Mountains.[20]

Admittedly, these were extreme individual cases where rural voters enjoyed between 19 and 425 times the legislative strength of their state's urban dwellers. A study of all states calculated the average value of the vote

[20]Baker, *The Reapportionment Revolution,* pp. 25-26.

in the smallest (under 25,000) and largest (500,000 and over) category of counties according to how closely the share of seats from each category of counties in the two houses of the state legislature corresponded to its share of the population. It showed that in 1960 (in the twenty-two states with large cities) the weight of the rural vote ranged from 1.3 to 30 times that of the urban vote, with the average overweighting of the rural vote in those states being 5 times. (See Table 3-2, columns 1, 2, and 3.) Furthermore, in another study which calculated overrepresentation by showing what percentage of the state's population was encompassed in the most sparsely populated areas which in combination could elect a majority in each house of the state legislature, it was found that in only two states with large cities (Massachusetts and Wisconsin) were both houses apportioned so that areas sending majorities had to have at least 40 percent of the state's population. In four such states, areas containing less than 15 percent of the population could elect a majority of the members in at least one house, while in seventeen other such states, areas with only one-third of the population controlled a majority of at least one house and in five states they could elect a majority in both. (See Table 3-2, columns 4 and 5.)

The severe overrepresentation of rural areas in state legislatures has now been eliminated. This was the result of a series of Supreme Court decisions beginning in 1962 that eventually interpreted the "equal protection" clause of the Fourteenth Amendment to the federal constitution as requiring that both houses of every state legislature must be apportioned on a population basis and that the population in each legislative district be substantially equal.[21] As Chief Justice Earl Warren stated in one of the set of cases that in 1964 nailed down this "one man, one vote" doctrine:

> Legislators are elected by voters, not farms or cities or economic interests. . . . And, if a state should provide that the votes of citizens in one part of the State should be given two times, or five times, or ten times the weight of votes of citizens in another part of the State, it could hardly be contended that the right to vote of those residing in the disfavored areas had not been effectively diluted. . . . Diluting of the weight of votes because of place of residence impairs constitutional rights under the Fourteenth Amendment just as much as invidious discriminations based on race or economic status.[22]

Consequences and Prospects of Fair Apportionment

Unfortunately for large cities, fair apportionment in the 1960s did not lead to substantial strengthening of their representation in the state legisla-

[21]See *Baker v. Carr,* 369 U.S. 186 (1962) and *Reynolds v. Sims,* 377 U.S. 533 (1964).
[22]*Reynolds v. Sims,* at 562, 566.

TABLE 3-2 Effects of Malapportionment on Relative Value of Representative Strength in State Legislatures

States with Large Cities	Weight of vote for members of legislature (1960)			Minimum percentage of population controlling a legislative majority (1961)	
	Counties under 25,000	*Counties 500,000 & over*	*Ratio*	*Senate*	*House*
Arizona	533	53	10:1	12.8	N.A.
California	562	63	9:1	10.7	44.7
Colorado	211	70	3:1	29.8	32.1
Florida	476	16	30:1	12.0	12.0
Georgia	182	12	15:1	22.6	22.2
Hawaii	228	67	3:1	23.4	47.8
Illinois	151	91	2:1	28.7	39.9
Indiana	133	69	2:1	40.4	34.8
Louisiana	177	105	2:1	33.0	34.1
Maryland	445	83	5:1	14.2	25.3
Massachusetts	277	102	3:1	44.6	45.3
Michigan	205	74	3:1	29.0	44.0
Minnesota	156	55	3:1	40.1	34.5
Missouri	174	69	3:1	47.7	20.3
New Jersey	356	76	5:1	19.0	46.5
New York	348	86	5:1	36.9	38.2
Ohio	242	87	3:1	41.0	30.3
Pennsylvania	317	85	4:1	33:1	37.7
Tennessee	162	49	3:1	26.9	28.7
Texas	156	45	3:1	30.3	38.6
Washington	141	88	2:1	33.9	35.3
Wisconsin	119	92	1.3:1	45.0	40.0

Source: Columns one, two, and three adapted from Gordon E. Baker, *The Reapportionment Revolution* (New York: Random House, 1966), pp. 34-45. Columns four and five adapted from National Municipal League *Compendium on Legislative Apportionment* (New York: The National Municipal League, 1962).

tures. In most states outside the so-called sunbelt of Florida, Texas, Arizona, and California, the lion's share of the seats that were taken away from rural areas went not to large-city constituencies, but to the suburbs. For it was the population of the suburbs rather than of large cities that had been growing most rapidly since the 1930s and thus was the most underrepresented in malapportioned legislatures that failed to reflect population shifts. Indeed, from 1950 to 1960 twenty-two, and from 1960 to 1970 twenty-three, of the nation's fifty-six largest cities showed an absolute decline in population while their suburbs continued to grow rapidly. Actually the population of over half of these largest cities is now smaller than that of the part of their surrounding suburbs located in the same state.[23] By 1960 in no state did the population of its largest city amount to 50 percent of the entire state and by 1970 in only one state—New York—did the population living in all cities of 50,000 and larger combined exceed that of the remainder of the state! In short, the invalidation of state legislatures not apportioned according to population came some 20 to 30 years too late for large cities to become chief beneficiaries, so that even with fair apportionment, large cities currently still face legislatures dominated in numbers not by sympathetic urban legislators but by varying combinations of suburban and rural ones.

Despite the failure to win control for themselves through reapportionment, large cities probably have made some gains from the shift of varying degrees of legislative power in most states from rural to suburban areas: First of all, although suburban representation has increased and will probably keep increasing, in only five states with large cities—New Jersey, California, Pennsylvania, Maryland, and Massachusetts—was the suburban population in 1970 an absolute majority of the state,[24] so that suburban legislators if they were united could control the legislature without allies. And in some "urban" states, the big-city delegations are still larger than the suburban ones. This means that suburban legislators will often need non-suburban support to achieve their own objectives, and they may choose to form coalitions with big-city rather than rural legislators and thus be willing to provide reciprocal support for these legislators from urban areas.

Admittedly, few suburban legislators are "bleeding hearts" for helping cities cope better with the problems generated by the low level of housekeeping services, slums, poverty, crime, and racial conflict. And many legislators from the suburbs represent constituents with anticity biases almost as strong as those traditionally held in rural areas. Many suburbanites feel that they have through their own efforts escaped the troubles of the cities and they do not want to be reminded of those troubles and be forced to give up increments of their income to help those they consider unwilling to help or incapable of helping themselves.

On the other hand, some problems of large cities, like inadequate mass transit, air and water pollution and shortages of "open spaces," are shared by the suburbs, giving their legislators incentives to support state programs to come to grips with them. Also, some of the older, "closer-in" suburbs are themselves already beginning to experience some of the problems of poverty,

[23]U.S. Bureau of the Census, *Statistical Abstract of the United States: 1974* (Washington, D.C.: U.S. Government Printing Office, 1974), Table 24, p. 23-24; Census of Population and Housing: 1970, *General Demographic Trends for Metropolitan Areas, 1960-1970,* Final Report PHC(2)-1 (Washington D.C.: U.S. Government Printing Office, 1971) Table 11, pp. 1-47 to 1-60 (hereinafter cited as PHC(2)-1).

[24]PHC(2)-1, Table 2, p. 1-25.

blight, and drugs that are associated with large cities. Furthermore, suburbanites are feeling the strain of high real estate taxes to finance their school systems and are therefore willing to support expanded state aid to local schools, from which large-city school districts will also benefit. Moreover, some suburbanites work in large cities or use city shopping, cultural, and recreational facilities, thus experiencing at first-hand certain kinds of unhealthy urban conditions and having a direct stake in their alleviation. Finally, because resistance to increased state taxes is probably not as strong among the better-educated, higher-income suburbanites as it is in rural areas, reapportioned legislatures will probably allow more and more states to adopt sales taxes and graduated income taxes that can generate additional revenues each year to permit expanded state aid of various sorts to all local governments including those of large cities.[25] Since the late 1960s, state legislatures have in fact been showing greater responsiveness to the needs of large cities through increases of state aid and the addition of some urban-oriented programs.

Role of the Governor

The governor is a key factor in determining how responsive state governments will be to the needs of large cities. For in almost all states, it is the governor who proposes new legislative programs, budgetary increases or decreases or other changes in grants to local governments, and a tax program to raise the necessary revenues. The legislature then proceeds to adopt, defeat, or modify the governor's proposals. Broadly speaking, governors, since they are elected on a state-wide basis and feel responsibility for conditions in all parts of their states including large cities, have been more sympathetic to urban needs than the average rank-and-file member of the legislature. Governors are likely to continue this posture and will probably find reapportioned legislatures more responsive to their leadership, within the limits of not giving large cities more favored treatment than suburbs and of not requiring continual large increases in state taxes.

The latter may turn out to be a very significant limit, especially for state governments already making a high tax effort. States that still lack one or more broad-based taxes, such as on income and sales, can raise large amounts of additional revenue by imposing them. In states that already have such taxes, the automatic increases in revenues generated at given rates are not proving sizable enough to meet the enormity of demands for increased state aid that are forthcoming from large-city and other local

[25]See A. James Reichley, "The Political Containment of Cities," in Campbell, ed., *The States and the Urban Crisis,* pp. 169-95. Of course, this analysis of legislative power based entirely on constituency characteristics of legislators is greatly oversimplified since with varying degrees of frequency in different states, party affiliations overcome the pull of constituency characteristics in influencing legislative voting.

governments. The capacity of state governments to channel significant additional funds to city governments is therefore largely dependent on the federal government's providing increased financial aid to the states. The most widely talked about proposals involve the federal government completely taking over the financing of certain expensive functions like welfare and medicaid, making available larger amounts of money through revenue-sharing for general support of state governments, and reducing the disincentives to increases in state income taxes by allowing credits against federal income taxes for the amounts paid in income tax to the state.[26]

[26]See, for example, Advisory Commission on Intergovernmental Relations, *Urban America and the Federal System,* chap. 1.

4

City Governmental Structures and Electoral Rules

City governmental decisions are made and carried out by various parts of a "formal governmental structure." Because the governmental structure of any particular large city is determined by some combination of state law, state constitutional provision, and home-rule action, no two cities have one that is exactly alike: Cities differ in the titles, legal powers, and responsibilities of the specific offices, governing bodies, and other agencies that constitute their governmental structure. They differ in how each of these offices, bodies, and agencies relate to each other in terms of legal superiority or subordination. Large cities differ in how the different positions in their governmental structures are filled and in how the various incumbents can be removed and replaced. Cities also differ in the procedures by which the whole structure of governmental offices and positions and legal powers itself can be changed.

These differences in structural arrangements and legal powers are not just neutral technical details. They almost always provide differential advantages and disadvantages to particular individuals and groups seeking to influence the content of city governmental decisions or to gain office for themselves or their allies. The exact allocation of authority in a particular city's governmental structure has great impact on the relative influence different officials can exercise over its decision-making process. For ultimately, binding city decisions are made when certain officials perform designated formal acts like the placing of a signature on a piece of paper or the casting of votes in a collective body. Each city's formal structure specifies whose signatures or votes are the controlling ones in making decisions binding on different matters, and cities differ widely in how such powers are assigned. How much influence a particular official can have over what regulations are enforced, over what taxes are imposed, and over who is appointed, hired, and fired will normally be greatly affected by whether the legal power to make the decision is in his own hands or in the hands of some hierarchical superior or some other official not in a hierarchical relation to himself at all.

Some readers of this book may question the importance assigned in this chapter to structures, legal powers, and legal rights as sources of political influence. They may believe that other kinds of political factors and that especially social, economic, and psychological forces are always much more "fundamental" to who can influence political decision-making most effectively. They may consider the allocation of formal authority to be an "irrelevant legalistic technicality."

Admittedly, legal powers and rights are not always determinative of actual influence. But they are never irrelevant. City officials and other city political activists think and talk constantly in terms of the legal powers, legal obligations, legal rights, and legal procedures applicable to the city government as a whole, to different officials and agencies, or to different categories of citizens. Furthermore, the awareness of the participants in a decision-making conflict of who has what legal powers or rights and of who is under what legal obligations shapes expectations about who should do what and hence conditions behavior even when formal authority is not being explicitly invoked. Finally, that conditioning is buttressed by the further awareness among urban political activists that trial courts stand ready to issue orders against official acts which exceed legal powers or violate legal rights, procedures, and obligations.

FORMS OF CITY GOVERNMENTS

All city governments are alike in that their building blocks consist of an array of "line," "operating," or "administrative" departments and agencies. The departments and agencies carry out particular specialized governmental functions, like police protection, fire protection, garbage removal, schooling, welfare, urban renewal, parks, recreation, etc. City governments are also similar in that they all have some kind of "central organs of control." These central organs of control are hierarchically superior to the departments and agencies and legally responsible for exercising varying degrees of direction and supervision over the performance of their functions. Because city governments differ in how these central organs are constituted, such governments are normally differentiated and categorized as "mayor-council," "council-manager," or "commission" forms.

Mayor-Council

The mayor-council is the most widely used form among large cities. All of the very largest cities of over 1,000,000 in population, three-quarters of those ranging from 500,000 to 1,000,000 and almost half of those ranging between 250,000 and 500,000 have a mayor-council type of general city government (Table 4-1). In these cities there is an independently elected mayor who is normally designated "chief executive officer of the city" and given responsibility to see that its laws, ordinances, and resolutions are "faithfully" or "efficiently" executed. The mayor also serves as the city's formal "chief of state" and ceremonial head.

The elected "city council," or "board of aldermen" as it is called in some cities, has legal powers to enact regulatory ordinances and local laws, to establish programs to be administered by the operating departments, to appropriate money for the various activities of the city government, to impose taxes, to condemn private property for public use, and, in general, to make decisions on how the governmental powers that are assigned to the city government by state law shall be exercised. Councils range in size of membership from four in El Paso and seven in New Orleans and in Columbus to forty-three in New York, forty-one in Nashville, and fifty in Chicago. (See Table 4–2.)

Most city councils elect their presiding officer, or "president," from their own membership. In a few large cities, however, including New York, Baltimore, and Atlanta, there is a "president of the city council" elected directly by the voters at large. A very few mayor-council cities—the most notable being New York—also have a second legislative body with certain limited powers, the most important of which is shared control with the council over adoption of the budget. In New York this body is called the Board of Estimate.

There are great variations in the specific legal powers assigned to mayors in different cities for the performance of their chief executive function and for providing general policy leadership to the council on legislative matters. Because of these variations a further distinction is usually made among mayor-council systems, between the so-called "strong-mayor" and "weak-

TABLE 4-1 Percent Mayor-Council Form by Population Size

Population Size	Number Mayor-Council	Total Cities	Percent Mayor-Council
Over 1,000,000	6	6	100
500,000–1,000,000	15	20	75
250,000–500,000	13	30	43

Source: *The Municipal Year Book,* 1968 (Washington, D.C.: The International City Managers' Association, 1968), Table III; *The Municipal Year Book,* 1972, (Washington, D.C.: The International City Management Association, 1972), Table 3/20.

TABLE 4–2 Large Mayor-Council Cities and Size of City Councils

Population Size	City	Size of Council
Over 1,000,000	Chicago	50
	Detroit	9
	Houston	8
	Los Angeles	15
	New York	43
	Philadelphia	17
500,000 to 1,000,000	Baltimore	19
	Boston	9
	Cleveland	33
	Columbus	7
	Denver	13
	Indianapolis	29
	Jacksonville	19
	Memphis	13
	Milwaukee	19
	New Orleans	7
	Pittsburgh	9
	St. Louis	29
	San Francisco	11
	Seattle	9
	Washington, D.C.	12
250,000 to 500,000	Akron	13
	Atlanta	19
	Birmingham	9
	Buffalo	15
	El Paso	4
	Honolulu	9
	Jersey City	9
	Louisville	12
	Minneapolis	13
	Nashville	41
	Newark	9
	Omaha	7
	Tampa	7

Source: *The Municipal Year Book,* 1968 (Washington, D.C.: The International City Managers' Association, 1968), Table III; *The Municipal Year Book,* 1972, (Washington, D.C.: The International City Management Association, 1972), Table 3/20.

mayor'' types. Certain textbook explanations specify some one particular characteristic that supposedly differentiates between these two kinds of mayor-council systems. But it is more useful to think in terms of the legal powers assigned to mayors of different cities placing them on different points along a strong-mayor to weak-mayor continuum. At the strong-mayor end would thus be a mayor who had specific legal powers to do all of the following: (a) Appoint and remove the heads of all the operating departments and agencies without the need of approval by the council; (b) Submit to the council an overall "executive budget" indicating the amounts proposed to be spent the following year by each department and agency, veto any changes made in this budget by the council with the mayoral veto being binding unless overridden by extraordinary council majorities (e.g., two-thirds or three-quarters), and have the budget deemed adopted if the council does not act within a certain period following its submission; (c) Submit to the council legislative proposals, initiate ordinances, and veto or item-veto those passed by the council, again with his veto being overridable only by extraordinary majorities; (d) Over the course of the year after a budget is adopted, transfer funds between categories within different departments or even between departments; (e) Reorganize and shift functions between departments, agencies, and staff units; (f) Serve a four-year term, indefinitely renewable.

Conversely, at the weak-mayor end of the continuum would be a mayor who had none of these powers and in addition suffered from the following infirmities: (a) His appointments and removals would need the concurrence of the council; (b) Some executive functions would be performed by independently elected officials. The executive officials most commonly elected in "weak-mayor" systems are comptrollers, treasurers, city attorneys or prosecutors, and city clerks; (c) Some or all operating departments would be under the direct supervision of council committees or of independent boards or commissions, whose members served long, overlapping terms, which might extend beyond the mayor's own term. The mayor would not be able to remove these board or commission members except "for cause," usually defined as "official misconduct," "gross neglect of duties," but not simple unwillingness to follow the mayor's directives; (d) Departmental budgetary requests would go directly to the council, which would formulate and adopt the budget. The mayor would not be in a position to raise or lower those requests or veto the adopted budget. In addition some operating departments would be entitled by laws to some fixed percentage of the taxes to be raised without any budgetary approval at all; (e) The mayor would be allowed to serve only a two-year term or be limited in the number of consecutive terms that he could serve or both.

The mayor of no particular large mayor-council city has legal powers that would position him directly on either pole of the strong-mayor—weak-mayor continuum: The mayors of Detroit, New York City, and Philadelphia are probably legally the "strongest." But even their city governments have certain administrative functions—for example, city planning in New York City—that are vested in semi-independent boards, and two cities also have at least one executive official besides the mayor—a comptroller in New York City and a city clerk and treasurer in Detroit—independently elected.

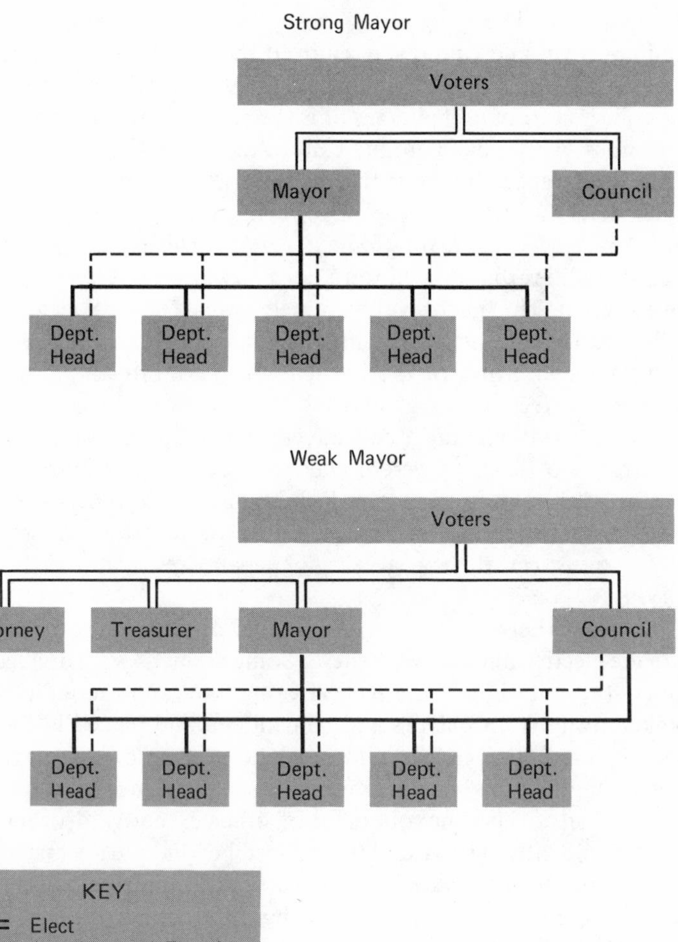

FIGURE 4-1 Diagram of Mayor-Council System

The legal powers enjoyed by the mayors of Cleveland, Boston, and Baltimore would also definitely position them near the strong-mayor end of the continuum. On the other hand, the legal powers of the mayors of Seattle, Milwaukee, and especially Los Angeles would clearly place them close to the weak-mayor end.

In Los Angeles, for example, all the important operating departments are under the control of citizen-boards, consisting of members serving five-year, staggered terms. These members are appointed by the mayor only with council approval and cannot be removed by him. Several departments are independent even of regular budgetary controls, having money to spend that is collected from user charges or is received as a fixed share of the city's tax revenues every year automatically. And although the mayor of Los Angeles can prepare an executive budget, the council has the power to change it in any way without the mayor being able to veto the changes.

Emergence of the Mayor-Council Form During colonial times, the few municipalities that existed were normally governed by a mayor and an elective council. The mayor was extremely "weak"—with legal powers that were limited to representing the municipality on ceremonial occasions and presiding over meetings of the council. Furthermore, the mayor was not independently elected, but chosen by the council itself or by the colonial governor. It was the council collectively that made appointments of such administrative officials as were needed, and council committees supervised the performance of administrative tasks. In addition to performing legislative and administrative functions, the mayor and the councilmen were usually also justices of the peace, trying legal cases that arose in the municipality.[1]

In the period between the Revolution and Jackson's presidency, mayors were made elective almost everywhere. Some councils were divided into two chambers (in imitation of the federal Congress), and the judicial function was taken away from mayors and councilmen and placed in the hands of elective or appointive judges. Independent election of the mayor did not greatly strengthen his powers over the performance of administrative functions. For at this time a number of other executive officers were also made independently elective and thus placed beyond the mayor's control.

A different set of changes in the structure of municipal government was made in many mayor-council cities during the second half of the nineteenth century. Disenchantment set in with elected officials because of the uncovering of widespread inefficiency and corruption in their conduct of city governmental affairs. As a result, control of newly established functions such as parks and libraries and even some existing ones like education were taken out of the hands of elective "politicians" and put under semi-independent "citizen boards" or "commissions." The members of these boards and commissions served only part-time and often without salary. To attempt to insulate them from the purportedly corrupting effects of "politics" even further, their terms were usually made overlapping and longer than

[1]This account of the emergence of mayor-council government is based primarily on William Anderson and Edward W. Weidner, *American City Government,* rev. ed. (New York: Henry Holt and Company, 1950), chaps. 14-15; and Herbert Kaufman, *Politics and Policies in State and Local Governments* (Englewood Cliffs, N.J.: Prentice-Hall, 1963).

those of the elective officials who appointed them, thus precluding the appointment of a new majority by the winner or winners of any particular election. The overall consequence of all these developments was that city governments came to consist of some dozens of semi-independent or completely autonomous offices and units.

The strong-mayor system was one reaction to the extreme fragmentation that existed in city governments at the turn of the century. It became clear that the splintering of city government into a multiplicity of independent and semi-independent offices and agencies did not immunize it against corruption. Indeed that splintering sometimes facilitated corruption by allowing the capturing of various administrative agencies by particular interests who were in the position to profit from the agencies' decisions. Many became convinced furthermore that this fractionizing of city government caused unnecessary waste, contradictions, and stalemates that interfered with the adoption by city governments of necessary programs to cope with demanding conditions.

In many cities reformers called for a reintegration of the legal powers of the city government through a strengthening of the mayoralty. These supporters of "executive leadership" argued that dispersion of governmental power made its exercise "invisible" and therefore irresponsible. They urged a concentration of legal powers in the hands of the mayor, who was a highly visible and elected official. Such concentration would thus promote accountability to the public for the performance of the city government and strengthen the coordination of what were even in the first decades of the twentieth century becoming the wide-ranging activities of large-city governments. A strong mayor could also be looked to as a source of affirmative leadership for the development of needed new programs and policies.

In most large cities that kept mayor-council systems these arguments were heeded. Over the course of the first half of the twentieth century, their mayors' position was strengthened by having their terms of office increased from two years to four years and by having their powers of appointment and removal broadened. Also, varying numbers of independently elected executive offices and semi-independent boards and commissions were abolished and their functions transferred to regular operating departments under the control of the mayor. Finally, mayors were granted additional legislative prerogatives such as the veto and were assigned responsibility for formulating an integrated executive budget.

These trends were not, however, universal. In some large cities that retained the mayor-council form of government, none or few of these changes were made, so that their mayors remained "weak." During this same period the division of the city's legislative body into two chambers fell into general disfavor in both strong and weak mayor-council cities, with the single-chambered council becoming the almost universal pattern.

Council-Manager Form

None of the nation's very largest cities of 1,000,000 population or larger, but one-quarter of the cities between 500,000 and 1,000,000, and almost half of those with populations between 250,000 and 500,000 are governed by "council-manager" or, as they are more commonly referred to, "city-manager" systems (Table 4-3). There is, under this type of city government, a small council, ranging in size from five to twelve members, vested with the same legislative powers normally held by councils in mayor-council cities (Table 4-4).

In council-manager cities there is no separately elected mayor to function as chief executive with independent legal powers and responsibilities for supervising and directing the city government's operating departments. Instead, the council appoints a city manager to serve as the "chief executive and administrative officer" of the city. The manager serves at the pleasure of the council and can be dismissed at any time. It is the manager who appoints and removes the heads of the operating departments and who is obliged to see that the city's ordinances are enforced. Members of the council are explicitly prohibited, " except for the purpose of inquiry," from dealing with any of the operating departments without going through the manager. The manager has the responsibility for preparing an executive budget, though that budget does not take effect unless approved by the council, and the manager cannot veto any changes that the council sees fit to make. Finally, the manager is usually given the right to attend council meetings and is charged to make any recommendations to the council concerning the affairs of the city as seem to him advisable.

Even in council-manager cities there is an official with the title of mayor, either directly elected by the voters (in, e.g., Dallas, San Diego, and Phoenix) or chosen by the council itself from among its own membership (in, e.g., San Antonio and Cincinnati). This mayor serves as a member and presiding officer of the council with a vote like the other members but not a veto. The mayor of a council-manager city also acts as the official head of the city government, representing the city on ceremonial occasions, signing legal instruments and documents, and usually having the legal power to take

TABLE 4-3 Percent Council-Manager Cities by Population Size

Population size	Number Council-Manager Cities	Total	Percent Council-Manager Cities
Over 1,000,000	0	6	0
500,000–1,000,000	5	20	25
250,000–500,000	14	30	47

Source: *The Municipal Year Book,* 1968 (Washington, D.C.: The International City Managers' Association), Table III; *The Municipal Year Book,* 1972 (Washington, D.C.: The International City Management Association, 1968), Table 3/20.

TABLE 4-4 Large Council-Manager Cities and Size of City Councils

Population Size	City	Size of Council
500,000 to 1,000,000	Dallas	11
	Kansas City	12
	Phoenix	7
	San Antonio	9
	San Diego	8
	Austin	6
	Cincinnati	9
	Fort Worth	8
	Long Beach	8
	Miami	4
250,000 to 500,000	Norfolk	7
	Oakland	8
	Oklahoma City	8
	Rochester	9
	Sacramento	8
	San Jose	7
	Toledo	8
	Tucson	6
	Wichita	5

Source: *The Municipal Year Book,* 1968 (Washington, D.C.: The International City Managers' Association, 1968), Table III; *The Municipal Year Book,* 1972 (Washington, D.C.: The International City Management Association, 1972), Table 3/20.

personal command of the police in times of emergency for the purpose of maintaining order and enforcing the city's laws.

Council-manager governments normally have few important administrative functions assigned to agencies that are not under the control of the manager. Such semi-independent or independent boards or commissions as exist—Cincinnati, for example, has a "board of health," a "public planning commission," and a "board of rapid transit commissioners"—are most often appointed by the mayor, though occasionally appointments are made by the council as a whole. With the exception of San Diego which elects a city attorney, in none of the large council-manager cities are there separately elected executive officials who head administrative departments.

Emergence of Council-Manager Government Sumter, South Carolina, was in 1908 the first municipality to have a "general manager" hired by its council. The first sizable city (over 100,000 in population) to establish a full-fledged council-manager government was Dayton, Ohio, in 1914. The council-manager system was seen as an alternative to the strong-mayor form for overcoming the fragmentation of authority that existed in city government in the first decades of the twentieth century and as a method of introducing "business-like" efficiency and economy into its operations. The idea was that the council would function in the manner of a

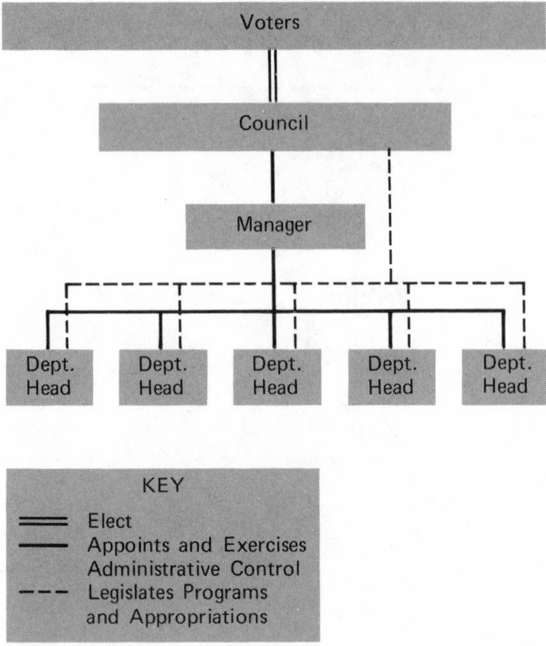

FIGURE 4–2 Diagram of Council-Manager System

business corporation "board of directors," setting general policies. The manager correspondingly would perform the role of a professionally trained administrator responsible for seeing that those policies were implemented in as technically neutral and efficient a manner as possible. "Politics" and policymaking would thus be separated from administration. Because all or almost all of the legal powers of the city government would be concentrated in the hands of a small council, the voters would have only a "short ballot" of names to consider at election time and thus be in a position to study the qualifications of the candidate so as to make a wise judgment in casting their votes.[2]

Although not a logically necessary part of a council-manager system, most cities that adopted it required that the council members be chosen in "nonpartisan elections." In such elections the ballots or voting machines are not allowed to show any party affiliation for the different candidates. This kind of "nonpartisanship" was supposed to provide additional protection against the intrusion of politics into the operation of the city

[2]See Anderson and Weidner, *American City Government*; and Kaufman, *Politics and Policies*.

government. To many reform-minded supporters of the city-manager system and "nonpartisanship," the term "politics" referred to the influence exerted by "party bosses" and the lower-status immigrants who provided much of those party bosses' bases of support. They saw the interests of the bosses and their immigrant followings as antithetical to those of the purportedly more "public-regarding" businessmen and middle-class people generally.

The council-manager plan was endorsed in 1911 by the National Short Ballot Organization—a civic reform group whose president was then Woodrow Wilson. In 1916 the plan was incorporated into the "model city charter" sponsored by the National Municipal League—another "good government" reform group. Between World War I and the decade following World War II, so many villages and small and middle-sized cities established council-manager governments that it became and still is the single most widely used form in the municipalities with populations between 25,000 and 250,000.

The very largest cities of over 500,000 in population have not found the council-manager plan especially attractive: Cleveland, after switching from a mayor-council to a council-manager government in 1921, switched back again and established a strong-mayor government in 1931. Cincinnati, one of the nation's largest cities then, adopted a council-manager plan in 1926 and has stuck to it. The handful of other large cities of over 500,000 that presently have council-manager governments were considerably smaller in population when they adopted the plan and retained it as they grew to large-city size.

Commission Form of City Government

No large city over 500,000 in population has a commission form of government. Memphis had one until 1968, when it abandoned the commission for a mayor-council form of government (Table 4–5). Three large cities exceeding 250,000 have a commission form of government—Portland, Oregon; St. Paul, Minnesota; and Tulsa, Oklahoma. All legal powers in a commission government are essentially vested in a small number of commissioners, usually five or seven (Table 4-6). Collectively, the commissioners make up the city's council and exercise legislative powers. Individually, each commissioner is the administrative head of a different department or set of related operating departments. As was the case in Memphis, commissioners are usually elected on a nonpartisan ballot. In some commission cities, each candidate runs to become head of a particular department or set of departments, while in other cities particular departmental responsibilities are assigned to each commissioner after the election by vote of the council.

TABLE 4-5 Percent Commission Form Cities by Population Size

Population Size	Number Commission Form Cities	Total	Percent Commission Form Cities
Over 1,000,000	0	6	0
500,000–1,000,000	0	20	0
250,000–500,000	3	30	10

Source: *The Municipal Year Book,* 1972 (Washington, D.C.: The International City Management Association, 1972), Table 3/20.

There is in a commission government no single official who functions as chief executive or administrative officer of the city with legal authority over the entire array of operating departments. One of the commissioners does carry the title of "mayor," and presides over the council and acts as the city's representative on ceremonial occasions. But a commission government mayor does not have any greater legislative or administrative powers than the other commissioners. In most commission cities (and in all *large* commission cities) this mayor is elected directly by the voters by running for a specifically designated ballot position. In some cities, however, the mayor is chosen by the council from among its own membership after the election, while in a very few cities the mayor is the candidate for commissioner who polls the largest number of votes.

Besides commissioners, commission cities sometimes elect one or more other officials, most commonly a city attorney. Normally commission cities also have a small number of semi-independent boards in charge of such functions as libraries, city planning, zoning appeals, etc.

Emergence of Commission Government Although there had been "commissions" serving temporarily as governing authorities of a few cities in the second half of the nineteenth century, commission government attracted widespread notice as a distinct form when the Texas state legislature authorized a commission charter for Galveston in 1901. Galveston had been hit by a tidal wave the previous year, causing major loss of life and widespread physical destruction and leaving the city government's finances almost exhausted. Since the existing "weak-mayor" government was showing itself incapable of coping with the emergency situation, a group of

TABLE 4-6 Large Commission Form Cities and Number of Commissioners

Population	City	Commissioners
250,000 to 500,000	Portland	5
	St. Paul	7
	Tulsa	5

Source: *The Municipal Year Book,* 1972 (Washington, D.C.: The International City Management Association, 1972), Table 3/20.

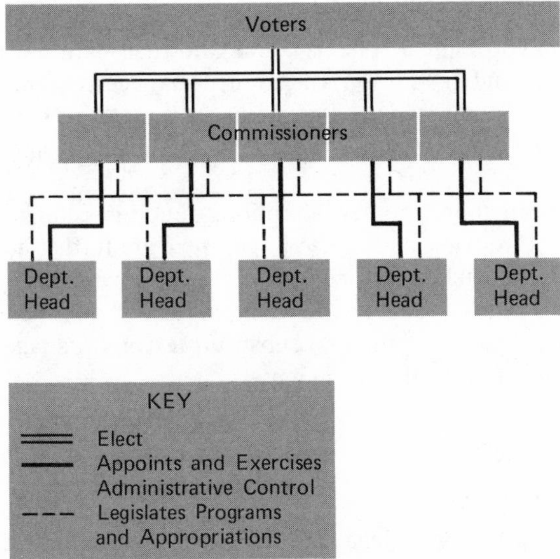

FIGURE 4-3 Diagram of Commission System

leading citizens constituted themselves as a new de facto government and began successfully to organize relief and rebuild the city. The action of the Texas state legislature, therefore, essentially only legitimated a form of government that had developed spontaneously during the emergency.[3]

The effectiveness of what became known as the Galveston Commission impressed other cities. Variations of the plan were soon adopted by Houston, Texas, in 1905, and by Des Moines, Iowa, in 1907, at which point it became known as the "Des Moines Plan" of city government. Because of its concentration of governmental powers in a small commission, the commission form appealed to reformers who were dissatisfied with the fragmentation of power in "weak-mayor" systems. Because of the small number of officials who would have to be elected, it also appealed to those favoring a shorter ballot. The newly developing "National Short Ballot Organization" publicized the commission form for a few years before it switched its support in 1911 to the council-manager plan.

In the years immediately preceding World War I, there were large-scale adoptions of the commission plan, so that by 1917 about 500 municipalities, particularly small ones, had adopted it in place of mayor-council systems. Thereafter the popularity of commission government waned, as the council-manager form gained favor. Those who were attracted to the commission's concentration of legal powers in a single body in contrast to the separation

[3]See Jewell Cass Phillips, *Municipal Government and Administration in America* (New York: Macmillan, 1960), chap. 11.

of powers of mayor-council systems could gain that feature with a council-manager system. And in addition, the council-manager system did not carry with it what were soon recognized as the disadvantages of having no center of administrative leadership and coordination under a single individual chief executive.

There have been almost no new adoptions of commission government by cities since the 1930s, while almost every year there are further abandonments. Des Moines itself switched to a council-manager government in 1949. San Antonio, New Orleans, Newark, and Memphis also abandoned the commission form in recent decades, the first substituting a city-manager system and the last three mayor-council governments.

DIFFERENCES IN ELECTORAL RULES

The machinery and other legal arrangements governing elections in city government also constitute part of its formal structure. Differences exist among large cities with respect to (1) the length of term for particular elective offices; (2) the boundaries of the constituency from which officials are elected to multimembered bodies; (3) whether a partisan or non-partisan general election ballot is used; (4) the machinery for nominating candidates; (5) whether provisions for recall election of incumbent officials exist; and (6) whether there exist provisions for referendum and initiative elections.

Length of Terms

Almost all large mayor-council cities elect their mayors, councilmen, and any other separately elected officials for four-year terms. About half of the council-manager cities and the remaining mayor-council cities elect officials to two-year terms. In the great majority of large cities, the terms of all elected officials expire simultaneously. The terms of councilmen in a few cities are, however, "staggered" or "overlapping," normally meaning that only half are elected at any particular election. And in a few cities, mayors and councilmen have different length terms, four years for mayor and two years for council or vice versa. (See Table 4-7.)

District vs. "At-Large" Constituencies

Obviously all candidates running for specific city-wide offices like mayor, separately-elected comptroller, president of city council, treasurer, clerk, and city attorney are voted upon by the electorate as a whole. Their constituency is therefore the entire city. Other city officials, like councilmen

TABLE 4-7 Length of Terms of Elected Officials in Large Cities, By Form of Government

Mayor-Council		Council-Manager		Commission
4-year terms	*2-year terms*	*4-year terms*	*2-year terms*	*4-year terms*
Akron	Buffalo[4]	Kansas City	Austin	Portland
Atlanta	Cleveland	Miami[2]	Cincinnati	St. Paul[4]
Baltimore	El Paso	Norfolk[2]	Dallas	Tulsa[4]
Birmingham	Houston	Oakland	Fort Worth	
Boston	Louisville[4]	Oklahoma City	Long Beach[3]	
Chicago	Minneapolis	Rochester[2]	Phoenix	
Columbus		San Diego	Sacramento[4]	
Denver		San Jose	San Antonio	
Detroit		Tucson	Toledo	
Honolulu		Wichita[1]		
Indianapolis				
Jacksonville				
Jersey City				
Los Angeles				
Memphis				
Milwaukee				
Nashville[2]				
New Orleans				
New York				
Newark				
Omaha				
Philadelphia				
Pittsburgh				
St. Louis				
San Francisco				
Seattle				
Tampa				
Washington				

Source: *The Municipal Year Book,* 1968 (Washington, D.C.: The International City Managers' Association, 1968, Table III, and *The Municipal Yearbook,* (Washington, D.C.: The International City Management Association, 1972), Table 3/20.

Notes: [1]Mayor has one-year term
[2]Mayor has two-year term
[3]Long Beach has three-year terms
[4]Mayor has four-year term

or commissioners who are members of multimembered bodies may be voted upon by the voters of the entire city or by only those residing in some geographic subdivision of it. When the candidates are voted upon by all the city's voters, they are said to run "at-large." The candidates who poll the largest number of votes city-wide are deemed elected. When the candidates are voted upon by only a particular subdivision of the city, they are said to be running in "district" or "ward-based" elections. The winners are then the candidates who polled the largest vote in each of the districts or wards into which the city is divided. Under a 1968 decision of the U.S. Supreme Court, districts or wards from which members of local governing bodies are elected must be substantially equal in population.[4]

About 60 percent of the large mayor-council cities but only a fifth of the council-manager cities elect all or most of their councilmen from districts or wards. About 70 percent of the council-manager cities elect all of their councilmen at-large. All the commission cities elect their commissioners at large. (See Table 4-8.)

"Partisan" vs. "Nonpartisan" Ballots

Slightly less than half of large cities with mayor-council governments hold "partisan" general elections for city offices. In partisan elections the different candidates are identified on the ballot or voting machine as "Republicans," "Democrats," or members of some third or other independent party. Almost all of the large council-manager cities and exactly half of the mayor-council cities hold "nonpartisan" general elections for city offices. One of the large commission cities holds partisan elections and the other two hold nonpartisan ones (Table 4-9). In nonpartisan elections party designations are prohibited by law from appearing on the ballot or voting machine to identify the candidates. The largest council manager city to use partisan elections is Rochester, N.Y., with a 1970 population of 296,233. Chicago has a hybrid electoral system in which members of the council are elected in nonpartisan elections, but other officials including the mayor are elected on a partisan basis. It should be noted now, although it will be fully explained in Chapter 8, that in some cities that legally have the nonpartisan ballot, parties are nevertheless active in city elections and the voters generally get to know the party affiliation of the different candidates even though the ballot doesn't show it.

In cities with partisan elections, a person gets his name on the general election ballot automatically if he is the nominee of an organization recognized as a party under the state election law. To qualify as a party an organization is normally required to have run a candidate for governor in the last gubernatorial election and to have polled more than a particular minimum percentage of the vote cast.

Being a candidate for office in partisan cities is not restricted only to party nominees: Independent candidates usually can also secure a place on the general election ballot beneath the party candidates. The typical requirement is filing a petition with election officials containing the signatures of a certain minimum number of enrolled city voters—a number set high enough to make it relatively difficult, but not impossible for candidates with a significant following to collect.

[4]See *Avery v. Midland County, Texas,* 390 U.S. 474 (1968).

TABLE 4-8 Method of Election for Councils in Large Cities

Mayor-Council Cities			Council Manager Cities			Commission Cities		
	Number at-large	*Number by ward*		*Number at-large*	*Number by ward*		*Number at-large*	*Number by ward*
Akron	3	10	Austin	6		Portland	5	
Atlanta	19		Cincinnati	9		St. Paul	7	
Baltimore	1	18	Dallas	3	8	Tulsa	5	
Birmingham	9		Fort Worth	8				
Boston	9		Kansas City	6	6			
Buffalo	6	9	Long Beach	8				
Chicago		50	Miami	4				
Cleveland		33	Norfolk	7				
Columbus	7		Oakland	8				
Denver	2	11	Oklahoma City		8			
Detroit	9		Phoenix	7				
El Paso	4		Rochester	5	4			
Honolulu		9	Sacramento		8			
Houston	3	5	San Antonio	9				
Indianapolis	29		San Diego	8				
Jacksonville	5	14	San Jose	7				
Jersey City	3	6	Toledo	8				
Los Angeles		15	Wichita	5				
Louisville	12		Tuscon		6			
Memphis	6	7						
Milwaukee		19						
Minneapolis		13						
Nashville	6	35						
New Orleans	2	5						
New York[a]	10	33						
Newark	4	5						
Omaha	7							
Philadelphia	7	10						
Pittsburgh	9							
St. Louis	1	28						
San Francisco	11							
Seattle	9							
Tampa	7							
Washington,	4	8						

Source: *The Municipal Year Book,* (Washington, D.C.: The International City Managers' Association, 1968), Table III and *The Municipal Year Book,* (Washington, D.C.: The International City Management Association, 1972), Table 3/20.

Note: [a]Two at-large seats for each of the five boroughs.

A few partisan large cities—the most notable being Philadelphia and New York—have special provisions governing general elections for their city councils in order to make it impossible for candidates of one party to capture all the seats. In Philadelphia, for example, whose council consists of ten members elected from districts and seven members elected "at-large,"

TABLE 4-9 Type of Ballot for Large-City Councilmanic Elections

Type of Ballot	Form of Government		
	Mayor-Council Cities†	*Council-Manager Cities*	*Commission Cities*
Partisan*	50% (16)	16% (3)	33% (1)
Nonpartisan	50% (16)	84%(16)	67% (2)
	100% (32)	100% (19)	100% (3)

Source: *The Municipal Year Book,* 1968 (Washington, D.C.: The International City Managers' Association, 1968), Table III.

Note: * Refers to national or local party labels.

†Data for Tampa and El Paso not available.

no single party can nominate more than five candidates for the at-large seats. In New York City, thirty-three councilmen are elected from councilmanic districts and another ten are elected nominally "at-large," two from each of the five boroughs that make up the city; no party is allowed to nominate more than a single candidate for each borough's two at-large seats.

In most cities with nonpartisan elections, a person gets his name as a candidate on the general election ballot by having first run in a nonpartisan preliminary or "primary" election. A number of nonpartisan cities such as Dallas, Phoenix, San Antonio, Newark, Denver, and Cincinnati have no nonpartisan primary per se: Would-be candidates can get their names directly on the general election ballot by filing a declaration of candidacy together with a petition signed by a certain minimum number or percentage of the city's enrolled voters. In Cincinnati, election is by plurality, so that the candidates polling the highest vote for a particular office or set of offices are deemed elected. In all other nonpartisan cities without a primary, a plurality is not sufficient and candidates are deemed elected only if they poll a majority, i.e., over half of all the votes cast for the office they are contesting. For any position for which no candidate receives a majority, a "run-off" election is subsequently held between the two candidates who had the highest votes.

In all large cities, general elections for city officials are held either in years when there are no national or state-wide elections or at a different time of year than elections for national or state office.

Nominating Machinery

In all partisan large cities, the nominees of each party for city office are chosen in a partisan "direct primary" election. To enter this primary, aspirants for a particular party's nomination must file a petition bearing the signatures of some stated minimum of that party's enrolled voters. In

TABLE 4-10 Partisan and Nonpartisan Ballot According to Form of Government

	Mayor-Council	Council-Manager	Commission
Partisan (national or local parties)	Akron Atlanta Baltimore Buffalo Chicago Honolulu Indianapolis Jacksonville Jersey City Louisville New Orleans New York Philadelphia Pittsburgh St. Louis Washington, D.C.	Kansas City Rochester Tucson	Tulsa
Nonpartisan (neither local nor national parties)	Birmingham Boston Cleveland Columbus Denver Detroit Houston Los Angeles Memphis Milwaukee Minneapolis Nashville Newark Omaha San Francisco Seattle	Austin Cincinnati Dallas Fort Worth Long Beach Miami Norfolk Oakland Oklahoma City Phoenix Sacramento San Antonio San Diego San Jose Toledo Wichita	Portland St. Paul

Source: *The Municipal Year Book,* 1968 (Washington, D.C.: The International City Managers' Association, 1968), Table III.

addition the would-be nominees normally must themselves be enrolled members of that party. In almost all large cities, partisan primaries are "closed," meaning that only enrolled members of a particular party are eligible to vote in their party primary to select who the party's nominee or nominees will be.[5]

To enter a nonpartisan primary, a would-be nominee must file a declara-

[5]In some middle-sized and small partisan cities, no direct primary is held and the party nominees for the general election are designated by a party committee or a party caucus, i.e., a meeting of enrolled party members.

tion of candidacy, usually accompanied by a petition signed by some minimum number or percentage of voters. Sometimes the would-be nominee must also pay a filing fee. All enrolled voters in a city are, of course, eligible to vote in a nonpartisan primary, regardless of their national or state party affiliations. The number of signatures required to enter either partisan or nonpartisan primaries is usually small enough to permit candidates with at least a minimal following to get on the primary ballot.

Recall Elections

In addition to elections for filling city governmental offices whose terms have expired or which have become vacant due to death or resignation, the charters of many large cities or applicable state law provide for the holding of special "recall" elections. These are elections by which incumbent elected officials can be removed from office before the regular expiration of their terms. The recall along with the "initiative" and "referendum" (to be discussed later in this chapter) were parts of the package of procedural devices promoted by the turn-of-the-century "good government" reformers to further "direct democracy" and strengthen direct control over governmental operations by the voters. The first large city to adopt recall provisions was Los Angeles, in 1903.

A recall election is initiated by depositing with election officials a petition signed by some minimum percentage of the qualified voters residing in the constituency from which the official being challenged was elected. The number of signatures required is much higher than that required for a candidate to enter a primary election—typically between 15 to 25 percent of those having voted for mayor in the last election. Once the petition is certified by the designated election officials to contain the proper number of signatures, the city council is obliged to call a special recall election.

Mayors have been recalled from office this century in Los Angeles (1909 and 1938), Seattle (1910 and 1938), and Detroit (1929), while city councilmen have been recalled in Pasadena and Long Beach, California (1934) and Fort Worth, Texas (1938).[6] In 1967 petitions were circulated to recall the then mayor of Detroit, Jerome P. Cavanaugh. Although for a long time highly popular, Cavanaugh had had his image tarnished by the major riot that took place in his city in 1967 and by the dissatisfaction about how it was handled by the city police. Also, Cavanaugh had lost prestige as a result of his defeat in a primary election for the Democratic senatorial nomination from Michigan and his publicized marital difficulties. Apparently a sufficient number of signatures was not gathered, so no recall election was held.

[6]Russell W. Maddox and Robert F. Fuquay, *State and Local Government*, 2nd ed. (Princeton, N.J.: D. Van Nostrand, 1966), p. 333.

Cavanaugh's term was to expire within a year and he did not seek reelection. In 1970 in Detroit, however, the four-person majority on that city's independently elected school board was successfully recalled. The precipitating factor for the recall campaign was the announcement of the Board's plan for achieving maximum racial balance in the city's schools. The overall school population in Detroit was then about 62 percent black and the Board planned to redraw the boundaries of school attendance districts in such a way as to end predominantly white student bodies in any of the city's high schools, including those in the almost exclusively white outlying areas.[7] In the summer of 1975, a recall election took place concerning Seattle's mayor, Wes Uhlman. The recall campaign was organized by the Seattle Firefighters' Union after Uhlman dismissed the city's fire chief following a severely critical report about the operation of the fire department.[8] The recall failed by a wide margin—77,009 to 44,741.[9]

Referendum and Initiative Elections

In national elections members of the public can vote only to select candidates. On the city level, however, the public can also use the vote to make governmental decisions directly. This is accomplished by adopting or rejecting propositions placed on the ballot through "referendum" or "initiative" procedures. Such referendum or initiative procedures are authorized by provisions of the city charter or state law.

A referendum is a procedural device by which a decision of a general city government is "referred" to the voters for their approval or disapproval. There are three kinds of referenda that are usually distinguished.

(1) *"Mandatory" or "compulsory" referendum* This is the kind held where state law or charter provision stipulates that a particular kind of decision of the governing body—normally the city council—cannot take effect unless also approved by a majority of the voters. Mandatory referenda are usually held on various kinds of charter amendments, bond issues, the granting of franchises to public utility and transportation companies, and on territorial annexations. The budgets of independent school districts are normally submitted to mandatory referenda, with the proviso, however, that even with the defeat of the budget, the school board in most states is authorized to spend certain minimal amounts to keep the school system operating.

(2) *"Optional" or "advisory" referendum* The optional referendum is one that takes place when the governing body enacts an ordinance or charter amendment, but itself chooses to provide that it will go into effect

[7]See *The New Republic,* September 12, 1970.
[8]*New York Times,* May 18, 1975.
[9]*New York Times,* July 3, 1975.

only if approved by the voters. An advisory referendum is one where the governing body simply asks for a nonbinding expression of opinion. With this kind of referendum the governing body can escape responsibility for making a controversial decision by passing it on to the voters.

(3) *"Protest" or "petition" referendum* Where provisions for protest or petition referenda are in effect, certain stated categories of ordinances or charter amendments enacted by the governing body cannot take effect until a stipulated period of time elapses—usually thirty, sixty, or ninety days. During that period a petition can be filed that has been signed by a certain minimum number of voters—e.g., 10–15 percent of the city's enrolled voters or those having cast a ballot for mayor in the previous election—calling for a referendum. If the petition is found valid, the ordinance or charter amendment in question cannot go into operation unless it is subsequently approved by a majority of the voters in a specially called election or at the next regular election.

Referenda essentially give the voters power to nullify a substantive decision desired by a city's governing body. Initiative is a procedure by which the voters can themselves "initiate" and impose substantive policy of their own on the governing body regardless of whether that governing body approves it. Voters begin the initiative process by drafting a proposed ordinance or charter amendment and securing, as in a petition referendum, a certain minimum of supporting signatures on a petition. The city's governing body is then required to place the proposal on the ballot at a special or at the next regular election. If approved by a majority of the voters, the proposal takes effect just as if it were enacted by the governing body itself. In a few cities, the city council is permitted to draft its own substitute proposal on the subject in question and place the substitute on the ballot along with the initiative proposal. If both receive majorities, the formulation that draws the largest number of votes is deemed adopted. Normally cities with initiative procedures deny the governing body the power to repeal an initiative-passed proposal for a stated amount of time after its approval, commonly from six months to two years.

Impact of Electoral Rules on Kinds of Individuals Recruited for Office

The formal rules according to which official positions are gained or conferred provide built-in advantages or disadvantages to certain candidates. Elective positions give advantage to persons who can develop a popular following. Appointive positions, especially if eligibility is limited to individuals who have particular kinds of professional qualifications—an M.D. degree, for example, to be commissioner of hospitals or coroner—

favor those who have certain kinds of technical training and achievements, whether or not they have a popular following.

If a position is elective, the particular boundaries of the constituency as well as other aspects of the nominating and electoral rules give advantage to certain would-be candidates rather than others. Election of councilmen by district may give advantage to candidates with characteristics that appeal to any ethnic, racial, religious, socioeconomic, or ideological groups that are sufficiently concentrated geographically to form a majority in particular districts, even if these groups are a minority city-wide. Election at-large, on the other hand, favors candidates with characteristics that appeal to or are at least not strongly opposed by city-wide majorities. Especially in recent decades, councils in cities with district elections have had more black councilmen than councils in cities with at-large elections.[10] This happened because the size of the black population was large enough to dominate a number of the councilmanic districts even though it was still a minority in the city as a whole. In cities that now have or are approaching having black city-wide majorities, district elections in the future may work to the advantage of white candidates, who would still be in a position to carry districts consisting of white neighborhoods, but might lose if forced to run city-wide against black opponents.

Whether the ballot is partisan can strengthen or weaken a candidate's position. The partisan ballot, as will be discussed in Chapter 8, favors candidates who have the support of party leaders with canvassing organizations. The nonpartisan ballot is advantageous to individuals who are unwilling to seek the backing of party leaders and especially individuals who are members of the minority party in that city. Nonpartisan ballots also favor those who have access to large sums of money to get their names known through advertising—something that is crucial in an election when party affiliation is unavailable to serve as a cue-giver.

Even such a seemingly technical point as whether the formal rules provide for majority or plurality elections can affect what candidates are selected. Majority elections preclude the nomination or election of candidates who do not enjoy the support of over half of the voters. Plurality elections, on the other hand, allow candidates to win nominations or public offices even if they appeal only to a minority in the electorate, as long as their vote is higher than anyone else's, which can happen if they are faced with two or more opponents. Thus, for example, in the New York City mayoral elections of both 1965 and 1969, the candidates with the most conservative appeal won the Democratic primary election with a plurality of the vote while a number of more liberal opponents were dividing the

[10]See Lee Sloan, "Good Government and the Politics of Race," *Social Problems,* 17 (1969): 161–175.

remaining majority among themselves. If the Democratic primary had required victories by majority vote, a run-off election would have taken place between the conservative front runner and the liberal opponent with the greatest number of votes. And in such a two-way contest, the latter would presumably have drawn a lion's share of the votes cast for the other liberal contesters, and won the nomination. Subsequent to these elections the law was changed to require primary winners in New York City to poll at least a 40 percent plurality in order to avoid a run-off. Obviously, the larger the field of candidates, the narrower the base of public support that may suffice to provide a pluarality.

The listing of "slates"—where candidates running for different offices indicate mutual support of each other—will often affect the chance of success of different candidates. For "slate" ballots sometimes allow candidates for council and other low-visibility offices to get elected on the "coattails" of a highly popular head of the ticket. These same candidates might lose if forced to run as unaffiliated individuals.

LOCAL TRIAL COURTS

Besides executive and legislative institutions, every large city also has a set of local courts. These are trial courts and have the legal powers to hear, try, and render decisions on the following kinds of cases:

1. Lawsuits between residents of the city over what are primarily private disputes over such matters as personal injury, property damage, violation of contractual obligations, ownership of property, divorces, adoptions, and inheritance. The courts here can order or deny the payment of damages by one contesting party to another, the restitution of property, or the granting of divorces, adoptions, etc., as the case may be. The provision of impartial forums for the adjudication of these private disputes is one of the oldest functions of government. If such forums did not exist, parties with unsettled disputes might resort to violence. Sometimes these private disputes are private only nominally, with one or both parties to the suit being city officials.

2. Criminal prosecutions against persons accused of violating the city's ordinances or regulatory codes including whatever parts of the state criminal law the city government is mandated to enforce within its boundaries through its own personnel. Such prosecutions are initiated by city police or by city, municipal, county, or district attorneys or prosecutors. In these criminal cases, the courts have the power to dismiss charges against the accused person or, after trial, to find him innocent or to convict him and impose monetary fines, probation, or imprisonment.

3. Legal actions directed specifically against city officials for various kinds of court orders or "writs." These legal actions can ask that particular officials be restrained from, or compelled to perform, some act, that some decision of theirs be reviewed and set aside, or that their holding of office be declared invalid. The court orders or writs themselves carry names like injunction, mandamus, certiorari, habeus corpus, quo warranto, or modern-day equivalents. The alleged grounds for the court order or writ being issued are usually that the act in question is specifically prohibited or required by the city's own charter, ordinances, or administrative regulations or by state or federal statutory or constitutional provisions. If granted by the courts as a result of litigation instituted by private citizens in so-called taxpayers suits or by other officials, these writs have the status of legal commands. The officials against whom they are directed are accordingly under obligation to obey, with disobedience being subject to contempt of court proceedings.

In actions against the city officials for injunction and other writs, local trial courts pass upon the legality or constitutionality of the acts and decisions of city officials and agencies directly. These courts can also do so during the trial of private law suits or criminal prosecutions. For if the legality of acts or decisions of city officials is called into question in any kind of case, a determination of validity of those acts or decisions then becomes necessary in order to dispose of the case.

Selection of Judges

The judgeships of local trial courts are most often elective, generally for terms of from four to eight years, on partisan or nonpartisan ballots. In a few large cities—e.g., Boston, Newark—some trial judges are appointed by the governor. The judges in California's large cities are originally appointed by the governor and thereafter run for election on a nonpartisan ballot against their own record without an opponent. Judges in New York City trial courts are in part elected on partisan ballots and in part appointed by the mayor. In Honolulu, judges of magistrates courts are appointed by the Chief Justice of the State of Hawaii.[11]

The Legal Status of Local Trial Courts

The legal relationship that obtains between local trial courts that operate within a large city and its general city government is complex. In terms of

[11]See *The Book of the States,* 1974–75, Vol. 20 (Lexington, Ky.: Council of State Governments 1974). Herbert Jacob, *Urban Justice* (Englewood Cliffs, N.J.: Prentice-Hall, 1973).

formal structure, none of these courts is a third branch of the city's general government in the same sense that state courts of last resort and the U.S. Supreme Court are independent third branches of their state governments and the federal government, respectively. Strictly speaking, local trial courts are a part of the state judicial hierarchy. Typically, a city's local trial courts are established by state legislation or by state constitutional provisions. Their organization, jurisdiction, and powers as well as the salaries of most of their judges are set by state action, not by city ordinance or charter provision subject to change by home-rule procedures. Furthermore, it is the state legislature and not the city's council that can impeach the judges of these courts. Finally, the decisions of these local trial courts are subject to appeal to and reversal by state appellate courts and state courts of last resort.

Nevertheless, these trial courts can properly be considered as de facto parts of the structure of large-city governments. First, the local trial courts in a particular city have a territorial jurisdiction approximately or exactly the same as that of the general city government and many of these local trial courts carry the city's name in their titles (e.g., Recorder's Court of Detroit, Baltimore Municipal Court, Municipal Court of Boston, N.Y.C. Criminal, N.Y.C. Civil Court, etc.). Second, the judges elected to these courts are chosen from essentially the same constituency as regular city officials and in the exceptional case of New York City, some trial court judges are appointed by the city's mayor. Third, the salaries of many of these local trial judges and of their staffs and the cost of providing courtrooms, supplies, and equipment are mandated upon and hence paid by the city government. Also, some cities, like New York, are permitted by state law to, and in fact do, increase the salaries of their trial judges above the amount set by the state. Fourth, the fines, costs, and other receipts collected by most of these trial courts go into the city treasury and, except in the small minority of cases where long sentences are imposed, convicted persons sentenced to imprisonment serve their time in city or other local, such as county, jails. Fifth, local trial courts are the only ones available in which city police and prosecuting attorneys can prosecute alleged violators of the city's ordinances. The efficiency of operation of these courts will thus have an important impact on the city government's entire law enforcement effort. Sixth, these local trial courts are the only ones available for securing judicial review of the decisions and the acts of city executive, legislative, and administrative officials for conformity with the city's own charter, ordinances, and regulations. Finally, despite the fact that all decisions of local trial courts are subject to review and reversal by higher courts in the state judicial system, in actuality these local trial courts operate with a very high degree of autonomy. Very few of their decisions are in fact appealed to higher state courts, and even fewer decisions of these local trial courts are ever successfully overturned at the state level.

LIMITS ON THE IMPACT OF FORMAL STRUCTURE

While a city's formal structure of government influences the process of decision-making, there are a number of reasons why it is not determinative of the nature and content of these decisions. The first major reason is that the specification of legal powers and obligations itself leaves large areas of discretion between the limits of what particular officials or agencies are required to do and what they are forbidden to do. Indeed, most political decision-making in cities consists of the attempt to influence the relevant decision-makers to exercise their discretionary authority in one particular way rather than in some other.

The advantages and disadvantages conferred upon different candidates for elective or appointive office by the formal structure of government and electoral rules are of varying weight. In any particular contest for an appointive or elective position, candidates disadvantaged by the formal structure may have sufficiently great appeal on other grounds to win. On the other hand, candidates given an advantage by the formal structure may run such a poor race that they lose. Furthermore, when all the candidates have the same favorable characteristics, as they often do since elective politicians tend not to waste their time running in constituencies where they are severely disadvantaged, the advantage of those characteristics cancels out. For example, once a councilman's district becomes predominantly black or predominantly Italo-American, non-blacks or non-Italo-Americans are not likely to put themselves forward in such districts as candidates.

The second major reason that a city's formal structure is not more determinative of what happens in its political decision-making process is that many of the key legal powers conferred by that structure on officials are shared powers. Thus the members of a city council or a commission or an independent board hold the legal power to make binding decisions collectively. In mayor-council cities, the mayor and the council also share certain powers which they can exercise only if they act jointly. In such situations, each of the officials involved has a share of the authority but no single one of them has it all. Each can influence the other only by means other than the assertion of the authority granted to them by the formal structure.

A third reason that an official's formal authority is not always determinative of his influence is that that authority may not be involved. Thus officials with superior legal powers may not be controlling the actions of subordinates because they are unaware that those subordinates are acting against their, the superior officials', preferences. Or, even if they are aware of their subordinates' noncompliant activities, superiors may decide that invoking their legal powers would be too costly to make it worthwhile: Superior officials may not consider the gain of securing compliance sufficient to justify taking the time and energy away from more important matters or they may feel that forcefully overruling or replacing subordinates would unduly disrupt their organizations or harm morale.

Similarly, officials or governmental agencies who are legally independent of top elected officials may choose not to assert their formal independence because they wish to be cooperative or to avoid sanctions. Chicago, for example, has many boards in its city government and also a number of important special districts which legally are independent of the mayor. However, throughout the 1960s and the early 1970s few of their officials insisted on exercising their independent authority in accordance with their own policy preferences when those policy preferences were known to conflict with strong preferences held by Chicago's Mayor Daley.

Likewise, a citizen's rights to civil liberties and procedural due process do not determine what will actually happen if the particular citizen involved is unaware of his rights or for other reasons chooses not to assert them. Thus, many trespasses by local officials on Supreme Court sanctioned civil liberties are not stopped because the victims do not know that what they are being subjected to constitutes violations or they may find it unacceptably costly to instigate the lawsuit in a local trial court that would be necessary to stop such violations. Also, persons accused of crimes are not always accorded the treatment that they have a legal right to receive. Often they are unaware of their procedural right not to give evidence against themselves or their rights to have legal counsel, a preliminary hearing, or a jury trial. Or, with significant frequency, they "choose" to waive such rights because they are too frightened to assert them or because they are promised or simply hope for leniency and better treatment if they are cooperative.

Finally, a city official's formal authority is not always determinative of his influence on the outcome of a decision-making situation because even when it is invoked, those against whom that authority is asserted may not comply voluntarily. Subordinate officials may, for example, drag their feet or even explicitly refuse to comply. Rioters may not disperse when ordered to do so. Striking civil servants may not return to work. Refusal to comply may be based on a rejection of the "legitimacy" of the authority being asserted or may be based simply upon a calculation that regardless of legal obligations, it is more profitable not to obey or on a combination of both. In that kind of situation, an official's formal authority will influence events only if he also has the legal powers and the de facto ability to impose forceful sanctions.

In sum, the distribution of authority and legal powers as reflected in a city government's formal structure is not equivalent to the distribution of actual influence. The structure of formal authority sets the general framework within which other types of influence on a city's political decision-making may operate. That framework is itself, of course, subject to change through the legal procedures that govern charter amendment and through changes in state legislation or relevant state constitutional provisions. But at any particular point in time, the structural framework defines the key decision-making points in a city government. It identifies the individual officials or bodies of officials who hold the legal power to control those points. It delineates how those officials come to hold their positions and how they can be removed. And the only way individuals and groups who themselves lack legal decision-making power can influence the decision-making process is by influencing those who do have such legal powers.

5

Cities and Other Local Governments

The city governments discussed in the previous chapter are only one type of local government exercising authority within the boundaries of large cities. Because those governments hold the broadest scope of local governmental authority and perform the widest range of functions, they are called the city's general purpose units of government.

But in addition to these "general purpose" city governments, there are also operating in every large city one or more so-called "special purpose" units of government or special districts. Furthermore, most large cities are part of counties that have separately organized county governments performing some urban-type functions within the city. And at least one large city, Miami, also forms a large portion of the jurisdiction of what is in effect a metropolitan level of government. Finally, very many large cities are represented on "metropolitan councils of government" that have various sorts of advisory powers over certain of their governmental activities. The allocation of functional responsibilities between the general city government and these other units of local government has an impact on the city government's decision-making and on its governing capacity and performance.

Large cities are also surrounded by a host of neighboring general purpose local governments, like villages, towns, and smaller satellite cities. These neighboring local governments have no legal authority to perform functions within the boundaries of the central city. But the activities of these neighboring governments nevertheless often "spill over" and have a de facto impact on the problems of the large cities they adjoin.

SPECIAL DISTRICTS

Special districts—or public authorities, boards, commissions, and corporations as they are also called—are units of local government that perform a single or a small number of related functions, but are administratively and fiscally independent of any unit of general government, such as city, town, or county.[1] These special districts are to be distinguished from semi-independent boards or commissions which, although independent of the mayor or other city chief executive, are formally part of and financed by the general city government. The geographic boundaries of special districts that operate within large cities sometimes are coterminous with the boundaries of the general city government. However, they sometimes overlie the city, extending beyond its boundaries to include the territory of neighboring cities, suburban areas, and even other states. In terms of the size of operating budgets, outstanding debt, or numbers of employees, a few special districts rival or are larger than some large-city general governments and even many state governments. (See Table 5-1.)

The most common type of coterminous special district that operates within large cities is the independently elected and financed school board. In all but nine of the largest cities of over 300,000 in population, the local public school system is run by such school boards, carrying titles like "The Chicago Board of Education," "The Detroit Board of Education," etc. The exceptions are Baltimore, Boston, Buffalo, Memphis, Nashville, New York City, Newark, and Norfolk (where the school boards are "dependent parts" of the general city government) and Honolulu (where the local public school system is operated by the state of Hawaii).[2]

The other very common type of coterminous special district in large cities is the "public housing authority." Such authorities construct and manage low-rent housing projects for low-income families and in some cities do the same for middle income families or undertake other kinds of urban renewal projects. All but eight large cities have independent public housing authorities ("St. Louis City Housing Authority," "Boston Housing Authority," etc.). The exceptions are Baltimore, Buffalo, Detroit, Louisville, Milwaukee, New York City, Norfolk and Phoenix, where the public housing agencies are part of the city government.[3]

No other kind of special district is as widespread as school districts or

[1]See U.S. Bureau of the Census, Census of Governments, 1972, Vol. 1, *Governmental Organization* (Washington, D.C.: U.S. Government Printing Office, 1973), pp. 12-14.

[2]See U.S. Bureau of the Census, Census of Government, 1972, Vol. 4, No. 2, *Finances of Special Districts* (Washington, D.C.: U.S. Government Printing Office, 1974); Vol. 3, No. 1, *Employment of Major Local Governments* (Washington, D.C.: U.S. Government Printing Office, 1974).

[3]See U.S. Bureau of the Census, *Finances of Special Districts.*

TABLE 5-1 Largest Nonschool Urban Special Districts in Terms of Expenditures (1971-72), Outstanding Debt (1971-72), and Number of Employees (1972)

Expenditures		Debt Outstanding	
Special District	*Amount (millions of dollars)*	*Special District*	*Amount (millions of dollars)*
Port of New York Authority	617	Port of New York Authority	1812
Chicago Transit Authority	200	San Francisco Bay Area Rapid Transit District	937
Metropolitan Water District of So. California	190	Mass. Bay Transit Authority	639
Mass. Bay Transit Authority	175	Metropolitan Water District of So. California	639
San Francisco Bay Area Rapid Transit District	152	East Bay (Alameda County, Calif.) Municipal Utility	152

Number of Employees

Special District	*Employees*
Chicago Transit Authority	12,521
Port of New York Authority	8,802
Southeastern Pennsylvania Transportation Authority	6,730
Mass. Bay Transit Authority	6,464
Chicago Park District	4,811

Source: U.S. Bureau of the Census, 1972 Census of Governments, Vol. 4, No. 2, *Finances of Special Districts* (Washington, D.C.: U.S. Government Printing Office, 1974); Vol. 3, No. 1, *Employment of Major Local Governments* (Washington, D.C.: U.S. Government Printing Office, 1974).

public housing authorities. In a few cities special districts operate parks (e.g., "The Chicago Park District"), and parking lots and garages (e.g., "Newark Parking Authority," "Philadelphia Parking Authority").

About a dozen large cities have special districts operating within them whose boundaries extend beyond those of the city. These are regional or metropolitan authorities that operate piers and other seaport facilities—e.g., "The Port of Seattle District," "Port of New York Authority" (which also operates airports, bridges, tunnels, and some mass transit). Chicago, Milwaukee, St. Louis, and Denver are parts of regional sewerage districts.

A very few cities are also within regional park districts, mass transit districts, and hospital districts.[4]

A dominant characteristic of special districts is their large or complete degree of fiscal autonomy. Indeed, this is often the one characteristic that distinguishes them from semi-independent boards and commissions that are part of the general city government. The fiscal autonomy of special districts means that their budget does not need the approval of, nor is it exclusively dependent on appropriations from some general unit of government like a city.[5] Most nonschool districts derive the revenues to finance their operations from "user" or "service" charges, such as bridge and tunnel tolls, transit fares, apartment rents, admission fees for recreational facilities, etc. All school and selected nonschool districts—e.g., regional sewage or park districts—have the legal power to impose taxes on real property within their jurisdictions. Essentially all districts—school and nonschool, coterminous and regional—also have legal power to borrow money by issuing bonds in order to finance the construction of capital projects such as school buildings, bridges, and airports. They may also receive grants and other kinds of subsidies from city, state, and federal governments.[6]

The Emergence of Special Districts

Special districts came into existence and continue to survive for various reasons: First, some functions or services, because of their character or because of economies of larger scale operations, require that they be performed beyond as well as within the boundaries of a large central city. The clearest example of such functions are transportation to and from the city, water supply and sewage disposal, and management of terminal facilities in a seaport which borders only in part on the city. The city government cannot itself perform the function because its legal powers do not extend beyond its boundaries. Typically, there is no general purpose metropolitan government encompassing the large city and often no county government whose boundaries coincide with the areas to be served and which is otherwise prepared to undertake the activity. An "overlying" or "regional"

[4]*Ibid.* The formally correct title of what was known as the "New York Port Authority" at the time of the 1972 Census of Governments is now the "Port Authority of New York and New Jersey."

[5]The Census Bureau, in order to classify a board, commission, etc., as an independent special district, must find that it has "independent fiscal powers . . . to (1) determine its budget without review and detailed modification by other local officials or governments, (2) determine taxes to be levied for its support, (3) fix or collect charges for its services, or (4) issue debt without review by any other local government." *Governmental Organization,* pp. 4–5, 62–73.

[6]See John C. Bollens, *Special District Governments in the United States* (Berkeley: University of California Press, 1957); Advisory Commission on Intergovernmental Relations, *The Problem of Special Districts in American Government* (Washington, D.C.: U.S. Government Printing Office, 1964); U.S. Bureau of the Census, *Finances of Special Districts.*

special district may consequently be the only means of providing the desired service in the area involved.

Special districts sometimes operate facilities that a general city government is not in a position to finance. This may be because that city's tax rate was close to or at statutory or constitutional limits or because city officials did not want the responsibility for raising additional taxes. The device of the special district also allows facilities to be built through borrowing that is not subject to the limits binding on city governments. Many independent housing authorities were formed in the depression period of the 1930s, when the city governments were so financially hard-pressed that even with federal grants and loans they could neither float more bonds nor impose additional taxes even temporarily to get new housing projects underway. Furthermore, assigning the performance of a function to a special district allows city officials more easily to shift the financing of a new facility or service from taxes on the general taxpaying public to user charges or fees paid by the direct users or beneficiaries.

Special districts often reflect the view that particular governmental functions should be "taken out of politics." This conviction is sometimes based on antipathy to political parties, elections, and "professional politicians," because of their association with corruption, self-seeking, inefficiency, etc. For others, taking a function out of politics is intended to remove it from the direct control of elected officials responsible to broad constituencies and to separate it from competition for funds with other city programs and activities. This maximizes the autonomy of those professional specialists who administer particular programs—e.g., professional educators for schools, medical doctors for health services.

The second half of the claim that special districts can take a function "out of politics" is that they perform it in a "business-like way." Over the past decades special authorities have been able to gain a widespread reputation for efficient, dynamic, competent, largely scandal-free administrative performance. In part this is because many facilities operated by special authorities are of the kind, as Sayre and Kaufman have put it, that

> "sell themselves": towering bridges and spectacular vehicular tunnels are impressive feats of engineering that speak for themselves. Neat and clean, if architecturally undistinguished, buildings and housing projects are good advertising, and some of them, such as the [N.Y.] Port Authority's international terminal at [Kennedy] Airport, are landmarks in design. Modern, well-lighted subway cars and buses, faster service, and brightly illuminated stations bespeak the competence and zeal of those who provide them.[7]

[7]Wallace S. Sayre and Herbert Kaufman, *Governing New York City* (New York: W.W. Norton, 1965), p. 338.

In part the reputation of special authorities is the result of their own highly organized and effective public relations activities and the favor they have enjoyed with newspaper editorial writers and other mass media personnel. This reputation for efficiency is bolstered by the freedom from "red tape" enjoyed by special authorities. They normally are not bound by the detailed requirements and procedures imposed on regular city agencies for purchasing supplies or letting construction contracts, which, while calculated to protect the taxpayers against embezzlement and other forms of self-enrichment, introduce long delays in obtaining the supplies and facilities needed. And many special districts also are not bound by regular civil service hiring procedures and maximum salary scales. The chief executive of the New York City Health and Hospitals Corporation established in 1970 to operate the city's eighteen municipal hospitals for example, was hired at a salary of $65,000 a year, which was more than that of the mayor. The Port of New York Authority traditionally has paid its high officials and managers generous salaries, particularly as compared to those received by regular city officials of similar rank and responsibilities.

Special authorities are sometimes stimulated by city officials who wish to "spin off" and reduce their responsibility for programs and functions that have become especially and chronically troublesome. Their "troublesomeness" is normally the result of a combination of complaints over the quality of service and difficulties of providing adequate financing to improve performance. Thus New York City's Health and Hospitals Corporation (which, strictly speaking, is only a semi-independent agency) was set up at the instigation of Mayor Lindsay only after years of repeated public complaints, newspaper exposés, and adverse reports by various investigative committees and bodies about the low level of patient care and the deterioration of the physical plant at the city's municipal hospitals.

Special districts are sometimes established by state legislatures at the initiation of state officials in order to take a particular function out of control of city officials.

Reduced Popularity of Special Districts

Although still popular, in recent years special districts have lost some of the aura of being virtually beyond criticism.[8] Complaints have been directed, first, against the remoteness from popular control of many authorities that perform important governmental functions. Appointive members of governing boards frequently serve for long terms with staggered expiration dates, so that newly elected officials who hold the power of appointment cannot replace the memberships of the boards even over the course of their entire term. Also some appointments are made by elective

[8]See, for example, the conclusions and recommendations of the Advisory Commission on Intergovernmental Relations, *The Problem of Special Districts in American Government.*

officials, like governors, whose constituencies are much larger than the city in which the districts exclusively or primarily operate. And even when the governing boards of special districts are formally elective, many members are originally appointed to fill vacancies. The members thus appointed then run for election as incumbents, often without opposition and at the bottom of the ballot, with few voters being knowledgeable about their record and performance.

There have also been more complaints in recent years about unequal distribution or "skewing" of resources that takes place when some districts which happen to have lucrative sources of revenue—e.g., highly-trafficked toll bridges and tunnels—generate large operating surpluses and then dispose of those surplus revenues by overly generous treatment of bondholders or by the construction of still other revenue-producing projects, whose need may be questionable. If these surplus revenues were under the control of the general city government, they could be made available to finance other needed governmental services which cannot pay their full way or are not revenue-producing, such as commuter railroads or welfare programs.

Third, complaints have been made about the fragmentation and increased difficulty special districts present in coordinating governmental functions within a particular city or metropolitan area. This results from having a multiplicity of agencies independent of one another and of the general city government performing related governmental functions.

Finally, complaints have been generated by the drop in quality of performance of some districts—like the New York Metropolitan Transportation Authority—which operate facilities (e.g., subways and commuter railroads) that are difficult and expensive to maintain properly and in addition do not have access to any lucrative revenue source.

Despite these recent complaints and some loss of popularity, special districts are not about to fade away. For almost all the factors that led to their development still are operating. What may happen is that any new districts and possibly some established ones may have their autonomy reduced. State legislatures may, for example, give city and state elected officials greater influence over their activities and force richly endowed districts to share some of their revenues with the city governments they overlie.

COUNTY GOVERNMENTS

Separately organized county governments operate and perform local governmental functions within some four-fifths of all large cities. The functions that different county governments perform vary. In essentially all large cities that have them, county governments are responsible for such routine housekeeping tasks as maintaining some local courts; keeping records of deeds, marriages, and other legal documents; and supervising the conduct of elections. County governments almost always are involved in running welfare programs for residents of the city they encompass. In addition, in about three-fourths of the cities with separately organized county governments, the county operates public hospitals. In some cities, county governments also administer public health programs, maintain county roads and highways and some recreational facilities, and prosecute persons accused of committing crimes anywhere in the city.[9]

Of course, county governments may perform a wider array of functions in any part of the county that lies outside the boundaries of the central city. This part of the county would normally include both suburban municipalities and so-called unincorporated areas where there are no municipal governments. These extra services can be provided on a special contract basis with suburban municipalities that want them or outside central city areas may be part of a special county "subordinate taxing district" which pays additional taxes for these services.

County governments raise the money to finance their activities primarily through real estate taxes. But they also raise revenues from sales taxes, "user charges" for use of their facilities, and from grants from their states or the federal government.

The large cities where there are no separately organized county governments fall into three groups.

(1) New York City, Philadelphia, Boston, New Orleans, Jacksonville, Indianapolis, and Nashville: These cities constitute parts or wholes of areas legally designated as counties (Counties of Bronx, Kings, New York, Queens, and Richmond; County of Philadelphia; County of Suffolk; Parish of Orleans; County of Duval; County of Marion, and County of Davidson, respectively). And in all but Nashville, there are certain typical county offices—such as district attorneys, county clerks, sheriffs, registrars of deeds—that exercise specified functions within these cities. But the counties overlying those cities have no separately organized governments, so that whatever county offices there are function essentially as parts of their respective city governments and are financed by them.[10]

(2) Denver, Honolulu, and San Francisco: These cities encompass areas legally designated as city-counties ("City and County" of Denver, of Honolulu, and of San Francisco, respectively). They each have only a single organized government and it functions primarily as a city government.

(3) Baltimore and St. Louis: These cities are located outside of any

[9]See U.S. Bureau of the Census, Census of Governments, 1972, Vol. 4, No. 3, *Finances of County Governments* (Washington, D.C.: U.S. Government Printing Office, 1974). and Vol. 3, No. 1, *Employment of Major Local Governments.*

[10]Although the County of Suffolk includes in addition to Boston, the cities of Chelsea and Revere and the Town of Winthrop, all county offices are financed exclusively by the Boston city government.

geographic area legally designated by their states as a county. There is a "Baltimore County" and a "St. Louis County," each with a county government. But the territory of these counties is geographically adjacent to and does not encompass the cities bearing the same name.[11]

City-County Consolidation

In most areas that have them, county governments were organized before cities developed within their territories. Except in New England where the "town" served that purpose, it was the county that since colonial days provided the minimal governmental services that were available locally in a basically agricultural society. These services consisted primarily of maintaining roads, keeping records, and operating local trial courts as state judicial districts. Thus for the most part, county governments served as mere administrative agents of the state government.

When population concentrations formed within counties, city and other municipal governments were normally established to provide additional services beyond those required in rural areas. The county governments simply continued to operate, performing the functions that they had previously been responsible for side by side with those performed by the new city governments. Gradually, as governing boards and other officials of counties became elective and were granted greater autonomy in the exercise of governmental powers by their states, counties became another unit of general purpose local government.

In almost all large cities where presently there is no separately organized county government, the consolidation of the city and county governments or the separation of the city from its county took place in the nineteenth century or in the first decades of the twentieth century.[12] Those who supported the "consolidation" or "separation" movements were opposed to the complexity and alleged inefficiency of having two general purpose local governments in the same area. They were also opposed to the obligation of central-city residents in many places of having to pay the same county tax rate as other county residents. These city residents, who were also served and taxed by their city governments, obviously needed and received fewer services from their county. From the end of the first decade of the twentieth century to World War II, all efforts to achieve further city-county consolidations failed. The necessary state enabling legislation or constitutional amendments could not be obtained, or the consolidation proposals were voted down when they were put to local referenda. In more recent decades, however, there has again taken place a complete or almost complete merger of the county government with the government of its

[11]U.S. Bureau of the Census, *Governmental Organization,* pp. 1, 14-15.

[12]New Orleans, 1813; Boston, 1821; Baltimore, 1851; Philadelphia, 1854; San Francisco, 1856; St. Louis, 1876; N.Y.C., 1898; Denver, 1902; Honolulu, 1907, while Hawaii was still a territory.

principal city in three large cities—Nashville, Jacksonville, and Indianapolis. In each case the new consolidated governments have operated essentially as city governments but over much larger geographic areas represented by their counties.

Consolidation of the Nashville and Davidson County governments in Tennessee took place in 1962. The consolidated government, officially titled the "Metropolitan Government of Nashville and Davidson County," is headed by an elective "metropolitan county mayor" and an elected 41-member metropolitan county council, most of whom are chosen from districts. This consolidated government provides one set of services to a "general service district" consisting of the entire county, for which all residents are taxed. These services include schools, public health, police, courts, public welfare, public housing, urban renewal, streets and roads, traffic, transit, library, refuse disposal, and enforcement of electrical, building, plumbing, and housing codes. The consolidated government provides an additional set of services (fire protection, intensified police protection, sewage disposal, water supply, and street lighting and street cleaning) to an "urban service district." This district consisted initially of only the city of Nashville, but allowed for expansion as other areas desired the extra services. The cost of these additional services is paid for only by residents of the urban service district.

The governments of Jacksonville and Duval County in Florida were consolidated in 1967 as the government of the "City of Jacksonville" under an independently elected mayor and a nineteen-member council, five elected at-large and the remainder from districts. As in Nashville, the new consolidated government provides certain "general services" throughout the county area and an additional set to an "urban service district" (initially consisting of the city of Jacksonville) for which extra taxes are assessed.

Finally, in 1969 the governments of Indianapolis and Marion County in Indiana were consolidated under a mayor and a council of twenty-nine members. This government of the "City of Indianapolis," or UNIGOV as it is often called, performs certain functions area-wide (e.g., planning and zoning, roads, transportation, and public works) and others (e.g., police, fire, sanitation) within the former boundaries of the city only.[13]

METROPOLITAN GOVERNMENTS AND COUNCILS OF GOVERNMENT

The only large city in the United States which has close approximation to a metropolitan government functioning within its borders is Miami, Florida. The characteristics that distinguish a metropolitan government from a city-county consolidated one like that of Indianapolis are two-fold:

[13]See John C. Bollens and Henry J. Schmandt, *The Metropolis: Its People, Politics and Economic Life,* 3rd ed. (New York: Harper and Row, 1975), chap. 11, for greater detail on these city-county consolidations.

(1) A metropolitan government functions as a separate level or "tier" of government. It performs "area-wide" type services over the entire metropolitan area but the central-city and suburban governments remain independently organized and continue to perform "local-type" services within their separate jurisdictions.

(2) A metropolitan government can provide services over a multicounty metropolitan area whereas a city-county consolidated government is restricted to the boundaries of a single county.

In fact, the Miami area's metropolitan government—or "Miami Metro" as it is often called—itself operates in only one county since it is actually a reorganized version of the government of the county within which Miami is situated. The official title of the Miami Metro is the "Metropolitan Dade County Government." In 1957, the then existing county government was restructured under a board of county commissioners and an appointed county manager and assigned greatly expanded powers. In 1963 provision was added for an elective mayor. This new metropolitan government was given authority to perform on a county-wide basis such functions as the construction of expressways; the regulation of traffic; the operation of mass transit, hospitals, public health, and welfare programs; flood, beach erosion and air pollution control; and the preparing, adopting, and enforcing of county-wide zoning and building codes and plans of development. These functions, to the extent that they had been performed previously at all, had been performed by the City of Miami and twenty-five other municipalities, each within its own area of the county separately. Even with the expansion of the powers of the county government, the Miami city government and those of the other municipalities were retained as separate entities. These local governments continued to perform those functions not taken over exclusively by the Miami metropolitan government.[14]

In the 1950s and 1960s, there were attempts to create what approached metropolitan governments in a number of cities, including St. Louis and Seattle, and all of them failed. The mechanism proposed in both St. Louis and Seattle was the establishment of a metropolitan area-wide special district, which would have had the powers to perform a multiplicity of functions on an area-wide basis. These proposals were defeated in popular referenda. The voters in the metropolitan area surrounding each of these two large cities did permit, however, the establishment of special districts to perform the single function of sewage disposal.

A full-fledged metropolitan government has existed since 1953 in Canada. It encompasses the city of Toronto and what were at the time of its establishment twelve surrounding suburban municipalities.

There are many more metropolitan or regional councils, conferences, and associations of governments than there are metropolitan governments.

[14] *Ibid.*, pp. 275-80; Edward Sofen, *The Miami Metropolitan Experiment* (Bloomington: Indiana University Press, 1963).

These metropolitan councils have the legal status of voluntary associations, whose membership includes the chief elected officials or other representatives of most or all of the municipalities (and sometimes counties) in the area. As voluntary associations, these councils have neither authority to enforce decisions nor the power to finance themselves through the imposition of taxes. What the councils do is provide a fairly regular opportunity over lunch or dinner or cocktails for discussion of common problems and for exchange of information about what each of the constituent units is doing in various spheres of activity. They also often employ research staffs, sometimes attached to the standing committees devoted to particular functional problems, which prepare studies and recommendations for dealing with area-wide concerns.

The first major council of government (COG) was organized in 1956 in the New York area under the title of "New York Metropolitan Regional Council." Because they feared loss of autonomy, both in New York and elsewhere, smaller constituent units were reluctant to join COG's. The idea consequently did not catch fire and only a handful of additional metropolitan councils were in operation by 1965. That year, however, the federal government provided a strong stimulus for COGs by making them eligible for federal grants under Section 701 of the Housing and Urban Development Act of 1965. Previously, the activities of the councils were financed entirely through dues from their constituent members. In 1966, an even stronger impetus for the creation of additional COGs was given by Section 204 of the Demonstration Cities and Metropolitan Development Act. This section stipulated essentially that no applications from big cities and other local governments for federal loans or grants under such programs as "open-space," hospital construction, airports, libraries, basic water supply and distribution works, sewer facilities, and highways or other transportation facilities would be approved unless first submitted for review by an agency that performed metropolitan or regional planning in the area where the project was proposed.

Since COGs were obvious candidates and were in fact designated to perform this function in many metropolitan areas, about 100 additional ones were formed in the five years following the 1966 act. When the area agency is a COG, local governments now have very strong incentives to join since otherwise they will have no "inside" voice in shaping the council's recommendations on either their own applications or the applications of neighboring governments for projects that would impinge on their own operations.[15]

[15]For a study of the New York Metropolitan Regional Council, see Joan B. Aron, *The Quest for Regional Cooperation* (Berkeley and Los Angeles: University of California Press, 1969). Bollens and Schmandt, *The Metropolis*, pp. 303–9, also provides a summary treatment of the activities of the councils. For the pre-1966 situation, see Advisory Commission on Intergovernmental Relations *Metropolitan Councils of Government* (Washington, D.C.: U.S. Government Printing Office, 1966).

IMPACT OF SPECIAL DISTRICTS, COUNTY AND METROPOLITAN GOVERNMENTS ON CITIES

The constellation of special districts and county or metropolitan governments that operate within cities or overlie them can have both positive and negative effects on the city government. If the powers to perform services or impose regulations that have a major bearing on the alleviation of key urban problems like slum poverty are outside the control of the general city government, its entire capacity to govern is weakened. For under these circumstances, the central-city government cannot coordinate programs for maximum effectiveness. For example, the success of a program dealing with urban slum poverty may depend on voluntary cooperation between the independent school board running the schools, the county-run welfare programs, and the city government. Any deadlocks that develop cannot be broken by appeal to a higher authority. Mayor Yorty of Los Angeles explained to the 1966 Ribicoff Committee how many key governmental functions in his city were performed by agencies other than the city government:

> . . . The mayor of Los Angeles has nothing to do . . . with the school system. We have an independently elected school board, with their own taxing power and they make up their own budget.
>
> Also, the mayor of Los Angeles has nothing to do with the welfare program. This is handled by the county for the State. So I am not involved in any of those programs either. We don't have a department of employment in the city. This is another state function, the State department of employment which is entirely separate and I have no jurisdiction over that.
>
> The health department is part of the county structure. Our effort to build a rapid transit system is through a State agency, with the members originally appointed by the Governor, but now with some local appointments, but still the transit district is much larger than the city.
>
> Our housing authority, while it is called a city housing authority, is nevertheless a State agency. . . .
>
> *Senator Ribicoff.* As I listened to your testimony, Mayor Yorty, I made some notes. This morning you have really waived authority and responsibility in the following areas: schools, welfare, transportation, employment, health, and housing, which leaves you as the head of a city with a ceremonial function, police, and recreation.
>
> *Mayor Yorty.* That is right, and fire.
>
> *Senator Ribicoff.* And fire.
>
> *Mayor Yorty.* Yes.
>
> *Senator Ribicoff.* Collecting sewage?
>
> *Mayor Yorty.* Sanitation; that is right.

> *Senator Ribicoff.* In other words, basically you lack jurisdiction, authority, responsibility for what makes a city move?
> *Mayor Yorty.* That is exactly it.
> *Senator Ribicoff.* What makes a city go round.[16]

On the other hand, it must also be said that the assignment of the responsibility for such highly expensive functions as education and welfare to other units of local government greatly relieves the pressures on the general city government's treasury. And it also gives its highest officials ample opportunities for disclaiming responsibility when things go wrong. Furthermore, although coordination based on cooperation may be difficult to achieve, such coordination is not always present and startlingly successful even where the general city government has legal jurisdiction over all the relevant activities.

The pattern most damaging to central-city governments is when other units of local government perform functions—like operating heavily used toll bridges and tunnels—that are lucrative producers of revenue, while these units also create undesired spill-overs for the city government to handle—like increased traffic congestion and need for off-street parking. This means that the surplus revenues generated are not available to the city government for financing other governmental programs, while at the same time the city must deal from its own funds with the undesired spill-overs these other units of government produce.

A normally desirable pattern for a city government is when a service that is inevitably used by commuters or other suburbanites—for example, subways, museums, or zoos—is under the control of a government such as a large county or regional special district, which has jurisdiction over those users. Such wider-jurisdiction governments can spread more widely the tax cost of operating the program and thus reach a larger proportion of its beneficiaries than could a city government. Finally, wide-ranging county governments or overlying special districts can be useful to a central-city government when they perform functions—like air and water pollution control, seaport improvement, operation outside city boundaries of major airports—from which the city profits, but which it could not perform itself because it is bounded by its geographic and legal jurisdiction. Sometimes performance of these kinds of area-wide functions—including water supply and sewage disposal—by a unit larger than the city can also result in economies of scale.

In the 1950s and early 1960s, a number of urban experts argued that problems like air and water pollution were typical of all urban problems and

[16]U.S. Senate, *Federal Role in Urban Affairs,* Hearings, before the Subcommittee on Executive Reorganization of the Committee on Governmental Operations, 89th and 90th Cong., 2d sess., 1966–67, pp. 671–72, 774.

hence that those problems could not be significantly alleviated without some form of government whose reach extended beyond existing municipal boundaries and encompassed the entire metropolitan area surrounding a large city. As Luther Gulick, the unofficial "dean" of good-government reformers, put it:

> . . . every one of these problems [slums, traffic congestion, mass transportation, urban obsolescence, migration, education, crime, water supply, air and water pollution, recreational and cultural needs] spreads out over an area broader than the boundaries of the local government in question. It is clear that our big urban complexes are now so closely tied together economically, socially, and structurally by daily human movements and activities that every problem is a "spill-over" from the next jurisdiction. Little can be done about one piece of such a problem. *Once an indivisible problem is divided, nothing effective can be done about it.*[17]

It soon became recognized, however—especially as campaigns for metropolitan government failed politically—that because various urban problems were found in many parts of a metropolitan area, no simple change of governmental structure, such as by adding a metropolitan area-wide layer, was magically going to eliminate these problems. In short, it became understood that whether the existence and operation of a special district, county government, or metropolitan government would, overall, be beneficial or harmful could not be determined in the abstract. It would depend on what were the specific gains and losses imposed on the city government, primarily in terms of strengthening or weakening its control, coordination, and finances. Sometimes a particular pattern would be beneficial in terms of one value but not beneficial in terms of another, so that the overall impact would depend on the exact "trade-offs."

Many times these trade-offs are difficult to determine in advance. Even the long hoped for panacea for city governments of a metropolitan taxing district whose reach would extend to the more affluent suburbs and purportedly bring extra revenues to hard pressed central-city treasuries might not turn out to have that result if it were actually put into effect. For if the allocation formula is determined by a governing board responsive to majorities in the overall metropolitan population, and as the population in the "outside central city" part of many metropolitan areas already has or soon will exceed the central city part, the redistribution of resources might turn out to be not from suburbs to central city, but vice versa.

[17]Luther H. Gulick, *The Metropolitan Problem and American Ideas* (New York: Knopf, 1961), p. 24.

NEIGHBORING LOCAL GOVERNMENTS

Neighboring general purpose local governments like satellite cities, suburban villages, and unincorporated areas have no legal powers to perform governmental functions within a large central city. The impact that these neighboring governments have on the city government is determined by how cooperative the neighboring governments are in dealing with shared problems and by whether they cause or fail to control conditions within their own boundaries that have undesirable "spill over" effects on their big-city neighbor.

Much of the contact between a large city and its immediately adjoining neighbors that requires cooperative agreement concerns routine housekeeping matters, such as construction and maintenance of facilities like highways, bridges, mass transit lines, traffic control signals, and parks that connect or straddle the boundaries of the two governments. Other relations between a large city and its neighbors involve the joint construction and operation of expensive public works, like water supply and distribution systems or sewage treatment works or airports, which are more economical to build on a scale that will take care of the total needs of the combined different jurisdictions. These arrangements are usually worked out on the basis of formal, written contracts, specifying the rights and obligations, including the financial ones, of the different contracting parties. Still other relations consist of the large city providing standard services—like water supply—to some or all of its neighbors from its own facilities for a fee, usually established on a contractual basis but sometimes within limits specified by state law. Finally, many large cities and their neighbors have "mutual assistance" pacts whereby one government will lend forces like police and firemen to help cope with emergency situations within the other's jurisdiction.[18]

Direct legal arrangements concerning the kinds of tangible activities are discussed above. Many arrangements are normally handled on a sporadic, ad hoc basis by the various functional specialists on "technical grounds"—i.e., highway people deal with highway people, water supply people with water supply people, etc. The major impact of these relations on a large city results from willingness of the neighboring governments to work out cooperative arrangements that are considered fair by the city government, financially and in other respects.

There is another important set of impacts on a large city from its neighbors. This comes from unilaterally determined governmental actions or inactions by these neighboring governments that may have spillovers that cause or aggravate problems with which the large city must deal.

[18] Advisory Commission on Intergovernmental Relations, *A Handbook for Interlocal Agreements and Contracts* (Washington, D.C.: U.S. Government Printing Office, 1967).

Traditional examples include failure of neighboring governments to control sources of water and air pollution that then flow downstream or downwind to damage the central-city's beaches, water supplies, air, and other aspects of the environment. Or a neighboring government may establish traffic patterns that by relieving congestion within its own boundaries, increase the traffic and congestion forced into the central-city's streets.

Also, in recent decades, suburban local governments (and suburban counties) adjoining large cities have increasingly limited entry into their parks, beaches, and other recreational areas to their own inhabitants, thus closing their facilities off to those living in the central city. This reduces the opportunities for enjoyment of city-dwellers and, directly or indirectly, their contentment with city living. It also puts pressure on city government to find by itself equivalent or substitute opportunities for recreation for its citizens.

A more subtle, but nonetheless extremely important, form of spillover from the actions of local governments surrounding large cities involves suburban zoning and other housing policies. One important set are the explicit ones that require large minimum lots for single-family housing and prohibit apartment or other multifamily dwellings, especially those designed for low or low-to-moderate income occupants. Another important policy is the implicit one that tolerates discrimination against selling or renting housing to blacks and other low status minorities. The impact of these suburban policies is obvious. First, they largely confine low-income families and the high cost of providing them with governmental services and benefits to the central cities. At the same time they attract to their own jurisdictions families with fewer needs and greater taxable resources. And second, they contribute to the steady increases in central cities of the proportion of the black population, thus creating conditions that aggravate racial tension and conflict and decrease the possibility of maintaining multiracial neighborhoods and schools.

The success of large-city governments in coping with these spillover problems produced by their neighbors has been much less than in working out housekeeping arrangements. Discussions of problems, directly or through the contacts made at "metropolitan councils," sometimes lead to improvement. The more effective recourse of large-city officials against the damaging "spill-overs" of their neighbors has been to appeal to a higher and thus more inclusive level of government. Accordingly, officials have asked their states or the federal government to impose restrictions on the activities producing the adverse impact that cities cannot themselves legally reach. Thus far, some states and especially the federal government have responded on such matters as air and water pollution and established standards that are binding throughout the state or nation, as the case may be. This promises to cut down the sources of pollution affecting cities, even when those sources lie outside their boundaries. And the Civil Rights Act of

1968 prohibits racial discrimination in housing everywhere, including the suburbs.

City officials have, in general, not succeeded in getting state or federal policies that would lead to greater opening up of the suburbs to the poor, whether white or black. The Supreme Court in 1974 ruled that suburban local zoning codes prohibiting multiple-family dwellings did not violate the equal protection clause of the Fourteenth Amendment[19] and ruled further in 1975 that central-city (Rochester, N.Y.) residents did not even have "standing" to sustain a lawsuit challenging a suburban zoning code because they could not show "demonstrable, particularized injury" to themselves as a result of the suburb's exclusionary zoning policies.[20] A few of the state courts have, however, struck down "large lot zoning" on the grounds that it bore no relation to the public health or welfare or safety of the community, which has been the traditional basis of zoning.[21] In 1968, the New York legislature established an Urban Development Corporation (UDC) with legal power to construct housing and other projects anywhere in the state, including suburban areas, without regard to local zoning regulations. This power to override local zoning became so controversial that the UDC chose not to become involved with any project in a locality unless at the request of local officials. By 1975, the UDC was moribund.

Similarly unhelpful to central-city governments was a 1974 Supreme Court decision holding that suburban school districts had no obligation under the equal protection clause to take black children from the central city into suburban schools or to exchange white for black children through cross-district busing in order to provide those black children the possibility of attending other than predominantly- or all-black schools. The question arises in cities where the proportion of black children in the central-city public school population is so high that there are not enough white children left to produce "racially balanced," de facto "unsegregated" student bodies. However, the Court did say at the same time that if plaintiffs for a central city or its school children can prove that the actions of suburban school districts intentionally contributed to the de facto segregated school attendance patterns in the central city, then school "boundary lines may be bridged" and "interdistrict relief" could be granted.[22]

Central-city governments were also disappointed by a 1973 Supreme

[19] *Village of Belle Terre v. Borass,* 416 U.S. 1 (1974).

[20] *Warth v. Seldin,* 422 U.S. 490 (1975). In the 1976 case of *Hill v. Gautreaux,* however, the Supreme Court ruled unanimously that it was permissible to order the federal Department of Housing and Urban Development to fund low-cost housing in the suburbs of a metropolitan area when the department had previously discriminated unconstitutionally by funding housing only in the central city's ghetto neighborhoods. See The *New York Times,* April 21, 1976.

[21] See Michael N. Danielson, *The Politics of Exclusion: Suburban Barriers to an Open Society* (New York: Columbia University Press, 1976), chap. 7.

[22] *Milliken v. Bradley,* 418 U.S. 717 (1974).

Court decision denying that unequal tax resources among school districts which allowed greater expenditures per pupil in wealthier (e.g., some suburban) than in poorer (e.g., some central-city) school districts was an unconstitutional denial of "equal protection" for the children who attended school in the poorer districts.[23] This case was decided after a few state supreme courts and lower federal trial courts had declared that state legislation basing the financing of public schools primarily on local property taxes was discriminatory against the poor and thus unconstitutional.[24]

State courts are still free, of course, to find that because of the inequality of resources it affords to different districts, school financing based on local property taxes violates state constitutional provisions.

[23]*San Antonio Independent School District v. Rodriguez,* 411 U.S. 1 (1973).

[24]The first and most notable case was that of the California supreme court, *Serrano v Priest,* 4 Cal. 3d. 584 (1971).

6

Cities and the Federal Government

Because cities owe their legal existence and scope of authority to state action, the federal government's influence on city decision-making and performance is bound to be less pervasive than that of the states. Article VI of the federal Constitution does, however, make that document and "the laws of the United States which shall be made in persuance thereof . . . supreme law of the land" and thus binding on cities as subdivisions and legal creatures of states.

There are no provisions in the federal Constitution that give the federal government explicit regulatory authority over city governments. But various constitutional provisions do impose explicit prohibitions on "state" and hence city action. Also, the Constitution does not preclude regulation of the activities of city officials when "necessary and proper" or "appropriate" for carrying out the explicit enumerated powers that the federal government does have or for enforcing federal prohibitions. And the Constitution also authorizes federal expenditure of money to provide "for the common defense and general welfare of the United States"[1] without excluding as an allowable means the financing of programs benefiting city governments. It is on some combination of the above provisions that federal influence on the cities is based.

[1]Article I, Section 8.

VEHICLES OF FEDERAL INFLUENCE

Constitutional Prohibitions

The body of the Constitution itself imposes few limits on city decision-making. One such limit results from the constitutional clause prohibiting cities[2] from "impairing the obligation of contracts."[3] Under this prohibition, attempts by cities to change provisions of such things as franchises granted to public utilities, tax concessions granted to businesses, or contracts made with employees or suppliers have been held invalid unless justified by some public emergency like war or economic depression. Still another restriction on city decision-making comes from the judicial interpretation that the "supremacy clause"[4] of the Constitution prohibits cities from taxing federal property, installations, or activities located within their borders. A final important constraint is derived from judicial interpretation that the "commerce clause"[5] prohibits regulations or taxes that discriminate against or "burden" "interstate commerce," such as by cities imposing a license tax on the sale only of goods manufactured outside the state or on out-of-state traveling salesmen.

The most important federal constitutional constraints on cities are the various guarantees of civil liberties, procedural due process for defendants in criminal trials, and equal protection of the laws. These guarantees rest on the language of the Fourteenth Amendment, which was passed after the Civil War. This amendment explicitly prohibits any state, including any city as a state subdivision, from making or enforcing any law abridging "the privileges or immunities of citizens of the United States," from depriving "any person of life, liberty, or property, without due process of law," and from denying to any person within its jurisdiction the "equal protection of the laws."

The Supreme Court has determined that included within the meaning of the term "liberty" as used in the Fourteenth Amendment are the First Amendment freedoms of speech, press, assembly, and "free exercise" and "nonestablishment" of religion. The Supreme Court has thus ruled that police arresting a speaker because his speech "stirs the people to anger, invites dispute, brings about a condition of unrest, or creates a disturbance"[6] is an infringement of the freedom of speech. The Court has also struck down as an infringement of free speech, a city's making permits to

[2]Hereafter whenever a restriction is said to apply to a "city," that term should be understood as standing for "a city as a subdivision of a state."

[3]Article I, Section 10.

[4]Article VI.

[5]Article I, Section 8.

[6]*Terminiello v. Chicago,* 337 U.S. 1 (1949).

speak on public streets or parks available to some groups but not to others, either arbitrarily or contingent on the content of the prospective speech,[7] or a city's prohibiting peaceful picketing in labor disputes or political controversies.[8] It has also called unconstitutional, banning the wearing of black armbands by schoolchildren as a form of antiwar protest when such wearing did not disrupt schoolwork.[9]

Under freedom of the press city governments have been restricted from such practices as banning or punishing with criminal penalties the publication, distribution, or exhibition of newspapers, books, movies, or leaflets of a political or religious nature.[10] Cities have also not been allowed to impose discriminatory taxation on particular newspapers[11] or to refuse to license movies because of such vague grounds as sacrilege, immorality, or harm to public order.[12] The protection of freedom of assembly has been held to restrict city officials from prohibiting an association like a labor union or a black interest group such as the NAACP from soliciting members door-to-door.[13] Under freedom of assembly such an association cannot also be forced to divulge for publication its membership lists since publicizing the names of members would act as a deterrent to persons joining.

The prohibition against interference with the "free exercise" of religion has been held to restrict city or local school officials from such policies as requiring schoolchildren to salute the flag if, like the Jehovah's Witnesses, they have religious scruples against such a ritual.[14] A city's preventing religious groups from distributing handbills or otherwise proselytizing on the streets has also been deemed a violation of the "free exercise" guarantee.[15] City and other local officials, under the constitutional ban against any "establishment of religion," are prohibited from such practices as allowing sectarian instruction on public school property during school hours.[16] Composing official—even if nondenominational—prayers to be recited by schoolchildren and requiring the reading to schoolchildren of passages from the Bible even if without comment, also have been declared unconstitutional.[17] On the other hand, city policies and regulations like subsidi-

[7]*Kunz v. New York,* 340 U.S. 290 (1951).

[8]*Thornhill v. Alabama,* 310 U.S. 88 (1940).

[9]*Tinker v. Des Moines School District,* 393 U.S. 503 (1969).

[10]See, for example, *Near v. Minnesota,* 283 U.S. 697 (1931) and *Beauharnais v. Illinois,* 343 U.S. 250 (1952).

[11]*Grosjean v. American Press Co.,* 297 U.S. 233 (1936).

[12]*Joseph Burstyn, Inc. v. Wilson,* 343 U.S. 495 (1952); *Kingsley International Pictures Corp. v. Regents,* 360 U.S. 684 (1959).

[13] *Thomas v. Collins,* 323 U.S. 516 (1945); *Staub v. Baxley,* 355 U.S. 313 (1958).

[14] *West Virginia State Board of Education v. Barnette,* 319 U.S. 624 (1943).

[15]*Martin v. Struthers,* 319 U.S. 141 (1943).

[16]*McCollum v. Board of Education,* 333 U.S. 203 (1948).

[17]*Engel v. Vitale,* 370 U.S. 421 (1962).

zing busing[18] or textbooks for parochial school children,[19] allowing school children to be dismissed early to attend religious instruction,[20] Sunday closing laws,[21] and the granting of property tax exemption to church property used solely for religious purposes[22] have been held not to constitute an "establishment of religion" and hence to be constitutionally allowable.

The Supreme Court has never ruled that every one of the procedural rights that persons are entitled to in federal criminal proceedings because of the Fourth, Fifth, Sixth, and Eighth Amendments are also incorporated within the meaning of "due process of law" which the states and therefore the cities cannot violate under the Fourteenth. But as a result of what the Court calls "selective incorporation," the vast majority of those rights have been made to operate against city police, prosecuting attorneys, and judges. Thus, city police and other investigatory personnel must observe the Fourth Amendment's prohibition against "unreasonable searches and seizures," refraining from searching premises or seizing evidence without a search warrant issued by a judge upon showing of probable cause that incriminating evidence exists at a particular place.[23] City police and prosecuting attorneys are bound during the detention of suspects by many of the Fifth and Sixth Amendments' guarantees, being prohibited from coercing confessions and being obliged to warn the accused of his right to remain silent and to have the assistance of an attorney before interrogation.[24]

City prosecuting attorneys and local trial judges are also bound not to infringe an accused's Fifth and Sixth Amendment rights during trial. These rights include the accused's being informed of the specific charges against him, to have counsel for his defense, and to have process for compelling witnesses to appear and testify.[25] They also require that any accused be allowed to refuse to testify and to have any illegally obtained evidence not admitted.[26] More, an accused person is guaranteed a jury trial if the maximum punishment that can be imposed for his offense exceeds six months,[27] a trial by an impartial judge and jury,[28] the right to appeal to higher courts for alleged errors of fact or law made at the trial, and not to have to submit himself to "double jeopardy"—i.e., stand trial involuntarily more than once for the same act or offence.[29] Finally, the equal protection clause

[18] *Everson v. Board of Education,* 330 U.S. 1 (1947).
[19] *Board of Education v. Allen, 392 U.S. 236 (1968).*
[20] *Zorach v. Clauson,* 343 U.S. 306 (1952).
[21] *McGowan v. Maryland,* 366 U.S. 420 (1961).
[22] *Walz v. Tax Commission,* 397 U.S. 664 (1970).
[23] *Mapp v. Ohio,* 367 U.S. 643 (1961).
[24] *Miranda v. Arizona,* 384 U.S. 436 (1966).
[25] Amendment VI, United States Constitution; *Washington v. Texas,* 385 U.S. 812 (1967).
[26] *Malloy v. Hogan,* 378 U.S. 1 (1964); *Mapp v. Ohio.*
[27] *Williams v. Florida,* 399 U.S. 78 (1970).
[28] *Duncan v. Louisiana,* 391 U.S. 145 (1968).
[29] *Benton v. Maryland,* 395 U.S. 784 (1969).

prohibits sentences that give a choice of a money fine or imprisonment—e.g., thirty dollars or thirty days—since such a sentence allows a more lenient penalty to those who can afford the fine.[30]

Apart from criminal proceedings, the due process clause of the Fourteenth Amendment applies to city governments the Fifth Amendment's prohibition against taking private property "without just compensation" or for other than "public use." And the Fourteenth Amendment's due process clause similarly requires city administrative officials to give a fair hearing to any aggrieved person who challenges the application to him of a regulation or tax or the denial of some benefit.[31]

Like the due process clause, the equal protection clause of the Fourteenth Amendment also imposes important restraints on city governments. As currently interpreted, equal protection prohibits city legislative, executive, or judicial officials from discriminating in favor of or against persons arbitrarily, as, for example, in imposing unequal tax assessments for similar property. It prohibits discrimination on such bases as color or ethnicity, as by maintaining intentionally segregated facilities like schools, playgrounds, or bus lines, or by interfering with the registration for or voting in primary or general elections by members of a particular race.[32] (Cities or local school districts are not, however, unconstitutionally denying equal protection by operating neighborhood schools attended predominantly or even exclusively by one race—white or black—as long as those unintegrated student bodies simply reflect unintegrated neighborhood residential patterns and are not the result of current or past discriminatory policies practiced by city or local school officials.)[33] The equal protection clause bans requiring enactment of a local "fair housing" law to be subject to a public referendum[34] (although it allows construction of low-rent housing projects to be subject to such a referendum).[35] Equal protection forbids discrimination on the basis of geographic residence, as when some sections of a city have greater representation in proportion to their population on its legislative body than others.[36] And because of the equal protection clause, city governments cannot discriminate on the basis of length of residence, making persons ineligible for welfare payments unless they have met minimum residency requirements.[37]

[30] *Tate v. Short,* 401 U.S. 395 (1971).

[31] See, e.g., *Goldberg v. Kelly,* 397 U.S. 254 (1970).

[32] *Brown v. Board of Education,* 347 U.S. 483 (1954); *Smith v. Allwright,* 321 U.S. 649 (1944); *Terry v. Adams, 345 U.S. 461 (1953).*

[33] *Keyes v. School District No. 1,* 413 U.S. 921 (1973); see also Harrell R. Rogers, Jr., "The Supreme Court and School Desegregation: Twenty Years Later," *Political Science Quarterly,* 89 (1974-75): 751-76.

[34] *Hunter v. Erickson,* 393 U.S. 385 (1969).

[35] *James v. Valtierra,* 402 U.S. 137 (1971).

[36] *Mahan v. Howell,* 410 U.S. 315 (1973).

[37] *Shapiro v. Thompson,* 394 U.S. (1969).

Statutory Regulation

Given that Congress is not assigned any express powers over cities, direct statutory regulation of city governments and officials is almost nonexistent. Congress can, however, regulate the activities of local officials when that regulation is necessary to carry out the enumerated powers that Congress has. Consequently, congressional regulatory legislation does reach city officials if they seek to undertake activities that would be prohibited even if performed by private persons. Examples include: operating radio or TV stations without compliance with federal regulations and securing a Federal Communications Commission license; operating an airport without compliance with provisions of federal aviation law; bridging a navigable stream or river in violation of congressional legislation and the rules of the Army Corps of Engineers; polluting interstate streams or rivers through discharge of wastes and sewage in violation of federal antipollution laws and regulations.

Practically the only congressional regulation of the conduct of local officials per se has been through the various post-Civil War and contemporary civil rights acts. The provisions of these acts are all based primarily on the Thirteenth, Fourteenth, and Fifteenth Amendments. The few surviving provisions of the post-Civil War acts thus make it a federal crime for any local official "in the selection or summoning of jurors," to exclude or fail "to summon any citizen on account of race, color, or previous conditions of servitude."[38] It is similarly a crime for such an official "under color of any law, statute, ordinance, regulation, or custom, willfully [to subject] any inhabitant of any State, Territory or District to the deprivation of any rights, privileges, or immunities secured or protected by the Constitution and laws of the United States. . . ."[39] Under this provision, for example, a local sheriff can be prosecuted in the federal courts for beating a black prisoner to death, thus depriving him of his right not to have his life taken without "due process of law."[40]

Of the contemporary civil rights legislation, the Civil Rights Act of 1964 allows the Justice Department to bring suits for injunction against local officials ordering them to desegregate any segregated public facilities or public schools or colleges that they might own, operate, or manage. And one title of the Civil Rights Act of 1965 authorizes, in effect, the superseding of local election officials by federal "voting examiners" and prohibits the use of literacy tests and related devices in certain areas.

[38]Title 18, U.S. Code, 1970, ed., §243. The statute on which this section is based was originally enacted in 1875.

[39]Title 18, U.S. Code, 1970 ed., §242. The statute on which this section is based was originally enacted in 1870.

[40]See *Screws v. United States,* 325 U.S. 91 (1945).

All the preceding kinds of congressional regulatory legislation are restrictive of the actions of local officials, their purpose being the furtherance of nationally defined objectives such as the protection of the rights of black citizens. There are, however, many regulatory statutes passed by Congress whose purpose is to help officials of local government. The most important single category consists of statutes that define as federal crimes certain activities that are also crimes in large cities under the regular state criminal law. Most often the constitutional basis for making the activity a federal crime is that the facilities of "interstate commerce" are involved in its commission. Thus under Congress' power to regulate interstate commerce, federal statutes have outlawed:

1. Kidnapping when the victim is transported across state lines.
2. Prostitution when the procurer transports a woman across state lines.
3. The interstate shipment of slot-machines or gambling records, tickets, slips, etc.
4. The interstate shipment of handguns, rifles, or shotguns to individuals.
5. The transporting across state lines of explosives or possession of explosives so transported with the knowledge or intent that they would be used to blow up any building or vehicle.
6. The crossing of state lines or use of facilities of interstate commerce such as telephones to incite, organize, encourage, or take part in riots.
7. The teaching of the use, application, or making of a firearm or explosive with the knowledge or intent that it would be used in a civil disorder obstructing commerce.
8. The obstruction or interference with a law enforcement officer or fireman performing his official duties during such a civil disorder.
9. The crossing of state lines to avoid prosecution or confinement after committing a felony.

This kind of federalizing of a crime helps local police and prosecutors in part by allowing federal investigative personnel like the F.B.I. to enter the case. It also helps by allowing federal attorneys to undertake prosecutions in federal courts where sometimes fewer elements need to be proved for a conviction under the state or local statute. The Congress' "taxing power" has also been used to "federalize" crimes. The most important example is the outlawing of the purchase, sale, or possession of narcotics or marijuana, except in or from a package with federal tax stamps.

In still another attempt to assist local law enforcement officers, Congress under the Omnibus Crime Control Act of 1968 exempted them from the absolute prohibition against wiretapping contained in the Federal Communications Act of 1934. The 1968 Act authorized the principal prosecuting attorney of any political subdivision, such as a city, to apply to a local trial judge and the judge to grant a warrant approving wiretapping to secure information relating to any crime dangerous to life, limb, or property, which is punishable by imprisonment for more than one year.

Federal Grants-In-Aid

Federal financial aid programs to cities are based primarily on Congress' so-called "spending power." The spending power derives from Congress' constitutional authority "to lay and collect taxes . . . to pay the debts and provide for the common defense and general welfare of the United States."[41] As Congress has exercised it since the founding of the country and as the Supreme Court eventually ruled in 1936,[42] this clause permits the spending of federal monies not only in the substantive areas which Congress can regulate under its various enumerated powers but also for any purpose that comes within the meaning of the broad terms "common defense" or "general welfare" of the United States. Although some limited and sporadic forms of federal assistance to local governments date to the very beginning of the Republic, it is the year 1932 that constitutes, as Roscoe C. Martin put it, "a sort of geological fault line" in the development of financial relationships between the federal government and large cities.[43] With the exception of highway aid which was begun in 1916, all the major urban-oriented grant programs that are currently in existence have been enacted since 1932.

The main urban problem areas for which there were federal grant programs in fiscal 1974–75 are: poverty and unemployment (public assistance or "welfare" grants, medical assistance grants, food stamps, antipoverty grants, comprehensive manpower assistance grants); inadequate housing and physical decay (urban renewal, low-rent public housing, model cities, rent supplements, and neighborhood facilities grants); education (elementary and secondary education grants); crime (law enforcement assistance grants); water pollution (waste treatment works construction grants, water and sewer facilities grants); health (hospital and medical facilities construction grants); and transportation (federal aid to highways and urban mass transportation grants). The grants in these specific problem areas have since 1972 been supplemented by general revenue-sharing payments.[44]

[41]Article I, Section 8.

[42]*U.S. v. Butler,* 297 U.S. 1 (1936).

[43]*The Cities and the Federal System* (New York: Atherton Press, 1965), p. 111.

[44]It should also be noted that none of these grant programs is "urban" in the sense of benefiting large cities exclusively. Large cities are direct or indirect beneficiaries of each of these programs and normally have received larger sized grants under particular programs than other local governments. But local governments other than those of large cities are also eligible for grants and are recipients of benefits. Figures comparing the allocation of federal monies for particular programs for large cities and other local governments are not available.

It should be understood that not all of these "urban" grant programs provide for the grant payment to be made directly to city governments. Under some programs, the grant is made to the state government, either for eventual redistribution of a part or all of it to city governments or for the state itself to operate a particular program that deals with a problem found in large cities. A few grant programs benefit city governments indirectly by providing subsidies or other payments to individuals (e.g., food stamps) or private groups (e.g., grants to community corporations under the Economic Opportunity Act of 1964) in large cities to help them cope with conditions that constitute problems for city governments.

Because only some urban grants are paid directly to city governments, while others are paid to the states and still other grants go to private individuals and groups, it is impossible to determine the total amount of federal grant money that is actually spent to help large cities. The U.S. Census Bureau's *City Government Finances* reports only federal grants made directly to local governments. In fiscal 1973–74, federal aid to the nation's largest cities of over 300,000 in population (excluding Washington, D.C.) comprised $2,293,944,000 or some 10.6 percent of their aggregate general expenditures, up from .7 percent in 1951–52.[45] This represents a dramatic 99-fold increase in the aggregate amount of such grants—one that has been 15 times as fast as the rise in those cities' general expenditures (Figure 6–1).

Because grants under some of the very largest programs that benefit cities, including public assistance, elementary and secondary education, medical assistance, highways, and food stamps are not paid to city governments, these Census Bureau figures obviously understate the amount of federal money spent seeking to ameliorate undesirable conditions with which city governments must cope. In order to make an exact calculation, it would be necessary to add to the direct federal grants the portion of federal grants to states that are "passed through" to local governments and the payments that go directly to private individuals and groups in large cities. These figures are not, however, available in published census reports on city governmental finances. What is available is the total amount spent by the federal government on the kind of grant programs that directly or indirectly benefit large cities; for fiscal 1973-74, that total for major programs was $33,172,000,000. (See Table 6–1.) This total, of course, included monies retained by state governments as well as monies that went to local governments and individuals in locales other than large cities.

Impact of Federal Grants on Cities. Like state grants-in-aid, federal grant programs influence city governmental performance by allowing them

[45]Calculated from U.S. Bureau of the Census, *City Government Finances, 1951-52* to *1973-74.*

TABLE 6-1 Overall Size of Selected Federal Aid Programs Benefiting Large Cities, Fiscal 1973-1974 (in million of dollars)

Commerce and Transportation	
Highways	4,489
Urban mass transit	348
Airports	243
Community and Regional Development	
Urban renewal	1,205
Model cities	466
Community services administration (formerly community action)	622
Education, Manpower, and Social Services	
Elementary and Secondary education	1,665
Comprehensive manpower assistance	1,137
Emergency employment assistance	598
Health	
Medicaid	5,818
Income Security	
Public assistance	5,423
Food stamps	2,779
Housing payments (HUD)	1,116
Law Enforcement and Justice	639
General Revenue Sharing	6,624
Total	33,172

Source: U.S. Bureau of the Census, *Statistical Abstract of the United States,* 1975 (Washington, D.C.: U.S. Government Printing Office, 1975), Table 422.

to undertake a level of effort or a range of programs that otherwise would not be possible without an increase in city taxes and that might not be possible at all. Some federal grant programs, such as highways, welfare, primary and secondary education, and general revenue-sharing simply "support" or subsidize functions that have traditionally been performed by city governments. Other grant programs like low-cost public housing, urban renewal, community action, and manpower training have stimulated city governments to undertake new programs that the cities lacked the will, imagination, or financial capacity to establish and maintain on their own.

The conditions normally attached to federal grants also influence the recipient city government by obliging it to comply with various procedural or substantive requirements in the administration of the aided program. Traditional examples of such requirements are the use of the merit system

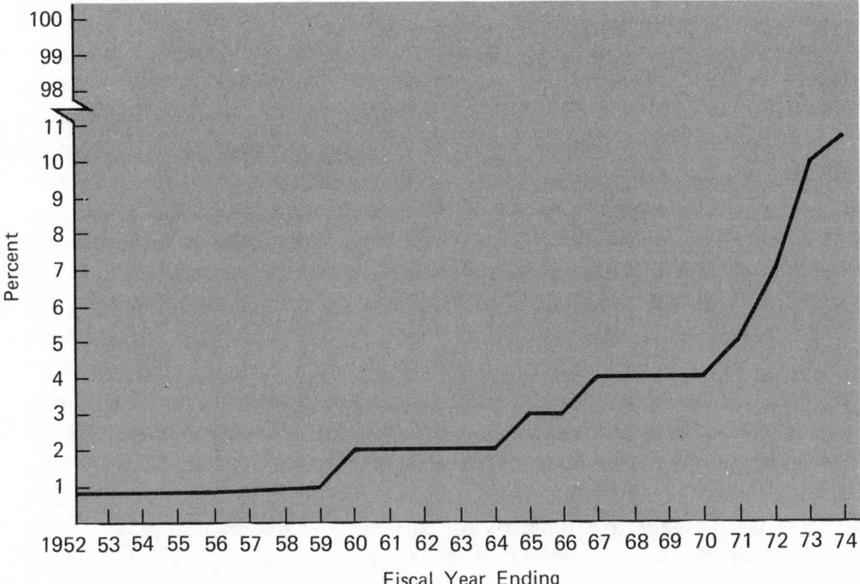

FIGURE 6-1 Direct Federal Aid to Large-City Governments As Percentage of General Expenditures, 1952–1974. (Cities of Over 300,000 in Population, Excluding Washington, D.C.)

Source: Calculated from U.S. Bureau of the Census, City Government Finance, 1951-52 to 1973-74.

to hire employees in federally funded programs and the maintaining of certain standards in accounting and in auditing of the funds spent. Newer requirements have been the developing of comprehensive plans by the recipient local governments showing the future development of programs in a particular functional field, such as education or public health, or how particular construction projects would affect the overall physical development of a city or its entire metropolitan area. The Civil Rights Act of 1964 made additional conditions for the continuation of any grant program: nondiscrimination in the administration of aided activity or facility on account of race, color, or national origin and nondiscrimination in employment practices with respect to race, color, religion, national origin, or sex. And beginning in the early 1970s, Congress attached provisions to education bills that imposed various restrictions on the use of federal funds for busing school children in order to achieve racial balance. All of these grant conditions are normally enforced by federal administrators in charge of the different programs, and failure to comply with requirements may lead to those administrators terminating the grant. But grant conditions can sometimes also be enforced by injunctive suits brought by aggrieved private persons who claim that particular conditions are being violated by city administrators.

Finally, it cannot be denied that some federal grant programs have influenced city governments by unintentionally worsening rather than improving problems with which cities must deal. The most striking illustration of this is the massive interstate highway program which damaged the tax base of many cities by destroying tax-paying property to make way for the various roads and also destroyed the city's stock of older, low-rent housing. The highway program at the same time facilitated the flight of car-owning, middle-income taxpayers to the suburbs and increased the problems of traffic congestion in downtown areas by encouraging commuting by car rather than by mass transit. Similarly, while one of the objectives of the urban renewal program and different public housing programs was to improve the supply of housing, the number of low-rent units razed as part of urban renewal projects typically exceeded the number of low-rent units that have been built on the renewal sites. For much of the time, private developers build office buildings, shopping complexes, and luxury apartments rather than housing that could be afforded by the poor.[46] Also, the absence of federal standards or minimums with respect to what size welfare payments are available in different cities led to some nonurban, and especially southern nonurban, states keeping their level of payments at only one-third to one-half that available in the large cities of urban states. Many city officials believe that such great disparities in the size of welfare payments have provided strong incentive for poor people to migrate to, remain in and increase the financial burden of large cities.

Despite these restrictions on their freedom of action and the negative side effects of a few urban grant programs, city officials, on the whole, look upon them with great favor. Indeed, the chief complaint of city officials is that federal grant programs are all greatly underfinanced. This underfinancing, city officials insist, exists both relative to the expressed objectives of the authorizing legislation—especially such grandiosely phrased ones as "to eliminate blight in urban areas," to provide a "decent home in a suitable environment for every American family," or "to combat the problems of poverty"—and relative to the perceived needs of their own cities. City officials are increasingly expressing the view that only through massive infusion of larger amounts of federal funds to city governments by means of categorical grants, block grants, or revenue-sharing will large-city governments be able to survive financially.[47]

[46]See, for example, Scott Greer, *Urban Renewal and American Cities* (Indianapolis: Bobbs-Merrill, 1965).

[47]See e.g., U.S. House of Representatives, *Federal-State-Local Relations, State and Local Officials,* Hearings before a Subcommittee of the Committe on Governmental Operations, 85th Cong., 1st Sess. (1957); U.S. Senate, *Federal Role in Urban Affairs,* Hearings before the Subcommittee on Executive Reorganization of the Committee on Governmental Operations, 89th and 90th Cong. (1966-67); U.S. Senate, *Creative Federalism,* Hearings before the Subcommittee on Intergovernmental Relations of the Committee on Governmental Operations, 89th Cong., 2d Sess. (1966); U.S. Senate, *How 45 Selected Jurisdictions View Revenue-Sharing,* Subcommittee on Intergovernmental Relations of the Committee on Governmental Operations, Committee Print, 93rd Cong., 2d Sess. (1974).

The other complaints city officials have about federal grant programs are minor: (1) The application procedures for the program are sometimes unduly complicated and clumsy, requiring the filing of many separate and sometimes extremely lengthy applications to different agencies for grants in related areas; (2) There are delays in receiving word on whether an application has been accepted and sometimes even in obtaining the actual cash payment; (3) Not enough grant awards are made directly to city governments: some of the grants go directly to the states which then proceed to reallocate them according to the states' own determination of the relative needs of different local governments, and some—like community action grants—go directly to private groups and institutions, thus bypassing city governments completely and denying city officials any formal way of imposing their judgment on the necessity, desirability, or relative priority of the projects being funded; and (4) The requirement of multiple and advance clearances at different stages of implementation introduces excessive delay in the completion of projects.[48]

Differences in Grant Administration Federal grants are allocated to recipients on a "formula" basis, a "project" basis, or some combination of the two. Formula grants are allocated to states or their cities or school districts according to formulas which take into account certain prescribed numerical factors—i.e., the relative share of the nation's population as a whole, some relevant age group, or poor families. Depending on the program, they may include fiscal need as measured by per capita income or the size of the area or the number of miles of roads. Each eligible recipient is entitled to a certain size grant, resulting from the formulas being applied to the total sum of money appropriated by Congress for that fiscal year. The public assistance and medical assistance grants programs are special cases of formula grants because they are "open-ended," meaning that there is no ceiling on the total amount that can be spent under these programs; the applicable formula specifies for what percentage of the state's payments for public and medical assistance the state will be reimbursed, whatever the total amount of the reimbursement turns out to be.

"Project grants" are allocated in response to applications that request financial assistance for particular proposals or projects. Federal grant administrators use their discretion in approving or rejecting applications, according to the merits of the proposed projects, whether they meet federal requirements, and subject to the total amount of funds that has been appropriated. Combined "formula-and-project" grants are made in response to specific applications, but a general formula sets maximum or minimum limits on the proportion of total grants that can be allocated to any one state or its cities. Among urban grant programs, public assistance

[48]See Jeffrey L. Pressman and Aaron B. Wildavsky, *Implementation* (Berkeley and Los Angeles: University of California Press, 1973).

and medical assistance, law enforcement assistance, and elementary and secondary education grants are distributed primarily according to a formula, while urban renewal, hospital construction, and highway aid grants are given out on a "project" or "formula-and-project" basis.

Both formula and project grants usually carry "matching" requirements on a fixed or variable percentage basis. For example, grants for regular highways require that the state or locality "match" or contribute out of their own funds 50 percent of the total cost of the project and those for interstate highways that the state or city match 10 percent. Urban renewal projects normally carry a one-third matching provision. The few grant programs that have variable matching requirements make the contribution required from the recipient government dependent on some measure of its relative fiscal capacity or need: Thus grants for hospital construction require variable matching from one-third to two-thirds of the federal funds; projects in states with the lowest per capita income provide the smaller percentage and those in states with the highest per capita income provide the larger percentage.

Often grants also carry "maintenance of effort" requirements. These condition the payment of the federal money on the recipient government's continuing to provide from nonfederal sources at least the level of expenditures of some prescribed earlier period.[49]

Categorical Grants vs. Block Grants and Revenue-Sharing Until 1972 all federal grant programs in existence were "categorical," meaning that the funds had to be used for the specific purposes or "categories" specified in enacting legislation. In 1964 Walter W. Heller, then the chairman of the President's Council of Economic Advisors, proposed that the federal government begin to distribute a specified portion of federal income tax collections each year as block grants to state governments to be used for whatever purposes were designated by the states. This distribution was to be over and above the system of categorical grants.[50] Beginning in 1964, numerous "revenue-sharing" bills were introduced in Congress for such block grants to the states and in some instances to local governments like those of large cities.

In 1972 Congress passed the State and Local Assistance Act, or general revenue-sharing act, as it became commonly known. Congress appropriated funds for five years, providing payments to state and local governments at an annual rate of $5.3 billion in fiscal 1972 and reaching a rate of $6.3 billion by fiscal 1977. The size of each state's allocation was

[49]All these distinctions among grant programs are fully explained in Advisory Commission on Intergovernmental Relations, *Fiscal Balance in the American Federal System,* Vol. 1 (Washington, D.C.: U.S. Government Printing Office, 1967), Vol. 1, Chap. 5, and U.S. Senate, *Federal Programs of Grants-in-Aid to State and Local Governments,* Committee on Governmental Operations, Committee Print, 91st Cong., 1st Sess. (1969).

[50]See Walter W. Heller, *New Dimensions of Political Economy* New York: W.W. Norton, 1967), chap. 3.

determined by a complicated "three factor" formula that took into account population, relative per capita income, and tax effort or a "five factor" formula which adds urbanized population and state income tax collections. Two-thirds of each state's allocation was automatically passed through to its general purpose local governments—i.e., counties, townships, villages, and cities—on the basis of the "three factor" formula. The formula's intent was to compensate for relative poverty in the population and to reward high tax effort. Local governments were given wide leeway to spend their allocations on such items as police, fire protection, building code enforcement, sanitation, streets and roads, mass transit, health, recreation, and libraries.

Large-city governments favor revenue-sharing, both because of the funds they receive and for the essential lack of restrictions on how those funds can be spent. City officials do complain, however, that they expected revenue-sharing payments to supplement grants under categorical aid programs, whereas such categorical grants were cut back since the institution of revenue-sharing, and that the allocation formula was not weighted to sufficiently compensate large cities with concentrations of slum poverty. Futhermore, the officials of some large cities complain that even under the existing formula, they were penalized by "ceiling" and "floor" provisions in the law governing the size of payments: The ceiling provision limited any city's entitlement to no more than 145 percent of the state-wide average local per capita entitlement, even if its low per capita income and/or high tax effort would under the general allocation formula have entitled it to more. (See Table 6-2.) The floor provision guaranteed every county, township, village, or city no less than 20 percent of the state-wide average per capita entitlement regardless of the operation of the allocation formula, thus distributing extra moneys to jurisdictions whose per capita income and tax effort would not otherwise merit them. Since the total distributions for any particular year were a fixed number of dollars, such unmerited distributions decrease the size of the pot from which other, more needy local governments can draw.

TABLE 6-2 Allocation Reductions Due to 145 Percent Ceiling (Selected Major Cities)

City	Amount of Reduction	Percent of Actual Allocation
Baltimore	$6.6 million	25
Cincinnati	1.1	13
Detroit	4.8	12
Philadelphia	28.3	57
St. Louis	9.7	68

Source: Advisory Commission on Intergovernmental Relations, *General Revenue Sharing: An ACIR Re-Evaluation* (Washington, D.C.: U.S. Government Printing Office, 1974), p. 29.

Spokesmen for the urban poor also criticize revenue-sharing when it is used as partial substitution for categorical grants. They point out that the federal government has had a better record than city governments in allocating moneys to improve the conditions of the slum poor minorities—something it was able to do by directly targeting funds to them through categorical grants. These spokesmen are concerned that revenue-sharing funds, because they can be allocated for a broad array of programs by city governments, are more likely to be used for purposes favored by a city's politically dominant groups rather than those favored by its deprived minorities.[51]

In 1973 and 1974 two sets of categorical grants were consolidated into so-called "block grants" or "special revenue-sharing." The Comprehensive Employment and Training Act of 1973 (CETA) repealed and replaced the Manpower Development and Training Act of 1962 and the manpower training provisions of the Economic Opportunity Act of 1964. The Housing and Community Development Act of 1974 (HCDA) authorized community development block grants as a replacement for previously separate urban renewal, model cities, basic water and sewer facilities, neighborhood facilities, and other community development-type categorical programs. Both the CETA and the HCDA made all cities and counties above a certain size (100,000 for the first and 50,000 and 200,000, respectively, for the second) eligible for "entitlements" under different formulas. However, the would-be recipients of such entitlements would be required to file satisfactory plans for the expenditure of the funds before they received them.

As with general revenue-sharing, spokesmen for large city governments and for the urban poor have complained about the switch from categorical to block grant or special revenue-sharing programs. The central complaint is that because funds will now be distributed primarily on the basis of formula-generated entitlements rather than individual project applications, many more city and county jurisdictions will be receiving grants than previously was the case, thus reducing the amounts left to be allocated to large central cities.[52]

[51]For a balanced discussion of the pros and cons of revenue-sharing, see Advisory Commission on Intergovernmental Relations, *General Revenue Sharing: An ACIR Re-evaluation* (Washington, D.C.: U.S. Government Printing Office, 1974). For an acute analysis of how the form of federal aid influences the internal politics of the recipient government, see Jeffrey L. Pressman, *Federal Programs and City Politics* (Berkeley: University of California Press, 1975).

[52]For a more extensive discussion of the implications of the shift from categorical grants to various forms of revenue-sharing, see Jeffrey L. Pressman, "Political Implications of the New Federalism," and Robert D. Reischauer, "General Revenue Sharing—The Program's Incentives," in Wallace E. Oates (ed.), *Financing the New Federalism* (Baltimore, Md.: Johns Hopkins University Press, 1975).

POLICY ORIENTATION OF THE FEDERAL GOVERNMENT

Broadly speaking, the federal government has in the past four decades exercised its influence so as to assist large-city governments to cope with their problems. Admittedly, the federal court system capped by the Supreme Court is part of the federal government, and some court decisions have proven burdensome to city officials. For example, the Court's expansion of protection for defendants in criminal trials may have made it more difficult to secure convictions against those in cities who commit crimes. The Court's increased intolerance of any kind of racial segregation in city facilities and the lower courts' consequent ordering of school desegregation plans including the use of busing have caused rancorous conflict in some cities and may have accelerated white flight to the suburbs. And through its interpretation of the "establishment of religion" clause, the Court has stopped city schools from continuing what had traditionally been considered relatively innocuous, semi-religious rituals like praying and Bible reading. Yet even in these areas the constraining court decisions applied nationwide and did not have any antibig city bias per se.

Most of the federal government's actions have, however, been either not constraining or positively helpful to cities: The federal government has imposed only the barest of statutory regulation of city governments. The federal government has "federalized" certain crimes that occur in cities so as to lend federal law enforcement forces in dealing with them. And most importantly, the federal government has established the growing variety and magnitude of grant and loan programs that directly and indirectly subsidize city governmental operation. It is these financial subsidies that already allow city governments to provide higher levels of performance than they could otherwise do with their own locally raised revenues. And it is the future size of these financial subsidies that will have the heaviest impact on determining whether the level of performance in most large cities will continue to decline because of lack of financial resources or whether their capacity to alleviate undesirable conditions and to check adverse trends can be increased. The remainder of this chapter will therefore concentrate on analyzing past trends, bases, and prospects for federal financial support of large cities.

Party Differences and Urban Support

Although the long-term trend in federal financial assistance to large cities has been upward in the past four decades, the expansion of the federal government's role has not been smooth and continuous. Rather, the establishment of new programs and the sharp increases in funding have come mainly in spurts, the most important ones being between the years 1933 and 1937 during the Roosevelt Administration and between 1964 and 1968 in the Johnson Administration. The single most important factor underlying the federal government's responsiveness to the financial needs of large cities has been having in office a Democratic president serving with a Congress that had heavy Democratic majorities.

The President's importance comes from the fact that it is he who provides in his messages to Congress and his annual budget most of the major proposals that Congress seriously considers for new or for expansion of existing grant programs and for increased spending levels. The President's proposals are not, of course, all actually invented by him nor are the amounts proposed for different programs in the budget that he submits to Congress set by him on his own: Many ideas and all the original budgetary requests concerning urban affairs come to the President from the executive branch departments and agencies administering urban programs—notably Housing and Urban Development (HUD), and Health, Education and Welfare (HEW), and, to a smaller extent, Justice and Labor. New ideas also come from White House advisors and specially appointed task forces.

But it is the President himself who decides which of those proposals he will make part of his own legislative program and thus make a special effort to have enacted by Congress. And it is the President who, with the help of the Office of Budget and Management, passes on the original budgetary requests from the departments and agencies and sets the final figures in the budget presented to Congress.

Presidents Roosevelt, Truman, Kennedy, and Johnson—all Democrats—were inclined to propose and support new and expanded urban programs and to ask for sizable appropriations increases to fund those that were already in effect. Presidents Eisenhower, Nixon, and Ford—all Republicans—were more inclined to consolidate rather than expand and sometimes even to cut back and scrap some existing programs and to keep spending levels from rising abruptly from what they had been in previous years.

Congress itself does on rare occasions consider proposals for major additions to or expansions of urban grant programs that are originated by its own members and do not constitute a part of the President's legislative program. This happens most often when the President and majorities in Congress belong to different parties. Even then, however, the President's support or at least acquiescence is almost a prerequisite for any major increases in federal financial assistance to cities; the President can normally defeat congressionally-enacted proposals with a veto, since vetoes can be overridden only by a very difficult to attain two-thirds vote in both the House and the Senate. Various presidents have also claimed the right to "impound," i.e., not spend, funds even after they were appropriated by Congress with the President's signature or over his veto; the Congressional

Budget and Impoundment Control Act of 1974 may, however, have all but eliminated presidential impoundments that Congress opposes.[53]

Though typically it is the President who originally proposes additional help for cities, it is Congress that disposes: For Congress is the body that has the legal power to make the final decisions on whether and with what kinds of modifications presidential legislative proposals will be enacted into law. And Congress is the body that determines the extent to which the moneys actually appropriated and thus legally available for spending coincide with the amounts requested in the President's budget. Within Congress too, the party differences have been clear. In recent decades it has been the bulk of the Democratic members of the House and Senate who have been willing to vote for new and expanded urban programs and for larger spending and the bulk of the Republican members who have not. An examination was made of all those roll-call votes on urban-aid issues that were among the "key votes" selected annually between 1945 and 1974 by the Congressional Quarterly, Inc., a nonpartisan organization that publishes the *Congressional Quarterly Weekly Report* and other reports and books analyzing Congress.[54] These key votes were not necessarily the votes on bills on final passage. They are intended to represent the most significant decisions made in the consideration of bills, which are sometimes motions to amend or recommit in order to expand or contract the coverage of a program or to decrease or increase its appropriations.

As Figures 6–2 and 6–3 show, on forty-four "key" urban votes taken in the House between 1945, when the Congressional Quarterly began keeping score, and 1974, a majority of all the Democratic members who voted cast their votes in favor of the prourban position in every one of the forty-four instances. One the other hand, in thirty-seven out of the forty-four cases, a majority of the Republicans who were voting took the antiurban position. Similarly, in twenty-eight "key" urban votes taken in the Senate during the same time period, a majority of the voting Democrats was in favor of the

[53]See Public Law 93-344, Title X.

[54]The Congressional Quarterly "key votes" on which this analysis is based are by number and year: in the House, #6 of 1945, #2 of 1946, #2 of 1949, #1 of 1954, #6 of 1955, #4 of 1956, #6 of 1957, #2 of 1960, #4, 6 of 1961, #1 of 1962, #3, 5 of 1964, #3, 5, 8, 9, 10, 12 of 1965, #2, 9, 11 of 1966, #3, 4, 7, 8, 12 of 1967, #7, 11 of 1968, #3, 10 of 1969, #1, 5, 9, 10 of 1970, #3 of 1971, #4, 7, 12, of 1972, #8, 10 of 1973, #10, 11, 15 of 1974; and in the Senate, #2, 4 of 1948, #2 of 1949, #4 of 1955, #1 of 1960, #3, 4 of 1961, #2, 3, 5 of 1963, #4 of 1964, #3, 10, 11, 13 of 1965, #3, 8 of 1966, #9 of 1967, #8, 11 of 1968, #7 of 1970, #5, 14 of 1971, #11, 14 of 1972, #2 of 1973, #4, 14 of 1974.

Full details on each of these votes can be found in *Congress and the Nation,* Vol. 1 (1945-64) (Washington, D.C.: Congressional Quarterly Service, 1965), "Key Votes," pp. 38a-97a; Vol. II (1965-68) (Washington, D.C.: Congressional Quarterly Service, 1969), "Key Votes," pp. 5a-41a; Vol. III (1969-72) (Washington, D.C.: Congressional Quarterly Service, 1973), "Key Votes," pp. 5a-47a; *Congressional Quarterly Almanac,* 1973 (Washington, D.C.: Congressional Quarterly Service, 1974), pp. 929–41, *Congressional Quarterly Almanac,* 1974 (Washington, D.C.: Congressional Quarterly Service, 1975, pp. 973-85.

prourban position on all but two of the twenty-eight votes while a majority of voting Republicans voted against, on all but ten. (See Figure 6–2) Inspection of Figure 6–3 will also show that the majorities from the two parties for and against urban programs typically were not marginal ones, but represented sharp differences between the dominant Democratic and Republican point of view. The difference in the average level of support for urban programs in the period 1945 to 1974 was between 76 percent for the Democrats and 28 percent for the Republicans in the House, and between 75 percent for the Democrats and 38 percent for the Republicans in the Senate.

It should be noted that the difference between the dominant Democratic

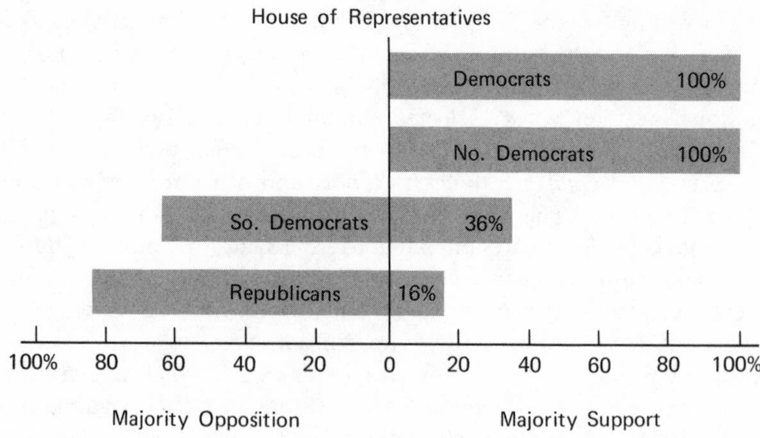

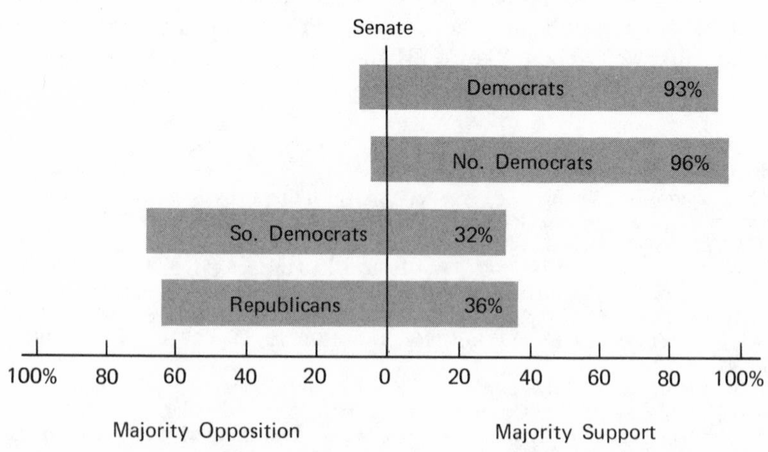

FIGURE 6-2 Majorities in Support and in Opposition of Urban Legislation on Selected Key Votes, 1945-1974, by Party, and for the Democratic Party, by Region.

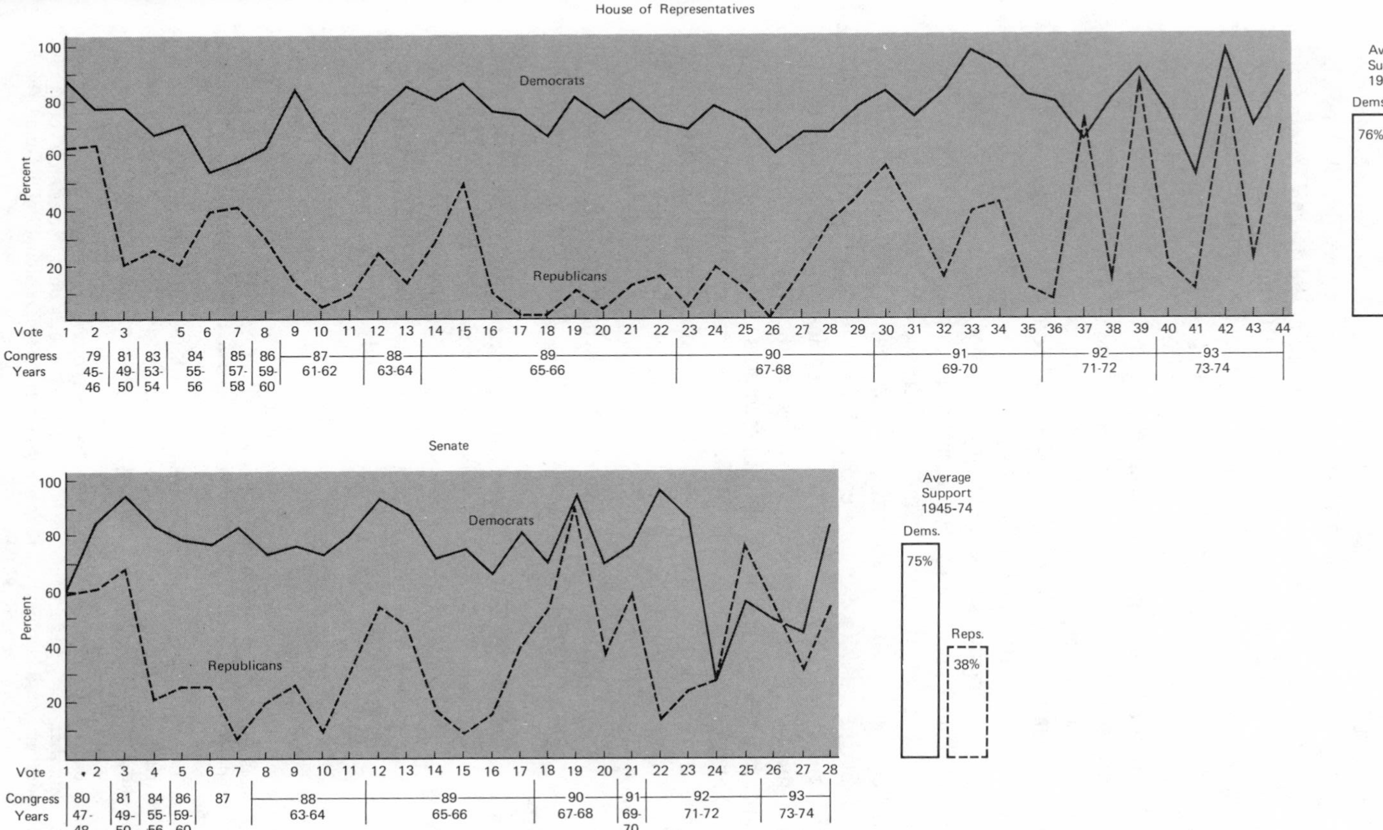

FIGURE 6-3 Percentage of Democratic and Republican Members of Congress Supporting Urban Legislation on Selected Key Votes, 1945-1974.

and dominant Republican positions on urban issues becomes even more striking if the votes of those Democrats defined as "southern"[55] by the Congressional Quarterly Service are not included in the overall Democratic totals but are treated separately. Since the late 1930s majorities of this bloc of southern Democrats have voted more consistently with the Republicans than with the remaining "northern" Democrats[56] on urban issues. On the key votes already referred to, a majority of "southern" Democrats voted with a majority of their northern Democratic brethren in support of the urban position only sixteen out of forty-four times in the House, giving an average level of support of 45 percent, and nine out of twenty-eight times in the Senate, giving an average level of support of 47 percent (see Figures 6–2 and 6–4). Thus, the plotting of urban voting scores of the northern Democrats alone raises the average support level from 76 percent to 94 percent in the House and from 75 percent to 90 percent in the Senate and therefore shows even more accurately the very dramatic difference on urban issues that has existed between the "nonsouthern" or "national" Democratic party and the Republican party (see Figure 6–5). This dramatic difference indicates also that regardless of whether their constituencies were urban, suburban, or rural, most northern Democratic members of the House voted in favor of urban programs while most Republican members voted against. This is not to say that the kind of constituency had no influence: Within each party, support for urban programs was normally greatest from representatives and senators from the most urban districts and states, slightly less from those whose districts and states were suburban, and least from members with the most rural constituencies. The difference in urban support within each party according to type of constituency has been sharply less, however, than the difference between parties.[57]

Given these very strong characteristic positions on urban issues of northern Democratic, southern Democratic, and Republican members of Congress, a necessary condition for a particular Congress to enact prourban legislation proposed by a prourban President has been the existence and large size of a Democratic majority. Accordingly, in the four years since

[55]CQ defines as "southern" all those Democrats coming from the states of the old confederacy—Alabama, Arkansas, Florida, Georgia, Louisiana, Mississippi, North Carolina, South Carolina, Tennessee, Texas, and Virginia—and the two border states of Kentucky and Oklahoma.

[56]CQ defines as "northern" all other Democrats, whether they are in fact from the "North," strictly speaking, or from the Midwest, West, Pacific coast, etc. It is with these meanings that the terms "southern" Democrats and "northern" Democrats are used in this book.

[57]For an explanation of why the Democratic party has been the prourban and the Republican the antiurban party and an analysis of the relative impacts on congressional voting of party, constitutency, and ideology, see Demetrios Caraley, "Congressional Politics and Urban Aid," *Political Science Quarterly,* 91 (1976): 19-45.

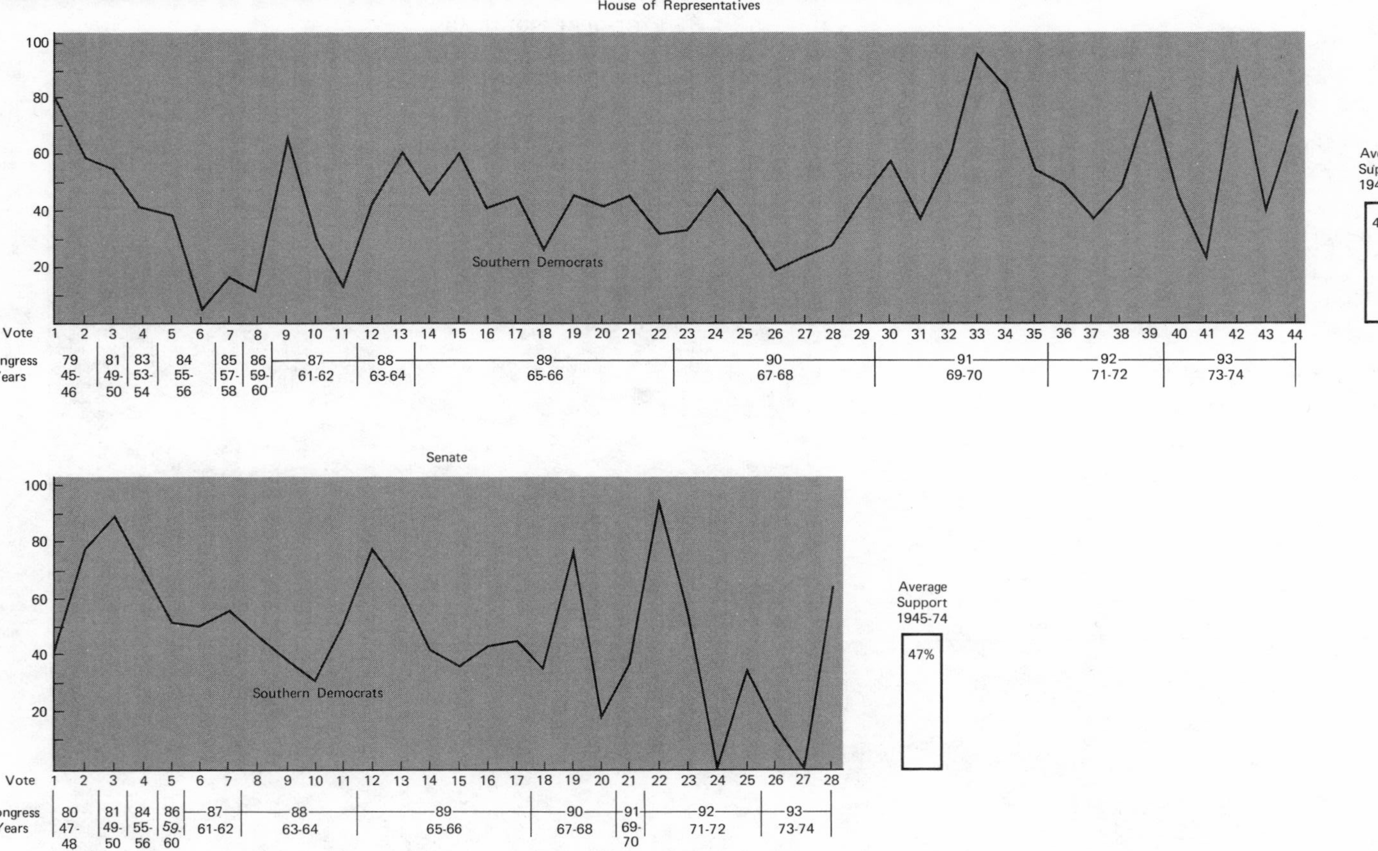

FIGURE 6-4 Percentage of Southern Democratic Members of Congress Supporting Urban Legislation on Selected Key Votes, 1945-1974.

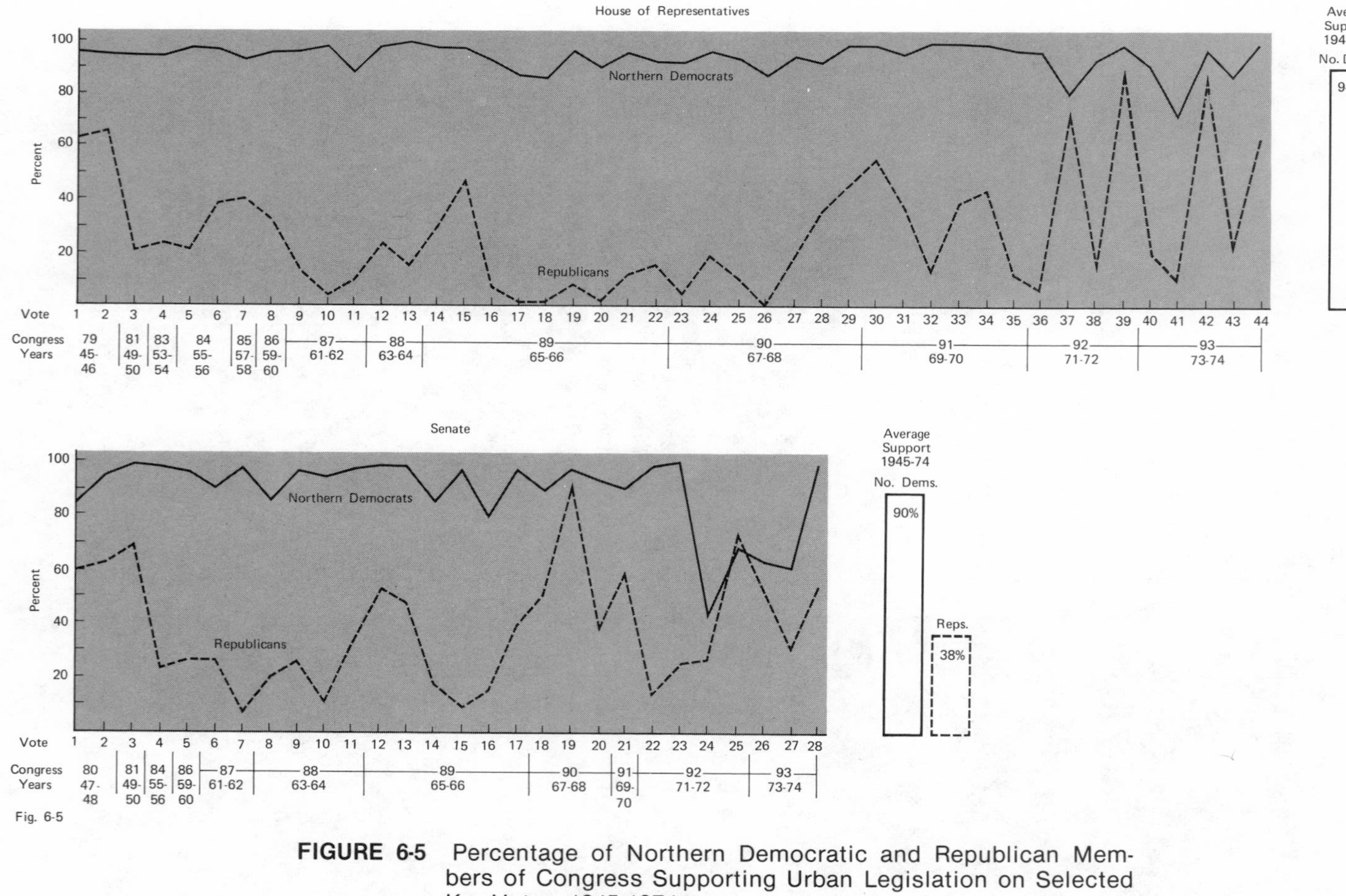

FIGURE 6-5 Percentage of Northern Democratic and Republican Members of Congress Supporting Urban Legislation on Selected Key Votes, 1945-1974.

1945 with Republican majorities in Congress (1947–48, 1953–54), no new urban-aid programs were passed and only one old program was expanded. The converse is not true, however, and prourban positions did not fare equally well in all the years that the majorities were Democratic. Consistent success for prourban positions in Congress depended on the Democratic majority being sizeable enough so that even with large-scale southern Democratic defections, enough Democratic votes were left from the preponderant majorities of northern members who consistently supported the prourban stand and from the varying-sized minorities of southern Democrats who voted with them to constitute majorities on the floor. On a few occasions, the majorities also required the votes of the handful of Republicans who deserted the dominant antiurban point of view of their party and voted for the prourban position.

Party Differences in Action: A Contrast of the 87th and 89th Congress

An analysis of two specific sessions of the House of Representatives may make clearer the impact of differences in the distribution of seats between parties from Congress to Congress. During most of[58] the 87th Congress —the Congress that was elected with President Kennedy in 1960 and was in session 1961–62—there were 263 Democrats and 174 Republicans in the House of Representatives. This line-up gave the appearance of the House being safely in the control of the prourban Democratic party. And the Democrats did in fact have nominal control, being able to elect members of their party as speaker of the House and as chairmen of the various standing committees. The appearance was, however, deceptive as only 159 of the Democrats were northern and 104 came from the South. The result was that the total number of 174 Republicans plus 104 southern Democrats greatly exceeded the number of 159 northern Democrats so that "working control" of the House—as President Kennedy used to refer to it—with respect to enacting urban legislation was largely in the hands of the Republican-southern Democratic, antiurban, "conservative coalition". Thus on two issues that led to an urban key vote—passage of the Emergency Educational Act of 1961 and the attempt to establish a Cabinet-level Department of Urban Affairs and Housing—the prourban position lost, even though northern Democrats voted in favor by 97 percent on the first and 87 percent on the second. On both these votes, heavy southern Democratic majorities joined the near unanimous Republicans to defeat the nominal Democratic House

[58]"Most of" because through deaths and resignations, the number of northern Democrats, southern Democrats and Republicans changes slightly over the course of a Congress.

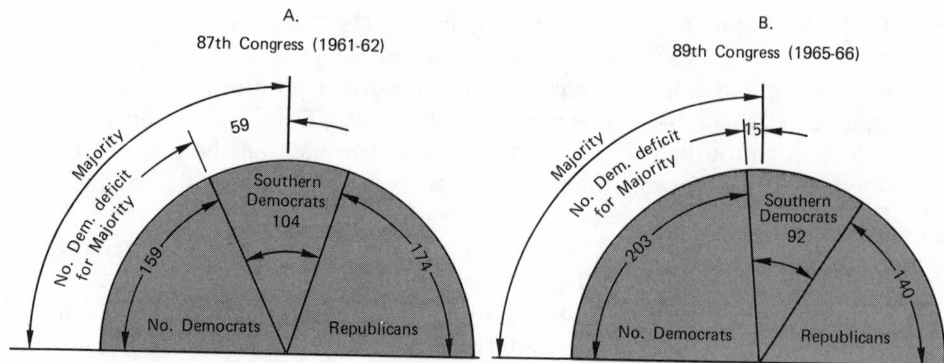

FIGURE 6-6 Distribution of Seats by Party and for Democratic Party, by Region, House of Representatives, 87th and 89th Congress

majority party.[59] Only on the third key vote—that on passage of the Emergency Housing Act of 1961—where 66 percent of the southern Democrats voted with a 98 percent northern Democratic majority, did the nominal majority win out.[60] In short, for the northern Democratic supported, prourban position to prevail, some two-thirds of the southern Democrats had to shift from their characteristic, longterm stance and vote with their nonsouthern colleagues (Figure 6–6A). Since this rarely happened on key or other votes, almost no urban programs were voted upon favorably by the House in the 87th Congress.

A sharp contrast to the 87th Congress is the 89th, which was elected in 1964, during President Johnson's landslide victory, and served in 1965–66. When it began, the 89th Congress had 140 Republicans and 295 Democrats, of which only 92 were southerners and 203 were from outside the South. This meant that the total number of Republicans and southern Democrats combined barely exceeded that number of northern Democrats alone. It also meant that when only a small minority of 20 percent of the southern Democrats voted with the rest of their party, the northern Democratic, prourban position prevailed in roll-call votes in the House (Figure 6–6B).

[59]H.R. 8990, Emergency Educational Aid Act of 1961, authorizing grants for school construction, etc. Question, under "Calendar Wednesday" procedures, on whether bill should be considered. Consideration rejected: 170-242. Democrats (D) (164-82) (Northern Democrats [ND] 132-4, Southern Democrats [SD] 32-78; Republicans [R] 6-160. H. Res. 530, Resolution disapproving President Kennedy's Reorganization Plan No. 1 of 1962 to create Cabinet-level Urban Affairs and Housing Department. Resolution of disapproval agreed to 264-150. D 111-137 (ND 18-124, SD 93-13); R 153-13.

[60]H.R. 6028. Passed 235-178. D 210-38 (ND 141-3, SD 69-35); R 25-140.

The 89th Congress consequently saw the passage of the Elementary and Secondary Education Act, medicaid for recipients of public assistance, the Department of Housing and Urban Development Act, rent supplements and expansion of other housing programs, model cities, and the expansion of antipoverty programs. On the key vote on each of these issues a majority of the voting Republicans and (with one exception on Medicaid) a majority of southern Democrats took the antiurban position. But each time the number of northern Democrats available to vote favorably was so large that with only minority support from southern Democrats (plus sometimes a small handful of Republicans), the prourban position won.[61] On only one key urban vote during the 89th Congress did the conservative coalition come out the winners—that to delete funds for rent supplements from a supplemental appropriation act. This happened when an unusually small number of northern Democrats turned out on the floor to vote and in addition an unusually large percentage of those northern Democrats—some 15 percent—voted with the conservative coalition, a combination of factors that caused the postponement of rent supplements funding for a few months.[62]

The line-up of forces in the House for the two years of the 89th Congress was exceptional, the Democratic party not having enjoyed such large majorities since the early Roosevelt Congresses of 1933–38. The typical House situation since 1939 has been something like the line-up of the 87th or the first Kennedy Congress or worse. Prourban majorities have therefore been difficult to put together in the House most years, even though it has almost always been under nominal Democratic control.

In the 1974 congressional elections the Republicans suffered sharp defeats, creating a potentially very prourban House of 204 northern Democrats, 87 southern Democrats, and 144 Republicans. But unlike the 1930s and the 89th Congress of the Johnson Administration, the 94th Congress

[61]H.R. 2362, Elementary and Secondary Education Act of 1965, providing grants to school districts with large numbers of children from low-income families. Passed 263-153. D 228-57 (ND 187-3, SD 41-54); R 35-96. H.R. 6675, Social Security Amendments of 1965, establishing "medicare" for the aged and medical assistance or "medicaid" for public assistance recipients and other medically needy. Passed 313-115. D 248-42 (ND 189-2, SD 59-40); R 65-73. H.R. 6927, Department of Housing and Urban Development Act, establishing cabinet-level department. Passed 217-184. D 208-66 (ND 170-10, SD 38-56); R 9-118. H.R. 7984, Housing and Urban Development Act of 1965, extending public housing, urban renewal, etc., and providing for "rent supplements" to low-income families. Motion to recommit to delete rent supplements provisions rejected 201-208. D 72-204 (ND 21-163, SD 51-51); R 130-4. S. 3708, Demonstration Cities and Metropolitan Development Act of 1965, authorizing "model cities" grants. Passed 178-141. D 162-60 (ND 141-11, SD 21-49); R 16-81. H.R. 15111, Economic Opportunity Act amendments of 1966 continuing program and authorizing appropriations for 1967. Motion to strike enacting clause (thereby killing the bill) rejected 156-208. D 49-193 (ND 5-159, SD 44-34); R 107-15.

[62]H.R. 11588, General Supplemental Appropriations Bill. Amendment to delete funding of rent supplements in fiscal 1966 accepted 185-162. D 86-160 (ND 24-141, SD 62-19); R 99-2.

(1975–76) served with an antiurban Republican president who could nullify less than a two-thirds majority strength in both Houses of Congress with his veto. Two dramatic examples of the huge weight of a presidential veto were President Ford's disapproving in 1975 the "emergency [public service] jobs appropriation bill" and the "emergency housing bill." Although on the first bill 99 percent of the northern Democrats and 79 percent of the southern Democrats (as well as 13 percent of the Republicans) voted to override, the veto was sustained by five votes. On the second bill, 95 percent of the northern Democrats and 71 percent of the southern Democrats (as well as 13 percent of the Republicans) voted to override; that attempt failed also, by 16 votes.[63]

The Senate in recent decades has not been as antiurban in voting behavior as much of the time as the House. Although since World War II the combined total of Republican and southern Democratic senators has always exceeded the number of northern Democrats, during this period aid to education, mass transit, expanded housing, and other kinds of prourban bills that could not be enacted in the House did pass in the Senate.

Prospects for Increased Federal Aid to Cities

Looking to the future, what are the prospects for any greatly increased federal financial help to cities? There will probably be proposals in the years ahead to establish additional kinds of programs purported to provide new or more effective remedies for urban problems and to increase the overall level of urban funding, through expansion of categorical grants or of revenue-sharing, or both. There will most likely also be proposals to redesign ongoing programs that are widely felt not to be working well or to be producing undesirable side effects. At least over the short-run future, there is little reason to doubt that under Democratic presidents and northern Democratic controlled congresses, there will be a greater probability of new programs, greater additional spending, and proportionately more federal aid channeled to cities than under Republican presidents or Republican-southern Democratic conservative coalition controlled congresses.

What the longer-term prospects are for drastic increases in federal spending to help solve the problems of large cities is more uncertain: The basic factor here is the decreasing proportion of the nation's population that lives in large cities, particularly in the older large cities of the East and Midwest which are experiencing the greatest difficulties and financial needs,

[63]H.R. 4481, Emergency Jobs Appropriations, Fiscal 1975. Passage over the President's veto. Rejected 277-145 (282 required for two-thirds). R 19-123; D 258-22 (ND 192-4; SD 66-18). H.R. 4485, Emergency Housing Assistance. Passage over the President's veto. Rejected 268-157 (282 required for two-thirds). R19-122; D 249-35 (ND 186-9; SD 63-26).

and the increasing proportion living in the suburbs. This will result in a steadily decreasing number of members in the House of Representatives who will be representing large-city districts. The impact of the 1960–1970 population shifts on the distribution of House seats through reapportionment caused a decrease of 7 percent—from 110 to 102—in those seats primarily representing central cities of 50,000 or larger in population, and an increase of 26 percent—from 104 to 131—with basically suburban constituencies. The nonmetropolitan constituencies dropped 16 percent—from 155 to 130—while the number of seats from mixed constituencies rose from 66 to 72. (See Figure 6–7.) The strength of House representation from city constituencies not only remained smaller than the total nonmetropolitan strength, as before, but it also became smaller than the total suburban strength.

What this long-term shift in types of districts is likely to do to the policy complexion of the House of Representatives is difficult to predict: Thus far Democrats from suburban districts have been voting almost as strongly prourban as members from central-city districts. If the Democratic party can maintain its present relative strength among suburban constituencies and if any additional suburban Democrats that are elected continue to share the policy outlooks of the central-city representatives who will still be the dominant contingent in the northern Democratic membership, sources of support for urban programs will not be fundamentally weakened. Indeed, to the extent that rural Republicans and rural southern Democrats are replaced by suburban Republicans and suburban southern Democrats, the resistance to urban programs from the conservative coalition may actually weaken to some extent. If, on the other hand, the bulk of the new suburban seats can be captured by the Republican party, the low-spending, antiurban, conservative coalition forces in the House will be strengthened.

The impact of present population trends on the Senate is more difficult to nail down: Senators in general, and even Democratic senators from urban states, will inevitably be recognizing the increasingly suburban nature of their overall constituencies. Therefore, even those who personally may be prourban may be less able politically to afford this stance.

If the historical attachment to the Democratic party continues to weaken in the South and the emergent pattern of more two-party, competitive congressional politics spreads, most of the more conservative and antiurban southern aspirants for House and Senate seats may run as Republicans. Since so many present southern Democrats are conservative and antiurban, the election of individuals with such outlooks as Republicans rather than Democrats would have no effect on the amount of congressional support for urban programs. However, the distribution of seats between Democrats and Republicans might then be more indicative of the true relative strength of the different policy positions with which these parties have been traditionally associated.

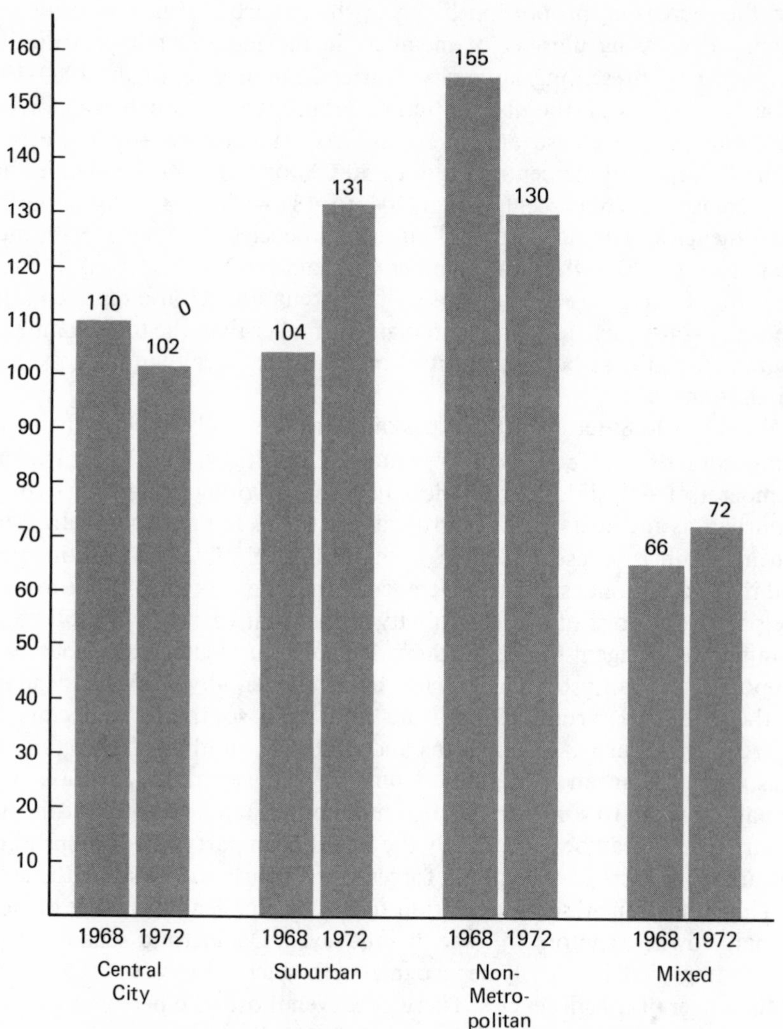

FIGURE 6-7 Distribution of Seats in House of Representatives by Type of Constituency, 1968 and 1973

Source: Calculated from *Congressional Quarterly Weekly Report,* April 6, 1974, p. 878.

The increasing suburbanization of the population, finally, may affect the intensity of presidential leadership that will be forthcoming for increased federal assistance to cities. For in a nation whose suburban population will be increasingly in a position to outvote its big-city citizens, even Democratic presidents, let alone Republican ones, may not find it electorally profitable to assign their highest policy and budgetary priorities to programs that are perceived as basically benefiting large cities.

In short, the most probable long-term impact of the decline in the share of the nation's people living in large cities will be that most additions to, expansions of, and increased spending on urban programs probably will be on those that will interest and benefit suburbs as much as or more than large cities, e.g., increased aid to education, mass transit, intercity rail transportation, environmental pollution, and revenue-sharing based on formulas that are also favorable to suburbs. On the other hand, those urban programs intended to improve the social and physical conditions of the poor, and especially the black, urban slum-dwellers, will most likely receive treatment varying from only marginal improvement to "benign neglect."[64]

This outcome is not inevitable: The extent and conditions under which a set of policies and programs can be adopted by the federal government and be funded at a sufficiently high level to prevent large cities from becoming "slum ghettoes" will be discussed in the concluding part of this book.

[64]Space does not permit taking into account in the analysis the factor of suburban diversities. It should be noted, however, that not all suburbs are problem-free white, upper-middle-class residential havens. Some suburbs—especially those that are older and closest to central cities—are already experiencing increases in crime, poverty, physical deterioration, and ghettoization. Members of Congress from constituencies that include such suburban areas may turn out to be a source of long-term support even for programs aimed at alleviating the pathologies associated with slum poverty.

7

Epilogue: Remaining Bases of Autonomy for City Governments

Given the heavy legal, administrative, and financial involvement by states and the federal government in the operation of large-city governments, can these city governments any longer be regarded as important loci of independent decision-making? Or are city governments increasingly becoming more like mere administrative agents for higher levels of government?

Although cities have no ultimate constitutional authority since all the powers they exercise must be delegated to them by their states and theoretically can be limited or withdrawn at any time, city governments do have substantial de facto independence to conduct their affairs. First of all, state and federal legislation and constitutional provisions leave wide areas of discretion within which city governments can make policy and program decisions on a day-to-day basis. Admittedly, in some cities and especially with respect to some program areas heavily aided by conditional grants from the states or the federal government or both, the areas of discretion are less wide than in others. But in virtually all cities and all program areas, important real choices exist that can still be made by city officials.

Second, the relations between city governments and their states and the federal government are not ones of continuous conflict where the exercise of influence by the higher level governments necessarily restricts the freedom of action of the city. It has already been pointed out that the primary consequence of state and federal grants has not been to control city governments; it has been to permit them to operate on a local level with local determination of large parts of their content, programs they otherwise could not finance at all or would have to run at a reduced level. Relationships between functional specialists in city, state, and federal governments are most often ones of cooperation and mutual helpfulness where the specialists at the higher governmental levels have a shared interest with their city colleagues in having the function they are responsible for be performed as effectively as possible. As Pressman summed it up:

> . . . donors depend on recipients both to produce a supply of fundable applications and to implement programs on the local level. . . . Donor and recipient need each other. . . .[1]

Third, city officials have varying degrees of ability to resist compliance with state or federal policies to which they are strongly opposed. Given the few state and federal officials in different program areas relative to the number of local governmental units that exist, it is difficult for such officials to monitor the activities of city governments, spot violations, and bring them to an end. Despite federal policies enunciated by the Supreme Court in the 1950s and early 1960s against segregation of public schools or Bible-reading, for at least a decade thereafter these practices continued in those areas where local officials backed by strong public opinion were strongly committed to them. Similarly, despite the Supreme Court's enunciations of procedural protections for the accused in criminal cases, police and prosecutors in many jurisdictions continued with forbidden practices, in the secure knowledge that few if any cases would ever reach and be reversed in higher level courts and especially the Supreme Court. Even the seemingly effective sanction of withdrawing or suspending grants if the conditions attached to them are not observed is a two-edged sword: Such withdrawal will defeat projects that the grant-giving officials at the higher level of government are committed to bringing about and may well hurt the clients of the grant-aided programs more than the city officials administering them.

All this is not to say that state and federal officials cannot ultimately enforce policies they feel strongly about if they commit sufficient time, energy, and manpower to exercise constant supervision and follow-up inspections. And even the imposition of formal sanctions like cut-off of grant funds or securing of court injunctions and the use of military force have all been occasionally employed. But it is to say that the policies, rules, and regulations of state and federal officials are not self-enforcing. These higher officials will have to incur costs to see that they are implemented—

[1]Jeffrey L. Pressman, *Federal Programs and City Politics* (Berkeley: University of California Press, 1975), pp. 106–7.

usually the more intensely the particular policy or rule is opposed, the higher will be the cost of its enforcement. Accordingly, higher officials have incentive both not to originally impose and also to later modify decisions that city governments find extremely distasteful.

Furthermore, city governments and officials are not simply passive objects of the influence of the states and the federal government. With varying degrees of success, city officials themselves try to influence the formulation and administration of federal and state policies affecting their activities. Elected city officials individually, through staff members stationed in the national and state capitals, and through interest groups like the U.S. Conference of Mayors or various state leagues or conferences of cities, lobby with the President, with their state governors, and with congressional and state legislative leaders.[2] Also, associations of local officials with different professional specialties, like social workers, public health officers, highway supervisors, etc., try to influence state and federal administrative practices, and less frequently, legislative policies dealing with their specialties.

Finally, state and federal urban-oriented policies are not developed in a vacuum by officials who have little contact with or awareness of local conditions and needs. Both state legislatures and Congress are composed of members elected from localities, or in the special case of the United States Senate, from states. Those members whose constituencies include large cities often use, either on their own initiative or at the request of city officials, whatever leverage they have to influence legislation or its administrative implementation in the direction desired by their city's government.

In short, the increasing involvement of the states and the federal government in the operations of large city government is not an example of the usurpation of the latter's powers. Rather, it is another example of the traditional pattern in American government that if a serious problem is to be solved, all levels of government must join in a cooperative effort to cope with it. Exclusive of foreign and military affairs, essentially no major problem or function is any longer the sole responsibility or province of any one governmental level. As Morton Grodzins put it:

> The federal system is not accurately symbolized by a neat layer cake of three distinct and separate planes. A far more realistic symbol is that of the marble cake. Wherever you slice through it you reveal an inseparable mixture of differently colored ingredients. There is no neat horizontal stratification. Vertical and diagonal lines almost

[2]See Suzanne Farkas, *Urban Lobbying: Mayors in the Federal Arena* (New York: New York University Press, 1971); and Donald H. Haider, *When Governments Come To Washington: Governors, Mayors, and Intergovernmental Lobbying* (New York: Free Press, 1974).

> obliterate the horizontal ones, and in some places there are unexpected whirls and an imperceptible merging of colors, so that it is difficult to tell where one ends and the other begins. So it is with federal, state, and local responsibilities in the chaotic marble cake of American government.[3]

Indeed, the more important question is not whether state and the federal government are becoming excessively involved in the traditional functions of large-city governments. The question is whether without greater involvement, city governments will have the capacity to meet the demands directed toward them for improved performance and the alleviation of pathological conditions.

[3]Morton Grodzins, "Centralization and Decentralization in the American Federal System," in Robert A. Goldwin, ed., *A Nation of States* (Chicago: Rand McNally, 1963), pp. 3–4.

III

INFLUENTIALS IN CITY POLITICS

Part III goes beyond explaining the constitutional, legal, and structural setting within which city governments operate. This part concentrates on the characteristic resources, strategies, and tactics of influence—i.e., the politics—used by different participants in a large city's decision-making process in order to impress their views on city policies and programs. Some of these participants are official city governmental decision-makers—e.g., mayors, city managers, councilmen, judges, administrators, and bureaucrats. Other participants, such as party leaders, social and economic notables, interest group leaders, mass media elites, and the general public try to exert influence while being outside the formal institutions of city government. At the end of Part III, there is an overview of how the influence process in large cities operates in general.

8

City Party Leaders

When questioned by a state investigating committee in 1900 about his influence in New York City government and politics, Richard Croker, then the de facto chief of the New York County Democratic organization (Tammany Hall), replied:

> "...there are others who have their influences [in New York City], but probably none to such an extent as me...."

When further asked whether it was not a fact

> "that practically all heads of departments in the city meet at the Democratic club every evening?" Croker modestly answered, "yes, sir."[1]

Upon taking office in 1932, the new mayor of the City of New York, John P. O'Brien, was asked by press reporters who his police commissioner would be. O'Brien replied, "I don't know. They haven't told me yet." Everyone present understood that the "they" referred to the Tammany party chiefs.[2]

Both examples above illustrate the great, perhaps dominant influence that party leaders exercised in the politics of large cities some forty to

[1]New York State Legislature, *Report of the Special Assembly Committee Appointed to Investigate the Public Offices and Departments of the City of New York and the Counties Therein Included* (1900), I:329,331.

[2]Quoted in Alfred Connable and Edward Silberfarb, *Tigers of Tammany* (New York: Holt, Rinehart, & Winston, 1967), p. 286.

seventy years ago. Many readers may believe that this is the way the system still operates. Indeed, probably more misconceptions exist about the role and influence of party leaders than about any other category of urban political actors.

Since an accurate understanding of the influence of other kinds of politically active individuals and groups in city politics requires a more realistic conception of the current status of party leaders, this chapter will attempt to explain both how and why urban party chiefs exerted such great influence in the past and how and why in almost all large cities that influence has now greatly declined.

THE NATURE AND STRUCTURE OF URBAN PARTIES

Political parties are organizations that make nominations for public office and contest elections. Party leaders are those persons who serve on the important governing committees or occupy the influential leadership positions in such organizations. Although the specific names of these committees and leadership posts vary in different cities depending on state law (and occasionally on party rules as authorized by state law), the party units in large cities typically carry titles such as Ward Committee, County or City Committee, or County or City Executive Committee. The leaders are known as Ward or Assembly District Leaders or County or City Chairmen or Leaders. None of these party positions normally pays any regular salary.

Every large city is divided by law into voting precincts or election districts as they are sometimes called. These units are geographical areas containing the number of voters that can be handled conveniently on election day at a single polling place. The polling place is where the residents of the precinct go to register and cast their votes in city as well as state and national elections. The voting population of a precinct can vary from 200 voters in some California cities to 2,000 in certain Massachusetts cities, with the typical figure ranging from 600 to 900.

Each precinct or election district selects, usually by direct primary or occasionally through a precinct caucus of the party members, one or more committeemen and committeewomen. These precinct committeemen are the lowest-ranking officials of the party, though they are more accurately described as party workers than party leaders.

The next wider unit of party organization is the ward or assembly district, which consists of the smallest number of precincts that make up the constituency of some elected *public* official, usually a city councilman or state assemblyman. Each ward or assembly district selects ward leaders or assembly district leaders who are the basic party leaders within the city. The ward or assembly district leaders are chosen in a direct primary election by the enrolled party members who live in the ward or district or are elected by a caucus of the precinct or election district representatives. The ward or district leaders are usually empowered to appoint "captains" for each precinct. In actual practice, the captains and the precinct leaders are likely to be the same persons.

Collectively these ward leaders or assembly district leaders normally constitute the party's county or city central or executive committee, which appoints a county or city chairman or leader, who is the chief urban party leader. (see Figure 8-1.) There are, however, other variations. In Texas, for example, the county executive committee is elected directly by the qualified party voters of the county through direct primary; in Michigan, the party's

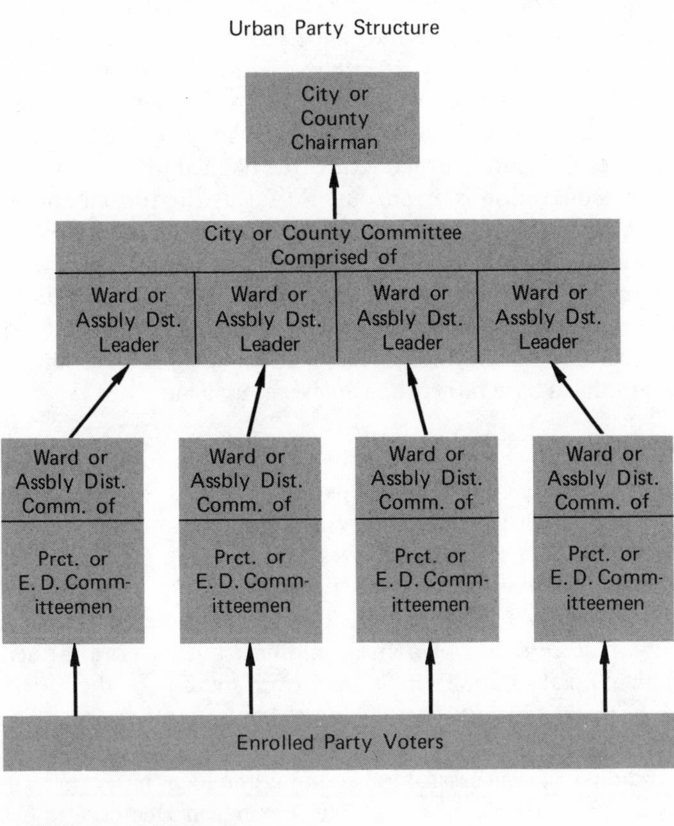

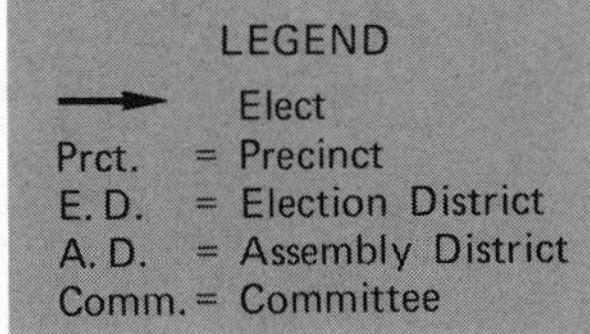

FIGURE 8-1 Diagram of Urban Party Structure.

successful nominees for public office choose the county party officials.[3] In New York City, which consists of five counties, there are party executive committees, leaders, and chairmen for each county, but no overall city committee or city chairman or leader.

These city and county party officials nominally are part of the state and national party organizations, but in fact they enjoy almost complete autonomy, especially in elections for city officials. V. O. Key, Jr., has summed up the interrelation among the different party officials and committees as follows:

> The party organization is sometimes regarded as a hierarchy based on the precinct executive and capped by the national committee, but it may be more accurately described as a system of layers of organization. Each successive layer—county or city, state, national—has an independent concern about elections in its geographical jurisdiction.
>
> The entire [party] structure is often likened to a military hierarchy, yet the conception is erroneous. So far as the formal authority goes the national chairman cannot issue directions to the state chairmen or the state chairmen to the county chairmen. Though the levels of party organization are intimately interrelated, the linkage is from the bottom up rather than from the top down. . . . Advancement in the political organization tends to be an expansion of influence from a geographical base rather than an ascent up a ladder.[4]

Side-by-side with the party's legally defined structure, committees, and leadership positions, exist the various party "clubs." These clubs, which have the status of private, voluntary associations, normally have a headquarters or "clubhouse" which serves as a meeting place for the various party officials, workers, would-be officials, and favor-seeking constituents in the particular ward or district. Party clubhouses and headquarters are usually in store fronts or office buildings, but in more affluent areas, they can be in hotel suites. There is great overlap between the officers of the club and the party officials from that area. Under some state laws and party rules, if there is more than one party club in a ward or district, only the club whose candidate was successful in becoming the local party official can use the party label in its name, as in "The Lexington Democratic Club." Its insurgent competitors must employ some variation in naming its club, e.g., "The J.F.K. Reform Democrats."

[3]See Hugh A. Bone, *Grass Roots Party Leadership* (Seattle: University of Washington Bureau of Governmental Research and Service, 1952), p. 159.

[4]V. O. Key, Jr., *Politics, Parties, and Pressure Groups,* 5th ed., (New York: Crowell, 1964), pp. 316, 328.

"OLD-STYLE" PARTY MACHINES AND BOSSES

Old-style party leaders used to be crucially influential actors in large cities because of their control of the nominating process. The leaders' organization was called a machine because with machine-like regularity, it could normally produce pluralities for its preferred candidate regardless of that candidate's qualifications or stand on the issues. At the hey-day of old-style party leaders and machines, most large cities were dominated by one party, i.e., their electorates typically voted consistently either Democratic or Republican. Control of who was nominated by the dominant party, therefore, essentially constituted control of who was elected to office.

In the nineteenth century nominations were made by local caucuses or primary assemblies. These were meetings in each ward or other subdivision of the city that selected (1) party officials, (2) candidates for offices such as city councilman whose constituency was the ward or subdivision, and (3) delegates for a city-wide convention to pick candidates for mayor and other city offices. The local caucus method of choosing nominees facilitated control by city party leaders. The incumbent leaders, for example, determined the "roll" or "check-list" of party members entitled to vote. Thus these party leaders could keep names of people who were unlikely to support the choice of the party leaders off the lists. They could also leave on the list names of persons who had moved away or died thus creating "voting stock" that the leaders could have cast through stand-ins. The party leaders called the caucuses whenever they pleased, often on short notice (so-called snap primaries), and at a time and place inconvenient to possible opponents. In the conduct of the meeting, the party leader functioning as presiding officer could refuse to recognize persons likely to propose opposing slates of candidates or rule their motions out of order. Opponents could also be intimidated by the presence of squads of strong-arm men loyal to the machines.[5] The usual locations of the caucuses themselves were not such as to encourage idealistic, antimachine members to come and stand up for their principles: Bryce reports that of the 1007 primaries and conventions held in New York City to nominate for the elections of 1884, 633 took place in drinking saloons.[6] The counting of ballots was in the hands of the leaders' henchmen who could stuff in more ballots or falsify the count on the rare occasions that such tactics were necessary to carry the organization slate. Since the party was at that time still a private association, it was no more illegal to commit this kind of fraud than it is today in the election, for example, of a college fraternity officer.

[5]The best description of all these techniques can be found in James Bryce, *The American Commonwealth, I* (New York: Macmillan, 1889), esp. 70-71.

[6]*Ibid.*, p. 81.

With the institution of the direct primary in the first and second decades of the twentieth century, the ground rules changed. For the most part, however, the party leaders managed to adapt creatively. The numbers of party rank-and-file whose votes were important increased and opposition slates could not easily be kept off the primary ballot. The party leaders turned then to ingratiating themselves with individual voters by offering them in exchange for their votes, various kinds of tangible and intangible benefits like personal friendship, favors, services, and, occasionally, cash.

To distribute inducements and keep the system running, the party leaders maintained a fully-staffed organization of precinct workers who cultivated the loyalty of the voters, ideally on a block-by-block, house-to-house, 365 days-a-year, 24-hours-a-day basis. What this involved is well explained by George Washington Plunkitt, a butcher's helper who rose through the party ranks in New York City at the turn of the century from precinct captain to district leader:

> . . . [Y]ou have to go among the people, see them and be seen. I know every man, woman, and child in the Fifteenth District, except them that's been born this summer—and I know some of them, too. I know what they like and what they don't like, what they are strong at and what they are weak in, and I reach them by approachin' at the right side.
>
> For instance, here's how I gather in the young men. I hear of a young feller that's proud of his voice, thinks he can sing fine. I ask him to come around to Washington Hall and join our Glee Club. He comes and sings, and he's a follower of Plunkitt for life. Another young feller gains a reputation as a baseball player in a vacant lot. I bring him into our baseball club. That fixes him. You'll find him workin' for my ticket at the polls next election day. Then there's the feller that likes rowin' on the river, the young feller that makes a name as a waltzer on his block, the young feller that's handy with his dukes—I rope them all in by givin' them opportunities to show themselves off. I don't trouble them with political arguments. I just study human nature and act accordin'.
>
> . . . [T]he fellers that go through college and then join the Citizens' Union. . . . I watch the City Record to see when there's civil service examinations for good things. Then I take my young Cit in hand, tell him all about the good thing and get him worked up till he goes and takes an examination. I don't bother about him any more. It's a cinch that he comes back to me in a few days and asks to join Tammany Hall. . . .
>
> What tells in holdin' your grip on your district is to go right down among the poor families and help them in the different ways they need

> help. I've got a regular system for this. If there's a fire in Ninth, Tenth, or Eleventh Avenue, for example, any hour of the day or night, I'm usually there with some of my election district captains as soon as the fire engines. If a family is burned out . . . I don't refer them to the Charity Organization Society, which would investigate their case in a month or two and decide they were worthy of help about the time they are dead from starvation. I just get quarters for them, buy clothes for them if their clothes were burned up, and fix them up till they get things runnin' again. It's philanthropy, but it's politics, too—mighty good politics. . . . The poor are the most grateful people in the world, and, let me tell you, they have more friends in their neighborhoods than the rich have in theirs.
>
> If there's a family in my district in want I know it before the charitable societies do, and me and my men are first on the ground. . . .
>
> Another thing, I can always get a job for a deservin' man. . . . I know every big employer in the district and in the whole city, for that matter, and they ain't in the habit of sayin' no to me when I ask them for a job.[7]

Excerpts from Plunkitt's diary show still other services he performed:

> 2 A.M.: Aroused from sleep by the ringing of his doorbell; went to the door and found a bartender, who asked him to go to the police station and bail out a saloon-keeper who had been arrested for violating the excise law. Furnished bail and returned to bed at three o'clock.
>
> 8:30 A.M.: Went to police court to look after his constituents. Found six "drunks." Secured the discharge of four by a timely word with the judge, and paid the fines of two. . . .[8]

The machines thus built up generalized goodwill through friendship; opportunities for self-fulfillment; unsolicited charity for those destitute or confronted by special emergencies; jobs; intervention with the courts, the prosecutors, or the police. The goodwill and sense of obligation created by these favors could be converted into reliable blocs of votes in support of the organization slate on primary day. It was the party representative who became, as the Boston ward-leader, Martin Lomansy, explained to the muckraking journalist, Lincoln Steffens, the "somebody"

> . . . in every ward . . . that any bloke can come to—no matter what

[7]William L. Riordon, *Plunkitt of Tammany Hall* (New York: Dutton, 1963), pp. 25–28.

[8]*Ibid.*, pp. 91–92.

he's done—and get help. *Help you understand; none of your law and justice, but help.*[9]

Conditions Conducive to Party Machines

Party machines operated successfully when large numbers of rank-and-file voters were prepared to trade their vote for this kind of friendship and other personal services and favors. Many voters living in large cities in the decades bracketing the turn of the century were willing to do just this. Sizable proportions of these big-city populations were unskilled workers, conscious of being highly replaceable in their jobs, and hence valuing the support of party leaders who could influence public or private employers. Also, many of these same workers were immigrants or children of immigrants, lonely in a strange and even hostile new social environment and understandably appreciative when powerful figures like party leaders demonstrated concern for their welfare. It did not matter that the motives of the party leaders were not altruistic—that they sought the votes of the immigrants to strengthen their own positions. What did matter was that the party boss cared at a time when almost no one else did.

There is some question about whether these newly arrived European immigrants were any more vulnerable to the blandishments of the machine than the unskilled and uneducated native-born WASPs, who were flocking to cities from rural America. Although one contemporary observer of urban parties, James Bryce, put forth the theory of the especial susceptibility of immigrants to boss rule,[10] another contemporary observer, Moise Ostrogorski, disputed it:

> Almost all the men of sound judgment whom I have been able to consult . . . of American stock themselves and some of very old stock protested against the theory according to which the "ignorant foreigners" are the great culprits. . . . My personal observations have only confirmed me in their view. No doubt, the newly naturalized citizens are, for the most part, ignorant, but the proportions of ignorant electors of American origin is not less great. The wretched immigrants are easily bought [by the machines], but the poor natives of the country are exposed to the same temptations, and not only the poor ones.[11]

[9]Quoted in *The Autobiography of Lincoln Steffens* (Chautauqua, N.Y.: Chautauqua Press, 1931), p. 618.

[10]See Bryce, *The American Commonwealth,* Vol. 1, esp. p. 67.

[11]Moise Ostrogorski, *Democracy and the Organization of Political Parties, Vol. II: The United States,* Abridged (New York: Anchor, 1964), p. 222.

To a large segment of city populations, the vote had little intrinsic value, since the issues stressed in elections at that time had little to do with ameliorating their social conditions. The government was as yet a regulator and extractor, but not much of a benefactor. And, given the low general level of education that prevailed and the absence of communications media easily available even to the illiterate, there was little basis for a voter to make an independent judgment even if he were motivated to ignore the advice of the party leaders, which was normally not the case. The importance of this absence of competing voting cues should not be underestimated: Even at the height of the machine, there was a distinction between the "delivery wards" and the "newspaper wards." The latter were middle- and upper-class areas where the reading of newspapers was widespread and which could not be counted on to be safely "delivered."

Sources and Uses of the Party Machines' Income

To continue in operation and remain solvent, the machine needed an income to fund the favors distributed to the voters and, perhaps more important, to compensate the party workers and the party leaders themselves for the time and energy they devoted to their party tasks. This income took many forms. The machine received substantial amounts of cash from "assessments" on, or "kickbacks" from, the salaries of those to whom it had provided routine government jobs. Bryce reports that the going rate in his day was anywhere from 1 to 5 percent of the jobholder's salary.[12] It also received cash for "campaign expenses" from those nominated for important elective office. Paradoxically, the more certain the chances for victory in the election, the larger the sum of money that appeared to be needed for campaign expenses. The machine charged legitimate businessmen varying amounts for such special privileges as franchises to operate street-railways, gas, water, or electric utilities, variances from zoning regulations, contracts for business with the city government to pave streets or erect public buildings. The machine also often received payments for protecting illegal enterprises like gambling casinos, houses of prostitution, after-hours taverns, etc. And through inside information from city officials, the machine leaders were presented with opportunities for personal financial gain through "honest graft." As Plunkitt explained the concept:

> There's an honest graft, and I'm an example of how it works. I might sum up the whole thing by sayin': 'I seen my opportunities and I took 'em.'

[12]Bryce, *The American Commonwealth,* I, 84.

> Just let me explain by examples. My party's in power in the city, and it's goin' to undertake a lot of public improvements. Well, I'm tipped off, say, that they're going to lay out a new park at a certain place.
>
> I see my opportunity and I take it. I go to that place and I buy up all the land I can in the neighborhood. Then the board of this or that makes its plan public, and there is a rush to get my land, which nobody cared particular for before.
>
> Ain't it perfectly honest to charge a good price and make a profit on my investment and foresight? Of course, it is. Well, that's honest graft.
>
> . . . I'm lookin' for it every day in the year. I will tell you frankly that I've got a good lot of it, too.[13]

Finally, the machine's leaders sometimes resorted to "dishonest graft," such as outright stealing from the public treasury.

Although much of the machine's cash income went to pay for its favors and services to the voters, enough remained in the pockets of the party leaders to give them generous remuneration for their party activities. Most of the turn-of-the-century, city-wide bosses managed to become millionaires and multimillionaires.[14] Even Plunkitt, who was never more than a second-echelon party leader, allowed that:

> If you hear people say that I've laid away a million or so since I was a butcher's boy in Washington Market, don't come to me for an indignant denial. I'm pretty comfortable, thank you.[15]

To the lower-level party workers who manned the precinct organizations went more modest rewards: Moderate-sized cash payments for "election day expenses" (some of which had to be passed on to the voters); low-level jobs for themselves with the city government—preferably "no-show jobs" that carried a salary from the city treasury but did not require the holder to "show" at the city agency during working hours, thus giving him freedom to devote full time to party business; jobs for themselves with private companies that did business with the city; jobs for their spouses, children, or other relatives; opportunities for small-scale honest graft or dishonest graft or both; and the possibility of eventually becoming a high-level party leader or receiving a nomination to an elective office or an appointment to appointive office, perhaps the most sought-after of which was a judgeship. As Ed

[13]Riordon, *Plunkitt,* pp. 3-4.

[14]See Harold Zink, *City Bosses in the United States* (Durham, N.C.: Duke University Press, 1930), p. 143.

[15]Riordon, *Plunkitt,* p. 7.

Flynn, the leader of the Bronx County Democratic Party between the 1920s and 1940s, observed in his memoirs, "The appointments are few, but the hopes are many."[16]

Bosses and City Politics

Old-style bosses had great potential influence on city governmental policies. The bosses often had been responsible for the nomination of key elected officials like the mayor and members of the city council and had sponsored many of the commissioners that were appointed by these elected officers. Boss Croker of New York City, for example, frankly admitted to a state investigating committee that he did not recall any "member" or "important officer" of the incumbent city administration who had not been "discussed" with him or whose appointment was not "agreeable" to him.[17] All these officials, consequently, had reason to feel some sense of obligation to the party leaders. Also, the party leaders held a potent sanction in their power to deny renomination to city elected officials and to bring about the dismissal of appointive officials through the party leaders' influence on the appointees' elective superiors. On those issues where they chose to do so, the bosses could use their influence on the holders of different elective offices in the executive and legislative branches to overcome the separation of powers and other fragmentation of authority in the city's formal governmental structure.

Nevertheless, even at the height of their power, party leaders did not function as city-wide equivalents of totalitarian rulers dictating all aspects of the city's substantive policies. For the most part, these party officials were concerned with jobs, appointments, and contracts and with those elements of policy that gave opportunities for self-enrichment rather than with the substance of policy in general. As Ostrogorski put it:

> The use which the boss makes of his extensive and penetrating power by no means, however, affects the whole of political life: this use is confined to his requirements as an exploiter of the industry of elections. He does not try . . . to assert his power over the polls in general, to control all the manifestations of political life. All his designs on the commonwealth amount, in fact, to running the elections as he likes, putting his followers in all the places, keeping out his opponents . . . and realizing the material profits attaching to these places and to the influence which they procure. The line of public policy to be adopted, in itself, is a matter of indifference to the boss.[18]

[16]Edward J. Flynn, *You're the Boss* (New York: Collier, 1962), p. 38.
[17]New York State Legislature, *Report of the Special Assembly,* I, 328.
[18]Ostrogorski, *Democracy and the Organization of Political Parties,* II, 207.

THE DECLINE OF PARTY STRENGTH

The image of the invincible, tightly organized, corrupt, old-style political machine still lives on, particularly in the minds of certain editorial writers looking for devil-figures against which to crusade. And it is also kept alive by elective party and office-holding politicians who sometimes find it strategically convenient to brand their opponents as spineless "tools" or "creatures" of the satanic, boss-dominated machines. For as Ed Flynn, the Bronx County Democratic leader put it: "The 'leader' you don't like . . . is a 'boss' and the 'organization' you don't like . . . is a machine."[19]

Despite the stereotype of party strength, the reality is otherwise: Only one large city, Chicago, had in the 1970s a party organization that could be classed as a powerful city-wide machine. In a few other cities, there were "submachines" that could generally dominate electoral outcomes in particular neighborhoods, generally those with high concentrations of low-income black, Puerto Rican, Mexican-American, or Appalachian white populations. But in the vast majority of large cities, party leaders presided over weak, faction-ridden, skeletal organizations that were financially hard-pressed, and devoid of active ward and precinct workers. Unlike in earlier decades, these organizations were unable to control primary fights for party office or nomination to city elective office when faced by strong opposition. In recent decades, party organizations with even the greatest reputations for invincibility—New York's Tammany Hall and the Pendergast machine of Kansas City being two classic examples—have gone down in bitter defeat.

The Atrophy of Party Organization

The old-style machine was based on every precinct or election district being manned by an active party worker who maintained continuous contact with his voters. Although there is no compendium of the current staffing of urban parties generally, the relevant studies that exist of party organizations in cities all point in the same direction: That almost everywhere the party organization in reality consists of little more than a chairman and a handful of ward or district-based leaders. On the basis of his recent summary of the available evidence, Frank Sorauf has described the typical city party organization as follows:

> An active chairman and executive committee, plus a few associated activists, who in effect make most of the decisions in the name of the party, who raise funds, who seek out and screen candidates (or approve the candidates who select themselves), and who speak locally for the party.

[19]Flynn, *You're the Boss,* p. 248.

> A ward or precinct organization in which only a few local committeemen are active and in which there is little door-to-door canvassing or other direct voter contact. . . .
>
> A distinctly periodic calendar of activities marked by a watchful waiting or general inactivity at other than election times.
>
> Nowhere here does one find the serried ranks of party foot soldiers.[20]

In the days of Plunkitt, heated primary contests took place over the filling of precinct committeemen positions. In recent decades not only are there almost no contests for the posts, but so few candidates normally even bother to come forward to place their names on the ballot that many of the committee positions are left vacant. The city and county chairmen and the other few persistent activists are therefore forced to fill as many of the vacancies as they can by appointment. Even in areas where the precinct positions are nominally filled, the precinct captains may do little beyond distributing campaign literature from door to door in the few weeks before elections, perhaps make a few telephone calls on election day to remind people to vote, and help in transporting voters to the polls, if they do even that. All the evidence suggests that Robert L. Morlan's twenty-five-year-old description of Minneapolis precinct captains applies much more generally today:

> On rare occasions a few of the more earnest ones may do some doorbell ringing.
>
> The average precinct captain has no personal political following and is unlikely to possess even such an elementary tool as a list of the registered voters of his precinct. He is not in the least concerned over the danger of a competitor developing sufficient strength to take over his job, for his job in most cases means nothing to him and he would be happy to be relieved of it.[21]

Shrinkage of Available Rewards. The basic reason that full time armies of party workers are no longer available is that the party leaders have few, if any, rewards to provide for time-consuming, burdensome, and largely menial old-style precinct activity. Municipal as well as state and federal civil service systems in most cities have left only a handful of governmental jobs for party leaders to bestow on party workers and their relations. Eldersveld's study of Detroit, for example, found that only 10 to 12 percent of the

[20]Frank Sorauf, *Party Politics in America,* 2nd ed. (Boston: Little, Brown, 1972), p. 77.

[21]Robert Morlan, "The Unorganized Politics of Minneapolis," *National Civic Review* (November, 1949), pp. 485–90. See also Bone, *Grass Roots;* Samuel J. Eldersveld, *Political Parties* (Chicago: Rand McNally, 1964).

Democratic and Republican precinct activists (or their husbands in the case of women) had any type of governmental job.[22] Costikyan reports that the maximum percentage of city government job holders among captains and workers in any club in New York County was 35 percent and that more often it was between 10 and 20 percent and frequently even less. A different study of New York County Committeemen in 1960 showed that only 5 percent were on the public payroll.[23] Plunkitt foresaw that civil service was going to destroy the "patriotism" of party workers and hence sap the foundation of the whole system of machine politics that he was used to:

> First, this great and glorious country was built up by political parties; second, parties can't hold together if their workers don't get the offices when they win; third, if the parties go to pieces, the government they built up must go to pieces, too; fourth, then there'll be h_____ to pay.[24]

Some supportive evidence for "Plunkitt's Law" comes from sociologist Phillips Cutright who compared the activities of precinct committeemen from two cities which had great similarities with respect to population, median family income, homeownership, proportion of population living in rural areas, and party regulations. The cities differed in that one had a large volume of local patronage available (with partisan local elections) and one had no local patronage (with nonpartisan local elections). Cutright concluded that there was a "clearcut relationship between local [precinct] political activity and the local reward system" with precinct workers in the high patronage city doing more polling of the precinct to register the voters, doing more door-to-door "selling" of candidates, and handling more requests for assistance from the voters than their opposite numbers in the nonpartronage city.[25]

Furthermore, most cities now prohibit assessment of salaries of civil servants, require competitive bidding for contracts for the purchase of supplies or for construction projects, and subject city accounts to careful auditing procedures. This leaves few opportunities for party leaders to profit from "honest graft" and those party leaders lack the wherewithal to

[22] Eldersveld, *Political Parties*, p. 279.

[23] Edward M. Costikyan, *Behind Closed Doors* (New York: Harcourt, Brace, and World, 1966), p. 86; Robert S. Hirschfield, Bert E. Swanson, and Blanche B. Blank, "A Profile of Political Activists in Manhattan," *Western Political Quarterly*, 15 (1962): 484-506. Raymond E. Wolfinger argues to the contrary that in the late 1950s in New Haven, there was a sizable number of patronage positions in the city government whose holders were expected to contribute time for party work during elections. *The Politics of Progress* (Englewood Cliffs, N.J.: Prentice-Hall, 1974), p. 81.

[24] Riordon, *Plunkitt*, p. 13.

[25] Phillips Cutright, "Activities of Precinct Committeemen in Partisan and Non-Partisan Communities," *Western Political Quarterly*, 17 (1964): 93–108.

compensate party workers for election day duties and other activities in cash. Indeed, party leaders find their responsibilities not only financially unremunerative but also at times too financially burdensome to continue. Ed Flynn, writing as long ago as 1947, explained that holding his position had been expensive, both in direct contributions to the organization and in feeling compelled to lend money without high probability of repayment to organization members in financial difficulties.[26] Edward Costikyan, who succeeded Carmine De Sapio in 1961 as New York County Democratic Leader, voluntarily retired from that post only two-and-one-half years later in large part because of the financial drain involved from the job. As Costikyan explained in his memoir:

> Despite the Tammany myths, movement up the leadership ladder within the Democratic Party in New York County does not make you rich. In point of fact, it has been a costly venture for me. Because—at the end—I spent half my time on political activities, my income suffered. Time spent in politics is not compensable, as is time spent by a lawyer on his clients' affairs. Overworked partners cannot fail to take into consideration the frequent absences of a junior on political gambols. . . . [and] my share of the firm income was fixed accordingly. . . .
>
> Finally, there were direct political expenses—tickets, trips, conventions, carfare, lunches. Prior to my election as county leader, like most district leaders I paid such expenses myself, completely. . . . In my last year [as County Leader], over and above the reimbursement I received of some $450, I spent well over five times that amount of unreimbursed after-tax income on politics—my checkbook showed over $700 in tickets to dinners and political affairs alone.[27]

Of course, some party leaders do also hold salaried elective office in city government such as city councilman or alderman, or serve as state assemblyman from within the city, or, more occasionally, like the late Charles Buckley of the Bronx and William Dawson of Chicago, have a seat in Congress. Also, when the mayors have no rule against it, some party leaders hold salaried appointive city offices such as deputy commissionerships or memberships on certain boards. Further, there are "special guardianships" and "refereeships" awarded to lawyers in estate cases that bring sizable fees for the amount of time spent. In some cities these go only to lawyers who are active in the party organization. Lucrative sponsorships of urban renewal projects or government-subsidized private housing also occasion-

[26]Flynn, *You're the Boss,* p. 241.

[27]Edward N. Costikyan, *Behind Closed Doors* (New York: Harcourt, Brace, and World, 1966), pp. 345–46.

ally have found their way into the hands of party leaders or their close friends and associates. Then too, most party leaders are not as rigid as Costikyan about precluding the possibility of their income being enhanced by the extra business that their known relationships to city officials may bring their law firms, insurance brokerships, or building construction companies.

A few party leaders are corrupt and therefore are willing to take cash payments for attempts to influence governmental policies. But party leaders have decreasing influence over governmental decisions as compared to city officials or career civil servants. Consequently, the bribery that does occur usually takes place between the seeker of the favor and the immediate maker of the decision—e.g., the housing inspector, the purchasing agent, the policeman on the beat—without the intervention of party leaders.

Substitutes for Tangible Payoffs. Since the party organization has a scarcity of tangible, financial payoffs to distribute to its leaders and workers, other incentives must operate to keep together the small core of leaders and active workers that now constitute the party organization in most cities. For the leaders, the intangible rewards might include: the "fun of the game"; the opportunity to be "on the inside" in the making of important decisions on who is to run for public office; the desire to be in an advantageous position to run for office themselves; commitment to the success of the party as an important instrument for promoting their version of public welfare; and the development of first-name acquaintances with important city (and sometimes state and national) officials. Costikyan, despite the many frustrations he suffered, ends his political party valedictory with a chapter entitled, "I'd Do It Again," explaining that although "on a strictly material cash accounting basis, the political account shows a substantial debit balance," "on an over-all accounting . . . including the intangible values," his balance came out on the credit side:

> The experience was incomparable. Crisis, struggles, arguments, opportunities to make a difference, if only a small one, were a common, even a daily occurrence. The pressures of all kinds to which I was subjected, I think, gave me a capacity to deal with practical problems which I would never have developed in any other way.
>
> . . . [P]olitics is the one area in which its participants have the repeated opportunity to make serious moral and intellectual choices between competitive alternatives, although in one's daily life such choices are relative rarities. . . .
>
> In addition to learning about competing principles, and what they were, and what values should be attached to them, . . . I learned a great deal about appraising the characters of our associates. . . . we

> acquired some understanding of people, and their prejudices, and how to distinguish erratic brilliance from genuine quality. . . .[28]

Few of the incentives available to party leaders are available to the precinct workers who moreover must do the more routine, menial tasks of canvassing, registering, and otherwise maintaining contact with the voters. For these rank-and-file precinct workers various degrees of motivation are supplied by: friends or relatives who have asked them to turn out; admiration for or attraction to a particular candidate; strong feelings on an issue; the pleasure of associating with like-minded people; opportunities to make and develop friendships; the diversion it creates for housewives or for men in dull, undemanding occupations; the belief that "contacts" can be made that may provide some benefit in the future; the chance to promote a cause but without the visible impact available to party leaders. There also appears to be an element of habit and inertia: 15 percent of the Democratic and 22 percent of the Republican precinct workers in Eldersveld's study of Detroit indicated they received *no* satisfactions from their party activities and hence would miss nothing if they ceased being active.[29]

All this means that party workers and, to a smaller extent, party leaders currently have little strong incentive to remain continuously active. Thus, there is rapid turnover of party activists, reflecting changing candidates and issues, the press of business and family life, and improved opportunities for socializing elsewhere.[30] Party leaders admit the "desperate struggle" to fill precinct leadership positions, which also forces them to put up with ineffective and, sometimes, even insubordinate precinct captains. As one party leader explained to Eldersveld:

> Voluntary organizations have a very difficult time keeping their members, let alone disciplining them. We cannot punish them for we lose them to our opponents.[31]

Costikyan reports the following conversation with one of his colleagues about what could be done with precinct captains who refused to man the polls at 6 a.m.:

[28] *Ibid.*, pp. 346–49.

[29] Eldersveld, *Political Parties,* Table 11.1, p. 278.

[30] In Detroit, almost 50 percent of the precinct activists in 1956 had begun working only recently. *Ibid.,* p. 276. In a study of county chairmen in (admittedly nonurban) Oklahoma, Samuel C. Patterson found that 47.5 percent of the Democrats and 81.6 percent of the Republican incumbents had held office two years or less and only 8.5 percent of the Democrats and 1.7 percent of the Republicans had been chairman more than ten years. "Characteristics of Party Leaders," *Western Political Quarterly,* 16 (1963): Table V, 342.

[31] Eldersveld, *Political Parties,* p. 116.

> '. . . fire them.'
>
> 'Yeah!' I said, 'fire them and then what do we do?'
>
> To this there was no answer. There was no waiting line of anxious applicants begging for appointment to a captaincy. In fact, over half the districts then had no captains. This is the unanswerable problem when one seeks efficiency in a modern volunteer political party—if you fire someone, then what do you do?[32]

In a few middle-income areas, particularly in New York City and certain parts of California, the parties have tried to solve the problem of recruitment and retention of workers, at least for preelection periods. This they have done by providing a year-round offering of social events by the local clubs, such as boat-rides, dances, picnics, along with the opportunity for ideological gratification in various discussion forums of "great issues" and unlimited opportunities for ego-satisfaction by creating myriads of committees, usually with chairmanships for anyone who is interested.[33] But the appeal of even such activities has proved to be short-lived, with precinct organizations in the new-style, middle-class-dominated, reform areas in cities finding it just as difficult to retain active workers as do the "old-line," ward organizations.[34]

Increased Voter Resistance to Party Organization

At the same time that because of the atrophy of their ward and precinct organization the party leaders find it increasingly difficult to reach the voter, the voter himself has become much more resistant to casting his ballot as the party leaders wish. This increased unwillingness to give his vote to the organization results from the following factors: (1) The organization no longer provides the favors and services that it once did, and the favors and services it still is capable of providing are no longer as inherently valuable, both because of the rise in the general standard of living and because of the availability of enlarged benefits and services from government agencies as a matter of right; (2) The growth in the perceived utility of the vote as a means of furthering governmental policies ameliorating one's life situation; (3) The availability to the voter through radio and especially television of additional cues for deciding how to cast his ballot; and (4) The strengthening of the values in our political culture favoring voter "independence."

[32]Costikyan, *Behind Closed Doors,* p. 86.

[33]See James Q. Wilson, *The Amateur Democrat* (Chicago: University of Chicago Press, 1962).

[34]See, e.g., Joseph P. Lyford, *The Airtight Cage* (New York: Harper & Row, 1966), esp. pp. 141-53.

Decrease in Quantity and Value of Organization-Disbursed Benefits. The reduction in the party's cash income and access to patronage jobs not only weakened its own organization, but also contracted the range of services and favors that it could lavish on the voter. The private charity that the machine bestowed on voters was expensive to maintain—too expensive for the hand-to-mouth financed present day party organizations. And if the organization cannot even provide jobs to motivate its own workers, it has few that it can spare for the voters.

Second, except in the many low-income neighborhoods that still exist in large cities, the Christmas turkey, the bucket of coal (or its modern equivalent), friendship and concern from a party leader, and similar kinds of personal favors are not highly valued. Indeed, these may be resented, not only by the increasing proportion of the population that has middle-class values and occupations, but even by the "successful working man."[35] Furthermore, for the poor, the unemployed, the elderly, the infirm, and the other downtrodden in today's society, there are available as a matter of right, governmental programs providing welfare and unemployment insurance payments, old-age assistance, municipal hospital care, and antipoverty projects on a scale that even the richest of the old-style machines could never have financed.

Paradoxically, the very number and complexity of governmental welfare programs sometimes provide party workers with new, even if small, opportunities to do favors and generate good will. This involves giving advice as to whether a person is eligible for a particular program, or by helping him complete an application, or by interceding on his behalf to hasten action on a request or application. Some neighborhood party organizations also conduct rent clinics giving free legal advice in landlord and tenant disputes and relocation cases. Here too, however, the neighborhood legal services projects operating out of storefronts under Antipoverty Act funding have in recent years institutionalized the provision of free legal advice and assistance to the poor and therefore made legal advice at the clubhouse more superfluous.

Enlargement in the Utility of the Vote. The positive value to the voter of his vote has also been enlarged. City governments (as well as state and federal) no longer perform only caretaker functions. Almost everyone understands that city government policies and programs can make a significant impact in alleviating the conditions causing most of the problems felt in urban areas. The voter consequently has great incentive to vote for those candidates he perceives as being most likely to adopt beneficial policies and not for those whose party sponsors have been the most "friendly." The voter has also learned to use the vote to express disfavor for certain disliked

[35]See Robert E. Lane, *Political Ideology* (New York: Free Press, 1962).

groups or practices by voting against candidates and officials that are favorable to them.

Availability of Alternative Voting Cues. The availability of radio and especially of television brings candidates and their appeals through news programs and paid advertising directly to the home of every voter. Consequently, even the voter who is too bored or illiterate to read about them now has more basis for making a choice than the "word" from his precinct captain. Before the advent of the broadcasting media, word-of-mouth endorsements were almost the only source of advice for the large proportion of the population who were not serious readers of political news. The potential impact of present-day media is well illustrated by a story told by Banfield and Wilson about a Chicago precinct captain who called on a voter to find him with three newspapers spread out on the floor and the TV set on. The captain was greeted with the remark, "What can you tell me that I don't already know?"[36]

Strengthening of "Independence" in Voting. Although difficult to document, there is evidence of a changing political culture. A lower value has been placed on party regularity in elections and a higher value on each voter having personal opinions and making up his own mind about whom to vote for on the merits. This change in cultural values most likely is related to the general rise in the level of education among city voters.

Writing at the turn of the century, Ostrogorski complained that the doctrine of "party regularity" and voting the "straight party ticket" was held in the United States with the intensity of religious dogma.[37] Many voters, even "of the better element," felt compelled to support the "yellow dog"—Ostrogorski's term for the completely unqualified candidate—if he was endorsed or run by the party organization.[38] In contrast, a poll in the 1960s found that only one person in ten took the "party regularity" position by disagreeing or strongly disagreeing with the proposition that "the best rule in voting is to pick the man regardless of his party label." On the other hand, 82 percent of the sample agreed or strongly agreed that the voter should vote for the man instead of the party.[39] And the increasing frequency with which candidates of different parties get elected to different offices in the same particular election shows that many voters carry out their "vote for the man, not for the party" feelings. Indeed, so strongly do many voters resent any attempt to influence their vote, that the appeal of a

[36]Edward C. Banfield and James Q. Wilson, *City Politics* (Cambridge, Mass.: Harvard University Press and the M.I.T. Press, 1963), p. 123.

[37]Ostrogorski, *Democracy and the Organization of Political Parties,* II, 173.

[38]*Ibid.,* II, 224-26.

[39]The exact percentages were as follows: Strongly Agree, 23 percent; Agree, 59 percent; Agree-Disagree, 6 percent; Disagree, 9 percent; Strongly Disagree, 1 percent; Don't Know, 2 percent. Jack Dennis, "Support for the Party System by the Mass Public," *American Political Science Review,* 60 (1966): 600–615.

party worker on how to vote may under some conditions be resented and boomerang.

The Nonpartisan Ballot

In about three-fifths of the large cities another factor that has led to a decline in party strength is that there are electoral systems requiring the nonpartisan ballot. In these nonpartisan cities, party designations or symbols are prohibited by law from appearing on the primary or general election ballot. The Seattle City Charter, for example, words the prohibition as follows:

> . . . Nothing on the ballot shall be indicative of the source of the candidate. No ballot shall have printed thereon any party or political designation or mark, and there shall not be appended to the name of any candidate any such party or political designation or mark, or anything indicating his views or opinions.[40]

Origins and Rationale of Nonpartisanship. The first large city to adopt nonpartisanship was Boston, in 1909. The "nonpartisan" ballot was part of a package of procedural devices that were introduced during the last two decades of the nineteenth century in order to "reform" urban political systems, particularly by weakening the influence of parties and party leaders. Other parts of the package included: direct primaries; initiative, recall, and referendum provisions; the short ballot; "at-large" elections; the city manager; merit systems; and timing of municipal elections in the spring or in odd-numbered years so as not to take place simultaneously with state and national ones.

The chief supporters of these antiparty reforms were middle-class, college-educated professionals, merchants, and small manufacturers, primarily of mugwump-Progressive point of view.[41] They appear to have been motivated by the following, not always consistent, set of beliefs: Party organizations were intrinsically corruptible and corrupting, leading to stealing from the public treasury, taking graft in exchange for favors and special privileges to businessmen, and protecting prostitution, gambling, after-hours liquor, and other forms of vice in violation of the law; Party organizations often placed wasteful incompetents in elective and appointive positions and prevented "high-quality" individuals, like themselves, from

[40]Article XVIII, sec. 1, Charter of 1962.

[41]See Richard Hofstadter, *The Age of Reform* (New York: Knopf, 1955), chaps. 4–6; Eugene C. Lee, *The Politics of Nonpartisanship: A Study of California City Elections* (Berkeley and Los Angeles: University of California Press, 1960), pp. 28–30; Willis D. Hawley, *Nonpartisan Elections and the Case for Party Politics* (New York: Wiley, 1973), esp. chap. 2.

becoming available for public office, since such individuals would not want to consort with the type of people associated with political parties; Partisan elections caused the voter to cast his ballot blindly according to his traditional attachment to one or another of the national parties, whose principles and policy stands had no relevance to issues of city government, and this prevented him from choosing the candidate "best qualified" on the basis of ability and honesty.

As a turn-of-the-century reformer saw it:

> . . . [A] city . . . has nothing whatever to do with general political interests; party political names and duties are utterly out of place there. The questions in a city are not political questions. They have reference to the laying out of streets; to the erection of buildings; to sanitary arrangements, sewage, water supply, electrical supply, to the control of franchises and the like; and to provisions for the public health and comfort in parks, boulevards, libraries, and museums. . . . . . . [T]he men who import political considerations into [what is] management are to be opposed.[42]

According to Henry L. Stimson, one of the most famous of the turn-of-the-century reformers, who eventually served twice as Secretary of War and once as Secretary of State, "there was always a policy which was best for all the people, and not good merely for one group as against another. . . The best political leadership . . . appealed not to class against class or to interest against interest, but above class and beyond interest to the good of the whole community of free individuals.[43] So frequently did the reformers use the term "good government" in their antiparty arguments that they were derisively referred to by the party people as "goo-goos."

The Effects of the Nonpartisan Ballot. Even in nonpartisan cities, the existence of local units of the national parties is not legally proscribed, so that party leaders are still to be found within the cities' boundaries as members and chairmen of county, city or ward committees. In a few "nonpartisan" cities, such as Chicago, Cleveland, Boston, Cincinnati, and Kansas City,[44] the nonpartisan ballot has not prevented party leaders and

[42]Andrew D. White, "The Government of American Cities," *The Forum,* December, 1890, reprinted in E.C. Banfield, ed., *Urban Government* (New York: Free Press of Glencoe, 1961), pp. 213–16.

[43]Henry L. Stimson and McGeorge Bundy, *On Active Service in Peace and War* (New York: Harper, 1947), p. 81.

[44]The situation has been very complicated in Cincinnati and Kansas City in that in addition to Republican and Democratic party leaders, there have been leaders of what until recently were strong local parties, the "City Charter Committee" in Cincinnati, and the "Citizens' Association" in Kansas City, which selected slates and ran campaigns. For many years Republican leaders in Kansas City worked in alliance with the Citizens' Association and Democratic leaders in Cincinnati worked in alliance with the Charterites. In Chicago, the nonpartisan ballot is used in elections to the Board of Alderman, but not for the mayoralty.

organizations from continuing to operate in a de facto partisan manner, slating candidates and campaigning for their election. Voters generally get to learn who each party organization is supporting and what is each candidate's national party affiliation through the mass media and campaign advertising. To the extent that the sympathies of the voters are overwhelmingly in favor of one party, the nonpartisan election in these cities functions as the equivalent of a direct primary for the dominant party, which in city-wide constituencies is almost always the Democratic party. The result is that while a Republican is almost never elected, registered Republican voters are free to participate in the election and thus can promote the fortunes of one or another of the aspiring Democrats.

In the larger number of nonpartisan cities, however, not only does the ballot not indicate party affiliations, but the sentiment among the majority of the electorate deems it improper for parties to play major roles in elections for city offices. As a result, party leaders and their organizations do not attempt to organize and campaign for party slates, and candidates are lined up and campaigns are led by nonparty groups. Some of these groups are short-lived and ad hoc, forming before each election in order to support particular candidates, with titles like "Citizens' Committee for John Smith." Other groups are more continuing, functioning as private, "slate-making" associations for election after election. They are the "Good Government Leagues," "Volunteers for Better Government," "Citizens Organized for Responsible Government," etc. Both the ad hoc and continuing groups are normally dominated by businessmen, professionals, newspaper publishers and editors, civic group staff members, and others of similar characteristics.

Of course, in some of these de facto nonpartisan cities, would-be candidates simply select themselves and run their own campaigns with the help of their friends and other volunteers. To the extent that finances are available to these nonparty groups and individual candidates, they hire public relations firms and employ television, radio, billboard, and newspaper advertising.

In the cities where campaigns for city offices are organized and led by nonparty groups or by individual, self-selected candidates, party leaders usually participate only to the extent of endorsing their preferred candidates. They may occasionally provide financial contributions and, even less often, may lend the behind-the-scenes support of their canvassing organizations. Frequently, party leaders stay out of such de facto nonpartisan elections completely. Limited participation by party leaders appears to be the typical pattern in cities like Seattle, Milwaukee, Denver, and perhaps increasingly, Los Angeles, while complete abstinence seems to prevail in Houston, Detroit, Atlanta, and Dallas.[45]

[45]The preceding categorization of nonpartisan cities is based primarily on Charles R. Adrian, "A Typology of Nonpartisan Elections," *Western Political Quarterly,* 12 (1959): 449-58; Charles E. Gilbert and Christopher Clague, "Electoral Competition and Electoral

THE CURRENT IMPACT OF PARTY LEADERS

As the preceding analysis attempts to make clear, city party leaders are no longer dominant or even highly influential actors in the politics of any but a few large cities. With the atrophy of their organizations, the increased voter resistance to following their preferences, and the development of nonpartisan elections, party leaders have lost the near monopoly they once held over the crucial nominating step in the electoral process. Since their hold on nominations to city offices was their chief resource of influence under the old-style machine system, having lost that, they lost their most powerful sanction over the actions and decisions of city officials.

On Nominations and Elections

This is not to say that in formal or de facto partisan cities party leaders have become completely impotent in matters of nomination and election. The party leaders, even with their weakened organizations, still possess first-hand knowledge of the technical routines involved in running for office. They know, for example, how petitions must be drawn to escape invalidation by the election authorities, the dates petitions can begin to be circulated and the dates they are due. They have at least a handful of workers available at the clubhouse who have circulated petitions in the past and hence know which of the voters are friendly, loyal, or cooperative enough to sign them again. Although their precinct and block organizations are not fully manned, party leaders are likely to have more personnel available for canvassing and getting voters out on primary day for their endorsees than do most unendorsed candidates, who normally need to build an organization from scratch. Furthermore, given not only these actual advantages enjoyed by the organization but also the overinflated image of its power that many would-be candidates still have, many primaries are uncontested so that the candidates endorsed by the party leaders are automatically nominated. With respect to general elections, the vote is strongly influenced by many factors not under the party leaders' control. But door-to-door canvassing does affect voting turnout. Therefore, in a closely fought campaign, party help may be determinative.

The key point is that in real nonpartisan cities the party leaders have only a marginal role, if any, in nominations. Even in partisan cities they have become primarily endorsers of and providers of a small amount of manpower to self-selected candidates rather than recruiters of nominees to

---

Systems in Large Cities," *Journal of Politics,* 24 (1962): 323-49; James Q. Wilson, "Politics and Reform in American Cities," *American Government Annual, 1962–63* (New York: Holt, Rinehart, & Winston, 1962); and *City Politics Reports* (Cambridge: Joint Center for Urban Studies, various dates, mimeo).

city office. Furthermore, when faced by a challenge to their endorsees, the party leaders are now far from certain to win. Party leaders are especially vulnerable to defeat when the office is a highly visible one like the mayoralty, with a city-wide constituency, and when the challenger is an incumbent who has not made himself highly unpopular with any sizable segment of the population. For example, competent incumbent mayors, like Robert F. Wagner of New York in 1961, or James J. Tate of Philadelphia in 1967, ran successfully for renomination against the opposition of most of the party leaders. A mayor can use television and press coverage normally given to his office as well as billboard and other kinds of advertising to reach the rank-and-file primary voter. He can form an effective campaign organization from among loyal supporters on his city hall staff and in the executive departments. He is likely to attract the backing of at least some party leaders who are antagonistic to the dominant group, who feel some special loyalty to him, or who predict that he is likely to win in any event and wish to be on the winning side. He can raise campaign funds from previous backers who are still loyal or obligated to him and who also believe he has a good chance to win and want to build up special credit by providing financial support. And an incumbent mayor can often get editorial support and favorable coverage from the newspapers, particularly if he can define the issue (as he frequently can) as a fight between "corrupt party bosses" who seek to control the city for their own selfish ends and a "noble, clear, public-minded reform-type official" who simply wants to insure that the city remains free from the "clutches" of the bosses for the benefit of "all the people." Furthermore, such an incumbent mayor is in a good position not only to win his own renomination in the primary but he can sometimes also bring in on his coattails candidates for other city offices and even for party positions, those who ran as part of his slate.

Party leaders are in a favorable position, however, when an incumbent has lost popularity either among the general public or among the enrolled voters of his party who are eligible to vote in the primary—e.g., St. Louis' mayor Raymond R. Tucker in 1965 or New York City's Vincent Impellitteri in 1953 and John Lindsay in 1969[46]—and the party leaders themselves are supporting a high-quality candidate. Party leaders are especially strong, furthermore, when a candidate is running for nomination to a low visibility office like city councilman, in a small constituency where television cannot be used effectively to reach the voter and newspaper coverage is likely to be thin. This is particularly the case when the nonparty candidate lacks a well-known family name to attract attention or the kind of magnetic personality that generates admiration and attracts a host of enthusiastic volunteer

[46]Lindsay was defeated for renomination by the Republican party in the 1969 primary campaign but was able to be reelected mayor by running on the Liberal party ticket.

door-to-door canvassers or when for any reason the candidate is short of campaign funds. Under these conditions the party leaders with even small numbers of dependable workers and their family, friends, and acquaintances are still in a good position to outvote their opponents and make their choices stick.

Influence on Policymaking

The impact of party leaders on the substance of city governmental policies is even more limited than their impact on nominations and elections. First of all, there is no evidence that modern party leaders are intrinsically interested in general questions of substantive policy any more than were their old-style predecessors. Eldersveld found that only 7 percent of the Detroit area party workers mentioned "concern for social and economic problems and issues" first as the reason for having become active in party work and only 23 percent mentioned that reason at all![47] Of the party leaders, only 29 percent of the Democrats and 10 percent of the Republicans felt that "ideological or issue satisfactions" were what they would miss most if they ceased their party work,[48] and only one-third emphasized "issue strategy" even during campaigns, in specifying their conception of their organizational task as party officials.[49] In Costikyan's account of the factors considered by party leaders when choosing candidates, the candidate's probable stand on policy questions is not even mentioned.[50] Included in the factors Costikyan does list are: "Financial ability of the candidate;" "Can he make a speech? Can he campaign? Does he get along with people? Has he any sense? What's his political background? Is he known in the district? How long has he lived there? What's his private life like? Can he win? Who will be happy if he's nominated, besides him?"[51]

City party leaders, in short, appear still to be persons with a strong fascination in the mechanics of negotiations and campaigns for nominations, elections, and appointments, but without an equally strong need to intervene and have their views prevail on matters of general governmental policy. There are, however, certain exceptions: Party leaders are constantly alert to changes in policies that immediately affect them and their organizations, such as election procedures, regulations of party organization, and the creation, elimination, or setting of qualifications for types of positions that the party leaders have been instrumental in filling. Party leaders are also likely to intervene when governmental policies will affect their own

[47]Eldersveld, *Political Parties,* p. 127.
[48]*Ibid.,* p. 278.
[49]*Ibid.,* p. 541.
[50]Costikyan, *Behind Closed Doors,* esp. chap. 9.
[51]*Ibid.,* p. 128.

districts exclusively, as in the construction of roadways, public buildings, urban renewal projects, or governmental housing, and especially if the community is united against the project or the project will cause a displacement of constituents who have been part of the leaders' traditional basis of support. When governmental agencies are not rendering a sufficiently high level of service in their district in such things as garbage collection, law enforcement, or school facilities, a party leader may also try to affect city decision-making. Occasionally, party leaders may try to influence officeholders to adopt general policies of city-wide application that they, the party leaders, have become convinced will be highly popular with the general public and hence make their vote-getting task easier in the next election.

By far the most frequent interventions by party leaders in the policy-making process concern not what the substance of new policies should be, but how existing policies are to be applied to particular individuals in the party leaders' constituency. Sayre and Kaufman have given a catalogue of the specific kinds of exceptions and special treatment that can be involved:

> Some . . . are so familiar they need no rehearsal here—evasion of penalties for traffic violations, a son helped out of trouble with the law, the tolerated violation of the Building Code, the immunity of a bookmaker from arrest and prosecution, and similar dispensations. But there are less heralded types of [interventions], too, many of which have nothing to do with violations of the law. Applications for licenses, for example, are sometimes speeded on their way through administrative channels at the behest of a party functionary ingratiating himself with a constituent. A tax assessment may be modified. The terms of a franchise may be eased or reinterpreted. Specifications in a construction contract may reduce the contractor's cost. . . . A tenant unable to make a landlord fulfill his obligations under rent control laws, and too unfamiliar with administrative processes to press his claim through the appropriate public offices, may find an informed and sympathetic spokesman and champion in a party leader.[52]

Of course, the party leaders' attempts to influence policies are not always successful, since officeholders very often have both the incentive and capacity to resist. Elected and appointed city officials have policy preferences of their own as well as an interest in a clean, scandal-free administration. Career bureaucrats and employees have a stake in uninterrupted routine and uniformity of treatment for all. For as has been explained,

[52]Wallace S. Sayre and Herbert Kaufman, *Governing New York City,* (New York: Norton, 1965), pp. 457–58.

incumbent mayors show increasing ability to win renomination and reelection even without the support of the party organization. Furthermore, line commissioners are increasingly being drawn from the personal followings of the successful candidates, from the career bureaucracy, or from some outside source of subject-matter experts. Consequently, few city officeholders are likely to feel any overwhelming sense of gratitude to the party leaders or to feel greatly intimidated by the possibility of being subjected to negative sanctions. Indeed, the resources of elected officeholders have grown so much, relative to nonoffice-holding party leaders, that in very recent years mayors—for example, Daley of Chicago and Wagner and then Beame of New York—have dominated their respective party organizations rather than the other way around. Costikyan tells that most of his admittedly infrequent attempts to register a party position on general policy with city officials were "not only disregarded, but I felt, resented."[53]

On some occasions, however, elected city officials may have won with the support of the party leaders and thus, out of a sense of gratitude and feelings of good fellowship from having worked for a common cause, be predisposed to cooperate, particularly when the costs are not high. Furthermore, the elected officials' popularity may not be so extraordinarily high as to make them feel certain that they have nothing to lose by permanently alienating the party leaders and risking a primary fight. Also, the party leaders, through their greater influence over the reelection prospects of district-based councilmen, or by themselves being councilmen or state legislators, may be able to retaliate against overly resistant executive officials by blocking or crippling their policies in the city's or state's legislative bodies.

In short, party leaders clearly do not dominate urban political systems nor do they run their policymaking machinery from smoke-filled back rooms. Their resources are such that when they seek to influence policies in a partisan city, they will normally receive a respectful, sympathetic, and even friendly hearing. But they come to officeholders, particularly citywide elected ones like mayors or to high appointed officials, as petitioners and claimants, not as commanders issuing orders that are certain to be obeyed. The party leaders' success will normally depend not on coercive powers but on how closely their objectives are shared by officeholders and on the calculation by these officeholders of how much support compliance with the leaders' wishes will cause them to gain and lose with other influential actors in the system, including the general public.

Implications of Party Decline

In conclusion, what are the implications of this decline in the influence of party leaders and organizations for the overall functioning of city govern-

[53]Costikyan, *Behind Closed Doors,* p. 289.

ments? Clearly, with the virtual disappearance of old-style machine practices, there has been a large-scale improvement in the honesty, efficiency, and impartiality with which large-city governments operate.

There is some question about whether these changes are the direct result of the weakening of the parties or whether they would have occurred anyway as a result of a changing political culture that attaches greater value to honesty, efficiency, and impartiality in the operations of city governments. A greater commitment to what can be called "procedural good government" is evidenced by the increased intolerance shown by the voters, by the mass media, and by high city officials to such things as outright stealing, bribery, incompetence, obvious waste of city resources, or favored treatment for those with "pull." Accordingly, it can be argued that whatever the exact cause-and-effect relationship historically, even if parties could again somehow be strengthened, there would be no necessary reintroduction of machine-style corruption.

In any event, to whatever extent the decline in party strength has eliminated corrupt and wasteful practices in city governments, this decline is a gain for the overall health of the system. To the extent that the decline of party strength has also reduced the party leaders' role in nominations and elections and thus their capacity to influence governmental decisions even in noncorrupt ways, it is not clear that the consequences have been altogether beneficial. This holds true with respect to the qualities of individuals coming forth to run for office, with respect to facilitating the voters' use of the ballot to promote their policy ends, and with respect to preventing widespread alienation among the city's low-income neighborhoods.

As Bryce pointed out in accounting for the great influence of the parties in the late nineteenth century, a leading characteristic of our city (and state and national) political systems is the overwhelmingly large number of elective offices to be filled.[54] These offices cannot fill themselves: Some flesh-and-blood human beings must spend the time, energy, and money that are necessary to find and have the names of candidates placed on primary or general election ballots and to promote their election among the general public. The reduction in the influence of party leaders does not mean that officials now emerge spontaneously and freely as some kind of direct, unencumbered expression of the public will. What it does mean is that nonparty political actors are now exerting much of the influence previously in the party leaders' hands. These other political actors include incumbent officials, newspaper publishers, editors, and other media people, downtown business and professional groups, ethnic group leaders, labor (especially civil service union officials, individuals with famous names, and people who themselves or through their friends have access to large sums of cash for buying TV time, campaign literature mailings, and the services of public relations and advertising agencies and private poll-takers.

[54]See Bryce, *The American Commonwealth,* Vol. 1, chap. 61, "What the Machine Has to Do."

Probably the largest net beneficiaries of this shifting of influence have been those persons with great individual wealth to invest in campaigns, a by-product being the great reduction in the possibility of nomination and election, certainly to city-wide office, of individuals without substantial money resources. For in the days of strong parties, potential candidates who themselves lacked access to money for campaign expenses were not automatically "unelectable" since the party had money resources of its own. Furthermore, before the development of TV and other media-centered campaigns, the overall amount of money needed was dramatically smaller. And because the party's income came from a broad base—kickbacks from city employees, padding of contracts, sale of a variety of favors, etc.—no individual large contribution was indispensable and therefore no particular large contributor had excessively great leverage over a candidate in a campaign or as an official if he were elected.

Apart from giving greater play to the influence of money, it can also be argued that the weakening of party leaders in nominations and elections of city officials has reduced the influence of those actors who, with the exception of incumbent officials themselves, are the most familiar with the workings of governmental institutions and hence in the best position to judge what qualities are most suitable in candidates for public office and to find persons possessing them. Party leaders who presided over strong organizations had, for example, a sizable pool of potential candidates among the active party workers and lower-level leaders whose abilities and personality characteristics they could observe at first-hand. The party leaders could test these aspiring politicians in less important elective positions and then sponsor for nominations to more important offices only those who had proved to be the most competent. Because the party leaders had a stake in the general reputation of the party, they had incentives to find candidates who would enhance that reputation rather than detract from it. They could also slate tickets balanced on ethnic and racial grounds so that elections could become integrative rather than polarizing devices. Finally, the party leaders could concentrate on the selection of candidates more easily than incumbent officials could. And they may also have been less wary to develop promising candidates for elective office than are incumbent officials, who may see new attractive personalities as potential competitors for their own jobs or for jobs to which these officials aspire.[55]

[55]Or so on this last point argues one party leader, Costikyan, attributing the shortage of high-quality Democratic candidates in New York during the early 1960s to Mayor Robert Wagner having dominated his party and blocked the path of anyone who might rival his vote-getting abilities (*Behind Closed Doors,* p. 294). Costikyan's argument is plausible in theory and his specific illustration may be correct. But since in real life all party leaders do not follow Costikyan's example of regarding himself only as a "talent scout" and never as the "talent" and since many party leaders do aspire to elective office (and there is no reason that they should not), any particular party leader may have no less incentive to block potential attractive rivals than any particular incumbent official.

Apart from the question of a candidate's competence, if the voter is to use his vote to influence the substance of governmental policies, it is crucial for him to know to what policy ends the candidate's competence will be directed. In the days of strong parties, it was possible for the voters to have a choice between different sets of candidates running as a team for all of the city executive and legislative offices being contested. Each set of party candidates was put forth by a continuing organization having an established general reputation and it was presumed to stand behind a common program. If elected these candidates could be expected to feel a sense of joint responsibility sufficient to work together from the different positions to which they were elected and thus have a good chance of putting their promised program through. If they did not help each other perform well, they knew that they might be held collectively responsible and all voted out of office. And such party-nominated and party-elected administrations were often able to recruit commissioners through the party, who would have the incentive to control the operating bureaucracies from the point of view of the overall administration.[56] Also, party leaders helped to develop the team spirit by exerting their informal influence to keep any would-be errant party-sponsored officials in line. The party whose candidates were not elected, on the other hand, had sufficient cohesion to stay "alive" between elections and offer criticism of the administration in power for their mistakes and other malefactions.

With the decline of party strength, even partisan campaigns are becoming increasingly media- and publicity-centered. They are often managed by public relations firms that concentrate on playing up the personalities of the candidates running pretty much as individual political entrepreneurs rather than what they will do as part of an administration. Candidates in nonpartisan elections, moreover, often avoid substantive issues, either remaining silent so as not to possibly alienate anyone or talking in bland generalities about why they are "best qualified" to serve.[57] Furthermore, the voter finds it difficult to use his vote even to indicate general satisfaction or dissatisfaction with the performance of the incumbent administration. With the great fragmentation of authority in city governments and with the different officials having largely been elected on their own, operating independently while in office, and possibly even belonging to different parties in partisan cities, it may be impossible to tell who was actually responsible for the good things that happened or the bad.

Also, there may be no alternative candidates who represent an identifiable set of "outs" who have continuity, a known collective position, and whose election could thus be expected to produce some different departures

[56]See Theodore J. Lowi, *At the Pleasure of the Mayor: Patronage and Power in New York City, 1898–1958* (New York: Free Press, 1964).

[57]See Charles R. Adrian, "Some General Characteristics of Nonpartisan Elections," *American Political Science Review,* 46 (1952): 766-76.

in policy and program. And given that officials are aware of all these impediments to the voter being able to cast his vote to express dissatisfaction with the officials' performance in office—i.e., to engage in so-called "protest voting"—they may not feel a great need to take into account how the public is likely to react to their decisions when making them.

This line of argument rejects, of course, the basic rationale of nonpartisanship—that there are no real, legitimate political issues in city governmental decision-making and that the policy process can become a problem-solving operation in which technical "experts" discover an optimum solution that will be agreeable and beneficial to the community as a whole. It assumes instead that since particular policies almost never distribute benefits and costs equally to everyone and since different policies distribute these inequalities differently, there will be conflicts about what policies should be adopted. And it also assumes that in a democracy, elections should be structured so as to afford the voter the maximum opportunity for using his vote to bring about the election of those candidates who are likely to adopt policies most favorable to his point of view.

The growing sense of alienation in low-income neighborhoods is at least in part related to the disappearance in almost all large cities of the local precinct captain with his motivation and ability to intervene with lower levels of the administrative bureaucracy on behalf of aggrieved constituents, even if they were members of a low-income group. Certainly, this growing alienation results predominantly from the increasing gap between expectations of what city governments can and should do to improve these neighborhoods and the personal conditions of those who live there and what the actual conditions are like. But some of this alienation is probably a consequence of those urban dwellers without high income or education not perceiving any established, nonviolent means for influencing city institutions to be more responsive to their needs, thus feeling frustrated, and "turning off" on the system.

Of course, neighborhood party workers never had the power to bring about any basic changes in levels of services and other conditions in particular neighborhoods. But they often were able to cut through bureaucratic "red tape" to rectify specific complaints, i.e., the removal of accumulated garbage on the streets, the towing away of abandoned cars, the installation of needed traffic control and street lights, the cleaning up of playgrounds, etc. Party workers were also able to find jobs for the unemployed, intervene with the police or the courts, and in various ways express a concern for the problems of the downtrodden, which was probably seen as coming in some way from the political system itself. And by making sure they were registered to vote, party workers politicized the normally apolitical lower classes. Perceiving the "system" to be "responding" to their needs, if even in only these very limited ways, probably helped to avoid the feelings of complete despair and powerlessness that many slum-dwellers now seem to hold about their ability to influence governmental institutions to ameliorate their conditions of life.

In recommending the establishment of "neighborhood action task forces" and "neighborhood city halls" to serve as easily accessible mechanisms for helping residents of low-income neighborhoods to get action from city administrative agencies on specific grievances, both the National Advisory (Kerner) Commission on Civil Disorders and the National (Douglas) Commission on Urban Problems implicitly recognized the value of the function that used to be performed by old-style party workers.[58] It remains to be seen whether such neighborhood task forces or city halls will be widely established in large cities; whether their staffs will include persons who actually live in those neighborhoods and are personally known to their residents; whether they will be able to develop the kind of leverage on middle- and lower-levels of administrative agencies that old-style party workers had; and whether neighborhood residents, not having the kind of sanction they had over party workers in being able to refuse to "deliver" their votes, will accept such units as spokesmen for their own interests rather than define them as mere "cooling" or "peace-keeping" machinery to protect the interests of the mayor and other city officials.[59]

It must, of course, be conceded that if party leaders had in the past always performed their functions honestly and responsibly—had they, for example, even in political recruitment rewarded with nominations those most deserving in terms of competence and party service as opposed to friends and cronies, and had they intervened with administrative agencies only to help legitimately aggrieved constituents rather than also to protect criminals and extract opportunities for personal self-interest—the antiparty forces could not have been as successful as they were in weakening parties and introducing nonpartisan electoral systems. The point here is that crooked or stupid party leaders are no more inevitable than crooked or stupid officials, bureaucrats, businessmen, professors, college students, etc. Consequently, with the present widespread acceptability of the "procedural good government" ethos, the operation of civil service and other procedural reforms, and the permanent elimination of most of the conditions that underlay the highly manipulable voter, the chance of even strengthened

[58]See United States National Advisory Commission on Civil Disorder, *Report* (New York: Bantam, 1968, chap. 10; National Commission on Urban Problems, *Report* (Washington, D.C.: U.S. Government Printing Office, 1968), Pt. IV, chap. 2.

[59]For the Boston experience, see Eric A. Nordlinger, *Decentralizing the City: A Study of Boston's Little City Halls* (Cambridge, Mass.: M.I.T. Press, 1972).

party leaders—if a strengthening of party organizations were somehow possible—being able to function as dictatorial, city-wide bosses running the city's decision-making apparatus from smoke-filled rooms and reintroducing large-scale corruption to large cities is probably infinitesimally small.

9

City Mayors

City hall officials like mayors, city managers, and councilmen are unique among urban political actors. It is these officials who possess the final authority to make the legally binding decisions about the content of city government policies and programs. It is they who also have the right to direct and supervise the performance by subordinate officials and employees of the implementing actions that become the policy outputs—i.e., the regulations, benefactions, and extractions—of large-city governments. In making and supervising the implementation of city governmental policies, these city hall officials function in a two-fold capacity: First, as independent actors of influence seeking to embody in those policies their own personal preferences, goals, needs, and interests; and second, as targets for, and reflectors of, the influence attempts and goals, needs, interests, and preferences of other actors within the system. Although city hall officials have in common that collectively they *are* the top decision-making element of the city government, rarely does that cause them to participate in the urban policy process as a single cohesive group. Rather, they come to the policy process in their special capacities as mayors, city managers, and councilmen, with different responsibilities, different perspectives, and different resources shaping the nature and extent of their participation. This chapter will examine the participation in city politics of mayors, and the next chapter will look at city managers and city councilmen.

MAYORAL ROLES

The mayor of a large mayor-council city is likely to be its single most influential political actor. In all cities, it is the mayor who serves as "chief of state" and thus symbolizes the unity of the city as an organized community. And except in council-manager systems, it is also the mayor who, because of charter-based duties, custom, and broadly-held public expectations, has come to be looked to as the city's chief problem-solver, crisis-coper, and responsible "person-in-overall-charge" of the operation of its government. Although the exact legal specifications of the mayor's total powers and responsibilities vary from city to city, in mayor-council systems he must essentially play five major roles—"city ceremonial head," "chief city executive," "chief city legislator," "chief city ambassador," and "supreme city emergency-handler." In the performance of each of these functions, the mayor usually has opportunities to make an impact on the content of the city government's policies and programs.

City Ceremonial Head

Traditionally, because he is its "chief of state," the mayor acts as the city's preeminent formal representative on a variety of ceremonial occasions: He greets and receives distinguished visitors at city hall and gives them a key to the city (or some less expensive equivalent thereof). He lays cornerstones for major public or private buildings and cuts ribbons when important projects are complete and ready to be opened for use. He attends an unending series of breakfast, luncheon, dinner, and after-dinner meetings, celebrations, and testimonials as guest of honor or principal speaker. He issues proclamations commemorating the anniversaries of certain events, launching charity drives, or otherwise designating special "days" or "weeks" in honor of different groups or organizations.

Although the mayor's time-consuming ceremonial activities may not immediately appear to offer opportunities for influencing policy output, they do so in at least three respects: First, because of the overall shortage of time and press of other business, the mayor attends some functions but not others. The mayor thus is directly conferring valued intangible benefactions on selected individuals and groups by lending his own personal prestige to occasions in which they have an interest and by symbolizing that the city itself deems the occasions and those associated with them worthy of special recognition. Second, the mayor can use his ceremonial activities to try to build up generalized goodwill, on which he might be able to draw in the future for the promotion of his own policies and programs. And to the extent that a celebrated occasion has an intrinsic importance apart from the mayor's participation, the mayor's prestige is replenished and possibly augmented by his being visibly associated with it. Third, the mayor very often has a chance during ceremonial occasions to make remarks in favor of some specific policy he is pursuing that will reach the immediate audience or, through the mass media, even a wider public.

Chief City Executive

The mayor of almost every large mayor-council city is designated by its charter as "chief executive officer of the city" and in varying language is required to see that the city's laws, ordinances, and resolutions are "faithfully" or "efficiently" executed. These bits of formal authority give him some claim to direct and supervise how, within the limits of local and state (and sometimes federal) legislation, the officials and employees in the operating departments carry out the city government's existing policies and programs. To the extent that the mayor is formally "strong," he will have appointed most of the heads of departments and other key executive officials without the necessity of approval by the council. As a result those officials may share the mayor's general policy outlook and perhaps also feel some further obligation to comply with his wishes out of a sense of personal loyalty. If the mayor is strong enough also to have the unrestricted right to make removals from office, he will probably be able to prevent at least outright defiance and disobedience from his immediate formal subordinates. When the mayor's formal strength includes responsibility for the preparation of an executive budget, and particularly if the city's legislative body is not allowed to make changes in that budget without extraordinary majorities, he has a theoretically powerful tool for setting the relative level of intensity at which different policies and programs can be implemented. This gives him a highly useful sanction for encouraging a generally responsive frame of mind among executive officials with an interest in adequate funding of the operations of their departments, which is to say most of them.

The possible array of formal powers available to the mayor for performance of the chief executive part of his role is impressive. But it must be remembered that even the strongest mayor has various independent agencies, boards, and commissions that are not under his formal control performing important functions within the city (e.g., the school board, the housing or redevelopment agency, the civil service commission, community corporations). In addition, in a quarter to a third of the large cities, the mayor is formally "weak" in that he suffers from one or more of the following infirmities: Not the mayor, but citizen boards or commissions serving staggered, fixed terms have the power to appoint the heads and are directly responsible for the running of important operating departments nominally subject to the mayor. Whatever appointments the mayor can make need the approval of the city legislative body. Removals from office by the mayor also need such approval or must be "for cause" after filing of charges and a hearing. The mayor has no right to prepare an overall executive budget; each department can submit its budget requests directly to the legislative body or to some special financial board of which the mayor is only one member (for example, St. Louis, Milwaukee). Furthermore, all mayors must rely for the implementation of their policies on operating departments staffed almost exclusively by civil service protected employees whom they cannot dismiss and replace except for the most flagrant instances of insubordination or inefficiency and even then only with the greatest difficulty.

The greatest obstacle to the mayor's converting his formal authority as chief executive into full control over the operating departments is not his shortage of legal powers, however important that shortage is in many instances. The greatest obstacle is his unavoidable lack of knowledge about anything more than a tiny fraction of what those departments are doing. A mayor has neither the time, the energy, nor the means for discovering the thousands of choices being made in the name of the city government by his subordinates while implementing general policies and programs. Thus, he cannot know whether choices and alternatives were available that he would have preferred but that they rejected. Furthermore, the mayor is not able to decide personally the matters that he considers most crucial, or would so consider if he knew about them, and then insure that the thousands of implementing decisions and actions performed by the operating departments be within their scopes. This is because instead of having opportunities to concentrate on such guiding or directing decisions of his own choice, the mayor's agenda is largely filled by issues that are brought to his attention by others—gross scandals or inefficiencies uncovered by the mass media; inter- or intradepartmental conflicts in which at least one party has an interest in appealing to the mayor; contemplated departmental courses of action that need the mayor's formal approval; and projects for which a departmental official needs the mayor's help in negotiating with powerful political actors outside the executive branch, such as the council, the state legislature, or private groups.

The mayor's influence on the activities of the operating departments is thus marginal rather than central: Most departmental activities simply go on unchanged or with changes introduced without any reference to the mayor. Even the budgetary authority of a strong mayor, which theoretically should give him great influence in imposing his own priorities on the allocation of funds among different programs and departments, in fact does not. For it is limited primarily to passing on the size of proposed and normally small increases to the total amounts approved the previous year. In other words, no mayor actually makes up his budget by redetermining every year the priority that each department or program should get in receiving funds for its operation. The great bulk of the money approved by the mayor is simply a continuation of the previous year's budgetary "base" which is taken as a given. His priorities can only affect the relative size of the increases over (or in some cases decreases from) that base granted to the different departments and programs. But even then the increases or decreases must be made within the double constraint of having to approve funds to meet "uncontrollable" increases in costs for various programs regardless of priority and of not being able to approve sufficient funds even for programs carrying his highest priority when the funds are not available within the city's overall anticipated revenues.[1]

Occasionally the mayor does intervene in the operations of a department on his own initiative. He may direct that some specific item that has come to his attention be handled in a certain way. He may demand more energetic action in dealing with an outstanding problem. Or, in a field in which he has special competence or a pet interest, he may even require a specific change in policy. Also, a mayor such as Richard Daley of Chicago, who has been in office a generation, can impose not only official but unofficial sanctions on the bureaucracy through his position as head of the Democratic party machine and thus does not tolerate obstruction from within his bureaucracies.[2] But given the press of all the mayor's duties, free time and energy for such interventions are rare, and when they take place by the typical mayor, it is far from certain that the desired action by the operating department will be actually forthcoming. The more common response is for the operating bureaucracy to provide reasons why "It's never been done that way before," meaning that the bureaucrats do not intend to change their existing practices to accommodate the mayor unless he forcefully and continuously follows up on their expected compliance. This he seldom is undistracted or unbusy enough to do. In the words of one big-city mayor, trying to get his policies carried out by the operating bureaucracies gave him the feeling sometimes that "I'm pushing my shoulders against a mountain . . . my feet are churning away and the mountain won't budge."[3]

Chief City Legislator

The charter of no city actually terms the mayor its "chief legislator." But the mayor's usual charter-based duties start him out with an important formal share of the city's legislative authority. He must, for example, report annually to the legislative body on the "state of the City" and give to it

[1]See Arnold J. Meltsner and Aaron Wildavsky, "Leave City Budgeting Alone!" in John P. Crecine, ed., *Financing the Metropolis* (Beverly Hills: Sage, 1970); and John P. Crecine, *Governmental Problem Solving* (Chicago: Rand McNally, 1969).

[2]See J. David Greenstone and Paul Peterson, *Race and Authority in Urban Politics* (New York: Russell Sage Foundation, 1973).

[3]Lindsay, quoted in Nat Hentoff, *A Political Life: The Education of John V. Lindsay* (New York: Knopf, 1969), p. 146.

information and recommend measures that he considers necessary or expedient. The mayor also often has power to veto and sometimes item-veto ordinances, and it is the mayor's right in the majority of large cities to submit an executive budget (whose amounts normally cannot be increased, changes to which he can veto, and that in some cities is deemed adopted if not acted upon by the legislators within an allotted span of time).[4] But more than formal powers, it is the typical inability of city legislative bodies—like all contemporary legislatures in complex, rapidly-changing societies—to generate their own agendas that insures the mayor will in fact be the chief continuing source of major proposals that the council considers. It is the mayor who speaks for the operating departments which have much better access to information about the nature of current problems and also better staff for developing, reviewing, and integrating ideas and suggestions for dealing with those problems into concrete legislative proposals than the council. Furthermore, all new programs, substantial changes in existing programs, structural reorganizations, appropriations for the departments under the mayor's control, as well as any new taxes to raise the money to fund those programs and operate those departments, need legislative authorization. The mayor must therefore formulate and submit a constant stream of legislative proposals for the council just in order to perform his job as chief executive.

The council does not always approve. True, most of the mayor's legislative proposals are of such minor routine nature or promote such overwhelmingly accepted purposes in such noncontroversial ways that they are quickly adopted. Indeed, many mayoral proposals have only token mayoral interest attached to them and merely represent the technical legislative needs of the departments. But if the mayor does have real interest in a proposal and that proposal is controversial or for other reasons opposition develops within the legislative body, his resources for overcoming that opposition are strictly limited. In partisan cities, where the council majority is of the same party as the mayor, he may be able at times to draw on feelings of party loyalty or commitment to the success of his administration. In rare cases like Chicago, in which there is still a strong party organization and the mayor is essentially the party chief, he can also threaten such actions as refusing to give jobs to followers of uncooperative councilmen, possibly discharging non-civil service protected followers already on the public payroll, and even opposing and preventing the councilman's own renomination. And in any city, particularly if the mayor is highly popular and doesn't mind running the risk of turning occasional opponents into permanent enemies, he may be able to use his superior access to the mass media to take the conflict between himself and the council to the public and

[4]In a few cities the mayor has additional formal legislative powers like introducing ordinances (Boston) or serving as presiding officer of the council (Chicago, El Paso).

to make it look like a fight between the "good [i.e., his] guys" seeking to promote an unquestioned public good against the "bad [i.e., council] guys" motivated by narrow, selfish, parochial, or party, interests. To the extent that the councilmen don't like to be treated disapprovingly by the mass media or are afraid that such treatment might hurt their chances for reelection, they may back down. But most frequently, the only tool available to the mayor is simply persuasion, and if his councilmanic opponents refuse to be persuaded into ceasing their opposition, there is normally nothing the mayor can do about it.

Chief City Ambassador

By custom, because he is regarded as the city official most capable of speaking for the city government as a whole, but even more importantly because of needs arising from the performance of his other functions, the mayor serves as the city's chief ambassador to outside political entities. Specifically, he is its paramount negotiator with neighboring municipalities and special districts and, most importantly, with the state and federal governments. Given the city government's dependent legal status, many of the new or changed regulatory, benefactory, and particularly extractive (i.e., tax) programs that the mayor as chief executive wants the operating departments to undertake and as chief legislator will ask the city legislative body to approve, first need to be authorized by changes in state law. The mayor will normally incorporate these changes into an overall legislative package to be presented to the governor and the state legislative leaders at the beginning of each legislative session. In addition, the mayor will usually make one or more well-publicized pilgrimages to the state capital, "hat-in-hand" as the mass media will put it, to plead personally for increased state grants-in-aid or taxing authority for his city. As Mayor Lindsay humorously, but nonetheless accurately, described New York's version of this ritual:

> . . . the Mayor and the Governor have a special tradition of commemorating the major religious holidays in the Judaeo-Christian tradition. Each December, sometime around Christmas and Chanukah, the Mayor writes the Governor a letter outlining the fiscal needs of the city for the coming year and describing the severe consequences that will result if the city does not receive a fair share of the taxes collected from the city and state. The Governor then acknowledges the needs of the city and describes the financial pressures on the state that will make such help unlikely.
>
> In April, at about the time of Easter and Passover celebrations, the Mayor makes a pilgrimage to Albany, the state capital, to present the case for additional city money. The legislative leaders greet this

> request with a level of enthusiasm traditionally reserved for the bearer of such tidings. Then, at the last minute, the ritual ends with a sudden burst of intensive negotiations, and stop-gap measures are applied to carry over the crisis to the next year. . . .[5]

Finally, the mayor will be watching bills affecting the city that are being promoted within the state legislature by other political actors. He will be supporting those he considers beneficial and asking the legislature not to pass or, at later stages, the governor to veto, those that he considers harmful.

Increasingly, in recent years, the mayor must also journey to Washington. There he will appear before congressional committees, most often explaining the nature and urgency of urban problems and testifying in favor of bills authorizing new programs of benefit to cities and against cut-backs in spending for existing programs. In the national capital, the mayor may also intervene with executive branch officials including the President. This is in order to encourage them to propose new or expanded urban programs to Congress, to ask that his city be treated more generously in the distribution of monies available under established grant programs, or to urge that, at least, the processing of its grant applications be speeded up. Besides this individual lobbying a mayor may also support and sometimes provide leadership for the efforts in Washington undertaken by the three mayoral interest groups—the "Big 10" group of mayors, the U.S. Conference of Mayors, and the National League of Cities—as well as by other nationwide, prourban interest groups like the National Urban Coalition.[6]

The potentialities for the state and federal (and sometimes neighboring local) governments to help or hinder the mayor are great. But the resources available to him as chief ambassador for influencing their actions are close to nonexistent. None of the mayor's formal, charter-based powers invigorate his ambassadorial task. He rarely has informal inducements to offer to, or negative sanctions to impose upon, those he is trying to influence. In 1966, for example, Mayor Lindsay announced that if the New York State Legislature did not authorize New York City to impose an income tax on its own residents and on commuters, he, Lindsay, would "have to take it to the people." Upon hearing the mayor's threat, one suburban Nassau County legislator remarked, "I can't believe he is serious about this. If he came out to Nassau County and campaigned against us, it would be a plus for us."[7]

The mayor's chief reliance must therefore be based not on threats, but on

[5]John V. Lindsay, *The City* (New York: New American Library, 1970), p. 177.

[6]See Suzanne Farkas, *Urban Lobbying: Mayors in the Federal Arena* (New York: New York University Press, 1971); Donald H. Haider, *When Governments Come to Washington: Governors, Mayors, and Intergovernmental Lobbying* (New York: Free Press, 1974).

[7]Quoted in Woody Klein, *Lindsay's Promise: The Dream That Failed* (New York: Macmillan, 1970), p. 124.

persuasion and goodwill. When the mayor of a partisan city and the governor happen to belong to the same party and are not personal or factional enemies, or potential competitors for the same elective office, the governor may be disposed to be as helpful as possible to his party colleague. But this help can only be given within the limits imposed by the governor's own difficulties in raising extra revenue and gaining the cooperation of the state legislature. Responsiveness on the part of the governor may be in exchange for the mayor's being able to influence state legislators to provide support for some of the governor's own legislative proposals. But again it is the governor in consultation with the leaders of the legislature, not the mayor, who will determine what the state's level of help will be.

In Congress, the mayor's testimony will buttress the efforts of those senators and representatives who are already predisposed to help the cities. Whether and to what extent favorable congressional action is actually forthcoming, however, will depend much more on the intensity of the President's support, on the division of seats in the two houses between the "liberal" (primarily northern Democratic) and the "conservative" (primarily Republican and southern Democratic) coalitions, and on the general mood or "temper" in Congress and in the country at the time toward new or expanded spending for urban problems, than on any intrinsic persuasiveness in the mayor's remarks.

The President, like a governor, may well be disposed to help a mayor of his own party look good, particularly if that mayor was an early supporter of the President for the party's nomination, and in any event, large-city populations are major elements of the President's electoral constituency. But the President has his own order of priorities in proposing or budgeting for new or expanded federal programs including those having to do with foreign and military affairs and other nonurban matters. He may also have other objectives that conflict with providing large amounts of money to cities, such as controlling inflation or reducing budget deficits. And since the President has his own problems in getting Congress to acquiesce to his wishes, he may not be able to bring about expanded spending for cities even if he is convinced of their need. In addition, every large-city mayor is essentially in competition with all others for available, and always scarce, funds under existing grant programs. The President cannot, therefore, become unduly partial towards the needs of any one city or its mayor. The mayor as the city's chief ambassador to the President is thus dependent upon the federal government's assessment of what can be provided to the city, and the mayor has few resources to influence these calculations.

Supreme City Emergency-Handler

Over and above his more formally defined responsibilities, though at times in connection with them, the mayor has come to be looked upon as the city's supreme emergency-handler. The public has come to expect him to deal personally with any occurrences that sizable numbers of the city's people consider seriously threatening or damaging and that no one else appears to be preventing, controlling, or alleviating satisfactorily. The mayor is required by the public and particularly by the mass media (and occasionally even by charter language formally designating him "conservator" of the city's "peace") to do or say something about municipal emergencies such as riots, crime waves, natural or man-made disasters, breakdowns in city services, or scandals in the city government. Increasingly, the mayor is also expected to take some action in areas where he does not have official jurisdiction: He may need to act on strikes of nongovernmental employees such as newspapermen, dock workers, construction workers, opera singers, or employees of governmental agencies not under his control such as many school systems or transit authorities. He normally must deal with threatened moves by large employers away from the city, intended closings by the federal government of military installations within the city, or even desertion of the city by one or more of its major baseball clubs or football or basketball teams.

In some emergency situations the mayor will be able to invoke formal powers or apply governmental remedies in order to influence the course of events. In other emergencies, he will largely be restricted to bringing the prestige of his office to bear in personal appeals to the parties involved, encouraging them to reach agreement or otherwise refrain from doing damage to the city. Sometimes this kind of activity by the mayor will succeed, with a strike being settled on terms that he suggests, the threatened flight of a company being cancelled, or the closing of a military installation at least being postponed. At other times the mayor will be able to accomplish nothing more than a demonstration of concern and effort.

MAYORAL POLICY STYLES

Every mayor performs the five core roles just discussed in some fashion. However, the extent to which that performance will actually influence the substance of his city's governmental policy varies from mayor to mayor. A mayor's influence will vary, for example, according to the specific legal powers and other resources at his command and according to the resistance displayed by those he is trying to influence. A mayor's influence will also vary according to his personal "policy style," i.e., his personal inclination toward imposing his particular views on the city's policy process. Robert Dahl has shown, for example, how New Haven Mayor Richard Lee's style made him a much more influential mayor than his immediate predecessor. And Jeffrey Pressman has explained how much less influential John Reading's style made him as compared to John Houlihan, his immediate predecessor as mayor of Oakland.[8] Though probably no mayor displays the same policy style on all occasions and some may change their style over time, most mayors show a clear tendency toward one of three distinguishable types: the "caretaker and policy mediator," the "policy innovator and champion," and the "opportunistic policy broker."

Caretaker and Policy Mediator

The mayor who sees himself as a passive "caretaker and policy mediator" makes no strong attempt to impose his own personal views on the policy process. He goes through the motions of performing his official or otherwise prescribed or expected functions, either unaware of, or uninterested in, how that performance will influence policy. His overriding concern is to preside over the continuation of programs that the city government has traditionally carried out and to ward off interruptions to ongoing routines. Such a mayor avoids or ignores demands for change unless change becomes almost universally agreed upon as necessary; he then adopts the substance of the change others demand. In cases of disagreement, this type of mayor will usually encourage the parties at odds to reach an agreement for him to ratify or, as a last resort, he will simply propose a compromise between the opposing points of view. Alan Altshuler's description of a past Minneapolis mayor, P. Kenneth Peterson, shows the traits of a caretaker and policy mediator mayor:

> [The mayor] does not actively sponsor anything. He waits for private groups to agree on a project. If he likes it, he endorses it. Since he has no formal power with which to pressure the Council himself, he feels that the private groups must take the responsibility for getting their plan accepted. He never attempts to coerce aldermen. Instead, he calls them into his office to reason with them. . . . The Mayor has let citizens' groups use the facilities of his office to work out solutions to certain pressing and highly controversial problems. Such solutions are often then seized upon by him and by the Council and adopted without amendment.[9]

Ralph Locher, who served as mayor of Cleveland from 1962 to 1967,

[8]Robert A. Dahl, *Who Governs?* (New Haven: Yale University Press, 1961); Jeffrey L. Pressman, "Preconditions of Mayoral Leadership," *American Political Science Review,* 66 (1972): 511-24.

[9]Alan A. Altshuler, "A Report on the Politics of Minneapolis," (Cambridge, Mass.: Joint Center for Urban Studies of the Massachusetts Institute of Technology and Harvard University, 1959, mimeo), sec. II, pp. 14-15.

could also be classified as a caretaker and policy mediator type of mayor. Locher has been described as a "tragic figure" who

> exhibited no sense of innovation and daring. He surrounded himself with inflexible leaders of the past. He turned his back on opportunity for a new opening to the poor and to black constituents. . . . Even the business community became estranged from him.
>
> While Cleveland's problems called for bold moves against racism and poverty, Locher was concerned with putting utility wires underground and getting children to pick up candy wrappers. No large creative projects came out of his administration. His tenure was a holding action, and risk was avoided whenever possible.[10]

Norris Poulson, mayor of Los Angeles from 1953 to 1961, also appears to have been a good example of the caretaker and policy mediator, doing little to impose his will on the conduct of the city government.[11] Samuel W. Yorty, who defeated Poulson for reelection in 1961 and thus is not an unbiased observer, has related that:

> When I came into office I found out why Mayor Poulson had gotten along with little friction. He let the Council take control and of course if the Mayor didn't stand up for his objectives there wouldn't be much friction. . . . The apparent harmony was all due to the Mayor letting things slide and letting the council have its way on nearly everything.
>
> The city was run by the civil service general managers of the departments who never met together in any coordinated fashion or checked with the Mayor. They spent bond funds and did everything else pretty much on their own. As a result there was no unity of approach and things were going off in every direction.[12]

Policy Innovator and Champion

Almost the exact opposite of the "caretaker and policy mediator" type is the mayor who is strongly oriented to responding aggressively to problems with policies incorporating solutions that he personally prefers and thinks will do the job. This "policy innovator and champion" kind of mayor need not also be the "inventor" of the new policies himself—he normally will

[10] James V. Cunningham, *Urban Leadership in the Sixties* (Cambridge, Mass.: Schenkman, 1970), pp. 79-80.

[11] See, for example, Charles G. Mayo, "The 1961 Mayoralty Election in Los Angeles," *Western Political Quarterly,* 17 (1964): 325–37.

[12] Quoted in Ed Ainsworth, *Maverick Mayor* (Garden City, N.Y.: Doubleday, 1966), p. 46.

have no time for that. But because he becomes known as a "mover" and "shaker," he serves as a magnet attracting large numbers of ideas for innovations from a variety of political actors, including subordinates on his staff and in the operating departments, interest group leaders, professors, foundations, etc. Once such a mayor determines that a particular policy is the best solution for a problem, he pushes as hard as he can for its adoption with those whose approval or cooperation is necessary. The spur to this kind of policy innovation and championing may be empathy with those experiencing the problem, the strong desire to have the city move in the direction of certain goals to which he or supporters of his are ideologically committed, the psychological appetite to be personally dominant in the operations of the city government, or any combination of the above.

Perhaps the classic example of the "policy innovator and champion" mayor was New York City's thrice-elected (1933, 1937, and 1941) Fiorello H. La Guardia. La Guardia's concept of the mayoralty was simply that *his* policies should *always* prevail in *every* area of government activity. As Sayre and Kaufman tell it, La Guardia:

> . . . had a great zest for innovation, a strong pride in his own initiative, forcefulness in arbitration, and a marked distaste for passive mediation.
>
> When La Guardia became Mayor (at age fifty-two), he had looked at the office as a goal for fifteen years. Impatient waiting and striving had simply whetted his appetite for the leadership opportunities he saw in the office; deference to party leaders, to the Board of Estimate, or to other institutions of influence had no place in his view of the mayoralty. . . . His intention from the first was to make himself as Mayor a highly visible chief executive, a symbol of energy and motion, accepting responsibility in all things as a weapon against his opponents, seeking to be omnipresent and omniscient and invincible.
>
> [La Guardia] made the fewest concessions to administrative autonomy, viewed his department heads with a skepticism bordering on suspicion, breathed down their necks with his close supervision, and was ferociously impatient with default. All problems were his to solve, the administrative agencies were his mere instruments.[13]

La Guardia's remote successor in office, John V. Lindsay, who was elected in 1965 and reelected in 1969, had a very similar concept of the mayoralty, wishing to be "out in front" on matters of policy and to have his point of view prevail generally. Lindsay's own term for this style was

[13]Wallace S. Sayre and Herbert Kaufman, *Governing New York City,* (New York: Norton, 1965), pp. 690-91; see also Charles Garrett, *The LaGuardia Years: Machine and Reform Politics in New York City* (New Brunswick, N.J.: Rutgers University Press, 1961).

being an "advocate mayor,"[14]—one who is willing to attack problems and propose solutions for dealing with them, even if they are controversial. An assistant of his described Lindsay as a mayor:

> . . . with a sense that problems have to be attacked in the open, even if the administration gets hurt in the process. *That's* the stiff-necked quality about Lindsay I admire. He knew he'd have to take an awful lot of political heat by letting all these problems come out in the open rather than making patch-up, short-term arrangements behind the scenes which would solve nothing basically. The thing is that he and his people are making attempts—even if they're sometimes half-assed—to really come up with solutions.
>
> And the mayor is on top of those attempts. . . . He said he was elected to change the city, and that's what he went on to do because that's what he *should* be doing.[15]

Among other recent mayors, Richard C. Lee of New Haven (1954–1970) demonstrated a policy innovator and champion style, particularly in providing aggressive leadership for that city's extensive physical rebuilding and urban renewal efforts.[16] So too did David Lawrence, mayor of Pittsburgh from 1955 to 1959, in his successful efforts to modernize and invigorate his city's downtown under the slogan of "Pittsburgh Rennaissance."[17] Henry W. Maier, the mayor of Milwaukee since 1960, has stressed the necessity for a mayor to "exercise the creative aspects of institutional leadership," to develop "a strategy related to the things people want and need," and to "show the people that he is fighting for their needs."[18] Jerome P. Cavanaugh, who served as mayor of Detroit from 1961 to 1969, once spelled out his own problem- and goal-oriented conception of the mayoralty as follows:

> I think all too often today the role of a mayor in a city is merely responding to a crisis in putting out fires. . . .
>
> But I really look at the role of a mayor as being one that exercises not only the legal responsibilities that he has, which are quite important, but really to exercise the degree of moral leadership that is needed in a community. By that I mean attempting to define a

[14]See, for example, Lindsay, *The City,* p. 25.

[15]Quoted in Hentoff, *A Political Life,* pp. 273–74.

[16]See, for example, Dahl, *Who Governs?*; Allan R. Talbot, *The Mayor's Game* (New York: Harper and Row, 1967).

[17]See Cunningham, *Urban Leadership,* pp. 48–50.

[18]Henry W. Maier, *Challenge to the Cities: An Approach to a Theory of Urban Leadership* (New York: Random House, 1966), pp. 180-81.

community's goals as articulately as you might be able to, and then moving a community toward the realization of those goals.

. . . And it is true that sometimes the mayor might have to espouse some very unpopular causes but I think this he must do if he proposes to attempt to cause that community to move forward.

What I am attempting to say is, the mayor is the man that probably should mobilize the conscience of a community. . . .[19]

Opportunistic Policy Broker

Somewhere midway on what could be considered as a continuum between the "caretaker and policy mediator" and the "policy innovator and champion" mayors is the type who is essentially a broker. Such a mayor responds to policy demands initiated by others and chooses policies to support or oppose opportunistically, in terms not primarily of his independent evaluation of their merits, but in terms of the resources and influence potential of the actors sponsoring or opposing them.

This "opportunistic policy broker" mayor is neither trying to avoid all policy decisions while presiding uninterrupted over housekeeping routines, nor is he attempting to make a maximum impact on the solution or alleviation of what he, himself, considers to be serious outstanding city problems. His main objectives are instead to win the approval of those who can help and to avoid displeasing those who can damage his own personal power position, especially his chances for reelection. Richard C. Daley, Chicago's mayor from 1955 to the 1970s, is probably the classic contemporary example of the opportunistic policy broker type of mayor. As Edward Banfield has described Daley's style and outlook:

> Any mayor of Chicago must "do big things" in order to be counted a success. It is not enough merely to administer honestly and efficiently the routine services of local government—street cleaning, garbage collection, and the like. An administration that did only these would be counted a failure, however well it did them. . . .
>
> Wanting to do "big things" and not caring very much which ones, the [mayor] will be open to suggestions. (When Mayor Daley took office, he immediately wrote to three or four of the city's most prominent businessmen asking them to list the things they thought most needed doing.) He will be receptive, particularly, to proposals from people who are in a position to guarantee that successful action

[19]U.S. Senate, *Federal Role in Urban Affairs,* Hearings before the Subcommittee on Executive Reorganization of the Committee on Governmental Operations, 89th and 90th Cong., (1966-67), pp. 635-36.

> will win a "seal of approval" from some of the "good government" groups. He may be impressed by the intrinsic merit of a proposal—the performance budget, for example—but he will be even more impressed at the prospect of being well regarded by the highly respectable people whose proposal it is. Taking suggestions from the right kind of people will help him to get the support he needs in order to win the votes of independents in the outlying wards and suburbs.
>
> For this reason, he will not create a strong staff of policy advisers or a strong planning agency. The preparation of policies and plans will be done mainly within those private organizations having some special stake in the matters involved and by the civic associations. Quite possibly, the [mayor] might, if he wished, assemble a technical staff of first-rate ability and, working closely with it, produce a plan far superior to anything that might be done by the private organizations and the civic associations. But a plan made in this way would have one fatal defect: its makers could not supply the "seal of approval" which is, from the [mayor's] standpoint, its chief reason for being. On the other hand, a plan made by the big business organizations, the civic associations and the newspapers, is sure to be acclaimed. . . . It is sure-fire, for the people who make it and the people who will pass judgment upon it are the same. . . .[20]

Robert F. Wagner, who served three terms between 1953 and 1965 as mayor of New York City, was another highly successful opportunistic policy broker. Although a number of notable new policies and programs were adopted by the city government during Wagner's administration with his backing, practically none was originally sponsored by Wagner himself. Like Daley, Wagner chose from the policy proposals originated and promoted by other influential actors and when serious controversy developed, Wagner just sat tight and waited until the distribution of power between the two sides became clear. He was fond of quoting, and obviously acting upon, the advice of his famous senator father, Robert F. Wagner, Sr., which was, "When in doubt, don't." Wagner's broker style became more widely appreciated after he left office and was contrasted with the style of his successor, John Lindsay. As one close observer of the mayoralty put it in the early years of the Lindsay administration:

> Wagner was not fully understood by the public, but in retrospect, his skills seem to be to have been all the more valuable. He was highly intelligent, extremely knowledgeable, and his mind worked almost like an I.B.M. machine. A proposal would be made to him, and thirty

[20]Edward C. Banfield, *Political Influence* (Glencoe, Ill.: The Free Press, 1961), pp. 250-53.

> seconds later, he'd tell you who'd be for it, who'd be against it, and how the opposition could be neutralized, if that were possible. But Lindsay . . . he doesn't figure out carefully enough in front who his allies and his opposition may be to specific proposals. Thereby he doesn't do enough planning with allies or potential allies, nor does he attempt to chip off the opposition. . . . Sure, Wagner procrastinated, but sometimes there was method in those maddening delays. He was waiting for the particular time when he could get a particular plan through.[21]

THE BIG-CITY MAYORALTY: AN OFFICE OF MASSIVE FRUSTRATIONS

Since the second half of the 1960s and into the 1970s the mayoralty of a large city has become an office of massive frustrations for its incumbent. The mayor, in the public mind, is the center of accountability and responsibility for all that goes wrong within the city while he receives little credit for anything that goes right. He is expected to find and impose solutions for the city's most pressing problems—poverty, crime, slums, drug addiction, pollution, insufficient housing, inadequate mass transit. And not only will the mayor be blamed for all of his own personal shortcomings, but, as Sayre and Kaufman report about New York's mayor, he is also "held hostage for the conduct of all other officials and all employees of the city, for their personal integrity, their wisdom in policy, and their efficiency in performance."[22]

Limited Formal Powers and Staff

Yet to satisfy these enormous demands and expectations, the mayor has only meager resources. Some problems will be beyond reach and some alternatives will be unavailable because the city government lacks the necessary legal authority from the state to deal with them. Within the city government, even a "strong" mayor's formal authority is circumscribed. Many administrative boards, commissions, or special districts operate independently in important substantive areas. The city's legislative body must give approval for the authorization of new programs and for the voting of taxes and the appropriation of funds. Even the departments and agencies that are formally under the mayor's control as chief executive often have built-in tendencies toward inertia and self-direction, and the mayor's shortage of time and energy place serious limits on the extent to

[21]Quoted in Hentoff, *A Political Life,* p. 108.

[22]Sayre and Kaufman, *Governing New York City,* p. 659.

which he can actually influence how they are implementing their programs and otherwise dealing with the city's problems. Mayor Lindsay's wife, Mary, described the pressure of the constant shortage of time to deal with all the problems facing him:

> It's impossible to realize the demands of being mayor until you live it. . . . John could work twenty-four hours a day, seven days a week, and he'd never be finished. So the most important thing is to set your priorities. He's been very tough in limiting his schedule of appearances, but he still gets home late nearly every night—usually around midnight—and he brings along a folder four inches thick with just the most essential stuff he has to work on. Some of that he may do in the car riding back and forth, some he roars through with his secretary at the office, but some he has to do here. We try to work it out so he can have dinner with the children *one* night a week. . . .[23]

A mayor normally has a staff to help him in the performance of his many tasks. In addition to the secretaries, stenographers, and clerks, he will have a small number of deputies, aides, and other assistants at city hall to handle such matters as press relations, appointments, speechwriting, and liaison with the council and perhaps the state and federal governments. The mayor will also be able to draw at times on the services of certain overhead agency chiefs like the budget and personnel officers and the heads of the planning or redevelopment agencies. He can hire outside consultants or appoint study commissions or task forces to make recommendations and develop solutions about specific problems. Also, in a small handful of cities, including New York, Philadelphia, New Orleans, and San Francisco, the mayor can appoint a "chief administrative officer" (also called a "city administrator," or "managing director") to aid him in the day-to-day supervision, management, and coordination of the operating agencies.

But in almost no city is the mayor's staff sizable relative to the demands of his office nor are the various elements of that staff integrated in a way to give the mayor effective control of his own decision-making agenda. Few mayors have staffs sufficient to protect them from having their desks flooded with unimportant matters. Nor do they have staff to enable them to find pivotal issues easily and pull them to their own desks for decision early in the decision-making stage, when alternatives are still realistically open and not after the issues have reached emergency or crisis proportions, with the mayor's options having been limited and his choice largely preordained. Finally, few mayors have staffs that insure that those important issues that do reach his desk are accompanied with full information, i.e., all the

[23]Quoted in Hentoff, *A Political Life,* pp. 104-5.

interested parties have been consulted, their different viewpoints explored, the strength of those viewpoints highlighted and the weaknesses exposed.

Furthermore, a mayor's staff usually is unequipped to follow up on a systematic basis and insure that the mayor's decisions are carried out by his subordinates as he directed and intended. Still less does the typical mayor's staff have the capacity to provide him with systematic evaluations of the effectiveness of existing programs or with long-range program planning and development for emerging social problems to which the public will expect effective governmental solutions. Perhaps still more rare is the mayor who receives from his staff what Sayre and Kaufman call "political help and advice, supplied by persons sensitive to and sensible about the mayor's full dimensional role in the city's political contest, aware of the subtleties of strategy in the timing and the boldness, the caution, or the finality with which the mayor uses, for his purposes of leadership, the resources of his office."[24]

Shortage of Money

Yet even if the mayor were to be given the formal powers and staff to dominate the city's policy process, there are basic reasons why he would remain frustrated in trying to satisfy the demands and expectations focused upon him. Essentially every important new program or expansion of an existing program to improve the city government's performance requires additional money. Occasionally, the city government will already have the authority to impose new, or raise existing, taxes; the mayor then need only be deterred from finding the additional money by the anticipated ire of rebellious taxpayers and the possible flight of upper-income residents and of industry to lower tax jurisdictions. However, most often the city will be taxing to the limits of its powers, and so the mayor's being able to provide new remedies for the city's problems will depend on the state legislature's approving additional or increased taxes or providing more state aid—something that hardly any state legislature ever does in the amounts requested. Furthermore, when the mayor looks to Washington for anything approaching the funds needed, he normally finds that, despite the emergencies in his city, the alleviation of urban problems is almost never assigned top priority in presidential or congressional politics. The result of this constant shortage of funds is that the problem-solving demanded of the mayor becomes almost exclusively restricted to crisis-management, fighting fires, plugging holes, i.e., treating symptoms with little or no opportunity to

[24]Sayre and Kaufman, *Governing New York City,* p. 668. John P. Kotter and Paul Lawrence conclude in their study of twenty mayors, that in only two of the twenty cases did the mayor create a staff "whose resources were significantly useful to him." *Mayors in Action: Five Approaches to Urban Governance* (New York: Wiley, 1974), p. 82.

eliminate the underlying conditions breeding or maintaining the problems his city faces.

Finally, when because of inflation in the national economy the cost of a given amount of services, supplies, and construction is steadily rising, or when because of economic recession the yields of given income and sales taxes are decreasing, or as in the 1970s, when both inflation and recession hit simultaneously, a city's incoming revenues become insufficient to cover even the costs of maintaining the preexisting and normally already inadequate level of services. The mayor under those circumstances not only cannot make advances in solving problems but his job becomes the more desperate one of simply "holding on" or "surviving," with his key decisions reduced to determining what magnitude of "shortages" or "cuts" will be imposed on the different departments and programs.

Mutually Conflicting Demands and Expectations

Still another major source of frustration for a large-city mayor is that he is the object of mutually conflicting demands and expectations. Thus it is almost guaranteed that any important measure he proposes will generate opposition. Many of these conflicting demands and expectations are peculiar to highly particular issues: There are, for example, conflicts between those who stand to benefit from various protections to public health, safety, morals, or welfare by means of certain regulations and those whose conduct is to be regulated; conflicts between taxpayers and officials over the level of increases in, and the kinds and exact mixture of, taxes to be imposed; conflicts among those seeking to gain exclusive, lucrative franchises or sponsorships of urban renewal or otherwise subsidized housing projects; etc.

The more fundamental and frustrating set of conflicting demands and expectations focusing on the mayor in the late 1960s and 1970s are, however, those that emanate from two broad but incompatible groupings that make up his constituency: One is the poor, lower-class slum blacks who are demanding better conditions and services, together with those middle-class blacks and upper-middle- and upper-class whites who support them because of empathy, a sense of noblesse oblige, or self-interest in keeping the city "cool." The other grouping consists of the lower-middle-class and working-class whites (and even some blacks) who themselves feel hard-pressed economically and don't see the city government doing anything for them. This latter group defines any vigorous efforts by the mayor to have the city do more for slum blacks as being at its expense, in terms of its tax dollars, its jobs, a reduction of housekeeping services in its neighborhoods to meet the heavy costs of slum and welfare programs, and a "deterioration" or a "takeover" of its neighborhoods when black people move in as a result of enforcement of open-housing policies.[25]

Especially because of the great shortage of money facing large-city mayors, it is almost impossible to satisfy one segment of this basically two-part constituency without alienating the other. For if the mayor ignores the demands of the slum blacks he increases their anger and frustration, may violate his own personal sense of fairness and justice, and also raises the risk of their grievances erupting in riotous and other violent ways. On the other hand, if the mayor assigns high priority to showing concern for and providing improvement in services and other programs for slum blacks, he alienates the white workers and middle class who feel that their interests are being ignored. New York's Mayor Lindsay admitted that what led to his near defeat for reelection in 1969 was "the common theme that for personal or ideological reasons I had neglected the middle class of New York City in favor of the Manhattan affluent and the poor, especially the black poor. Among many New Yorkers early in 1969 you were likely to hear something like this about my administration:

> John Lindsay doesn't care about the typical, hard-working man who lives in Brooklyn, Queens, or the Bronx. . . . He wants to keep the city cool, so he pays off the blacks with welfare and poverty money, and he ties the hands of police by letting his young assistants interfere with police who try to stop rioters and criminals. . . .[26]

Grinding Personal Strain

As a result of limitations on his formal powers, lack of time and adequate staff, shortage of money, and mutually conflicting demands and expectations directed toward him, however hard the mayor of a large city tries, and however much of a policy innovator and champion he may be inclined to be, his chances for bringing about any spectacular achievement are slim, while the chances of things going wrong are almost perfect. The frustration of not being able to achieve important objectives plus the pain of having to face endless financial and other crises subject the typical large-city mayor to great personal strain. Furthermore, the easy accessibility of mayors gives aggrieved members of the citizenry many opportunities to vent their grievances directly to the mayor in person—often using other than the most polite language—thus adding to the unpleasantness of the job. One

[25]For an analysis of the constraints that this kind of cleavage imposes on mayoral leadership, see Charles H. Levine, *Racial Conflict and the American Mayor* (Lexington, Mass.: Heath and Co., 1974).

[26]Lindsay, *The City,* p. 22.

indicator of the great personal strain that large city mayors are subjected to is the increasingly large number who decide that they've "had enough" and choose not to run for reelection. Former Mayor Jerome Cavanaugh explained his own decision not to seek the office again after eight years as Detroit's chief executive as follows:

> It is *expected* that the mayor deal with crises day after day. And this is one of the major factors contributing to the tremendous physical and mental frustration which eventually wears guys down in these jobs after eight years. You can't sit and think about what you should be doing in this city five years from now, or ten years from now, because you're dealing with the politics of confrontation constantly. It's the only political job in America in which that's true. *That's the job.* It's fine to deal with crisis and confrontation if you have the resources to meet them. But when all you have is a limited amount of money and a few programs, and you're long on rhetoric, that just isn't enough.[27]

Former Atlanta Mayor Ivan Allen, who also chose not to run again after eight years in office, told the enormous pressures he felt from the job:

> The mayor happens to be the one public official who is readily available to all the people he represents. It's just a short spin down to City Hall. . . . [B]eing involved in these daily confrontations will upset anybody's stomach after a period of time. You don't walk into the middle of a race riot without losing a few years off your life. You don't meet unruly entrances into your churches or anticipate takeovers by students of colleges, or go through a fireman's strike, or all the picketing and boycotting and demonstration that have come out of the racial issue [without its taking its toll].[28]

Some mayors especially resent the lack of privacy in the job. Mayor Lindsay once told a reporter:

> The thing I've found the hardest to get used to is the goldfishbowl life here. You can't go to the bathroom without being observed. There's no such thing as a private conversation or a private visit. You're being watched all the time.[29]

Furthermore, there is the pressure of constantly having to see people who have problems and who demand the opportunity to explain them directly to

[27]Fred Powledge, "The Flight from City Hall," *Harper's Magazine,* November 1969, pp. 71-72.

[28]*Ibid.,* p. 81.

[29]Klein, *Lindsay's Promise,* p. 105.

the mayor. And refusing too many requests for meetings runs the risk of developing a reputation for being arrogant. As Lindsay again has explained:

> They won't settle for the Buildings commissioner, or the Police commissioner or the chairman of the City Commission on Human Rights. They want to see me. They wait until I arrive at City Hall and get my ear. Or they can wait until I leave and catch me.[30]

And once the mayor listens to the complaints,

> The problem is that the answers I give to their legitimate questions cannot, by definition, be satisfactory, unless the demand is for a specific, relatively low-cost request like a traffic light outside a school or the acceleration of an already-approved project. Usually, however, the complaints are about more basic problems in the city. We don't have enough police. The garbage isn't picked up frequently enough. The subway system is a disgrace. . . . I listen to their inquiries and answer them the best way I can. But it won't do to say that every neighborhood wants more police—the questioner doesn't live in "every neighborhood," he lives in *this* neighborhood, and he does not want danger on *his* streets. . . . Meanwhile the [telephone] calls keep coming. . . .[31]

Former Mayor Eric Jonsson of Dallas—a city that also has a city manager—described the overall job of mayor as:

> Being . . . like walking on a moving belt while juggling. Right off you've got to walk pretty fast to stay even. After you've been in office a short time people start throwing wads of paper at you. So now you've got to walk, juggle, and duck too. Then the belt starts to move faster, and people start to throw wooden blocks at you. About the time you're running like mad, juggling and ducking stones, someone sets one end of the belt on fire. Now if you can keep the things you are juggling in the air, stay on the belt, put out the fire, and not get seriously injured, you've found the secret to the job. . . .[32]

Mayors come to feel consequently that there is no way of winning in their job; it is only a question of how fast they lose. Lindsay quotes former

[30]*Ibid.,* p. 143.
[31]Lindsay, *The City,* pp. 63-64.
[32]Quoted, in Kotter and Lawrence, *Mayors in Action,* p. 175.

New Haven mayor Richard Lee as telling him in 1968 when there was some question of whether Lindsay would be offered (he was not) a gubernatorial appointment to fill the New York senatorial seat vacated as a result of the assassination of Robert Kennedy:

> Take my advice, take the Senate seat. . . . You can't possibly win in your job; none of us can. Get out while you can.[33]

As could be expected, the large-city mayoralty is not an ideal steppingstone for higher office. Since World War II only some half dozen mayors of large cities have gone on to statewide or national elective office, and none has done so in recent years. And not achieving these higher offices has not been due to lack of desire: Kotter and Lawrence established that seventeen of the twenty mayors they studied had strong ambitions for moving on to the senate, their governorship, or the presidency, yet *not one* made it even to a desired nonelective post like a cabinet office. As they explain the pattern:

> In most cases, our former mayors did not lose elections to higher offices, they lost the fight for nomination. Many even failed to get into the nomination ring. They were just ignored. To the almost unbelievable frustration of some of the men in this study, the mayoralty turned out to be a "dead-end" job. No matter where they wanted to go, it was impossible to get there from the mayor's office.[34]

REMAINING OPPORTUNITIES FOR MAYORAL INFLUENCE AND ACHIEVEMENT

As was said at the beginning of this chapter, the mayor of a large city is likely to be its single most influential actor. Yet with all the constraints impinging on the mayor's exertion of influence, his opportunities for producing significant changes in city governmental policies and programs are severely limited. The great bulk of the activities constituting a city government's policies and programs go on from year to year either unchanged or changed at the operating level just as if the mayor did not exist. Still, some mayors do demonstrate a higher degree of success in getting a handle on the policy process and imposing their own personal stamp on the city government's operation, and they do so in essentially four ways.

First, by the differences in the quality and backgrounds of appointments that mayors make to head the various departments and to constitute their

[33]Quoted in Lindsay, *The City,* p. 24.

[34]Kotter and Lawrence, *Mayors in Action,* p. 239.

staffs. These can make a difference in the general "tone" of an administration, in its honesty and absence of corruption, in its responsiveness and willingness to change approaches if old ones are not working, and in its commitment to improving "productivity," i.e., making a greater impact and producing a higher level of services with a given amount of manpower and money.

Second, by the concern that different mayors indicate through their statements and other activities for particular problems and the particular marginal distributions they make of "new money" or of "shortages" through the budget. Over a number of years, these incremental changes in funding can accumulate and thus strengthen or weaken some programs and agencies more than others.

Third, by the difference in the ability different mayors show in raising new money through the selling to the state legislature, the council, and the electorate of the need for new taxes and through their "entrepreneuring" of grants from the state and federal government and from foundations. Cunningham, for example, shows large disparities in obtaining federal urban renewal and antipoverty grants among the four mayors he studied. While Mayors Locher and Daley were managing to obtain for their cities an average of only $.06 and $3.84 per capita in annual urban renewal grants over a selected span of years, Barr (of Pittsburgh) and Lee were getting $20.49 and $59.56. Similarly, while Locher and Daley were receiving an average of only $9.05 and $8.88 per capital in annual grants for antipoverty programs, Barr and Lee's cities were receiving $12.32 and $21.82 respectively.[35]

Fourth, by the different degrees of success mayors demonstrate in remolding demands and expectations from disparate parts of their constituencies. Basically, the public support that a mayor maintains depends on how closely his performance is seen to approach demands and expectations. If performance cannot be significantly increased, the level of frustration, and especially of righteous indignation, may be at least kept from rising by a mayor who is able to "educate" his public about the "harsh realities" preventing any sharp improvement, thus lowering its expectations. An example would be convincing slum blacks that because of incurable shortages of money or technological impossibilities, drastic and large-scale changes could not be made in their conditions regardless of the strong desire on the mayor's part to do so. Furthermore, in a city that is seriously polarized by conflicting demands and strong mutual animosities, a mayor's ability to change some of the attitudes causing the polarization and to generate broad public support for needed programs will have a difference: he can foster a spirit of reconciliation and reduce tensions; and he may be influential in getting certain programs adopted that had been blocked by

[35] See Cunningham, *Urban Leadership,* Table 4, p. 85.

animosity to the groups that were to benefit from them. An example of this kind of reshaping of attitudes would be a mayor's convincing lower-middle and working-class whites both that conditions in black slums were so deplorable that they warranted any special effort being made by the city to improve them and that those improvements need not be at the expense of those lower-middle- and working-class whites.

Even with maximum ability in all these areas, normally the only success open to a large city mayor is to help keep the city government from losing ground on most problems, while managing, with luck, to inch ahead in one or two areas where especially energetic efforts are made. Yet to accomplish even this, the mayor in terms of policy style, more and more appears to need the rare and high talents of having the instincts of a policy champion and innovator coupled with the strategic and tactical skills of an opportunistic policy broker.

The caretaker and policy mediator mayor will not be inclined to seize any of the opportunities to improve conditions. Since the current crop of urban problems are not self-correcting and when ignored only grow, this type of policy style will not deflect the adverse trends now operating in large cities. A pure policy innovator and champion mayor may dramatize the seriousness of conditions and create a greater sense of urgency about them, but such dramatization may raise expectations for dramatic improvement. If the mayor cannot follow through and produce the expected improvements, the result may be a level of frustration higher than before. And if part of a policy innovator and champion mayor's style is to ignore any opposition rather than to compromise while compromise is possible, that kind of policy champion mayor may succeed in alienating nearly everyone while causing his actual accomplishments to be nil. The opportunistic policy broker mayor may succeed in prolonging his tenure in office by supporting only those programs that earn him more credit than antagonism, but those programs may do little to improve conditions in the city.

The combined "policy innovator and champion" and "opportunistic policy broker" mayor will, on the other hand, have the motivation from his champion side to deal with the most pressing and serious problems, and from his broker side that mayor will also be ready to make the necessary trades and concessions to build up a sufficiently strong supportive coalition. Furthermore, even if his instincts tell him that a segment of the population of his city—like slum blacks—is so overwhelmingly deprived that it deserves the highest and perhaps the only priority in the allocation of new funds and effort, his strategic sense will tell him that acting completely on that instinct will damage his image of impartiality and earn him the reputation of being a special pleader for one group. Being "out in front" for "what's right" on all controversial policies that come up may be gratifying to the soul, but such a stance will quickly erode the majority support among electorates that is needed to stay in office and will seriously impede cooperation with other officials sharing decision-making authority with the mayor. Unfortunately for large cities, the tightening "fiscal crunch" they are experiencing in the mid-1970s may force mayors with even the combined talents of a policy champion and a policy broker to use them primarily in imposing budgetary and personnel retrenchment in such a way as to cause minimum damage to performance rather than initiate any new advances.

10

City Managers and City Councilmen

One-fifth of the very largest cities of over 500,000 in population and nearly half of the cities with populations from 250,000 to 500,000 have no separately elected mayor with legal powers to function as the city's chief executive officer. Instead, there is a city manager appointed by the city council who holds the executive powers of a strong mayor for supervising and directing the city government's operating departments. Not being an elected official, the manager is not the city's chief of state and does not serve as its ceremonial head. But although there is uncertainty and ambiguity about the extent to which he does or should, the manager usually acts as the city's chief legislator. Normally, the city manager shares the chief ambassador functions with the official designated as mayor, and also shares with the mayor and other leaders of the city council the responsibilities of supreme emergency-handler.

Based on his performance of the functions clearly assigned to him by the city charter as well as some that are not, the city manager frequently becomes the most influential actor in his city's policy process. The actuality of the city manager's high influence conflicts with the theoretical concept of the manager as essentially a technician who administers policies established by others and thus raises questions about the legitimacy of a nonelected official exercising such extensive influence in policical systems that are supposedly governed democratically.

Broadly speaking, city councilmen—or aldermen as they are also called —exhibit an opposite paradox. While city charters grant to their councilmen weighty powers for influencing the policymaking process of their cities, almost invariably councilmen play only a modest role. Most often that role consists of virtually ritualistic ratification of policy proposals that mayors, managers, and other executive agency officials have originated and sponsored.

This limited impact that city councilmen have, has serious implications for a city's policymaking process: It reduces the visibility and therefore the accountability of that process to the public. It lessens the amount of control to which city bureaucracies are subjected by elected officials. And it limits the ability of members of the general public to influence city policies through their legislative representatives.

CITY MANAGER ROLES

Chief City Administrator

In almost every large city, council-manager charter language designates the manager to be the city's "chief administrative" (San Diego), "chief administrative and executive" (Dallas), or "chief executive and administrative" (Cincinnati) officer and requires him to supervise the administration of the affairs of the city and enforce its ordinances and laws. The city manager is almost invariably given the right (held in mayor-council cities by "strong" mayors) to appoint the heads of the various operating departments without any need for the council's approval and is given the unfettered right to remove those department heads from office.

The city manager also has strong-mayor type authority to prepare and submit to the council an executive budget. Finally, to further stress the intended dominance of the city manager within the executive branch, most council-manager charters contain a clause explicitly prohibiting council members from interfering with the manager's appointments or removals and requiring council members, except for the purpose of inquiry, to deal with officials and employees in the operating departments solely through the city manager.

The city manager thus has potent formal powers for performing his function as the city's chief administrator. Furthermore, to the extent that he has had professional training and/or long experience in public administration, the city manager also can demand that his subordinates comply with his wishes because of his purportedly greater administrative expertise. But, like the mayor of a mayor-council city, there are factors that operate to limit his influence as a chief executive: The city manager too is subject to a shortage of time, energy, and information that places definite limits on how thoroughly he can control executive branch decision-making. Here, however, he is somewhat better off than most mayors, both because he is less distracted by ceremonial duties and because no city manager's city or executive branch is among the very largest in size. Second, in a few cities, some managerial appointees—for example, the chief of police in San Diego—do need to be confirmed by the council, and additionally in some cities—e.g., Dallas and San Diego—a removed official can demand a written statement of the reasons for the removal and a hearing before the city council or the civil service commission. Furthermore, unlike the case in certain strong mayor-council cities, the manager's budget can be changed by the council by majority vote, and the manager, who is not an independently elected official, cannot veto those changes. Finally, even in council-manager cities, there are normally one or more independent boards and commissions, such as Dallas' Park Board and City Plan Commission, Cincinnati's Board of Park Commissioners, Board of Health, and Board of Rapid Transit Commissioners, San Diego's Funds Commission and City Planning Commission, or San Antonio's Library Trustees, whose members are appointed by the mayor or the council and not by the manager.

An additional constraint on the city manager's performance of his chief administrator function is that occasionally the mayor of the city manager's city may not be content with acting merely as a ceremonial head and presiding officer of the city council and may insist on providing competition to the manager for direction of the operating departments. In San Antonio, for example, soon after the council-manager system was adopted in 1952, the mayor sought to take over the chief executive function himself and to turn the city manager into a sort of administrative assistant. But after a short running battle between the mayor and the manager, the council (which in San Antonio elects the mayor from its membership) replaced the mayor with another councilman who had no executive aspirations.[1] In smaller cities, competition between the manager and the mayor, particularly if the mayor is separately elected by the people, apparently occurs more frequently.[2] A more recent study reports, however, that in some cities, the mayor and the manager form what is essentially a noncompetitive team that provides policy leadership to the city government.[3]

City Legislative Leader

Although the city manager is the appointee of the council in a council-manager city, he nevertheless provides much of the leadership for the performance of the council's legislative tasks. Council-manager charters

[1]See Iola O. Hessler, *29 Ways to Govern a City* (Cincinnati: Hamilton County Research Foundation, 1966), p. 47.

[2]See Gladys M. Kammerer, "Role Diversity of City Managers," *Administrative Science Quarterly,* 8 (1964): 421-42.

[3]Robert P. Boynton and Deil S. Wright, "Mayor-Manager Relationships in Large Council-Manager Cities: A Reinterpretation," *Public Administration Review,* 31 (1971): 28-36.

usually give him the right to recommend to the council such measures as he may deem desirable, to report on the financial condition and needs of the city, to submit a proposed annual budget, and to prepare any other reports the council may request. In addition, in most cities the manager is entitled to attend all council meetings and take part in the discussions, though without having a vote.

The language in council-manager charters simply reflects the expectation that the city manager will be one important source of information and recommendation for the council's deliberations.[4] But the fact is that the manager of a council-manager city, like the mayor of a mayor-council city, is the only city official with fulltime, day-to-day responsibility for the overall operations of the city government. Because communications about problems and policies are directed primarily to him and because of his continuing contacts with the operating departments, he typically has the best access to information about developing problems and the staff for formulating proposals to deal with them. Furthermore, he is the conduit for many routine changes in city legislation desired by the various operating departments. Also, it is his proposed executive budget that sets the stage for legislative action on appropriations. For all these reasons, the manager's recommendations constitute the main part of the council's agenda, and these recommendations generally are taken seriously by the council and most of the time approved.

Still, the only weapon normally available to the manager for securing such approval is persuasion based on presumed expertise. And given the manager's subordinate formal status, even in trying to be persuasive, he must observe a certain etiquette: The manager does not, for example, propose a new policy at a public council meeting "cold," but "sounds out" the council informally beforehand to see what "will go." If the manager discovers that strong resistance exists among council members to his proposal, he does not "push" it beyond a certain point. Unlike a mayor, almost never does a manager attempt to go over the heads of the council to the public, both because he, himself, is probably convinced that becoming involved in a public controversy with the council is not an appropriate part of his role—the city managers' "Code of Ethics" specifically enjoins him to avoid such confrontations—and because if he did, the council might decide to fire him and replace him with another manager.[5]

[4]See Clarence E. Ridley, *The Role of the City Manager in Policy Formulation* (Chicago: International City Managers' Association, 1958), pp. 18–19.

[5]This formulation of the etiquette normally observed by city managers is based primarily on Ridley, *The Role of the City Manager,* whose findings are derived from questionnaires filled out by eighty-eight city managers and from interviews with approximately half of these eighty-eight. Among those completing the questionnaires were the city managers of ten of the large, council-manager cities. A more recent study of the city managers in small and middle-sized cities in the San Francisco Bay area finds similar self-denying but longevity-prolonging attitudes. See Ronald O. Loveridge, *City Managers in Legislative Politics* (Indianapolis: Bobbs-Merrill, 1971).

Other Functions

As has already been indicated, the manager does not serve as his city's ceremonial head. Council-manager charters explicitly specify that the mayor be recognized as the official head of the city for all ceremonial purposes, and city managers themselves appear to agree that they should be careful not to convey the impression to the public that they are out in front of the elected representatives:

> This frequently revolves around such matters as making sure that the mayor not the manager represents the city at official functions; the mayor not the manager sits at the head table when municipal officials are in the spotlight; the mayor not the manager rides in a position of honor in the parade.[6]

Neither charter language nor any empirical studies give hard data on the extent to which city managers act as their city's "chief ambassador" to other units of government. Since the mayor is formally recognized as the city's chief of state, he has some claim to represent the city, particularly when dealing with elective state and federal officials. On the other hand, the mayor, being a parttime offical, may prefer to let the manager carry the main burden of conducting the city's external relations. The sketchy evidence that exists suggests that the manager serves as chief ambassador to state and federal executive agencies, as in negotiating for grants under existing programs or for modification of administrative regulations. It also suggests that an elected official like the mayor normally deals with the governor and state legislative leaders, appears before congressional committees or, if the necessity arises, goes to see the President. Congressional committee hearings concerning urban policies, for example, rarely list city managers as having testified on behalf of their cities. Similarly, the lobbyist kept in Washington by San Diego—a council-manager city whose extensive military installations provide a large proportion of the city's income—is employed not by the manager, but directly by the mayor and council.[7]

As the official in overall charge of the day-to-day operations of the city government, the city manager is generally expected to provide recommendations to the council for coping with urgent, emergency problems. This expectation is sometimes reflected in charter language designating the city manager "chief conservator of the peace," a term applied to the mayor in

[6] Ridley, *The Role of the City Manager,* p. 52.

[7] David Greenstone, "A Report on Politics in San Diego," (Cambridge: Joint Center for Urban Studies of the Massachusetts Institute of Technology and Harvard University, 1962, mimeo). See also Hessler, *29 Ways to Govern a City,* pp. 59-64; and Kammerer, "Role Diversity."

mayor-council cities. The San Diego charter, for example, specifies that "In case of general conflagration, rioting, flood, or other emergency menacing life and property, the manager shall marshal all the forces of the different Departments of the City for the maintenance of the general security, and shall have the power to deputize. . . ."[8] On the other hand, council-manager charters also authorize the mayor in times of public danger or emergency and with the consent of council to take direct command of the police, maintain order, and enforce the laws, thus reflecting the further expectation that in times of supreme emergency, not the appointed manager, but an elected official be in charge.

IMPLICATIONS OF MANAGERIAL POLICY LEADERSHIP

Because the city manager is an appointive official and because the rationale of the council-manager plan stresses his role as a professionally-trained administrator responsible for implementing in a neutral way policies established by the city council, there has always been some uneasiness about the extent of the manager's actual participation in the formulation of city policies. The inventor of the council-manager plan, Richard S. Childs, and many early managers thought it appropriate for the manager to be a policy recommender. But other early supporters of the manager system believed that the promotion of policies by the manager would undesirably inject him into politics and would lead to his dismissal whenever those policies became unpopular.[9]

The first City Managers' Code of Ethics, adopted by the International City Managers' Association in 1924, stated flatly that "No manager should take an active part in politics." The context suggests, however, that the term "politics" was narrowly conceived to mean only involvement in elections and open controversies over policies with the council and not to mean all attempts to influence the substantive content of council policy-making. In the 1938 reformulation of the Code of Ethics, the original flat prohibition against politics was softened to "The City Manager is in no sense a political leader" and his responsibility to provide "the council with information and advice" in order that policy "may be intelligent and effective" was explicitly affirmed. The manager was, however, enjoined to encourage "positive discussions" on policy by the council instead of "passive acceptance of his recommendations" and, while informing the

[8]Article V, sec. 28, Charter of 1961.

[9]See Gladys M. Kammerer et al., *City Managers in Politics* (Gainsville: University of Florida Press, 1962), pp. 7-8. Also see Leonard D. White, *The City Manager* (Chicago: University of Chicago Press, 1927).

"community . . . on municipal affairs," to keep himself "in the background by emphasizing the importance of facts."[10]

The latest version of the Code, formulated in 1972, no longer contains any explicit statement of denial of a political role for the manager. It instead asserts that the city manager shall "submit policy proposals to elected officials [and] provide them with facts and advice for making decisions and setting community goals." There is also no longer any admonition to the manager to discourage "passive acceptance of his recommendations" by the council or to keep himself "in the background" when informing the public. The only limitation remaining in the Code on the manager's activities is that he "refrain from participation in the election of the members of his employing legislative body and from all partisan political activities which would impair his performance as a professional administrator."[11]

The doctrine of the council-manager movement has obviously changed to accommodate itself to the increasingly apparent reality that however much the city manager stays out of election campaigns and public controversies, he does not merely carry out policies established by others. Normally, the manager plays a leading role in the process by which those policies are made. As early as 1940, Stone, Price, and Stone, in their case study of fifteen council-manager cities, pointed out that:

> It is generally impossible for a city manager to escape being a leader in matters of policy, for it is an essential part of his administrative job to make recommendations. The most important municipal policy is embodied in the budget, and the city manager, of course, must prepare and propose the budget.[12]

In another study of three middle-sized (i.e., population of 50,000–80,000) council-manager cities, Charles Adrian similarly found that the manager and his administrator were "the principal sources of policy innovation and leadership."[13] Also, Ridley reports that all eighty-eight of the city managers responding to his questionnaire felt a "definite responsibility" to participate in policy; seventy-seven of the eighty-eight stated that as a matter of course they initiate policy; and the managers calculated that ideas

[10]For a fuller analysis of the changes in the International City Managers' Association concepts of proper managerial conduct, see Hugo Wall, "Changing Concepts of Managerial Leadership," *Public Management,* 36 (1954): 50-53.

[11]*City Management Code of Ethics* (Washington, D.C.: International City Management Association, 1972), p. 9.

[12]Harold A. Stone, Don K. Price, and Kathryn H. Stone, *City Manager Government in the United States* (Chicago: Public Administration Service, 1940), p. 243.

[13]Charles R. Adrian, "A Study of Three Communities," *Public Administration Review,* 18 (1958): 208-14.

filtered through or originated by themselves and departmental personnel accounted for 75 to 90 percent of all policies adopted by the city council.[14]

As the recent study by Loveridge explains:

> Exposed and required to do something about the problems of the city, the city manager cannot avoid initiating some kind of policy action. Because of such resources as time, expertise, position, and a near monopoly of technical information, the manager is likely to participate in decisions on how values should be allocated. The same resources again mandate the manager's participation in the promotion of chosen alternatives. . . . And, finally, implementation is the one activity that everyone agrees is the city manager's business; and, as students of public administration tell us, administrators have considerable discretion in interpreting legislation.[15]

The fact that the manager actively promotes policy proposals and that a large proportion of his recommendations are adopted is not in itself violative of American democratic ideology. Ridley reports that council members themselves expected their city managers to be "idea men" and not to have to be pushed for suggestions. Consequently, if managers did no more than list feasible alternatives for dealing with certain given problems, along with the advantages and disadvantages of each alternative, they would simply be helping the council to achieve its own ends. The critics of the council-manager system suspect, however, that managers do not, in fact, present to the council all the alternatives they know to exist. And the critics believe that the managers similarly do not always describe the disadvantages of their own recommendations as fully as the possible advantages. A number of city managers admitted to a University of Florida research team, for example, that "they had 'learned' to send only one proposal to the council because several alternatives would only 'confuse' the council members."[16] Furthermore, because not all problems are as visible to the council as to the manager, the manager's choosing not to call some matter to the council's attention almost insures that the council will not deal with it at all.

In short, given the city manager's near monopoly of information about problems and alternatives, relative to the part-time political amateurs who generally constitute the councils in council-manager cities, the manager is in a strong position on most issues to limit the range of possible policies that the council considers and to reduce the council essentially to the role of

[14]Ridley, *The Role of the City Manager,* pp. 3–4, 19.

[15]Loveridge, *City Managers in Legislative Politics,* p. 112.

[16]Kammerer, "Role Diversity," p. 434.

saying yes or no to his own policy recommendations. There is no firm evidence available that indicates how often managers do manipulate their councils in this fashion and thus cause them to adopt policies that they would otherwise reject if they had additional information or time for independent analysis of the logic of the problem. But when managers do this, there takes place a perversion of the principle of democratic accountability, with the policy preferences of appointed officials being imposed on elected officials rather than vice versa.

There is, ironically, another line of criticism of the city manager's policy leadership. This criticism is that however unduly strong that leadership may be on proposals he chooses to recommend, the typical manager because of temperament and training is primarily oriented toward "caretaker," "housekeeping," and narrowly managerial problems and fails to provide bold policy leadership for the solution or alleviation of the massive social problems that currently plague large cities. Most of the early managers had been trained as engineers. And although more contemporary managers are likely to have been graduates of university city manager programs or at least to have studied public or business administration,[17] they still do not appear to come to their jobs with any great awareness of political and social processes and issues or skills at forming political coalitions to support controversial programs. As Banfield and Wilson have explained:

> There are many exceptions, of course, some of them very conspicuous ones, but the impression is unavoidable that managers as a class are better at assembling and interpreting technical data, analyzing the logic of a problem, and applying rules to particular cases than they are . . . at manipulating people, either in face-to-face contacts or through the media of communications.[18]

Furthermore, these critics contend, even if a particular manager happens to be a socially-sensitive, "innovator-champion" type, he cannot be overly aggressive with the council in pressing for the adoption of proposals that will normally be controversial or expensive or both. This is primarily because he lacks the moral authority, the prestige, and the fixed term that comes from election to office. Nor, the critics continue, can he find extensive opportunities, as mayors do during election campaigns and at ceremonial occasions, for shaping public opinion to recognize the urgency of a problem or for building up the personal popularity to provide him with diffuse support despite his advocacy of policies that might not be universally

[17]See "An Analysis of City Managers," *Public Management,* 36 (1954): 5.

[18]Edward C. Banfield and James Q. Wilson, *City Politics* (Cambridge, Mass.: Harvard University Press and the M.I.T. Press, 1963), p. 174.

appealing. As Ridley warns, "Occasionally the manager finds that it is advisable to take a forward position in recommending a policy, but he cannot afford to get too far ahead of the council or the citizens. . . . In most of the highly controversial questions, managers hope that members of council will assume the initiative."[19] And finally, the critics claim that because neither members of the council nor other political actors can normally take up the slack left by these shortcomings in the manager's policy leadership, the result is status-quo oriented, unenterprising, socially-unresponsive city government.[20]

The most persuasive line of argument supporting the critics of the council-manager system is that since even with his larger resources, an elective mayor is not often effective in leading his city to establish policies that have a significant impact in the alleviation of its ills, a city manager, with his smaller resources, lower prestige, and inability to use all the roles the mayor plays in mutually supportive combinations, must necessarily be less effective still. Indeed, it is arguable that a council-manager system is no more conducive even to procedural good government than is a strong mayor with a competent chief administrative officer to whom he can delegate day-to-day supervision of the operating departments.[21] For those who accept this premise, the council-manager system appears to offer little clear advantage to large cities and yet carries the major disadvantage of preventing the chief advocate of policies, who is necessarily the manager, from being directly subject to the retaliation or approbation of the electorate.

It is perhaps for these reasons that the council-manager plan has not found wide favor in very large cities. In small cities or suburban villages having homogeneous communities and no severe outstanding problems demanding vigorous, expensive, or controversial solutions, managerial leadership has been more acceptable. Here the issues in local government are often what is the best—or at least a satisfactory—way to promote goals shared by the whole community. And frequently the resources are easily available to do it. Consequently the ability to assemble technical data to show that a particular proposal will accomplish desired objectives may be all the executive leadership that is required. And it is this kind of executive leadership that city managers have typically been best equipped to provide.

[19]Ridley, *The Role of the City Manager,* pp. 19–21.

[20]Part of this kind of criticism can be found in Duane Lockard, *The Politics of State and Local Government* (New York: Macmillan, 1963), pp. 446–49; and Banfield and Wilson, *City Politics,* pp. 182–85.

[21]See Wallace S. Sayre, "The General Manager Idea for Large Cities," *Public Administration Review,* 14 (1954), 253-58; Demetrios Caraley, *New York City's Deputy Mayor—City Administrator* (New York: Citizens Budget Commission, 1966).

CITY COUNCILMEN

It is in the city council (or, more exactly, in the hands of various-sized majorities of councilmen) that city charters vest the legislative power of the city. The legislative power is a large one. It normally involves enacting ordinances or local laws establishing new or changed city regulative or benefactory policies or programs. It extends to levying taxes or authorizing the borrowing of money and to taking, i.e., condemning, private property for public use. And it includes fixing the details of the structure of the city government and the salaries of its officials and employees and appropriating money for the city government's capital expenditures and current operations.

The councilmen can, of course, exercise their legislative power only within various limits set by relevant local, state, and federal laws and by constitutional and charter provisions. Furthermore, that exercise is further subject in mayor-council cities to a veto by the mayor, which is however overridable, usually by the vote of an extraordinary majority. And in certain cities the exercise of the council's powers with respect to specified categories of legislation (for example, special borrowing, basic structural changes in the city government) is subject to the approval of the voters in various kinds of public referenda.

Either by explicit charter grant or implicitly because of the necessity of having information in order to perform their law-enacting function, councilmen ordinarily also have the power to conduct investigations of any part of the city government or of other matters on which they may legislate. In this connection they can compel the attendance of witnesses and the production of various papers, records, and other evidence relevant to the inquiry.

Depending on the type of city government, councilmen may also have some nonlegislative powers over the executive branch. In manager-council cities the council appoints and removes the manager, and in some weak mayor-council cities, the council must approve the appointment and at times pass on the dismissal of mayoral appointees. Occasionally in weak mayor-council systems, the council even possesses supervisory powers over the operating departments. Finally, the councilmen ordinarily hold the "residual power" of the city, meaning the right to exercise any function deemed to be within the city's scope of governmental authority that is not assigned to other city officials or agencies.

The Exercise of Councilmanic Authority

Although the legislative authority vested in city councils theoretically should permit its members to become independent and perhaps even dominant forces in the determination of city policies, councilmen almost invariably play less stellar roles: They content themselves most often with routinely adopting policies proposed by mayors, managers, or other executive officials; they occasionally delay, amend, or reject such proposals; and only rarely do they adopt policies originated by their own membership. In certain weak mayor-council cities, councilmen do, however, sometimes gain a strong voice in administrative decision-making within the operating departments generally, and in all cities individual councilmen intercede with executive agencies on behalf of constituents or other clients.

Routinely Ratifying Executive Proposals. Although there are no statistical studies demonstrating the proposition, it is clear from newspaper accounts, case studies, and other impressionistic evidence that councilmen exercise their authority most often by routinely ratifying proposals of executive officials after fairly perfunctory, independent examination. Actually, this should not be too surprising. Most such proposals are uncontroversial, effecting technical changes in existing policies, promoting overwhelmingly accepted purposes, or containing details that are either too insignificant, too boring, or too complicated to make it worthwhile to exert the time and energy to master them in order possibly to come up with more desirable alternatives.

Of the approximately 2,100 local laws passed by the New York City Council in the eighteen-year period from 1938 to 1956, for example, some 30 percent gave names to streets, parks, and playgrounds, 25 percent made detailed alterations in the city's building code (such as changing the specifications for the valves to be used in certain kinds of construction work) and 12 percent transferred property from the jurisdiction of one city governmental agency or officer to another![22] In other words, fully two-thirds of the local laws adopted by the council of the largest city in the country concerned matters that not more than a handful of persons cared about. There is no evidence to indicate that the proportion of bills that deal with essentially trivial matters, but that because of state legislative or charter provisions or the language of past city legislation require formal legislative action, is any lower in other large cities.

Not all legislative proposals routinely adopted by city councils, however, concern minutiae. Some of the proposals establish important new benefactory programs, impose new regulations on vital areas of activity, levy additional taxes to support the normally increasing expenditures of the city government, or determine the sites of important new public facilities. Furthermore, the formal adoption of the annual expense budget is an act crammed full with policy implications and one that national and state

[22]Wallace S. Sayre and Herbert Kaufman, *Governing New York City* (New York: Norton, 1965), pp. 611-12.

legislative bodies have traditionally used to influence governmental outputs. Yet the number and size of changes that councils tend to make in the budgetary requests of the mayor, the manager, or departments—as the case may be, depending on the form of government—are amazingly tiny. The New York city council, in the same eighteen-year span previously referred to (1938–56), passed on nineteen expense budgets submitted by various mayors, totalling about $22 billion. The council made no attempt at all to cut the budget on fifteen of those nineteen occasions (during this period the council was not permitted to raise, but only to cut amounts), and the combined cuts sought to be made on the other four occasions amounted to slightly more than $3 million, or less than two one-hundredths of 1 percent of the money requested. Once again, there is no evidence to indicate that the New York City situation is atypical.[23] Banfield reports, for example, the following account of a Boston city councilman's experience in serving as chairman of a subcommittee to review a city budget of $100 million:

> When a department head came in, the usual question was: "How are you, Joe? Is there enough money for personnel in your budget? . . ."
>
> The first witness at my first hearing was the police commissioner.
>
> "Commissioner," I said, "would you like to give us the broad outlines of your programs for the year ahead?"
>
> "No," he said, "I would not."
>
> That was the tone of most of the hearings. . . .
>
> Usually one or two other councillors sat with me. Their contribution was largely social—calling people by their first names. When I would manage to work some witness into some kind of a pocket with questions about where the money was going, some councilman would interrupt.
>
> "May I ask a question, Mr. Chairman?"
>
> "Certainly."
>
> "Joe, how do you manage to do such a fine job with so little money?"
>
> "It isn't easy, but we try. . . ."
>
> When the hearings were over, I recommended about $500,000 in cuts. It was amusing to see what happened. The committee members were whimsical; they'd give me a cut for no reason at all, except, you know —"he's not a bad guy after all"—and then they'd deny me the next one. In that way they cut the $500,000 down to about $200,000 in subcommittee. Then on the floor that was cut down to about $100,000.[24]

[23]See, for example, the accounts of the influence of councils in Atlanta, Boston, Detroit, El Paso, Los Angeles, Miami, Philadelphia, St. Louis, and Seattle in Edward C. Banfield, *Big City Politics* (New York: Random House, 1966).

[24]*Ibid.*, pp. 41–42.

On the basis of his investigations in Cleveland, Detroit, and Pittsburgh, Crecine has explained why the influence of the city council on the budget is a limited one:

> . . . The primary reason is more one of cognitive and informational constraints than lack of interest. The city budget is a complex document when it reaches the council. The level of detail makes it virtually impossible to consider all or even a majority of items independently. The sheer volume of information to be processed limits the ability of a council, without its own budget staff, to consider the budget in a sophisticated or complex manner.
>
> Perhaps a more important computational constraint is the balanced budget requirement. If there is no slack in the budget the mayor presents to council, any increase the council makes in any account category must be balanced with a corresponding decrease in another account or with tax increase. So, in the presence of a revenue constraint, the council cannot consider elements of the budget independently as is done in Congress. . . .[25]

Delaying, Modifying, or Rejecting Executive Proposals. Councilmen also exercise their authority by resisting executive proposals, occasionally delaying, amending, and even rejecting them completely. For obvious reasons, councilmen are especially likely to be resistant to proposals that seek to effect structural changes that will redistribute authority away from the council and to executive officials. Thus, the Los Angeles council has consistently refused to approve the submission of charter amendments to the voters proposed by a succession of mayors and backed by various study commissions that would have strengthened the mayoralty, particularly by increasing its control and decreasing that of the council over the operating departments.

A second set of circumstances under which councilmen are likely to be more than normally resistant to executive proposals is when, in a de facto or de jure partisan mayor-council city, a majority of councilmen and the mayor are of opposite parties or of opposite factions of the same party. Of course, the councilmen's commitment to the continued operation of the city government will restrain them from rejecting proposals that are necessary to avoid breakdowns in city services. Resistance surfaces mostly with respect to proposals that appear to give the mayor electoral advantages but whose defeat will not cause any serious harm. In 1966 and again in 1967, for example, the lopsided Democratic majority of New York's city

[25]John P. Crecine, "A Simulation of Municipal Budgeting: The Impact of a Problem Environment," in Ira Sharkansky, ed., *Policy Analysis in Political Science,* (Chicago: Markham Publishing, 1970), pp. 291–92.

council refused to appropriate money to staff neighborhood "little city halls" as requested by then Republican (through self-proclaimed nonpartisan and later Democrat) Mayor Lindsay. They expected that he would use them to strengthen his following among the electorate by having the city halls perform the kinds of personal services and favors traditionally given out by Democratic clubhouses and councilmen.

In Philadelphia and New Orleans in recent decades, a machine-orientated Democratic faction controlling the council has at times dealt harshly with proposals of mayors who were elected to office with the support of their party's "reform" faction.[26] And in Newark after Kenneth Gibson was elected mayor in 1970, an anti-Gibson majority opposed the mayor's plan for conducting an independent audit of the city's books, opposed the creation of several new posts proposed by Gibson, and even refused to approve an application for a $1.5 million federal grant. The council charged that the federal monies would finance a personal political organization for Mayor Gibson.

Personal animosity toward a mayor or manager as a result of his personality characteristics is still another cause of resistance to certain of his proposals. Mayor Yorty, for example, so infuriated the Los Angeles council that in 1963 it cut entirely out of the budget the salaries for his five "field secretaries."[27] Some of Mayor Lindsay's troubles with the New York city council during his first year in office were apparently due to the manner in which he treated its members: According to one source, Lindsay had been ". . . arrogant, demanding, and totally uninterested in anyone else's problems. . . . He spent most of his time pounding the table and threatening people."[28] The councilmen became noticeably less belligerent during Lindsay's second year after the mayor had begun, among other things, to pay courtesy calls at their offices, to entertain them at cocktail parties at the mayor's residence, and to take care that members of the council were on the speaker's platform at any ceremonies that involved them or their districts. A study of council-manager cities found that councilmen were annoyed and became less accommodating in approving a city manager's recommendations if they perceived the manager as "blunt," "bullheaded," "inflexible," "somewhat snobbish," "cold and unfeeling," "proud and self-satisfied," "stubborn," "red-tape happy," "too formalistic and business-like," "undiplomatic," "arrogant," "looks down his nose."[29]

[26]See William H. Brown, Jr. and Charles E. Gilbert, "Capital Programming in Philadelphia," *American Political Science Review,* 54 (1960): 659-68; Hessler, *29 Ways to Govern a City.* For an analysis of the activities of an anti-mayoral faction in a small city, see J. Leiper Freeman, "A Case Study of the Legislative Process in Municipal Government," in John C. Wahlke and Heinz Eulau, eds., *Legislative Behavior* (Glencoe, Ill.: The Free Press, 1959), pp. 228–37.

[27]Ed Ainsworth, *Maverick Mayor* (Garden City, N.Y.: Doubleday, 1966), p. 186.

[28]*New York Times,* May 1, 1967.

[29]Jeptha J. Carrell, "The City Manager and His Council: Sources of Conflict," *Public Administration Review,* 22 (1962): 203-8.

A final cause of resistance to executive proposals is policy disagreement. Such disagreement may result from personal differences of opinion, but most often it arises from differences between the mayor's or manager's and the councilmen's felt constituency, which causes them to be more responsive to different sets of interests. A mayor or manager is elected by and/or feels responsive to a city-wide constituency. His proposals for spending or capital improvement or taxes are likely to represent an attempt to balance the needs of different parts of the city against each other and all the needs against the resources available. District-elected councilmen, on the other hand, want to modify the mayor's proposals in order to better satisfy the needs of their particular areas of the city. This may involve securing services and desired facilities or protecting these areas against projects that are considered dislocative or otherwise unpopular, however necessary it may be for them to be built somewhere. In St. Louis, for example, the mayor, according to Robert Salisbury, usually leads a coalition that proposes measures to improve the city's overall social and business climate, rehabilitate slums, and provide full city services throughout the city. The members of the Board of Aldermen, however, are:

> not particularly concerned with broad social or economic policy as such. [They are] concerned rather with the immediate needs of effective ward organization. . . . Jobs are crucial, but so also are specific contracts for building contractors, stop signs and parking regulations, assistance in getting into a public housing project, route location for a throughway, and so on. . . . [I]ndividual attention from the Board of Aldermen [is] achieved through a log-rolling system known locally as aldermanic courtesy. . . . Aldermanic courtesy does create conflict, since the granting of individual favors—e.g., a stop sign in front of a confectionery—often runs counter to broader policy concerns—e.g., a master traffic plan.[30]

Whereas the mayor and his downtown, large businessmen and middle- and upper-middle income supporters are "sympathetic to the needs for more tax revenue," the St. Louis aldermen, feeling responsive mostly to neighborhood small businessmen and lower-income homeowners, exhibit a "sharp antipathy toward any suggestions of increased tax rates."[31]

Similarly, in Philadelphia, the mayor and his planning and other executive aides normally propose capital budgets that stress the project needs of operating departments on an integrated basis over the long run. The councilmen, on the other hand, shift some priorities in order to bring about

[30]Robert Salisbury, "St. Louis Politics: Relationships Among Interests, Parties, and Governmental Structures," *Western Political Quarterly,* 13 (1960): 498-507.

[31]*Ibid.*

"regional [i.e., neighborhood] parity" in the short run distribution of projects being built. As Brown and Gilbert have related:

> Philadelphia's Council, dominated by one party, makes its capital program decisions in the closed caucus of that party, and the decision is reportedly characterized by a good deal of trading in which the party leadership is careful to see that everyone gets something to show his district, though no one gets all he wants. . . . Council's orientation to capital programming tends to be immediate and concrete rather than long-run and abstract. . . . Councilmen argue that *they* are the "experts" on scheduling since they know what the people want at the moment.
>
> Such abstract investment criteria as professional standards for service levels and facilities, or land use prescriptions, do not weigh heavily with Council. . . . Council prefers "visible" projects (*e.g.*, health centers over storm sewers), by which is really meant "politically popular," . . . It is clear that recreation centers, health centers, and fire stations have been especially popular in Council. . . .[32]

Like the St. Louis aldermen, Philadelphia's councilmen, and particularly those elected at-large, appear to feel more responsive than the mayor to taxpaying as opposed to project-demanding interests and so they usually make small cuts in the overall capital budget while reordering its priorities.[33] The policy differences between the council and the mayor can also be on very specific grounds: The Boston Council in recent years, for example, drastically reduced the amounts requested for purchase of police cars because the councilmen simply believed in their police "walking the beat."[34]

Enacting Council-Originated Proposals. On rare occasions, councilmen exercise their legislative authority by enacting into law measures originated and promoted by one of their own members. Such measures may come from a councilman who has a pet interest in a particular subject-matter or who decides to espouse the cause of some interest group seeking enactment of the legislation. An extra incentive comes if the councilman has an interest in seeking higher office and believes that the particular legislative measure will be perceived as socially useful or popular, thus providing him with good advertising and enhancing his reputation. In the post-World War II period in New York City, for example, councilmen originated important laws improving rent control, banning discrimination in the sale or rental of private housing, and restricting air pollution.

[32] Brown and Gilbert, "Capital Programming," pp. 664–65.
[33] *Ibid.*
[34] Banfield, *Big City Politics,* p. 42.

Intervening In and Supervising Administrative Operations. In all cities, councilmen occasionally influence the policy process by intervening on behalf of constituents or other favored parties to bring about some specific administrative decision. These interventions may be for such things as improved housekeeping services and facilities in certain neighborhoods, exceptions in the application of certain regulations, or the grant of some disputed benefit. In the handful of weak mayor-council cities (Atlanta, Los Angeles, Milwaukee, Minneapolis, and Seattle), councilmen have a more continuous and substantial impact on administrative decision-making: They have power to withhold approval of administrative appointments or removals; they share in the preparation or changing of the budget for the administrative departments without the possibility of a mayoral veto; and they serve on committees responsible for supervising the operations of particular departments.

In Atlanta, for example, committees of aldermen exercise significant amounts of administrative control over different city departments. Although the heads of the operating departments are nominated by the mayor, they can be elected to their posts only by the board of aldermen. And though the mayor appoints the members and chairmen of aldermanic committees, once they are appointed, the committee chairmen (and particularly the chairman of the finance committee, which controls the budget) manage to develop considerable independent power.[35] According to Banfield, "strong committee chairmen not infrequently dominate departments and function less as legislators than as administrators."[36] Similarly, in Los Angeles, where the council meets in session each weekday morning and in committee most afternoons, it is the members of the council that serve as the primary liaison between disgruntled citizenry and the operating departments. District branches of operating departments, for example, are in the habit of responding to requests of councilmen elected from that district without reference to their administrative superiors in the departmental headquarters. Each district's councilman becomes "the administrator of the city services in his district."[37]

> The councilmen are, of course, interested in the problems of their districts, not those of the city as a whole. The districts are big enough to be cities themselves (they range from 140,000 to 200,000 in population and up to 67 square miles in area). For the convenience of constituents, some of whom live so far from city hall that they would have to pay a toll charge to telephone it, most councilmen maintain a branch office staffed by a field secretary. A constituent who thinks the palm

[35]*Ibid.*, p. 23; Hessler, *29 Ways to Govern a City*, p. 18.
[36]Banfield, *Big City Politics*, p. 23.
[37]Quoted, *ibid.*, p. 84.

> trees along the street need trimming, who is bothered by a barking dog, or who wants bigger storm drains, calls the councilman, who takes the matter up with the appropriate city department. . . . As much as 25 percent of the work of a district public works office . . . is done at the request of a councilman and without any specific order from the board in charge of the department.[38]

In Minneapolis and Seattle, the various administrative departments operate largely under the direction of different standing committees. One result in Minneapolis is that levels of housekeeping services vary in different parts of the city; residents of wards represented on the council by senior aldermen on important committees enjoy better services than those less fortunately sited.[39] In Seattle, the committees have the power to clear the separate ordinances required to appropriate funds for the different departments and even to clear certain kinds of departmental purchases and hiring of personnel. So powerful are these council committees that they function as the normal channel of public access to the departments.[40] Indeed, with department heads tending to be more responsive to the council committee having jurisdiction over them than to the mayor, the executive branch has been described by one Seattle city planner as consisting of "a network of little administrative hierarchies, each with a council committee at its apex."[41]

CAUSES AND IMPLICATIONS OF COUNCILMANIC DOCILITY

To subject executive proposals to searching, critical review and possible revision and to exercise close supervision over administrative operations require large amounts of time, energy, information, and incentive. Councilmen usually have none of these to spare after attending to the essential routine business the council must deal with. Except for the few councilmen who hold leadership positions as presiding officers, floor leaders, or chairmen of key committees, being a councilman is not, in the vast majority of large cities, considered to be a full-time job with first claims on normal working hours. Almost all councilmen have other occupations, which provide their chief source of financial support and to which they devote most of their attention and energy. With a few notable exceptions like Detroit and Los Angeles, where the council meets daily, members of city

[38] *Ibid.,* pp. 83–84.

[39] Hessler, *29 Ways to Govern A City,* pp. 20-21,

[40] *Ibid.,* pp. 16–17.

[41] Quoted in Charles W. Bender, "A Report on Politics in Seattle," (Cambridge, Mass.: Joint Center for Urban Studies of the Massachusetts Institute of Technology and Harvard University, 1961, mimeo), sec. II, p. 18.

councils generally perform their legislative duties one afternoon, morning, or evening a week, with perhaps some extra time spent on committee meetings.

The pay for councilmen in most large cities guarantees that they would not be able to afford becoming full-time legislative officials even if they wanted to: In 1971, only Boston, Detroit, Los Angeles, Minneapolis, New York, Philadelphia, Pittsburgh, and Seattle paid $15,000 a year or more; councilmen in other mayor-council cities averaged $7,950 while those in council-manager cities were paid an average of $3,469 yearly.[42] In addition, most rank-and-file councilmen lack any staff assistance more extensive than perhaps a shared secretary to write letters, let alone not having any professional or research assistants to collect and integrate information for the performance of their legislative tasks. And the councilmen usually also lack individual offices in city hall at which to work. Furthermore, council committees almost never have the help of staffs who have developed expertise in the substantive areas with which they are concerned such as those attached to standing congressional committees. Still further, perhaps as a result of all the preceding, the individuals who become councilmen do not often seem to be highly industrious, intensely interested in, or highly skilled at, actively shaping public policy to accomplish specific policy objectives. Instead they tend to resemble the kind of legislators that John Wahlke and his colleagues have termed "ritualists" and that James D. Barber has called "spectators": Ritualists are legislators who go through the strictly necessary motions of attending meetings, voting, and performing other parliamentary routines for their own sake without much consciousness of the policy or power implications involved. Spectators are passive, submissive, unambitious individuals, who lack clearly defined political aims and whose chief objectives are simply to be accepted by the legislative group and to watch the legislative process as entertainment.[43]

Finally, even if some individual councilman has the inclination and therefore is willing to devote the time and energy and collect the information necessary to develop policy alternatives of his own, he is often deterred from doing so. The main deterrent is the belief that whereas "invisible" incumbency normally guarantees reelection, becoming identified with a policy that turns out to be controversial or unpopular will bring notice and

[42] *The Municipal Year Book,* 1972 (Washington, D.C.: The International City Management Association, 1972), Table 3/20, pp. 28-29.

[43] See John C. Wahlke et al., *The Legislative System: Explorations in Legislative Behavior* (New York: Wiley, 1962), pp. 249-52; James David Barber, *The Lawmakers: Recruitment and Adaptation to Legislative Life* (New Haven: Yale University Press, 1965), pp. 23–66. See also Kenneth Prewitt, *The Recruitment of Political Leaders: A Study of Citizen-Politicians* (Indianapolis: Bobbs-Merrill, 1970); and Robert Eyestone, *The Threads of Public Policy: A Study of Policy Leadership* (Indianapolis: Bobbs-Merrill, 1971) for data on the attitudes of some 425 councilmen from 87 cities in the San Francisco Bay area, but excluding San Francisco.

attract opposition that may lead to his defeat.[44] Banfield reports that even in a weak-mayor city like Atlanta, "in controversial matters aldermen are usually willing to let the mayor assume leadership and, of course, run any political risks."[45] Moreover, if a councilman opposes a mayoral policy when the mayor is a strong party leader, the party machine can be used to deny the councilman unopposed renomination. And even in a weak party or nonpartisan system, the mayor, with the help of the press, may be able to define the councilman as an "irresponsible obstructionist" and perhaps also stimulate and support candidates to run against him at the next election. In nonpartisan, weak-mayor Los Angeles, for example, Mayor Yorty supported candidates in 1965 against two members of the council who were his most violent opponents, and both these opponents were defeated.[46] Also, in certain cities councilmen may be under obligation to the mayor and his administration because they or their relatives or friends hold jobs or sell goods or services to the city government, the continuation of which is subject to the mayor's control. In New Haven, for example, Dahl reports that out of thirty-three members of the board of aldermen serving when he did his research, only a few appeared to be entirely free of some obligation to the city administration.[47] Similarly, in New Haven and other large cities, the aspirations of many members of the city legislative body to hold judgeships in the municipal courts, when these are in the mayor's power to bestow, dampen any enthusiasm for taking an active antiadministration role in the council.

Another deterrent to an individual councilman investing the time and energy to promote a policy of his own is the knowledge that unless he can convince at least a majority of his fellow councilmen to lend him their support, his impact on policy will still be nil, and his personal efforts wasted.

The major implications of this kind of councilmanic docility for the overall operation of the politics and government of large cities are at least three-fold. First, because of the very limited participation of the council in the original formulation or any basic reshaping of proposals, the conflict of ideas, consideration of alternatives, justification of different positions, and negotiations and compromises that are involved takes place primarily within the privacy of the executive branch. In a sense it could be said that the city's legislative process takes place in the executive branch and not within the legislative body. Indeed, it may be that in the aggregate, the greatest impact the council has on important general policies comes from the lobbying roles

[44]See Lockard, *The Politics of State and Local Government,* pp. 325, 333.

[45]Banfield, *Big City Politics,* pp. 22–23.

[46]See Ainsworth, *Maverick Mayor,* pp. 190–91.

[47]Robert A. Dahl, *Who Governs?* (New Haven: Yale University Press, 1961), pp. 251-52.

played by the few councilmen who hold leadership positions as presiding officers, floor leaders, or chairmen of important committees. Their lobbying involves support of or opposition to particular positions during executive branch consideration and before a legislative measure is officially proposed. The fact that these basic parts of the policy process do not take place openly in the council, which is a public forum, has important consequences: One such consequence is that individuals and groups in the general public who do not have privileged access to and inside information about the private, executive branch policymaking are neither kept well informed about the bases for various decisions or proposals nor are they given timely opportunity to intercede on behalf of some particular alternative being disputed or to ask for modification of some aspect or detail that they find particularly objectionable. Another consequence of the largely behind-closed-doors nature of city legislative policymaking is that even when a policy is formally adopted, it may enjoy little broad public support and only after it is in effect will the officials sponsoring it learn, sometimes to their discomfort, of opposition that exists.

Second, because of the limited attention given by the councils of all but a handful of large cities to oversight of administrative performance, only a single elective politician—the mayor—and in council-manager cities not even he, is available for controlling and directing the city's bureaucracies toward responsiveness to the actual needs and desires of segments of the general public. In contrast, federal bureaucrats know that they may be subjected to scrutiny not only by the president, but also by the elective representatives of the public who staff the congressional committees that have jurisdiction over the work of their the particular agency.

Third, because of the general lack of influence of their elected representatives on the city council, unorganized members of the general public have no ready access to effective, nonforcible, institutionalized means for trying to impress their interests, particularly neighborhood-based ones, on the content of key city decisions. The consequent feeling of powerlessness often results in alienation and sometimes leads to more forcible and disruptive means for trying to affect city governmental policy and operations.

11

City Administrators and Career Bureaucrats

Collectively, city administrators and career bureaucrats probably have greater influence over the policymaking process of large-city governments than any other category of influentials. The term "city administrators" refers to commissioners, directors, superintendants, etc., who have been appointed to head major city "line"[1] departments, e.g., police, fire, education, welfare, buildings, sanitation, highways and roads, housing, public works, health, hospitals, parks, traffic, corrections, and such key "overhead"[2] agencies as budget, personnel, law, and planning.

The city administrators who function as department heads have the legal powers to make decisions for their agencies and act as their chief spokesmen in dealings with other city agencies, with elected officials, with interest groups, with the mass media, and with their functional counterparts in the state and federal government. In almost all large cities, the heads of the line and overhead agencies serve at the pleasure of the appointing officer—typically the mayor or city manager—or for a fixed term of years. Below these department heads are the various deputy and assistant agency heads and the bureau, division, and section chiefs or managers who are in charge of the major subdivisions, field offices, and operating facilities of the departments. These officials are responsible for supervising the efficient operation

[1]Line departments and agencies are those that have direct contact with the public.

[2]Overhead departments and agencies do not normally deal with the public directly, but advise on, supervise, or service certain kinds of common activities that are involved in the internal workings of all line agencies.

of their respective parts of the department. In this connection, they promulgate rules translating departmental policies into more detailed instructions for their own units, originate budgetary requests, recommend promotions, and, in general, deploy their unit's work forces on a more day-to-day basis to accomplish its objectives. At the lowest, or operating, level of the various departments and agencies are the rank-and-file police officers, firemen, schoolteachers, social workers, building inspectors, engineers, medical doctors and nurses, attorneys, accountants, sanitarians, biologists, architects, planners, budget and management analysts, personnel specialists, librarians, secretaries, clerks, and manual laborers that compose the bulk of the work force of both the line and overhead agencies.

In all large cities the bulk of the bureau, division, and section chiefs and all of the rest of the operating personnel are civil service, merit system employees. These civil service employees are originally recruited and, most often, promoted on the basis of examinations testing their competence, and they enjoy protection against arbitrary dismissal during satisfactory service.[3] In the subsequent discussion the term "city administrators" will refer to the appointees at the top echelons of city government agencies and the term "bureaucrats" will be reserved for the career employees, usually at the middle and lower ranks, holding permanent civil service status.

INSTRUMENTS OF ADMINISTRATIVE AND BUREAUCRATIC INFLUENCE

Although it is the city's elected mayor and councilmen who possess the legal authority to adopt and promulgate binding city policies and programs, the nonelected city administrators and career bureaucrats are extremely influential in determining their operational content. First, city administrators and bureaucrats are normally delegated the authority to make decisions on the implementation of policies and programs. This gives them extensive opportunities both for fixing their details and for reshaping those they disapprove of, while translating them into concrete acts of governmental performance. Second, city administrators and bureaucrats are widely regarded as technical experts in their particular program areas. Consequently, it is their advice and proposals on which, often with only small degrees of modification, elected officials base their policy and program decisions in the first place. Third, city administrators and bureaucrats supplement their "inside" implementational and advice-giving influence with "outside" organized group activity seeking to impose their collective views on elected officials through such tactics as lobbying, public relations,

[3]In a few large cities, of which the most notable is Los Angeles, even some department heads are career civil service employees.

collective bargaining, and threatened or actual strikes. This is especially true of policies concerning their conditions of employment, but it also takes place when the perceived stakes are high enough on the policies and programs that constitute their regular workload.

Although similar in that neither holds elective office, the influence of city administrators and of career bureaucrats is not all of one kind. It should be understood that it is the bureaucrats and their values, much more than the administrators and theirs, that pervade the operating departments and agencies of large-city governments and impart to them their dominant characteristics. Admittedly, the city administrators hold the superior formal authority within the various city departments and agencies. But it is the bureaucrats who far outnumber the small number of administrators and who hold the middle-level and surround the higher-level centers of decision-making power. It is the bureaucrats who through long years of service have the first-hand, detailed knowledge of the past history of issues, of the lower-level decisions that are pending, and of the alternative lines of action that are open. It is the bureaucrats who essentially monopolize the performance of acts that constitute the direct implementation of policies and programs. It is the bureaucrats who originally draft almost all of the proposals that become the basis for the high-level departmental decisions and for departmental recommendations to elective officials. And it is the bureaucrats and their interests that are almost exclusively promoted by lobbying, public relations, collective bargaining, and threatened and actual strikes.

Influence Through Discretionary Implementation

Inevitably city policies and programs, as promulgated by city elected officials in charter provisions, legislation, or executive orders, are phrased in general language. Thus they leave varying, but almost always substantial degrees of ambiguity. Therefore, there is discretion in how those policies and programs are to be converted by administrators and bureaucrats into actual concrete performance. Sometimes, the higher elective officials lack the time or knowledge to work out policy and program in detailed form, being content simply to indicate purposes, objectives, and general means. Or sometimes, the factual contingencies are too numerous to make it feasible to specify and provide for in advance. Sometimes the policy decision itself may be an equivocal compromise. And sometimes, because of changed conditions, what might once have been an unambiguous instruction needs interpretation in the light of new circumstances.

The Detroit city charter, which is typical of charter, administrative code, or statutory language, assigns missions to major city departments in such broad terms as:

> do all the paving and repairing, cleaning and sprinkling of all streets, boulevards, alleys, public squares or places and bridges . . . (Public Works);
>
> control and manage all parks . . . conduct playgrounds and indoor recreational facilities . . . (Parks);
>
> [supply] the city with sufficient quantity of pure and wholesome water . . . (Water);
>
> prevent and supress the spread of infectious and contagious diseases within the city . . . (Health);
>
> have charge and control of all cases or persons applying for public aid in the city and the disbursement of funds for their relief . . . (Welfare);
>
> preserve the public peace and prevent crime, arrest offenders and protect the rights of persons and property . . . preserve law and order and enforce the laws of the state and the ordinances of the city . . . (Police).[4]

The generality of the language that constitutes their legal authority and the policy decisions they must implement thus provides city administrators and bureaucrats with legitimate opportunities for shaping the details of programs in ways that are not necessarily inconsistent with the objectives of the original policymakers. The high- and middle-level administrators and bureaucrats draft and promulgate the detailed rules and regulations that expand the language embodied in legislation or executive order into specific instructions defining the means to be used by lower-level operating personnel; they ask for and allocate money and personnel among the different subprograms and activities of the department and the various neighborhoods of the city, thus determining their relative intensity of performance;[5] they make determinations about equipment and facilities that need to be replaced; they settle disputes among lower-level bureaucrats; in response to appeals from the decisions of operating personnel, they make rulings about the application of policies in a specific case, thus fixing what become binding precedents about the detailed meanings of various provisions in legislation, executive order, or departmental regulation.

Much of the final choice-making on implementation of a program by a city's high-level administrators and especially by middle-level bureaucrats takes place under conditions of low visibility to the higher-level policymakers who originally promulgated it. As a consequence, these administra-

[4]Charter of the City of Detroit, 1963 edition, pp. 78, 84, 93, 103, 121, 130.

[5]For a case study of how middle-level professional street engineers, school administrators, and librarian-bureaucrats shaped important policies within their jurisdictions, see Frank S. Levy, Arnold J. Meltsner, and Aaron Wildavsky, *Urban Outcomes: Schools, Streets, and Libraries* (Berkeley: University of California Press, 1974).

tors and bureaucrats can influence policy by resolving ambiguities so as to further their own personal policy preferences. And they may interpret ambiguities so as to increase or protect their own personal power, prestige, security, or convenience, or possibly so as to not expand their workloads, even if in disregard or in defiance of their supervisor's objectives. In short, city administrators and bureaucrats are often in a position to reshape policies in the guise of implementation.

Furthermore, when they find certain decisions or policies set at higher levels highly unpalatable, administrators and bureaucrats can fail to put them into effect simply by dragging their feet. Often the higher city official will simply forget about or let the matter drop, rather than invest the time and energy necessary to overcome this kind of "protracted obstinance." Also, if the noncompliant city administrator or bureaucrat is effective and highly popular with public opinion, the mass media, influential interest groups, or all three, not only will a higher elective official like a mayor shrink from dismissing him, but a higher official might even have to comply with his subordinate's position in order to avoid getting an unwanted resignation.

For the most part, the rank-and-file operating personnel at the lowest levels of the city bureaucracies do not have occasion to exercise discretion that will have significant impact on urban policy outputs. In operating various city facilities and offices, providing concrete services, collecting taxes, enforcing various regulations, etc., lower-level bureaucrats engage largely in routine activity. The extent of underperformance of their jobs by these bureaucrats—both in quality and quantity of work—does, however, directly affect the level of services received by the public per dollar.

There are, in addition, a few "street-level"[6] bureaucrats whose functions do provide them with opportunities to make choices of vital significance:

1. Inspectorial personnel of different departments (e.g., health, fire, buildings, markets). Their largely unsupervisable failure to enforce regulations against violators either because of laziness, inefficiency, or corruption leads to highly uneven burdens of compliance among regulatees. If widespread enough, that failure of enforcement negates regulatory policies adopted by the city government altogether.

2. Welfare caseworkers. Their idiosyncratic leanings of openhandedness or tight-fistedness can determine whether particular individuals will be accepted as welfare beneficiaries, what level of payments they will receive, and whether various special grants will be awarded or denied.

3. Public school teachers, especially those in the lower grades in slum ghetto schools. Their attitudes, friendliness, energy, devotion, preparation,

[6]See Michael Lipsky, "Street-Level Bureaucrats and the Analysis of Urban Reform," *Urban Affairs Quarterly*, 6 (1971): 391, 409.

and effort will have a large impact on whether the students in their classes will come to look at schools as places of learning or as semipunitive custodial institutions.

4. Police officers. Their day-to-day discretionary acts decide not only such insignificant events as which from a massive number of traffic offenders actually will have to answer for their violations. They also determine more weighty matters: the extent and openness of illegal prostitution, drug-peddling, and gambling in various neighborhoods; the unnecessary "stopping-and-frisking" and excessive physical force to which various parts of the citizenry, especially in slum areas, will be subjected; and whether, in the process of police investigations of subjects, making arrests, or controlling mass demonstrations, various initial "incidents" will escalate into more serious disruptions including riots.[7]

Limits on Discretion. Although the opportunities for city administrators and bureaucrats to influence policies and programs in the process of implementation are wide, they are not complete. City administrators and bureaucrats must take into account that however infrequent and unlikely, there is a possibility that any of their decisions and actions may be monitored by the supervisory machinery of higher elective officials on those officials' own initiative and therefore any unauthorized deviations discovered. If the exercise of discretion has an adverse impact on the clientele they serve or other sizable segment of the public, complaints and disruptions may be generated against the administrators or bureaucrats in charge that, directly or through the mass media, might give the agency harmful unfavorable publicity and attract the attention and the intervention of higher city officials. This risk is especially great if that clientele has organized interest groups including community organizations—e.g., a local PTA—to act as its champion and spokesman. Indeed, the possible penalties of upsetting accommodations that have been worked out with an agency's clientele groups may be the most important limit that operates to restrain the discretion of city administrators and bureaucrats.

Finally, if the exercise of discretion appears arbitrary or clearly to fall outside the limits allowable by established procedural due process or the language of the delegated authority, appeal may also be taken to the courts. The courts can reverse the decisions of city administrators and bureaucrats and impose their own interpretation of what is required substantively or procedurally and, in cases of discretion that constitutes a violation of criminal statutes, may punish those involved.

Although all three of these controls combined probably lead to the review and overruling of only a tiny fraction of the implementing decisions

[7]For documentation of the discretion police have in carrying out their law-enforcement duties, see James Q. Wilson, *Varieties of Police Behavior* (Cambridge, Mass.: Harvard University Press, 1968).

made by city administrators and bureaucrats, their existence is important. They restrain administrators and bureaucrats in advance from engaging in certain kinds of discretion to which they may be inclined, but from which they can anticipate too great a risk of negative repercussions. But all three together cannot negate the unavoidable larger reality that, of hundreds of thousands of lower-level decisions and actions undertaken in the implementation of policies and programs, only a tiny fraction stands even the remotest chance of being overruled by higher authorities.

Influence Through Advice-Giving

City administrators and career bureaucrats also exert influence by the advice they give during the formulation of policies and programs. For obviously, since city elected officials must make decisions on a broad range of policy areas, they rarely can develop detailed knowledge in any particular one. Their decisions must therefore be based in large part on the information and recommendations provided by the administrators in charge of the agencies with the relevant substantive responsibility. Because of similar reasons, the policy decisions of appointed administrators—including decisions concerning what departmental recommendations they make to elected officials on particular problems, policies, programs, and budgetary needs—these are all heavily dependent upon advice and information prepared by career bureaucrats in the parts of the agency whose existing operations most affect or are affected by the matter under consideration. Because of the superior knowledge they are presumed to have acquired through long-term, continuous involvement in a particular program area, it is those career bureaucrats who are usually regarded as the city government's leading "subject-matter experts."

The advice given by city administrators and bureaucrats to higher officials influences the content of their policy decisions by, at the very least, its sheer quality—i.e., its having correctly analyzed the components of the problem and identified the issues, its imaginativeness in generating alternative solutions, and its accuracy in reporting facts about the current situation and about the likely consequences of possible changes. But that advice also influences the content of policies by its "slant." Agency administrators and most especially middle-level career bureaucrats are rarely, if ever, neutral in what policies they want to see adopted by the city government in program areas that constitute their agency's workload. Their advice will therefore normally reflect their own preferences, based both on their personal convictions about what policy is best for achieving their agency's or unit's official objectives and on their expectations of how various alternatives will affect their own personal or organizational power, prestige, security, convenience, workload, etc. Sayre and Kaufman have spelled out the tactics involved in using "slanted" advice to influence superior officials:

> . . . the amount and kind of information, the method of presentation, the manner in which alternatives are identified and appraised, and the making of, or abstention from, recommendations—all provide opportunities for the bureaucracies to impress their own discretion and preferences on the decisions as promulgated. . . . The useful techniques are many. The information [presented] may be incomplete, omitting data which point away from the preferred decision. It may be overdetailed, confusing the official until he is led to clear ground by the recommendation preferred by the reporter. The report may omit alternative solutions, driving exclusively at the bureaucracy's recommendations, or it may subject an alternative proposal to devastating criticism, while leaving the preferred solution unexamined. There are a hundred variations and combinations. The objective is constant: to guide the official's decision into the channels which the bureaucrats regard as wise and prudent.[8]

Counters to Advice-Giving Strategems. Even with the use of these advice-giving strategems, city administrators and bureaucrats do not invariably have their advice accepted by higher officials. Experienced high city officials are aware that recommendations from their subordinates are likely to be slanted and learn to make allowances to compensate for such distortions. Also, the more important the issue, the more likely that alternative and even competing information will be reaching these officials from rival administrators and bureaucrats, from affected interest groups, from the press and possibly other mass media, from the higher officials' own personal staffs (if they happen to have them), or from outside consultants and study groups that these higher officials may have appointed for the very purpose of securing more than a single line of advice. Last, much of the advice and recommendations from line administrators and bureaucrats carries direct budgetary implications. When those implications point to the need for sizable new funds, both city budget officials and higher elected officials, who must make the budget balance or vote tax increases, will be strongly motivated to find weaknesses in the original presentations.

On the other hand, most decisions that have to be made by higher city administrators and elected officials are on low-visibility issues that attract little outside attention or competitive advice and information to balance

[8]Wallace S. Sayre and Herbert Kaufman, *Governing New York City* (New York: W. W. Norton, 1965), pp. 420–21.

that received by their bureaucratic subordinates. And top administrators and elected officials infrequently have the time and energy to use the various means for developing such advice and information on their own. The result is that on only a minority of important issues are higher city officials in a position to do more than approve, reject outright, or make marginal changes in the recommendations presented to them from bureaucrats. Finally, to the extent that requests for new funds are for small increments over the existing budgetary base rather than sharp increases, higher officials are, in normal budgetary times, unlikely to invest sufficient time to inquire carefully into whether they are justified. But each annual increment, even if small, becomes part of the following year's base and typically no longer has to be justified. Thus the usual leverage that budgetary controls give to higher officials is simply to affect the rate of inevitable increases in spending.[9] In times of very severe financial crisis, however, every request for an increase may be questioned and the amounts in the previous year's budget may be frozen or even cut.

Influence Through "Outside" Lobbying, Collective Bargaining, and Striking

The influence that administrators and bureaucrats exert over the content of urban policy outputs through discretionary implementation and advice-giving comes from their capacity as insiders, that is, as strategically-placed individual members of city administrative agencies. Bureaucrats, with administrators sometimes as their covert allies, also influence policy outputs collectively as outsiders. This is done through organizations: of city employees generally; of the employees of particular departments, agencies, or functional specialties (e.g., sanitation men, police, firemen, transport workers); or of those city employees belonging to particular professions (e.g., school teachers, social workers, engineers and architects, doctors and nurses).

These organizations have the status of private voluntary associations. They take the form of fraternal or benevolent societies and, increasingly, of local unions affiliated with the national labor movement. As of the last systematic count in 1966, all but two of the cities of over 500,000 in population that reported statistics had organizations of city employees that were affiliated with national unions.[10] Major unions that represent city employees include the American Federation of State, County, and Municipal Employees (AFSCME), the National Education Association, the American

[9]See Aaron Wildavsky, *The Politics of the Budgetary Process,* 2nd ed. (Boston: Little, Brown, 1974), esp. chaps. 2 and 3.

[10]See *The Municipal Year Book, 1966* (Chicago: The International City Manager s' Association, 1966).

Federation of Teachers, the Transport Workers Union, the Teamsters, and the International Fire Fighters.[11]

In their organized, collective capacity, city bureaucrats use all of the standard influence techniques of non-civil service labor unions and other interest groups. The leaders of the various employee organizations lobby informally with the officials whose decisions they are trying to shape and appear to testify (and sometimes with followers to picket and demonstrate) at public hearings and other official proceedings held by city and state legislative bodies and administrative boards. They try through public relations activities to develop a favorable public opinion toward themselves and occasionally in large cities, they make active efforts to affect, through "endorsements," the outcome of city elections so as to reward officials who have been their friends and punish those who have been their enemies. The bureaucrats monitor the appointment process for the top supervisory posts in the agencies in which their membership is concentrated, primarily trying to veto any prospective appointees who do not come from the bureaucratic ranks. Their leaders participate at periodic intervals in collective bargaining sessions to work out agreements similar to the formal labor-management contracts signed in private industry. And, when negotiations do not succeed or provisions of past agreements are violated, the leaders of civil service unions tacitly or explicitly have their members withhold services by engaging in feigned illnesses, slowdowns, or outright strikes.

Strikes of city employees are illegal in all large cities outside the states of Hawaii, Pennsylvania, and Vermont.[12] Nevertheless, since 1965, the New York City government, for example, has been struck by its school teachers, transit workers, sanitation men, and welfare case workers. Additionally, it has heard strike threats, seen slowdowns, or both from police, firemen, and doctors and nurses in city hospitals. Newark, Detroit, San Francisco, and Kansas City have already experienced strikes of police or firemen, and it was a strike of sanitation men in Memphis that brought Martin Luther King, Jr., to that city where he was shot to death in the spring of 1968.

The city policies that bureaucrats normally try to influence through organized group activity are those governing the group members' conditions of employment, i.e., pay, hours, vacations, kinds and amount of work, promotion criteria, retirement eligibility and benefits, grievance machinery, and job protections. The civil service unions also concentrate on city policies bearing on the amount of control that higher officials can exercise over the operations and procedures of agencies in which their

[11] See David T. Stanley, *Managing Local Government Under Union Pressure* (Washington, D.C.: The Brookings Institution, 1972).

[12] The right to strike in these states is subject to various conditions and limitations. See Lee C. Shaw, "The Development of State and Federal Laws," in Sam Zagoria, ed., *Public Workers and Public Unions* (Englewood Cliffs, N.J.: Prentice-Hall, 1972), pp. 32–35.

members work. An example of this would be trying to specify the extent of, and especially the limitations on, the appointment, removal, or disciplinary power of these higher officials. In both of these categories, the central issue is not the best policy or program for achieving the agency's official objectives, but details of internal management. Here the interests of the rank-and-file and middle-level bureaucrats and the interests of the higher city officials are at times admittedly antagonistic. These higher officials may, therefore, not be persuaded to agree with the demands of the bureaucrats who are their subordinates. Through lobbying and other kinds of collective action, the bureaucrats essentially bypass the formal chain of command and take their demands directly to the ultimate, elective decision-makers at city hall or the state legislature.

Only infrequently do city bureaucrats have to appeal over the heads of their administrative chiefs and resort to organized group activity to try to shape the general policies and programs that constitute the regular workload of their agencies. The necessity to appeal arises most often to prevent some sharp departure from established, traditional courses being imposed by innovation-championing higher officials refusing to heed bureaucratic advice tendered through normal channels. Of course, large wage and fringe benefit increases won at the collective bargaining table have an implicit impact on policy and performance, as when funding those increases under a steady or declining budget forces a reduction in the size of the workforce and a consequent contraction in the level of services provided.

City elective and high administrative officials can, of course, choose to resist the demands of bureaucratic groups as asserted in lobbying and public relations campaigns and bargaining sessions much as they do those of non-bureaucratic interest groups. These officials have not yet, however, developed an effective counterstrategy for dealing with demands backed up by a strike or a serious threat of a strike. This is particularly true when the strikers or threatening strikers are from a large department performing services that are indispensable to the safety and health of the entire general public (e.g., fire, police, sanitation) or whose disruption, although not critical, is seriously discommoding to large numbers (e.g., schools, public transit, welfare). Furthermore, as this vulnerability to strikes becomes more and more apparent, the leaders of the bureaucratic groups are encouraged to hold out for greater and greater concessions when bargaining for pay increases and improvement of employee benefits for their members. Then the rank-and-file become increasingly predisposed to reject the terms tentatively agreed to by their leaders and threaten to strike if they are not improved upon, acting on the belief that "you get more by being impossible."[13]

[13]See A. H. Raskin, "The Revolt of the Civil Servants," *Saturday Review,* December 7, 1968, p. 89.

And still further, as strikes have proved successful in extracting employee benefits, their use has been threatened in order to impose the group's will on policy and program matters. Thus the New York City social workers who struck in 1965 were insisting not only on more pay, but also on improved staffing of welfare offices to give better service to clients; and in the New York City teachers' strike that extended through much of the fall of 1968, the issue was not primarily employee benefits like salary and hours, but community control of schools.

City ordinances and state legislation that prohibit strikes by city employees attempt to enforce that prohibition by a variety of devices. These include: court injunctions against violators; suspensions or automatic dismissals of strikers; prohibitions of salary increases or promotions for strikers for some stated period after the strike; imposition of fines against a striking group's treasury, and fining or imprisonment of its leaders. Although some of these penalties are severe, they are extremely defficult to invoke in such a way as to actually head off or end a strike: For mass dismissals or suspensions of the members of a city bureaucratic group who are either too numerous or too skilled to be easily replaced does not restore interrupted services.[14] Further, the deterrent effect of other legal disciplinary action against striking individuals is slight, since it is known in advance that an explicit or tacit condition for settling a strike is almost always that reprisals will not be undertaken and that bars against such things as pay increases will be ignored. Finally, the short jail sentences (e.g., two to three weeks) that normally are imposed on the striking group's leaders for defiance of court injunctions against the strike have little deterrent effect. They are slight enough to be absorbed without great personal distress and indeed may even reward the strikers' leaders by investing them with martyrdom and consequent increased prestige with their following. Similarly, the fines imposed on the group's treasury have usually been moderate, relative to its total resources, and thus far from devastating in their impact. The United Federation of Teachers, for example, was fined $150,000 for its 1967 school strike in New York City and $220,000 for its 1968 strike. (The maximum that could have been imposed was $620,000.) Since the U.F.T. had approximately 55,000 dues-paying members, the 1968 fine amounted to $4 for each member.

Nevertheless, if the frequency of disruptive strikes continues or increases, it is highly likely that more effective sanctions will be developed and applied. For as a general rule, power as naked and coercive as that represented by mass civil service strikes stimulates retaliatory forces that finally succeed in limiting it. Already, certain cities have both threatened and used

[14]On the other hand, if the group is small, the penalties can be effective. In 1965, sixteen New York City ferryboat officers and employees who struck in violation of the then operative Condon-Waldin Act were dismissed and replaced.

with some effectiveness against illegal strikes the suspending for some period of the union's "check-off" privileges—i.e., the automatic deduction by the city government of union dues from the employees' paychecks and forwarding to the union treasury. And given the increasing public displeasure over strikes that interrupt essential services and demand very costly wage settlements, courts may become more willing under existing or revised laws to impose heavy fines and prison terms for violations, particularly for flagrant defiance of court injunctions. Finally when, as in the mid 1970s, actual cuts in budgets and personnel must be made to bring the city budgets into balance, the credibility of mayors and city managers may be strengthened when they argue that the city cannot afford, and public opinion will not support, as generous improvements in wages and fringe benefits as in the past.

BUREAUCRATIC CHARACTERISTICS OF CITY OPERATING AGENCIES

The pervasive influence over the operating departments and agencies held by career bureaucrats is not exerted all in the same policy direction. Individual bureaucrats hold different substantive viewpoints, reflecting differences in their backgrounds, official responsibilities, and personal values and preferences. Bureaucrats do, however, tend to exhibit certain common traits in what can be called "operating style" and these impart to the city's departments and agencies the following set of dominant bureaucratic characteristics: reliability and impartiality in performance of routine functions; overformalism and red tape in application of standing rules; resistance to unfamiliar innovations; and empire-building.

Reliability and Impartiality in Performance of Routines

Because of varying combinations of training, constant practice, and long-term experience, city bureaucrats normally hold at least minimal competence and self-discipline to carry out the specific operations required by the policies and programs they are implementing. Consequently, most routine functions of city government are performed with a high degree of reliability and continuity.[15] This is to be contrasted with the situation in large cities at the turn of the century or in certain underdeveloped nations today,[16] where significant proportions of government employees were and

[15]See Max Weber, "Bureaucracy," in *Essays in Sociology,* translated by H.H. Gerth and C. Wright Mills (New York: Oxford University Press, 1962).

[16]See Ferrel Heady, *Public Administration: A Comparative Perspective* (Englewood Cliffs, N.J.: Prentice-Hall, 1966), esp. pp. 71–72.

are recruited on grounds other than technical competence and readiness to follow instructions. Instead such factors as faithful party service, family connections, ideological loyalty, or ability to bribe the appointing officer prevail. With such recruitment criteria, employees often are not able to perform their assigned functions without relatively frequent mistakes and other interruptions in providing their required services.

The minimum assured competence required for reliable performance of city governmental functions is fostered by the bureaucratic pattern of breaking down policies and programs into sets of relatively simple interlocking routines which can be learned without great difficulty. Thus the bureaucrats with the greatest knowledge and experience can work out what actions need to be taken upon the occurrence of various contingencies and incorporate their findings into as clearly defined rules of procedure as possible. Once these procedures are mastered at lower levels of the hierarchy, the program can be implemented without each employee on the operating level having to use up time and energy to think out what needs to be done with each situation as it arises or needing the technical expertise or judgment to decide the case on its "individual merits." When difficult or unusual cases come up, the lower-level city bureaucrat can search the files in order to find out how such cases were handled in the past or can request guidance from his presumably more knowledgeable and experienced superiors at higher levels of the hierarchy.

The bureaucratic implementation of programs by first converting them into sets of routines also promotes equal treatment of different individuals in similar situations. The standing rules of the city's operating bureaucracies normally specify how individuals possessing particular sets of officially recognized differentiating characteristics are to be treated. Minimum leeway is left, therefore, for exercising unduly favorable or unfavorable partiality on such bases as personal qualities unrelated to the official objectives of the program (e.g., the client's family background, religion, social standing), the momentary personal inclination of the bureaucrat (feeling of liking or disliking that particular client), or corruption (giving favorable treatment for receipt of monetary payment).

Overformalism and "Red Tape"

The very pressures within city bureaucracies that develop reliability and impartiality in the performance of routine functions often create habits of behavior among individual bureaucrats, especially on the lower levels, of overconformity with the most literal apparent meaning of rules for its own sake. Ideally, rules are to be followed because they have been thought out in advance to be efficient instruments for accomplishing program or organizational objectives. But the repeated performance of standardized procedures creates strong positive sentiments that become attached to the rules themselves. The result is that there takes place what has been called a "displacement of goals" whereby "an instrumental value becomes a terminal value"—i.e., conformity to the rules becomes an end in itself rather than simply a means toward effective performance.[17] For example, the supply bureau of a school system could reply to a letter from a school requesting order forms for various items, that the forms could not be requested by letter, but had to be requisitioned on the form the school did not have and was trying to get.[18]

Furthermore, continued tenure and even advancement in city bureaucracies are very often based more on successfully staying out of trouble than on creatively adapting rules to unusual situations. Accordingly, most lower-level bureaucrats learn early in their careers to become timid and play it safe by "going by the book," rather than to risk drawing criticism from their superiors by engaging in seeming deviation, even if the purpose is to better further the bureau or program objective.[19]

This kind of overconformity to the rules leads to three sets of consequences. First, under circumstances not envisioned when the language of the rules was drafted, the most literal application of those rules can lead to a defeat of those very objectives for which the rules were established. Second, to the extent that the client has the self-confidence and stubbornness to insist that his case should be treated as an exception, the lower-level city bureaucrat will normally seek to escape responsibility for any decision by passing the issue to higher authority. But this process of "passing the buck," i.e., sending the issue for consideration and clearance by higher authority, is very time-consuming. Thus final decisions are delayed in what is seen by the client as a maze of red tape. Third, because city bureaucrats insist that rules be applied literally according to whether the client fits into some predetermined category, while most clients desire "personal consideration" and a unique interpretation fitted to their special circumstances or problem, the client perceives the bureaucrats as being insensitive or worse.[20] When the client possesses lower status than the bureaucrat, he often feels that the bureaucrat is taking advantage of his powerlessness by unfairly pushing him around. And when the client possesses obvious higher social position than the bureaucrat, who at the moment is dominant—as when a wealthy businessman deals with a buildings department clerk—the client frequently feels that he is being unfairly domineered by a social inferior, thus defining the bureaucrat as being arrogant and haughty.[21] Furthermore, the resentment that results from both perceptions is compounded by the client's recognition that city bureaucratic agencies are normally monopolistic

[17]See Robert K. Merton, *Social Theory and Social Structure*, rev. ed., (New York: Free Press, 1957), pp. 197ff.

[18]David Rogers, *110 Livingston Street* (New York: Random House, 1968), p. 274.

[19]See Anthony Downs, *Inside Bureaucracy* (Boston: Little, Brown, 1967), p. 100.

[20]*Ibid.*, p. 69.

[21]Merton, *Social Theory*, pp. 202–4.

providers of various services. Therefore he cannot effectively punish what he considers to be insensitivity or arrogance by switching his patronage to a rival firm.[22]

Resistance to Unfamiliar Innovations

Related to the overformalism and red tape in the application of existing rules by lower-level bureaucrats is the strong resistance to unfamiliar innovations in policy, program, and technology by middle- and higher-level city bureaucrats. Even at these levels, the activity involved in supervising the implementing of ongoing policies and programs tends over time to become habitual, and these policies' implicit values and perspectives become internalized and made part of the individual bureaucrat's own personal value structure. As a result, that activity becomes satisfying to engage in for its own sake.

If the original policy was well-designed and the conditions it was meant to deal with remained the same, the tendency to continue ongoing policy would not have unsatisfactory consequences. But conditions are constantly arising in large cities that are significantly different from those that existed when the policy or program was originally formulated and those new conditions begin to interfere with the accomplishment of the policy's objectives. There is then a strong tendency for city bureaucrats not to perceive those new conditions, to insist that existing policies and programs are as satisfactory as ever, and to blame any undesirable shortcomings on an insufficient level of funding. This is especially so given the usual recruitment practices of large-city bureaucracies, which do not allow lateral entry into middle-level or higher bureaucratic positions to individuals who have not first given long service at lower levels of that particular bureaucracy. Thus in most cities, all police and fire lieutenants, captains, and officers of higher ranks have begun as plain patrolmen or firemen, all sanitation foremen and superintendents have begun as sanitationmen, and most general administrators have begun as clerks. These recruitment patterns largely screen out from the higher ranks individuals who might be disposed to see conditions from fresh perspectives and have closer awareness of, and possible identification with, the demands and aspirations of those feeling ill-served by existing city policies or programs. As Sayre and Kaufman have put it, "The virus of 'new blood,' that carrier of new doctrines and new technology, is . . . limited to the newest recruits, at the lowest rank, where its contagion can be slowed by the low temperatures of long indoctrination before freedom of movement is allowed."[23]

Given such recruitment and promotion practices, bureaucrats who reach

[22] *Ibid.*

[23] Sayre and Kaufman, *Governing New York City,* pp. 429–30.

the middle- and upper-levels of the city bureaucracies are likely to feel comfortable with their departments' traditional policies and programs. Innovations are therefore likely to be resisted because they are seen as requiring painful changes in habitual activity. The resistance seems to be greatest when the innovations involve value-laden deeper layers of behavior rather than shallower ones.[24] Innovations affecting such deeper layers would include, for example, law enforcement policies proposed to police that heavily reflect the values of social workers and sociologists or policies proposed to fire bureaucracies that emphasize not traditional fire-fighting skills but fire-preventive values expounded by engineers and similar technical specialists.

Innovations are also often resisted by bureaucrats because they almost always require extra work. In order to develop and secure approval for new policies and programs proposed to them, middle- and high-level city bureaucrats must generally invest the large time and energy drain of rethinking the matter at issue, of renegotiating agreements with a variety of interested parties, and of having to reactivate supportive coalitions and possibly countering new attacks from what may have become quiescent opponents. Anthony Downs has explained the situation as follows:

> . . . [the] established processes represent an enormous previous investment in time, effort, and money. This investment constitutes a "sunk cost" of tremendous proportions. Years of effort, thousands of decisions (including mistakes), and a wide variety of experiences underlie the behavior patterns a bureau now uses. Moreover, it took a significant investment to get the bureau's many members and clients to accept and become habituated to its behavior patterns.
>
> If the bureau adopts new behavior patterns, it must incur at least some of these costs all over again.[25]

And these costs must normally be borne by individual bureaucrats who already feel overworked and harassed in just coping with their existing responsibilities.

Third, besides the heavy organizational costs involved in considering and effectuating innovations, sharp policy or program changes can also lead to personal costs for individual bureaucrats. Such personal costs can involve increased workloads, losses of power and prestige, or disruption of comfortable ongoing relationships with colleagues, superiors, and supportive clientele groups. When these personal costs are certain and high, while the improvements to be brought about by the proposed innovations are only

[24]See Downs, *Inside Bureaucracy,* pp. 167–68.
[25]*Ibid.,* p. 195.

speculative, bureaucrats are especially likely to "dig in their heels" and resist intensely. Furthermore, bureaucrats cannot be certain about how successful or popular any innovations may turn out to be; therefore they also become concerned that any lack of success or popularity of new policies or programs will reflect adversely not on the original sponsors, but on themselves as the implementors. Finally, many bureaucrats see any proposal for change of policies and programs for which they are responsible as an implicit criticism of their own current or past performance and thus of their capabilities and competence.

Of course, policy and program innovations do take place at times within city bureaucracies despite all these reasons for built-in resistance. When, for example, performance of a city bureau or program falls so short of expectations as to draw the sustained attention and condemnation of higher officials, the mass media, and of large segments of the general public, city bureaucrats will often develop and provide those innovations necessary to ward off more painful ones being imposed from the outside. Furthermore, most bureaucrats normally will not oppose any innovations that promise not to decrease, but to enhance their own power, prestige, income, security, etc. Also, however careful the inbreeding, there are almost always some bureaucrats of the innovative type who manage to reach middle- and higher-rank and place a higher value on their unit's doing a better job than on avoiding additional work or disturbance to their ongoing relationships, particularly when those disturbances are minimal. Finally, a certain percentage of bureaucrats are, in Anthony Downs' parlance, "climbers" and "advocates" who are continually seeking to develop innovations that will justify an enlargement of the funds or organization under their control.[26] Downs calls this the "Law of Progress Through Imperialism: *The desire to aggrandize breeds innovation.*"[27]

It is not being argued here that bureaucratic inertia is the only, or even necessarily the dominant, factor in preventing more effective performance by large-city governments or that opposition by bureaucrats to proposed change is always pathological. First, resistance to change may sometimes be based simply on the knowledge of the bureaucrats that the required funds would not be forthcoming from higher city officials or, ultimately, from the public, and that any time and effort spent in considering, "fleshing-out," and supporting a particular change would be wasted.

Second, not every change that can be introduced into ongoing policies or programs will in fact improve the quality of city governmental performance: Resistance to some change may therefore be based on a city bureaucrat's superior knowledge of its unworkability even in terms of achieving its

[26] *Ibid.*, pp. 92–111, 190–200.
[27] *Ibid.*, p. 198.

originator's goals or purposes. Or the opposition may be based on a clearer perception by the bureaucrats of the unacceptable costs to other officially legitimized values and goals that the city bureaucrat has a responsibility to protect.

Empire-Building

The term "empire-building" refers to the tendency of most city bureaucrats to try to expand the size of their organization and budget, whether or not that proposed expansion is necessary to accomplish their official objectives. An "empire-builder" will also fight any proposed curtailment in size, functions, or legal jurisdiction for his department. The English writer C. Northcote Parkinson attributed this tendency to all bureaucrats and half-humorously built upon it a law, to the effect that "Work expands so as to fill the time available for its completion." Parkinson then derived as his law's major corollary that "In any public administrative department not actually at war, the staff increases . . . will invariably prove to be between 5.17 percent and 6.56 percent [per year], irrespective of any variation in the amount of work (if any) to be done."[28]

Whatever the actual annual rate of growth in large-city bureaucracies, there can be no denying that bureaucrats at all levels of the hierarchy have strong incentives to press for increases in the size and funding of their organization. First, since an expanding bureaucracy will require the creation of additional supervisory positions, it offers increased opportunities for advancement and reduces each supervisor's workload. Second, the prestige and power of the middle- and higher-level bureaucrats is in some varying, but significant, degree dependent on the size of the budget and personnel organization that they are administering. Consequently, every increase brings some additions of power and prestige; and the developing of a reputation for having secured disproportionately large increases as compared to other bureaucratic units, brings even larger ones. Third, expansion of a middle- or high-level bureaucrat's organization reduces the strain of managing it by maximizing the morale of its lower-level numbers. This is because they will recognize that almost all of them can improve their status instead of having to compete with one another for the smaller number of positions available in a stagnating or shrinking organization. Fourth, the bureaucrats, as specialists who have concentrated their energy and interest in some particular substantive area for many years, come to believe sincerely and ardently in the importance and desirability of the programs they administer. And at the same time, they are always able to see ways in which they can be implemented more effectively with additional personnel and funds. As Anthony Downs has explained:

[28]C. Northcote Parkinson, *Parkinson's Law and Other Studies in Administration* (Boston: Houghton Mifflin, 1962), p. 2.

> Each bureau develops an "expansionist" ideology, which typically emphasizes unresolved problems, unperformed services, and other indications of imperfection (though in an optimistic manner) to imply that the bureau is struggling manfully with its problems, but needs more funds to cope with them.[29]

Fifth, since the bureaucrats who are administering the various substantive programs are not also responsible for raising the money they spend, the financial difficulties being faced by city governments do not discourage asking for increased spending for any particular (nonbudget officer) city bureaucrat.[30]

Incremental rather than rapid building of the empire is the preferred mode for most city bureaucrats. For changes resulting from sharp expansion can normally not be absorbed into the normal pattern without hard work and the risk of disturbing comfortably settled arrangements and long-standing accommodations.[31] Indeed, there are even circumstances when bureaucrats become "shrinking violets"[32] and shun expansion, e.g., when the expected costs of the anticipated conflict that would be necessary to bring the expansion about exceed the benefits to be gained by the expansion, and when an expansion of jurisdiction and responsibilities would not be accompanied by a corresponding or more than corresponding increase in resources. As Levy, Meltsner, and Wildavsky have put it:

> Bureaucrats have long been accused of being empire builders. But the growth that is sought must be clearly understood. Is it growth that increases the resources of the organization in comparison with the demands placed on it? That is good. Is it growth that increases clients and services without corresponding resources? That is bad . . . Bigger is not necessarily better, and more may be monstrous unless there are excess resources left with which to reward loyal members.[33]

IMPLICATIONS OF BUREAUCRATIC INFLUENCE AND AUTONOMY

Under the classical theory of democratic government, appointed officials and career civil servants have no ultimate right to determine matters of general policy, but are supposed to be instruments for efficiently carrying out the policies and programs established by officials directly responsible to

[29] Downs, *Inside Bureaucracy,* p. 242.
[30] See *ibid.,* p. 103.
[31] See *ibid.,* p. 11.
[32] *Ibid.,* pp. 216–19.
[33] Levy, Meltsner, and Waldavsky, *Urban Outcomes,* p. 229.

the public through elections. Clearly, however, given the size, range, and complexity of operations of large-city governments, the few dozen elected city officials do not have the time, energy, or information to make all the important policy decisions themselves without the advice of the appointed administrators and bureaucrats. Of necessity some decision-making authority must be delegated to, and some reliance must be placed on the advice of, nonelected personnel, thus affording them opportunities for the exercise of influence. Democratic values can still be served as long as the following conditions are met: (1) Decisions made by administrators and bureaucrats fall within the limits of overall policy set by elected officials. (2) Discretion is exercised so as to further or at least not conflict with the objectives that the appointed decision-makers know or can find out are held by their relevant elective superiors. (3) The information, advice, and recommendations offered by administrators and bureaucrats are designed to facilitate the elective decision-makers' choices and are not seriously slanted toward some particular point of view in order to close their options.

The short-term appointed city administrators functioning as department heads (and their immediate deputies and assistants) are the key figures for ensuring that any decision-making or advice-giving within their agencies is meeting these conditions. Together with the mayor or manager who appointed them, these agency heads constitute "the administration" and have the chief responsibility for carrying over into the operations of the city government the will of the general public as registered in the most recent election and as expressed by its representatives in the city's legislative body.

Obviously there are too many different decisions on different matters that must be made within any department or agency for its head even to be aware of them, much less to give personal attention to each of them. This is especially so, given the distraction of his having to conduct much of the department's external relations. Much of the city department or agency head's formal authority therefore "leaks" out and is in fact exercised largely by the middle-level bureaucrats who are in charge of its various subdivisions and facilities.

Furthermore, given that most of these middle-level bureaucrats are likely to be long-term career employees, they may neither have similar policy outlooks nor feel any sense of personal loyalty to motivate them to exercise the "leaked" authority in accordance with the agency head's wishes. For most of these middle-level bureaucrats probably were not selected for their posts by the current agency head or were selected by him from a narrow list of eligibles (selected through a competitive promotion examination and seniority considerations) to which his choice was confined.

Also, most agency heads are "birds-of-passage" or "in-and-outers" who normally stay in office for only a few years. Besides lacking the time and energy and staff facilities for finding out how their subordinates are exercising their delegated authority, agency heads rarely have the opportunity to develop the detailed knowledge of their department's operations that is also a prerequisite for exercising close control. And because city agency heads are known by their career bureaucrat subordinates to be largely short-termers, on many matters of fundamental policy differences, those bureaucrats can prevail simply by outwaiting and outstaying their formal chiefs.

There are, of course, rare exceptions: On the day in 1935 that Robert Moses first became Parks Commissioner of New York City, he summarily fired the five existing borough park superintendents, along with their secretaries, stenographers, and aides. Moses then gave orders to his own personal assistants "to weed out—immediately—those headquarters employees who would not or could not work at the pace he demanded:"

> Unlike the [borough] commissioners and their personal secretaries, most headquarters personnel were protected by civil service, but that didn't help them much. Men who lived in the Bronx were told that henceforth they would be working in Staten Island; men who lived in Staten Island were assigned to the Bronx. Or they were given tasks so disagreeable that they couldn't stomach them. Women were treated no better. One ancient biddy, accustomed to spending her days . . . knitting in a rocking chair, refused to admit she was over retirement age and gracefully accept a pension. When a search failed to produce a birth certificate to disprove her story, she was ordered to work overtime—all night. Every time she tried to rest, she was ordered to keep working. She retired at 2 A.M.[34]

Finally, to avoid having to accept direction from unsympathetic superiors, some career bureaucrats in some cities have been able, through statutory requirement or, more often, through the creation of widespread public and mass media expectation of "career commissioners" or "promotion from within," to capture even the top-most posts in their departments and agencies for graduates of their own bureaucratic ranks. Such "career commissioners" may not even have the personal inclination to impose on their former bureaucratic colleagues the policies of elected officials when those policies are considered undesirable or threatening by the bureaucrats.

Most agency heads do seek to impose their preferences on at least some aspects of their agencies' operations. The motivation to do so can come from a sense of loyalty to their elected superiors resulting from personal

[34]Robert A. Caro, *The Power Broker: Robert Moses and the Fall of New York* (New York: Knopf, 1974), p. 368. Moses' whole career is a classic example of a high-level administrator who did not let any of his authority "leak" to his bureaucratic subordinates, while he, on the other hand, established for himself a position of almost complete autonomy vis-à-vis his elective superiors.

allegiance, friendship, or having been part of that superior's original campaign organization or following. It can also come from the ideological belief in ultimate control by elected city officials, from strong ideas of their own about what the content of specific policies and programs should be, from the personal need to be dominant in their own organizations, or from the desire to acquire a reputation for effective administrative leadership. And by forceful assertions of the authority of their office, the tacit or explicit threat of sanctions for any outright defiance, and, most of all, detailed following-up by themselves or by loyal members of any immediate staff to insure instructions are carried out as directed, agency heads can, if they feel strongly enough, at times succeed in eliciting the actions they desire.

However, the heavy influence of even the most forceful department heads will be felt only on that restricted segment of the department's whole range of activities which he feels is most important to him and on which he therefore chooses to concentrate his attention. And the policies that agency heads choose to concentrate on are not always necessarily those that coincide exactly with the mayor's top preferences. On the remainder of the city department or agency's activities where the agency head does not choose to focus his efforts, the career bureaucrats will have extensive opportunities to determine policies and programs. In these areas the bureaucrats will be able to exercise their administrative discretion with indifference to, or in defiance of, the preference of their superiors, to use information and advice to manipulate rather than to enlighten their appointed and elected superiors and even, given the conditions of low visibility under which they operate, to make decisions and perform acts that they know fall outside the limits of discretion set by high-level decisions.

City bureaucrats do not concede, of course, that any resistance to direction from, or divergences from the objectives of, or attempts to manipulate their elected or appointed superiors is based on their being "undemocrats" who do not believe in popular control through elections or who feel any selfish unwillingness to bear the personal costs implicit in new or otherwise unwanted policies. For the most part, the large de facto autonomy of middle-level city bureaucrats allows them to go their own way without having to explicitly reflect on or to offer justifications.

On those occasions when higher officials are insistent and explicit defenses must be provided, the bureaucrats are almost certain to argue that whatever actual issues exist are technical ones. The bureaucrats will therefore find technical objections to proposals that they oppose on policy or personal grounds. Or they may pretend that what are essentially political choices among conflicting values or the allocation of funds or who should bear the costs are also technical questions which should be settled on the basis of technical or professional expertise. And they argue that it is only they—

the professionals—and not elected officials or appointive superiors that have this expertise.

The overall result of the large-scale influence of middle-level city bureaucrats in shaping the content of policies and programs they are responsible for administering and in resisting direction from higher officials is that areas of operations exist within city governments that are largely beyond the reach of the ballot box and continue unaffected by changing currents of opinion as registered in elections. Such a state of affairs violates democratic theory. And it probably is in part responsible for city governmental performance that is not as efficient or productive nor as sensitive and responsive to the changing demands and problems of the city's general populace as it could be if that performance were dominated by city officials who regularly had to answer to that populace in elections.

12
City Trial Judges

City trial judges may not look at first impression as if they have any influence over a city government's general policy process. Judges have no legal powers to promulgate ordinances or executive orders embodying policy decisions that have general applicability throughout a city, nor do they function as advisors to city officials, such as mayors, managers, or councilmen, who have these powers. Judges also play no part in setting city budgets—an activity chock full of policy implications. And judges are not involved in the administrative activities that translate city policy and program decisions into governmental performance.

The way judges do have an impact on city policymaking is by trying lawsuits in which some city act or decision is challenged. Challenges are typically based on the claim (1) that the city government or some particular official exceeded its or his legal authority; (2) that the act or decision violated some state or federal constitutionally guaranteed civil liberty or civil right; (3) that the statute, ordinance, or other regulation as applied was incorrectly interpreted; or (4) that the act or decision did not comply with procedural requirements. Judges also influence a city's general policy process when their sentencing and other decisions on the disposition of criminal cases are part of a general pattern of strictness or leniency that renders a particular ordinance or regulation more or less enforceable. Because litigation has become a frequently used tactic of city political activists, including "public interest" law firms and community legal services sponsored clients, judges have in recent years had increasing opportunities to make decisions with policy significance.

THE NATURE OF JUDICIAL DECISION-MAKING

The job of city judges[1] essentially is to preside over the preparation for and trial of lawsuits, including criminal prosecutions and any taxpayers' suits filed against city officials. In the trial of lawsuits, judges make decisions in cases by ruling in pretrial stages and during the trial itself on various points of law that are raised by either of the parties involved. Judges also make decisions in both civil and criminal cases when they instruct the jury on what the law is that must be applied to the evidence in order to bring in a verdict for one or the other party. And if both the parties in a civil suit or the defendant in a criminal case waive a jury trial or if a jury trial is not provided for in certain other kinds of cases, trial judges also have to decide what the evidence proved or did not prove. Finally, trial judges decide on the sentences to be imposed on persons found guilty of crimes.

The independent influence of trial judges arises from the fact that the content of these decisions is not preordained. It is not always the case that, given the wording of a particular law or constitutional provision and given a set of factual happenings, only one outcome is possible. While making all their decisions on law and fact, therefore, trial judges are faced with varying degrees of choice and discretion. As Harry W. Jones explained:

> . . . No legal code, no aggregate of statutory directions and judge-made precedents, can ever furnish explicit and unambiguous commands for every conceivable case. . . . [O]n any account of the judical process, there is a substantial incidence of cases in which the law is unclear, that is, in which the judge has no clear mandate to decide one way or the other and must choose between the alternative decisions open to him on the basis of his own best judgment as to which decision is fair between the parties and sound as a matter of generally applicable public policy. . .[2]

Furthermore, even on the finding of the facts, the judge has opportunities for influence:

> . . . the trial judge is far from a passive bystander in a jury case. Through his rulings on questions of the admissibility of evidence, he controls or largely influences the testimonial data from which the jury will draw its inferences as to the truth of the plaintiff's and the defendant's competing versions of the facts of the case. The trial judge,

[1]As was explained in Chapter 4, strictly speaking there are no "city" judges, only judges in the state judicial hierarchy whose courts have jurisdiction over cases arising within the geographic area of large cities. It is the role of such judges that is being analyzed in this chapter.

[2]Harry W. Jones, "The Trial Judge: Role Analysis and Profile," in Harry W. Jones, ed., *The Courts, the Public, and the Law Explosion* (Englewood Cliffs, N.J.: Prentice-Hall, 1965), pp. 129–30.

> within certain more or less defined limits, may set aside the jury verdict in a civil suit and order a new trial of the case when he believes the verdict at which the jury arrived was capricious or wholly unsupported by the evidence before it. He may do this, too, in a criminal case if the jury comes in with a verdict of guilty . . .[3]

But it is in sentencing persons convicted of crimes and offenses that the trial judge has perhaps the greatest discretion:

> The judge's . . . responsibility [is] large, since the general statutory precept, more likely than not, will authorize a wide range of permissible treatment of the offender: "Punishable by fine not to exceed $10,000 or by imprisonment from one to five years, or by both . . ." is not an untypical sentencing provision of our day. In short, the legal rule merely fixes the outside bounds for the inescapable act of judicial discretion. Shall the offender before the court be sent to prison for five years, or one, or for some period in between, or is it perhaps appropriate that he be put in probation during good behavior and not be sent to prison at all? The trial judge must decide. Nowhere else in our society is one man invested with so awful a power over the life and freedom of another man.[4]

It is, of course, the decisions of the judges sitting on appellate courts, especially those on state courts of last resort or the U.S. Supreme Court, that are most often read about and are the most far-reaching and dramatic. But it should be recognized that trial courts have a much more continuous and, in the aggregate, perhaps a more pervasive impact on the operation of a city's policy process. First of all, it is the trial judges who always decide in the first instance how upper court doctrine as stated in landmark cases is to be applied to the particular facts presented by the case in court. And more importantly, it is also the trial judges who in fact function as "courts of last resort" or "supreme courts" for the vast majority of parties that appear before them. For only a small proportion (estimates vary from 1 to 5 percent and 1 to 8 percent)[5] of trial court cases are ever appealed; and of those appealed, only a fraction are decided differently than they were at the trial level. Furthermore, even with respect to the cases that are appealed and passed upon by higher courts, it is the original trial court judge who largely structures the legal issues to be decided by his rulings on pretrial and other

[3] *Ibid.*, p. 134.

[4] *Ibid.*, p. 139.

[5] See Kenneth N. Vines, "Courts as Political and Governmental Agencies," in Herbert Jacob and Kenneth N. Vines, eds., *Politics in the American States* (Boston: Little, Brown, 1965), p. 243.

motions, by his decisions on the admission of the evidence, and by his charge to the jury. And in general, findings of fact by a judge will normally not be reexamined on appeal unless such findings are completely unsupported by the evidence in the trial record.

SPECIFIC VEHICLES OF JUDICIAL INFLUENCE

Rulings on Whether Legal Authority was Exceeded

An aggrieved citizen can challenge the imposition on himself of a regulation or tax and through a taxpayers' suit can usually challenge expenditures, alleging that such a regulation, tax or expenditure exceeds the city government's substantive legal powers. Since the city as a municipal corporation is legally a mere creature of the state, it cannot undertake any policy or program unless it has relatively unambiguous positive authority to do so in its charter or in some provision of state legislation. In ruling on a challenge to some attempted exercise of city power, judges can decide that no charter or legislative language supports the policy or program in question and therefore can prevent the city government from carrying it out. Such things as attempts by different cities to impose or continue rent control, or to require that dates be stamped on milk containers, or to fluoridate the water supply, or to construct and operate facilities like bathing beaches and recreational piers, or to regulate the closing hours of taverns have been blocked by judges who ruled that the particular city's substantive powers were not adequate to sustain them.

The challenge coming before a court for decision need not be to the authority of the city government as a whole; the challenge may be only to the authority of some specific official or body to make a certain decision. And sometimes the challenge comes not from a private party, but from a different official or department who disagrees either with the content of the other official's decision or thinks that the matter is within the jurisdiction of his own agency, or both. In this latter kind of case, the judge acts as umpire between different city decision-making officials contesting each other's powers.

Rulings on Alleged Constitutional Violations

Even if a judge can find support for some challenged exercise of city power in the language of a positive grant of authority, he can still invalidate the policy, program or decision in question by deciding that it conflicts in the particular case with state or federal constitutional prohibitions.

One of the most far-reaching governmental decisions ever made was that issued by judges (ultimately at the Supreme Court level in 1954) declaring local government and school board policies requiring racial segregation in public schools to be in violation of the equal protection clause and hence invalid.[6] Later judicial decisions also outlawed segregation in other municipal facilities, such as garages, terminals, and ports, and even invalidated city charter amendments that would have required any local fair housing laws to be approved by a public referendum. It should be noted that challenges based on federal constitutional provisions are usually brought to federal trial courts.

Rulings on Challenged Statutory Interpretations

Statutes, ordinances, executive orders, and even departmental-level rules on which city policies and programs rest are necessarily written in general terms. Administrators and bureaucrats gain much of their influence from the opportunity to fill in the details of those policies and programs and apply them to concrete cases in the process of implementation. The final determination of whether a statute, ordinance, an executive order, or departmental rule is interpreted and applied correctly in any particular case does not, however, under the American principle of judicial review, belong to administrators and bureaucrats. It belongs to judges.

Thus any person who feels that a city regulation or tax is being imposed upon him or that a benefit is being denied him on the basis of an incorrect interpretation and application of a particular statute or ordinance has the right to challenge that interpretation in court. The person feeling aggrieved can refuse to comply with the regulation or tax and then resist prosecution with the defense that the regulation or tax was not intended to apply to him. Or he can petition for a court order to restrain the administrator or bureaucrat in question from enforcing the regulation or tax against him or to direct the relevant city official to grant him the benefit being withheld. In deciding as each case comes up whether or not a regulatory, tax, or benefactory law was meant to apply to a person in a particular set of factual circumstances, judges fix the outer reach of various city policies and programs.

Rulings on Compliance with Procedural Requirements

Judges can also influence city governmental decisions and policies by invalidating those they find were adopted or implemented without compliance with relevant procedural requirements. Normally this means that city officials will be held to following the procedures specified in their own

[6] *Brown v. Board of Education,* 347 U.S. 383 (1954).

charters, ordinances, or administrative regulations, and any additional procedural guarantees mandated by state or federal law or constitutional provision.

Apart from passing on the procedural regularity of substantive policy and program decisions, judges rule on challenges to the nomination and election of particular candidates. Judicial decisions often concern whether designating or nominating petitions conform to procedural requirements or whether contested ballots were valid or invalid. Judges occasionally rule on challenged appointments, passing on whether residence or other qualifying requirements for the post were met. Somewhat more frequently judges rule on dismissals, making the final determination on appeals from civil service or personnel commissions on whether a particular official had the power to effect a removal and whether procedural guarantees were followed.

Judges have their most pervasive influence over procedures in deciding on the propriety of the actions followed by police, prosecuting attorneys, and trial judges themselves in investigating, arresting, prosecuting, and actually trying people accused of violating criminal laws. For example, when formally charging a person at time of arraignment or at a habeus corpus hearing, a judge can rule that improper procedures were followed, dismiss the charges, and order the accused released. (A writ of habeas corpus directs police or other city officials who have a person in custody to produce him in court and specify the charge on which he is being held.) Just how drastic this kind of power is was illustrated by what happened in 1969 after a gun battle between police and members of the Black Africa Separatist Group in Detroit in which one police officer was killed. When the police and the county prosecutor presented ten arrested suspects for arraignment, the criminal court judge dismissed the charges against eight on the grounds that their arrests, the refusal of the police to let them call lawyers, and the administration without their consent of chemical tests to determine whether they had recently fired guns (the police claimed that the tests showed six had) were all unconstitutional.[7]

During a trial, judges can refuse to admit challenged evidence or can direct a verdict of innocent on the ground that the evidence offered, including any confession, was obtained by police or prosecutors as a result of the violation of an accused's procedural protections. After a conviction, occasionally a trial judge (though normally it is an appellate judge) can invalidate the verdict and order a new trial if his own independent examination of the record convinces him that illegal evidence was admitted or that other violations of state or federal procedural guarantees took place that prevented the convicted defendant from having received a fair trial.

It is through this kind of control over what practices will be allowed by

[7] *New York Times,* March 31, 1969.

police, prosecutors, and the courts that judges shape public policy on the degree of protection to be afforded to accused lawbreakers. The purpose of such protection is both to prevent inadvertent conviction of innocent parties and to guarantee a minimum of dignity and consideration in the treatment of suspects, whether they are guilty or innocent.

Sentencing

Another important way that judges influence city governmental policy-making is by the kinds of sentences they impose upon persons convicted of violating the city's criminal ordinances and statutes. Judges may choose between stated minima and maxima in setting the length of jail terms or the size of money penalties and they have almost complete discretion in deciding whether to suspend sentence or order it executed.[8]

A judge's sentencing decisions can have an important impact on the effectiveness of criminal and other regulatory laws. Persistently setting extremely lenient sentences for violations of certain kinds of regulations in plea-bargaining or after trial may, for example, cause the laws to lose their deterrent effect. Police or inspectorial personnel of other departments who are charged with the laws' enforcement may become so discouraged that they become less willing to make arrests or file reports and follow-up on the violation of these particular ordinances. City building departments officials often complain that landlords who even habitually violate safety and health codes are fined such insignificant amounts that it is more economical for the landlords to keep paying the fines, rather than to pay for making the necessary corrections and repairs. Police officials also attribute their own inability to drive prostitutes, numbers runners, narcotics pushers or other petty offenders off the streets to the refusal of judges to impose significant sentences upon those arrested and convicted.

Similarly, judges that consistently allow release of accused persons on low bail or no bail pending trial and then permit extreme delays in disposing of the case weaken the laws' deterrent effect. Part of the delay and backlog in disposing of criminal cases is, of course, due to a shortage of judges, courtrooms, and prosecutors. But to the extent that the trial judge himself permits avoidable delays to take place, thus increasing the chances for witnesses to become weary and unavailable and for evidence to become stale and unclear, the more likely it becomes that the offender will never have to answer for his actions. (Of course, high or no bail for arrested persons coupled with unavoidable delays in the disposition of cases would result in

[8]For one study showing the divergence in sentencing patterns among three large-city court systems, see Herbert Jacob and James Eisenstein, "Sentences and Other Sanctions in the Criminal Courts of Baltimore, Chicago, and Detroit," *Political Science Quarterly,* 90 (Winter, 1975–76): 617–35.

some innocent persons spending time in jails for crimes they did not commit.)

DISTINGUISHING CHARACTERISTICS OF JUDICIAL DECISION-MAKERS

Judges make decisions that serve as vehicles of influence on the urban policy process. In this respect they resemble mayors, managers, administrators, and bureaucrats. But judges also possess certain special characteristics as decision-makers that distinguish them from these other city officials.

Different Role Conceptions

Although sophisticated observers of judicial behavior now recognize that judges do exercise discretion and that judicial decisions can in fact influence governmental policy, judges normally do not conceive of themselves as "making policy" each time they decide a case. Rather, judges see themselves as "declaring the law."[9] As has been explained, what the law "is" in any particular case is not always clear; competing precedents may be equally relevant to a case, or the meaning of those precedents may be ambiguous, or a novel factual situation or legal issue may have arisen where no exact precedent exists. And this gives judges their basis for discretionary choice. But because of the judges' own role conceptions, which are reinforced by the expectations of other officials and the public and by the definition of their legal powers as being settlers of cases and controversies, city judges tend not to exercise their discretion self-consciously in terms of how best to promote their own policy preferences.

When the outcome is not predetermined, city trial judges tend instead to exercise their discretion by trying to interpret what the original writers of the law intended. And they also try to "do justice" for the parties involved in the particular case. As a result of these differences in self-concept and legal powers, judges will rebuff arguments based on naked policy grounds or tactics incorporating pressure or bargaining ploys. The appeals they will listen to will be those couched in legal form and language, where a particular outcome is argued to be most consistent with previously accepted legal principles, precedents, and rules of interpretation.

This is not to say that judges do not have policy and other biases and personal philosophies that may systematically color their perceptions of facts or receptivity to various kinds of legal arguments. In fact the particular personal outlook of an individual judge will often lead to his exercising discretion differently from other judges with different policy biases and

[9]See Herbert Jacob, *Justice in America* (Boston: Little, Brown, 1965), p. 184ff.

philosophies. The famous jurist, Benjamin N. Cardozo, once explained the play of a judge's personal philosophy in connection with a case that had come before his court:

> . . . A boy was bathing in a river. He climbed upon a springboard which projected from a bank. As he stood there, at the end of the board, poised for his dive into the stream, electric wires fell upon him, and swept him to his death below. In the suit for damages that followed, competetive analogies were invoked by counsel for the administratrix and counsel for the railroad company, the owner of the upland. The administratrix found the analogy that suited her in the position of travelers on a highway. The boy was a bather in navigable waters; his rights were not lessened because his feet were on the board. The owner found the analogy to its liking in the position of a trespasser on land. The springboard, though it projected into the water, was, none the less, a fixture, and as a fixture it was constructively a part of the land to which it was annexed. The boy was thus a trespasser upon land in private ownership; the only duty of the owner was to refrain from wanton and malicious injury; if these elements were lacking, the death must go without requital. Now, the truth is that, as a mere bit of dialectics, these analogies would bring a judge to an impasse. No process of merely logical deduction could determine the choice between them. Neither analogy is precise, though each is apposite. There had arisen a new situation which could not force itself without mutilation into any of the existing moulds. When we find a situation of this kind, the choice that will approve itself to this judge or to that, will be determined largely by his conception of the end of the law, the functions of legal liability; and this question of ends and functions is a question of philosophy.[10]

Analyses by political scientists of the behavior of judges on certain appellate courts show that they differed in their judgment of what the "law" required in certain kinds of cases according to their different political party affiliations, their different socioeconomic or ethnic characteristics, and their different occupational backgrounds.[11] In a study of nonunanimous decisions of some 300 federal supreme court and state court of last resort judges, Stuart S. Nagel found that:

> Democratic judges sitting on the same supreme courts with Republican judges were more prone to favor (1) the defense in criminal

[10]Benjamin N. Cardozo, *The Growth of the Law* (New Haven: Yale University Press, 1924), pp. 99-101.

[11]These studies are summarized in Jacob, *Justice in America,* pp. 105-7.

> cases, (2) the administrative agency in business regulation cases, (3) the private party in regulation of nonbusiness entities, (4) the claimant in unemployment compensation cases, (5) the broadening position in free speech cases, (6) the finding of a constitutional violation in criminal-constitutional cases, (7) the government in tax cases, (8) the divorce-seeker in divorce cases, (9) the wife in divorce settlement cases, (10) the tenant in landlord-tenant cases, (11) the debtor in creditor-debtor cases, (12) the labor union in labor-management cases, (13) the consumer in sales-of-goods cases, (14) the injured party in motor vehicle accident cases, and (15) the employee in employee injury cases, than were the Republican judges.[12]

Other studies show that judges differ greatly in the severity of the sentences they impose for particular crimes.[13]

Presumably differences in demographic characteristics and party affiliations of judges are in some way associated with or reflect differences in "personal standards of value."[14] These, in turn, carry over and influence, sometimes only unconsciously, a judge's discretion in deciding a case. On the other hand, studies also show that the vast majority of cases reaching appellate courts are decided unanimously.[15] This suggests the larger truth that judges really are trying to "declare the law" and are not simply making decisions best calculated to advance their own preferences on policy. Despite differences in background, in personal standards of value, and, presumably, in resulting policy biases, different judges most often do agree on what the meaning of the law is in a particular case and reach identical results when presented with the same precedents and the same factual situation.

Inability to Initiate Decisions

Unlike other city decision-makers, judges cannot take the initiative in making decisions in particular policy areas. City executives, legislators, administrators, and bureaucrats can reach out for issues to decide or can simply announce policy decisions on their own when they consider it expedient to change existing policy. Judges, on the other hand, must wait passively and can speak out only if outside parties happen to bring appropriate litigation before them in such a way that questions relevant to their

[12]Stuart S. Nagel, "Political Party Affiliation and Judges' Decisions," *American Political Science Review,* 55 (1961): 845.

[13]Jacob, *Justice in America,* pp. 86, 158-59; Jones, "The Trial Judge," pp. 139-42.

[14]Nagel, "Political Party Affiliation," p. 847.

[15]See, e.g., the studies summarized in Vines, "Courts as Political and Governmental Agencies," pp. 268–71.

policy preferences are raised. This means that practices may be going on in their city government that judges know, through personal knowledge or through the press, to be illegal or unconstitutional. But judges can do nothing to stop them unless some individual or group with "standing to sue" (i.e., with a direct personal involvement as a result of being substantially injured by such practices) and with access to a lawyer actually decides to institute a lawsuit challenging the illegality or constitutionality or unless some defendant raises it in a prosecution that comes before their courts.

Judges, cannot, of course, issue advisory legal opinions either "ex parte," meaning on their own, or in response to outside parties. And even if a complaining party does file a suit, judges may still on occasion be prevented from ruling on the issue raised, for prosecutors and other city officials may choose to stop prosecution or concede the claim of that particular litigant in order to turn the case "moot." This avoids the risk of having the legislation or administrative practice in question declared illegal or unconstitutional in a court of law, thus allowing it to continue against less litigious parties.

Weak Powers of Enforcement

Relative to other city decision-makers, judges have weak powers to enforce their own decisions. Of course, most judicial decisions are complied with voluntarily by the parties involved out of some combination of unreflecting habit, respect for the moral force of the law, or fear of such sanctions as attachment of property for failure to pay money damages or contempt of court for failure to obey a court order. And a few judicial decisions—like those dismissing charges and releasing a prisoner or ruling on the admissibility of evidence or sentencing convicted persons—are essentially self-executing. But when judges' decisions that are not self-executing meet opposition, their actual enforcement will depend heavily on the voluntary cooperation of city executive and administrative officials. As Jacob has written:

> Almost every court action requires support from an administrative agency. If a court awards damages to one party of a suit, an executive official must stand ready to enforce the court judgment. If a court issues an injunction, the police—another arm of the executive—must be willing to enforce it. When the courts declare a person in contempt, an administrative official must be willing to jail him until the courts set him free.[16]

Such cooperation from executive and administrative officials in enforcing judicial decisions is automatically forthcoming most of the time, partic-

[16] Jacob, *Justice in America,* p. 190.

ularly when the resistant party is a private individual or group. But when a judge's decision invalidates an executive decision or requires other changes in the behavior of city executive officials themselves, if these officials still feel strongly enough that their action was correct, they may resist.

Occasionally this resistance takes the form of outright defiance. But more often it involves the officials reinterpreting a decision so as to comply only with its letter rather than its spirit. It may also involve the filing of multiple appeals to higher courts and petitioning for "stay" orders to put off the time of compliance as long as possible. The threat of a contempt citation may aid the enforcement of a judge's decision when it is being resisted by a lone city administrator or bureaucrat. But such a threat is less useful against the determined resistance of a whole city administration, since the threat cannot be carried out without the cooperation of those to whom it is addressed or of their subordinates.

High Invulnerability to Pressure

Unlike other city decision-makers, judges are highly invulnerable to pressure. This is so both while they are making decisions and afterwards, in retaliation for decisions that are announced. First of all, judges have unusually long and secure tenure in office. Some judges are appointed for fifteen- to twenty-year terms or even for life (during good behavior). And even though most trial judges are elected for terms only moderately longer than mayors or councilmen, the etiquette in most jurisdictions is that incumbent judges are not opposed either in partisan or nonpartisan systems. In any event, a sitting judge has great advantages because of his public prominence and support of bar associations, so that almost no incumbent judge fails to be reelected. Those very few judges who do lose their offices in elections do so because of generally unsatisfactory performance on the bench rather than because of the policy content of their decisions. Even when judges are up for election, for example, they do not "campaign" by making speeches on policy matters.[17]

Second, judges are not subject to the normal hierarchical and budgetary controls exercised by mayors and councilmen over other city officials and employees. Judges usually enjoy strong state constitutional protection against suspension or dismissal, and there are usually also constitutional or statutory bans on any reduction in salary during a judge's term of office.

Third, judges are shielded from pressure by the widely held norms that favor the independence of the judiciary. The security of tenure and freedom from hierarchical controls already referred to reflect that norm. And so do the special ritualistic elements of court procedure: the imposing buildings that usually serve as courtrooms, the special dress, the honorific forms used

[17]*Ibid.,* pp. 97–101; Jones, "The Trial Judge," pp. 97–101; Herbert Jacob, *Urban Justice* (Englewood Cliffs, N.J.: Prentice-Hall, 1973), chap. 4.

to address judges, and the other kinds of special respect paid to them. These features, plus the requirement that parties who are attempting to influence a judge's decision-making must present their appeal deferentially, in open court and in traditional legal form, argument, and language, add to the judicial mystique.

In sum, all these protections of the independence of the judiciary serve to emphasize the distinctiveness of the judicial role and to allow judges, more so than probably any other city officials or employees, to make their decisions the way they personally think is right and without regard to possible retaliation from those they might offend.

High invulnerability does not mean complete invulnerability, however. As we have seen, given their own weak powers of enforcement, judges may feel self-pressured not to render a decision that is flagrantly at odds with the known preferences and values of city executive officials or of wide segments of the general public or both because of the risk it runs of not being complied with. Furthermore, judges know that their decisions can be appealed and reversed by higher courts, if those decisions lack sound legal foundation. Also, while such interventions are rare, judicial decision-making that persistently and over a long period of time goes counter to the general goals of elected officials and the dominant climate of public opinion may result in some forms of retaliation by legislative and executive officials. For example, legislative changes desired by judges for the structure of the court or of its jurisdiction may not be enacted. Increases in salary or better retirement benefits may not be granted. Additional funds for expansion of their supporting staff or for the appointment of more judges to reduce the load of the existing judges may be withheld. The legislature may even impose some restructuring or curtailment of jurisdiction that will reduce the powers of a particular court. Perhaps rarer still, judges who engage in bribery, corruption, or other serious misbehavior can be impeached, normally by the state legislature. In some states judges can also be removed from office after a special trial by a panel of fellow judges, and elective judges are usually subject to recall.[18]

THE OVERALL IMPACT OF JUDGES ON URBAN POLICYMAKING

We have seen how judges, in deciding lawsuits between particular contesting parties, have occasion to exert influence on urban policymaking. We have also seen in what respects judges, as decision-makers, are similar to and different from other city officials. Broadly speaking, this kind of decision-making by judges normally has sporadic and light impact on the substantive content of city policy and programs but more continuous and heavy impact on the procedural aspects of the policy process.

[18]Jacob, *Justice in America,* pp. 102–3.

On Substance of Policy

Overall, the influence of judges on the substance of city policy and programs is normally discontinuous, marginal, and "spotty" in coverage. Judges influence the substance of the urban policy process only as occasional vetoers of specific policy decisions that they find to be unsupported by positive grants of power, as marginal shapers of the detailed application of programs, and as partial determiners (through their discretion in fixing penalties) of the enforceability of particular regulations. The policy impact of judicial decision-making does not take place evenly all along the policy spectrum: Such vital policy decisions as spending levels for different programs, the rates of different kinds of taxes (up to, of course, the limits imposed by state law), the establishment or nonestablishment of a particular new service or facility are almost never successfully challenged in court. Either judges refuse to find that any private party has "standing" to sue or they rule that such matters are clearly permitted within the traditional discretionary authority of legislative bodies.

The kind of substantive matters often passed upon by city judges include: the application of zoning regulations; decisions on the location of public buildings or other capital projects, like highways and urban renewal projects; the use of the power of eminent domain to acquire the sites; the assessed valuation placed on particular property; and the exact kinds of conduct that various health, sanitary, and fair trade regulations are meant to restrict.[19] In these matters city judges not only may explicitly overrule the decisions of other city officials, but once they entertain such suits, judges often restrain the implementation of a challenged decision until the case is finally settled. During the long delays normal in large cities until cases have an opportunity to come to trial, the city officials may modify their original decision in order to end the controversy. Or a change of administration may take place that rescinds the decision in question, regardless of what the final judicial ruling might have been on its validity.

Another way that judges affect the implementation of substantive policy is by upholding an important city governmental act after a challenge. Judges place a "seal of legitimacy" upon the challenged policy, thus removing any widespread doubts as to its validity and permitting its implementation to take place more efficiently.[20]

On Procedural Aspects of the Process

Judges have a much heavier impact on the procedural aspects of the large-city policy process than on the content of its output. By being continuously

[19]Kenneth M. Dolbeare, *Trial Courts in Urban Politics* (New York: Wiley, 1967), chaps. 6 and 7; and "Taxpayers' Suits: A Survey and Summary," 69 *Yale Law Journal* (1960), 895–924.

[20]Dolbeare, *Trial Courts,* p. 116.

available to listen to and rule on complaints, judges play a key role in checking any tendencies of policymaking and policy-enforcing city officials to trespass upon civil liberties or ignore procedural regularities and protections are penalized within certain "civil libertarian—procedural due process" First Amendment freedoms of speech, press, assembly, and religion, judges protect individuals from the oppression of being subjected to regulations in areas of activity that involve a person's own sphere of individuality and taste. But more crucial to the continuation of a democratic government, these trial judges guarantee the openness of the policy process to criticism and to other nonviolent strategies and tactics that attempt to bring about change in the substance of city policy or programs or the replacement of city officials through elections. City officials might well succumb regularly to the temptation of trying to silence complaints against their performance. But one important deterrent is the knowledge that judges independent of their control stand ready to strike down any such limitations, regardless of how incapable the individuals or groups against whom they would be directed might be of protecting themselves by prevailing in political arenas like legislatures or elections where majorities rule.

And by passing on the correctness of statutory applications and by ruling on challenges to alleged arbitrary actions by city administrators and bureaucrats, judges promote a quality of government where persons with the same characteristics receive relatively equal and consistent treatment. There are preannounced general rules and no one needs to accept a restriction imposed on him or a benefit denied or withdrawn unfairly without being told the reason for the decision and given an opportunity to dispute in court the grounds on which it was made. Judges also sometimes soften the impact of a bureaucratic rule by interpretation, where its most literal application would cause great harshness, given the facts of a particular case.

Finally, by refusing in trials of accused violators of city ordinances and criminal laws to admit evidence gained through "unfair" means, as well as by requiring that such accused persons be provided with legal counsel and other provisions for conducting a vigorous defense, judges maintain a law-enforcement system highly protective of an accused.

In sum, judges insure that city policies are made, applied, and their violations are penalized within certain "civil libertarian—procedural due process" rules-of-the-game, rules which protect the weak and outnumbered as well as the strong and dominant. Judges can, of course, enforce such rules against voting majorities or against elected officials speaking for majorities only so long as judicial decisions based on civil libertarian—procedural due process standards continue to be widely accepted voluntarily. If any full-scale, prolonged assaults were to be launched against such rules by a unified body of elected officials with the support of dominant majorities among the public or by successful coup d'etatists of the left or right with dictatorial leanings, civil liberties and due process would be in serious jeopardy. For the present, however, most American governmental officials, and particularly most elected ones, appear to be committed to some form of civil liberties and procedural due process. City judges therefore can continue to enforce such rules-of-the-game against short-run, isolated incursions, and by doing so probably ward off even a greater number of attacks that are considered but never attempted. Thus city judges play a key part in maintaining the open, largely nonoppressive, and nonarbitrary qualities found in large cities' policymaking processes.

13

City Private Elites

Thus far we have discussed how party leaders and various kinds of city officials influence city governmental decisions. What these city influentials have in common is that they all hold some legally defined position within a city's governmental institutions or within what are, in effect, its "auxiliary" governmental institutions in partisan cities—the political parties.

In a democracy, political influence cannot be the monopoly of only those persons holding official public or party office. Accordingly, in large American cities private individuals, groups, and segments of the public also exert political influence. This chapter will examine how such influence is wielded by those private individuals—the social and economic notables and the leaders of its organized interest groups—whose resources give them the best opportunities to be influential in a city's politics. From these categories of individuals come a large proportion of what can be considered a city's "private elites." The following chapter will examine the role of an additional, special group of city elites—those who control the urban communications media. The chapter after that will turn to the question of what influence can be exerted on the policymaking process of our large cities by the nonelite, rank-and-file members of the general public.

GENERAL TECHNIQUES OF PRIVATE ELITES

Essentially all private elites exert their "outsider" influence on city governmental decisions through one or more fairly standard channels or techniques: direct lobbying of specific elective or appointed officials;

propaganda or public relations campaigns; electioneering for or against the election or appointment of particular persons to public office; litigation; and protest demonstrations or other direct action.

By direct lobbying is meant simply communicating views to city officials directly, either during public hearings or more privately by letter, telephone conversations, informal meetings and consultations, service as members of citizens' advisory or study commissions or as individual consultants. Public relations and propaganda campaigns entail the use of press releases and interviews, letters to the editor, newspaper advertisements, inspired stories or editorials, radio or television commercials, billboards, and direct mailings and telephoning to other members of the public, all with the purpose of arousing the opinions of a segment of the public in support of the policy goals sought and in the hope that officials will be responsive to any such public opinion generated. Electioneering involves trying to affect the outcome of a prospective election or appointment so as to place in office a candidate expected to be sympathetic to a particular point of view or to block one expected to be hostile. Litigation uses lawsuits and the courts in an effort to have some city official's act declared illegal or unconstitutional or to compel the performance of an act that such an official opposes. Demonstrations and other direct action refers to such practices as group picketing, marches, sit-ins, strikes, boycotts, civil disobedience, and the threat or actual use of violence against property or persons.

SOCIAL AND ECONOMIC NOTABLES

Much has been written in recent years about the influence of social and economic notables.[1] By "social notables" is meant individual members of upper-class families such as those listed in the "social registers" of various large cities, who normally hold that status by being descendants of individuals who achieved prominence or great wealth, or both, two or more generations earlier:[2]

> These families are at the top of the *social class* hierarchy; they are brought up together, are friends, and are intermarried with one another; and, finally, they maintain a distinctive style of life. . . .[3]

Members of these upper-class families are likely to have attended fashionable private schools, live in elegant neighborhoods, and belong to exclusive

[1]The term itself is Robert A. Dahl's in *Who Governs?* (New Haven: Yale University Press, 1961), esp. chap. 6.

[2]See E. Digby Baltzell, *Philadelphia Gentlemen* (Glencoe, Ill.: Free Press, 1958), p. 7; Dahl, *Who Governs?*, chap. 6.

[3]Baltzell, *Philadelphia Gentlemen,* p. 7.

clubs; the daughters of these families often "come out" at debutante balls.

By "economic notables" is meant individuals who have the greatest personal wealth in a city or who hold the top positions, like president or chairman of the board, in the companies with the largest volume of sales or profits or with the largest ownership of property in a city. Although these two categories are obviously not mutually exclusive, only a small minority of the "economic notables" in large cities are currently likely to be also among the city's "social notables."[4]

One school of thought has it that not only do these private elites participate in a city's policymaking process, but that they constitute an "establishment," "power elite," or "community power structure" that essentially runs the city government from behind the scenes. Floyd Hunter did most to popularize this view of the influence of business or economic notables in his book about "Regional City" (in reality, Atlanta, Georgia). Hunter argues that about forty individuals, meeting in downtown hotel luncheons, private clubs, or their own expensive residences, wielded the most "power" in Atlanta. Of these forty, eleven held top positions, like owners, chairmen of the board, or presidents in large commercial enterprises, seven in banking and investment firms, and five in industrial companies. The forty notables were the "big-wigs," "big wheels," "high moguls," and "fat cats" who, according to Hunter, dominated Regional City's political life:

> It is true that there is no formal tie between the economic interests and government, but the structure of policy-determining committees and their tie-in with the other powerful institutions and organizations of the community make government subservient to the interests of these combined groups. The governmental departments and their key personnel are acutely aware of the power of key individuals . . . , and they are loath to act before consulting and "clearing" with these interests. . . .
>
> The structure is that of a dominant policymaking group using the machinery of government as a bureaucracy for the attainment of certain goals coordinate with their interests. . . .[5]

These top business leaders were purportedly able to "enforce their decisions by persuasion, intimidation, coercion, and, if necessary, force."[6] They used a larger pool of second-tier, "understructure" men—the "fireballs," "hatchet men"—to serve as intermediaries and to actually implement the decisions reached at the top.

[4]See Dahl, *Who Governs?*, p. 68; Baltzell, *Philadelphia Gentlemen,* chap. 3.

[5]Floyd Hunter, *Community Power Structure* (Chapel Hill: University of North Carolina Press, 1953), pp. 101–2.

[6]*Ibid.*, p. 24.

The other, and by now much larger, school of thought in political science holds that although social and economic elites certainly have much more influence over city governmental decision-making than the average member of the general public, they do not dominate city politics. Rather, they meet with varying success in getting decisions that they want. This success depends on the issues, on how compatible their objectives are with the goals and preferences of elective and appointive city officials, on their own application, persistence, and skills, and on the extent and kind of opposition to them that mobilizes. In their study of New Haven, Robert Dahl and his colleagues concluded, for example, that the economic elites (who were decidedly more powerful than the social ones):

> far from being a ruling group, are simply one of the many groups out of which individuals sporadically emerge to influence the policies and acts of city officials. Almost anything one might say about the influence of the Economic Notables could be said with equal justice about a half dozen other groups in the New Haven community. . . . [S]ometimes the Notables have their way and sometimes they do not.[7]

Furthermore, the Dahl group found that even those notables who proved to have been influential, had been so in no more than a single issue-area of the three—party nominations, urban redevelopment, and public education—that were examined. Of the individuals who were determined to have exercised significant influence on a wider scope of issues, not one was an economic or social notable. All were elected or appointed city governmental officials: Richard C. Lee, New Haven's mayor for most of the period covered by the Dahl study; Lee's predecessor as mayor, William Celentano; and Lee's Development Administrator, Edward Logue.

Influence Resources of Social and Economic Notables

The chief resources which give social and economic notables their influence are a high sense of political efficacy, high prestige, contacts, and, occasionally, the economic sanctions they can impose.

The notables' high sense of political efficacy refers to a feeling that if they want to do so, they can by their actions influence the outcome of political events. A variety of studies[8] shows that such feelings of efficacy and self-confidence in dealing with governmental officials and the associated social and verbal skills necessary for communicating effectively with officialdom,

[7]Dahl, *Who Governs?*, pp. 72, 75.

[8]The studies are conveniently summarized in Robert E. Lane, *Political Life* (New York: Free Press, 1959), pp. 143–54; and Lester W. Milbrath, *Political Participation* (Chicago: Rand McNally, 1965), pp. 57–60.

are positively associated with the amount of a person's formal education, the size of his income, and the status of his occupation. In these areas, almost by definition, the notables score high.

To have prestige means essentially to have high capacity to evoke favorable attention, recognition, deference, willingness to associate, and similar positively charged feelings from other individuals and groups. For many and perhaps for most people in American urban society, individuals bearing upper-class names such as Rockefeller, Ford, Biddle, or those having extensive wealth or holding positions like board chairman or president in large, well-known business firms, carry this kind of high prestige. Accordingly, social and economic notables will normally be given more time and attention by officials than will the average citizen: David Rockefeller, for example, who is in the New York Social Register, is one of the world's richest individuals, and heads one of the two leading New York City banks, probably can get an appointment to see that city's mayor with only hours' notice. It is equally likely that a social and economic notable like Rockefeller can get to talk to the mayor on the telephone at any time, however busy the mayor might be and unavailable to "non-notables."

Besides giving them privileged access to officials, the prestige of the notables makes their remarks more likely to be published by newspapers and to capture the attention of the politically-attentive part of the public. Particularly on matters closely related to their own pursuits—for economic elites, policies affecting big businesses and for social elites, various cultural activities with which they are often identified—the views of the notables tend to carry special authority. This allows them to get sympathetic hearings for their own preferred policies and various kinds of modification of officially sponsored ideas in exchange for giving their "seal of approval" to the final policy adopted. Such seals of approval are especially valuable to city officials when they concern projects that, because of cost or other considerations, the business community could be expected to oppose. Mayor Lee of New Haven, for example, deliberately organized a Citizens Action Commission chock-full of economic elites to advise on his urban renewal projects. As Dahl tells it:

> The importance of the CAC in assuring acceptability for the redevelopment program can hardly be overestimated. The mere fact that the CAC existed and regularly endorsed the proposals of the city administration made the program appear nonpartisan, virtually nullified the effectiveness of partisan attacks, presented to the public an appearance of power and responsibility diffused among a representative group of community notables, and inhibited criticisms of even the most daring and ambitious parts of the program as "unrealistic," or "unbusinesslike." Indeed, by creating the CAC the Mayor virtually

> decapitated the opposition. The presence of leading bankers, industrialists, and businessmen—almost all of whom were Republicans—insured that any project they agreed on would not be attacked by conservatives. . . .[9]

In exchange, however, Mayor Lee had to abandon some projects or features of projects that he wanted, but that they would not have approved:

> . . . [T]he administration shaped their proposals according to what they expected would receive the full support of the CAC. . . . The Mayor . . . was particularly skillful in estimating what the CAC could be expected to support or reject.[10]

The notables' access to money allows them to hire the time, energy, and special skills of other people, such as staffs of public relations people, lawyers, and professional lobbyists. Such staffs can develop and justify proposals and conduct sustained lobbying or public relations campaigns or engage in drawn-out litigation. The notables can also use their money to make large campaign contributions to increase the chance of election of favored, like-minded candidates and to create a sense of obligation if those candidates are elected to office. Indeed, they can privately contribute to both opposed candidates so that the sense of obligation will exist whoever is elected. And their potential negative influence in this respect is probably even greater: For refusal of all of the economic elites to back a particular aspirant with campaign funds just about rules out any chance for succeeding in a primary or general election campaign to a city-wide office.

The notables can, if they themselves are criminally inclined and believe the promulgator of the decision in question is likewise, use their money to try to purchase a favorable policy outright with bribes. When the implementation of a city policy requires the investment of nongovernmental funds—as with urban renewal plans needing private sponsors to undertake construction or cultural centers needing the subscription of large amounts of private wealth—social and economic notables can draw on their own wealth or that of their friends or foundations they control to help the program to succeed. Or they can refuse to participate and allow it to fail.

The social and economic elites normally have "contacts" among high city officials which enhance their ability to reach the relevant decision-makers for the policy in which they are interested. Social and economic notables with offices in the "downtowns" have frequent opportunity to develop at least some kind of acquaintance with city officials that then saves

[9]Dahl, *Who Governs?,* p. 133.
[10]*Ibid.,* p. 137.

them from having to approach those officials on some matter of policy cold. Such contacts come from meeting city officials in their clubs and trade associations or during commemorative events, speaking engagements, memberships on advisory boards, or routine relations with government agencies in connection with their businesses.

The chief economic sanction that economic elites have in today's large cities is the threat to move their companies, with the jobs that they provide and the taxes that they pay, to another jurisdiction. That threat is employed implicitly by the business community as a whole continuously, with city decision-makers being aware that increases in taxes may speed the movement of industry to the suburbs or to cities in lower-tax areas. The more dominated a city's economy is by a few firms, the more powerful such a threat is. The threat can be used explicitly by a specific economic elite, however, only on occasion. The best occasion is when a new tax or tax increase hits particularly heavily at his company or when existing facilities have become inadequate, thus necessitating some kind of move and making more credible the possibility that the firm will in fact relocate out of town unless certain concessions in tax rates, assessments, favorable sites in a renewal project, or less restrictive regulation of its kind of activity are granted. And it can only be used by firms whose assets are easily transferrable to other areas, not by businesses like department stores, utility companies, banks, or newspapers, who either operate under franchises not transferrable or who could not replace their clientele in new areas.

The other major kind of economic sanction is held by investment bankers. For they can threaten not to purchase or market a city's bonds at all or to do so only at higher interest rates or they can downgrade the quality-rating of city bonds if the city does not live more frugally. New York City's investment bankers did this with great fanfare in 1975, insisting that the city cut services, freeze civil service salaries, and lay off employees. Investment bankers are in an especially good position to influence special district-type public authorities, because most authorities lack taxing powers and thus depend almost entirely on their ability to borrow money by floating bonds on favorable terms to raise capital for new facilities. The authorities can thus sometimes be pressured into shunning facilities, however much needed in the city, which do not bring in large operating revenues.

In smaller cities and small towns many local officials are part timers, most people are personally acquainted with one another, and control of wealth and credit is typically in fewer hands. There, leading businessmen and bankers may also use as a sanction an ability to affect the economic security of individual officeholders or their relatives.[11]

[11]See, e.g., the classic study, *Middletown,* by Robert and Helen Lynd (New York: Harcourt Brace, 1929).

Built-In Dampers on the Influence of Social and Economic Notables

Although the assets of social and economic notables are imposing, built-in dampers also exist which limit both the extent to which these assets are committed to attempts to influence city governmental decisions and the success that any commitment can assure.

First, city politics is typically not the primary interest of social and economic notables. Their regular working (or leisure) day is filled with non-political pursuits. Only occasionally do city decisions have specific, tangible, and clearly identifiable consequences for their central interests. To the officers of national corporations who are managers of branches located in a city, for example, local governmental decisions are usually unimportant. As corporate nomads, out-of-towners by origin, transferred every few years from city to city, usually having their own homes in a suburb, and oriented toward "making it" someday to the company's headquarters, branch executives develop little emotional involvement to what is going on politically in the city to which they are currently assigned. Even the taxes paid to the city government or possible increases being considered will almost certainly constitute only a tiny fraction of the operating costs of their plants. And unlike the case of owner-proprietors of earlier days or of contemporary small businessmen, any increased taxes will not cause a decrease in their own personal income.

Furthermore, the wealth of the corporation is not in the hands of the branch managers to invest in the political arena. The branch manager's:

> role is usually defined by headquarters. Proconsular in his position, each major commitment to the local community must be reviewed by his superior and every cent of his war chest accounted for. Powerful as he may be in the imaginations of local citizens, his power is usually the passive force of a bureaucratic instrument, part of a larger . . . machine.[12]

The old-style proprietor businessman could commit funds without caring about boards of directors or other superiors, but not most present executives. Similarly, a corporation's entire financial resources, however vast, are not all available for politics:

> A corporation may be worth millions, but its policies and liquidity position may be such that it cannot possibly bring these millions into

[12]Scott Greer, *The Emerging City: Myth and Reality* (New York: Free Press, 1965), p. 155.

> play to influence the outcome of a community decision—even one in which the corporation is vitally interested.[13]

For executives stationed at the corporation's headquarters city, local governmental policies and programs often appear trivial, marginal, or unrelated to the corporation's activities:

> In light of the corporation's national or [international] function, the chief advantage of *this* city, *this* community, may be no more than the residential preferences of the top staff and a relatively minute investment in a building or two.[14]

As the president of a major industrial concern headquartered in Philadelphia put it to an interviewer:

> It makes little difference to us what happens in the city. We do not have our homes here [they live in the suburbs]; we have no large plants located within the city limits; we have only an office building that we can close at any time that conditions within the city become too oppressive.[15]

Second, even if social and economic elites have incentive to try to influence city governmental policies, the "opportunity" and other costs for acting on that incentive are usually high. Opportunity costs are the value to be secured from foregone alternative uses to which a person's time, energy, and other resources might be devoted. Current corporate executives are busy people, very much actively involved in the day-to-day operations of their firms.[16] They constantly must make important internal decisions and cope with business problems. Becoming involved in a campaign to affect city governmental policy is distracting from their central pursuits and consumes large amounts of time and energy and attention that most businessmen feel is more productively spent on their own company's affairs and in advancing their own careers. Consequently, even when they do become involved in a policy conflict, their investment of time and energy may be too slight to make a difference. As Norton Long has explained:

> Again and again the interviewer is told that the president of such-

[13]Nelson W. Polsby, *Community Power and Political Theory* (New Haven: Yale University Press, 1963), p. 120.

[14]Greer, *The Emerging City,* p. 155.

[15]James Reichley, *The Art of Government* (New York: Fund for the Republic, 1959), p. 61.

[16]Donald A. Clelland and William H. Form, "Economic Dominants and Community Power," *American Journal of Sociology,* 69 (1964): 511–21.

> and-such an organization is doing a terrific job and literally knocking himself out for such-and-such a program. On investigation a "terrific job" turns out to be a few telephone calls and, possibly, three luncheons a month. The standard of "terrific job" obviously varies widely from what would be required in the business role.[17]

Furthermore, getting involved in politics on a controversial issue is often considered by economic notables to be bad public relations for their firms, particularly when the position preferred by the notable can be made to appear in conflict with that most beneficial to the general public. Also, for social notables who prize their exclusivity, becoming involved in city politics means having to associate with and in some respects treat as equals city officials and employees whom they regard as social inferiors.

Third, when social and economic notables do become involved in the city's political affairs, they are not always all on the same side. Various business firms are affected by city decisions in different and even contradictory ways. Some are property owners, some are renters; some engage in regulated activity, some profit from the regulation of competitors or other firms with which they must deal; some are subject to special proposed taxes; some sell to the city government or use its services, while others do not; some are in competition with others over the award of lucrative construction contracts or urban renewal sponsorships. Economic and social notables have different ideological beliefs about what kinds of policies are desirable or undesirable in principle. Not all businessmen, for example, oppose governmental regulation or higher taxes when necessary to permit spending for improvement of city governmental services or amelioration of the conditions of the poor, particularly when it is perceived as necessary to keep things cool.[18] Obviously when the elites are thus divided, their resources are used in opposition to one another and the view of any particular elite loses its authoritative quality, even when it bears on a policy closely affecting business.

Fourth, when opposed by nonelite political actors including city officials, the assets and resources of social and economic notables are not always weighty enough to prevail. The flattery of being able to accommodate and develop some degree of acquaintanceship with an upper-class personage or business notable may be pleasant for some city officials or employees. But it is unlikely to be important enough to cause such officials and employees to ignore statutory responsibilities, strong policy preferences of their own,

[17] Norton Long, "The Local Community as an Ecology of Games," *American Journal of Sociology,* 64 (1958): 257–58.

[18] See, e.g., Robert E. Agger, Daniel Goldrich, and Bert E. Swanson, *The Rulers and the Ruled* (New York: Wiley, 1964); R. Joseph Monson, Jr., and Mark W. Cannon, *The Makers of Public Policy* (New York: McGraw-Hill, 1965).

or the views of individuals and groups that can exert heavier sanctions than withdrawal of the privilege of name-dropping. Furthermore, most city officials and employees are not listed in the social register. Therefore, they may not be impressed favorably by a socially prestigious name, or they may even be impressed negatively by any perceived attempts to trade on and claim deference because of family background, instead of from achievement in the political arena or arguments based on the "merits" of the issue. Also, the opposition of businessmen to such policies as tax or spending increases is severely discounted since that opposition is expected and also is visibly self-serving.

Finally, on any showdown which pits the interests of the social or economic notables against the interests of broad publics or the policies perceived by city officials as necessary for the success of their administrations, the notables are in a position of severe weakness: For the notables must always have only a tiny fraction of the ultimate sanction in city politics —namely, the vote. Thus, even on the cutting issue of taxes, businessmen can complain and forecast dire consequences for the city's economy if business and property taxes are raised further. But this kind of defensive action serves at most only to slow the rate of increase, not to stay or retard it. As Sayre and Kaufman have written about the influence of the economic notables in New York City:

> . . . the department stores and other merchants, for example, protested against, but could not block, an increase in the general sales tax. . . . Stock-transfer and payroll taxes disliked by these [plutocratic] groups have not been lifted or even lightened. Holders of the city's bonds traditionally prefer to prevent increases in the city's borrowing capacity in order to protect their investments, but the number of activities exempted from the bond limits has nevertheless increased, and the limits themselves are higher than they ever have been. Likewise, the assessed valuation of property has risen higher than ever before. . . . And though the spokesmen for business groups are among the most vehement critics of rising municipal expenditures, the city's budget is over 50 percent larger [in 1965] than it was in 1958. . . .[19]

And lack of success in this instance is not the result of lack of trying:

> Charges of waste, inefficiency, and spending beyond the city's means are loud and insistent [from the economic notables], and those who make the accusations give every sign of *wanting* to reduce the

[19]Wallace S. Sayre and Herbert Kaufman, *Governing New York City* (New York: Norton, 1965), xxxviii.

> level of expenditure and service. From the available evidence, it appears that they do not prevail because they *cannot* prevail, and not because they refuse, in the last analysis, to use their political resources to attain the ends they profess.[20]

Of course in a crisis such as occurred in 1975, New York City officials did reduce expenditures in order to win the cooperation of investment bankers to avoid default.

The Overall Impact of Social and Economic Notables

Whether the overall impact of social and economic notables in city policy-making is deemed heavy or light depends on the benchmark one is using for measuring. If the benchmark is Hunter's "dominance," then the impact of the notables is relatively light. If however the benchmark for measurement is not dominance, but the influence of the average member of the general public, the impact of the notables, and especially of the economic notables, is considerable. Dahl admits that although the influence of New Haven's social notables was in any absolute sense very small, they were still clearly overrepresented as officeholders relative to their numbers in the general population. This was by as much as thirteen times overall and twenty-seven times in the agencies dealing with urban redevelopment.[21] Furthermore, in most large cities, social elites are heavily concentrated and thus massively overrepresented on boards of trustees or commissions that oversee the city's hospitals, parks, concert halls, art and other museums, and universities.[22]

The impact of the economic notables is clearly even heavier. Dahl found that in the field of party nominations, education, and urban redevelopment, these economic notables held twenty-six times the offices that they should have held if represented according to their proportion in the overall population and in urban redevelopment alone, they held fifty-five times the number. Indeed, in urban redevelopment one out of seven top leaders—which Dahl defines as "participants who were successful more than once in initiating or vetoing a policy proposal"—and nine out of nineteen minor leaders—"participants who were successful only once in initiating or vetoing a policy proposal"—were economic notables.[23]

[20]*Ibid.*, xlix, note 9.

[21]Dahl, *Who Governs?*, pp. 64–65.

[22]See Edward C. Banfield and James Q. Wilson, *City Politics* (Cambridge, Mass.: Harvard University Press and the M.I.T. Press, 1963), p. 249; Baltzell, *Philadelphia Gentlemen;* Peter B. Clark, "The Chicago Big Businessman as a Civic Leader," in Linton C. Freeman, ed., *Patterns of Local Community Leadership* (Indianapolis; Bobbs-Merrill, 1968), pp. 77-78.

[23]Dahl, *Who Governs?*, p. 73.

Different studies of city politics show that businessmen also have been active in cities other than New Haven in the post-World War II era in shaping and implementing redevelopment plans for the city's downtown central business district (CBD), out of all proportion to their numbers in the general population. Until very recently, the economic notables appear to have had much greater influence than any other nongovernmental actors immediately affected, especially the slum poor or the small businessmen who inevitably become displaced by CBD redevelopment programs. As a result, the implementation of urban renewal in large cities has been much more a blight-eliminating program for the CBD than any large-scale effort to improve housing for the poor.[24]

The overall impact of economic notables in other areas of city policy where their active cooperation is not necessary for a program's success, is more uncertain, as few detailed studies exist to provide bases for confident generalization. Apparently, however, it is less on other matters than on redevelopment policies for the central business district. On welfare benefits and regulations, education of ghetto children, crime and law enforcement, health and hospital care, big businessmen seem to have little continuous influence. And in all cases, businessmen are likely to have the greatest degree of success on low visibility issues where the public is indifferent, where the money cost to the city for complying with their claims is low, where potential opposition to their objectives fails to develop, and thus where going along with what the businessmen want becomes for city officials the course of least resistance.

In certain large cities in the South and Southwest like Dallas, El Paso, Houston, Atlanta, and Phoenix, big businessmen may, however, be more powerful generally than they are in the rest of the country's large cities and on a wider range of issues. According to Edward Banfield, in El Paso:

> [I]t is the businessmen who have the greatest influence in the conduct of affairs. . . . Most of those elected to office in El Paso are themselves businessmen who believe, along with most middle-class El Pasoans, that "What's Good for El Paso Business Is Good for El Paso." Ordinarily, there is no need for the business community to bring any pressure on city hall: the elected officials do what the businessmen want without being asked. If need be, however, business can draw upon a stock of influence it wields as the biggest source of financial support in election campaigns. . . . The few most important businessmen . . . try, almost always successfully, to keep those politicians who have particularly close ties to the unions out of local

[24]See Scott Greer, *Urban Renewal and American Cities* (Indianapolis: Bobbs-Merrill, 1965).

> office. . . . They also do what they can to see that officials have the "right attitude" on assessments, tax rates, off-street parking, highway location, traffic control, and similar matters.[25]

In these cities the lower-class voting population is relatively smaller than in the northern cities, both because annexations have allowed the central cities to keep middle-class, suburban-style residents within their legal jurisdictions and because less of the lower-class population is mobilized and politically self-conscious. Since city elections in those cities are often nonpartisan, neither party organization nor party affiliation provide motivation to get the less probusiness segment of the community to the polls. And organized labor is too weak to provide an alternative mobilizing device. But most of all, as Banfield indicates for El Paso, in these cities the dominant "political culture" among the general public appears to place the highest value on business growth, success, and profits. This outlook thus provides widespread support for initiatives by economic notables to promote policies benefiting business and to curb policies that would unduly tax or regulate business or provide protections or advantages to workers, unionized or not, let alone to the poor generally.

In all cities, of course, economic notables have great additional impact on the operation of the city government indirectly, through the aggregate consequences of their private business investment and locational decisions. Decisions to expand or build new office buildings or plants in the city or to move to the suburbs; decisions to risk profits by reaching out to find, train, and employ the hard-core unemployed; decisions to try to build or finance housing within the means of low- or middle-income families—all these private business decisions directly affect the environment of city governments by influencing various key conditions and problems that ultimately generate demands for governmental policies or provide resources making implementation of such policies more or less possible.

A Special Breed of Economic Notables: The Foundation Executives

A special case of economic notables is foundation executives. These executives control organizations that are geared not for making profits, but instead for spending money to advance the public good. The base of the foundation executives' influence in city politics has long been their financing of studies of city operations, policies, and programs by professors, civic groups, research leagues, and other nonprofit agencies. In more recent decades, the foundations have also been exerting more direct influence both

[25]Edward C. Banfield, *Big City Politics* (New York: Random House, 1966), pp. 73–74.

by financing the carrying out of demonstration or pilot programs by city governments and semigovernmental, nonprofit corporations and by financing the activities of various groups that seek to exert influence on city governmental policies through organized protest as well as through other means.

According to most foundation executives, their influence is only of a facilitative kind, making possible projects that city officials, scholars, or community groups themselves have thought up, but otherwise lack financial resources to carry out. The foundations deny that they use the leverage of their great financial resources to impose their own ideas upon, for example, responsible city officials. But since the resources of even the largest foundations—Ford, Rockefeller, Sloane, Carnegie—are not unlimited and are indeed meager relative to the cost of the unprovided services being demanded at any time of city governments, the foundation executives must make choices about the projects for which they will provide grants. Normally the foundations do not specify in advance exactly what kinds of projects they are willing to fund, but define their purposes in highly general terms like "advancing human betterment," "opening opportunities," "redistributing power," and invite applications. But this practice, as Marris and Rein have explained about the Ford Foundation's involvement in community programs:

> simply reduced the negotiations to a guessing game, in which the cities arrived by elimination at the answer the Foundation had first thought of. Even in the specification of programmes, where the Foundation was genuinely open-minded, the fertility of human invention could not match the opportunity. In search of fresh ideas, the drafters of the proposals in the cities could only turn, after all, to the Foundation itself, to discover what it would accept as relevant and new. The programmes which gained currency came to look very much alike, and they bore the stamp of the Public Affairs staff's analysis, more than the communities' first thoughts.[26]

In short, by deciding that certain governmental approaches or kinds of programs and certain kinds of problems are worthy of support but not others, the foundation executives insure greater concentration of effort on the approaches and problems in which they are interested. This they do not only by their direct funding, but also by the prestige and stamp of unimpeachable validity that they assign to those approaches and problems that are fashionable at any one time in foundation circles. This makes them

[26]Peter Marris and Martin Rein, *Dilemmas of Social Reform,* 2nd ed., (Chicago: Aldine, 1973), p. 123.

more likely to be imitated by different cities and agencies regardless of direct financial support.

It should be noted that the Tax Reform Act of 1969 prohibited tax-exempt foundations from spending money directly for lobbying or electioneering. During consideration of the bill in Congress, some strong objections were raised also to foundations subsidizing organizations that engage in political activities like protests. The language of this Act plus the possibility that more stringent restrictions might be legislated in the future have, consequently, made foundation executives more cautious in the 1970s about the kinds of outside group activities that they will finance.

LEADERS OF POLITICAL INTEREST GROUPS

Still another set of city private elites consists of the leaders of its organized political interest groups. These interest groups are private, voluntary associations of individuals (though sometimes the individuals represent firms or other organizations), whose collective purpose is to further or protect one or more shared interests, at least partly through influencing city governmental decisions.

Bases of Organization

Major bases of organization for city interest groups are their occupational, problem- or functionally-oriented, ethnic, territorial or neighborhood, and good government interests.

Occupational Interests. In all large cities there are groups organized on the basis of the common interest of those engaged in particular kinds of work, trade, or business. Thus plumbers, accountants, engineers, electrical contractors, builders, carpenters, garage operators, truck drivers, barbers, pharmacists, insurance salesmen, real estate brokers, real estate operators, morticians, lawyers, medical doctors—these and individuals pursuing numerous other occupations normally have their "trade associations," "professional societies," and "labor union locals." These groups attempt self-regulation and protection of their trade or business from encroachments by groups providing competing services. But they also engage in efforts to defeat suggested city governmental policies having an adverse effect on their lines of work and urge the adoption of city policies that would appear to confer special advantages. Very often, in addition to groups organized along the lines of particular businesses or trades, there are so-called "peak" associations. These represent the interests of business organizations in general, like chambers of commerce or commerce and industry associations, or of labor unions generally, like central labor councils, or central trade and labor councils.

Problem- or Functionally-Oriented Interests. Large cities also have interest groups whose interest is in some particular social problem and the conduct of the related city governmental functions or programs. Such groups carry names like "City Housing Association," "Community Service Organization," "Citizens Committee for Children," "Health and Welfare Council," "National Welfare Rights Organization," "Committee for Clean Air," "Park Association," local "Urban Coalitions," and, of course, city-wide and local "Parent-Teacher Associations" and "United Parents Associations."

Ethnic Interests. Still another category of interest groups consists of those built on interests growing out of common and usually minority and lower-status, racial, religious, or ethnic background. Thus, in nearly all large cities there are NAACP, Urban League, and CORE chapters as well as newer, shorter-lived groups to speak for the rights and interests of black people. In cities like New York, Los Angeles, and El Paso, similar groups exist to look out for the interests of individuals of Puerto Rican and Mexican descents. In the last decade, an "Italian-American Civil Rights League," was formed in New York City to protest purported harassment of Italians and their stereotyping by public agencies by use of such terms as "Mafia" and "Cosa Nostra." There are in many cities Jewish "Anti-Defamation Leagues" and "Congresses" and "Rabbinical Boards," and various Catholic "Organizations of Charities." These and other committees are ready to protest discrimination against persons of their ethnic background or against city governmental policies that permit activities that are offensive to their religious principles. Some Catholics, for example, find offensive such things as city hospitals disseminating birth control information and devices or performing abortions.

Territorial or Neighborhood Interests. Interest groups also exist in large cities whose interests center on the character of a particular territorial area. Many large cities have, for example, a downtown development association or equivalent. New York even has the "Fifth Avenue Association," identified with a particularly important street. All cities have improvement or taxpayers or homeowners organizations made up of residents and businessmen in various neighborhoods or blocks. Until recently, these neighborhood organizations were almost exclusively in middle-class areas. They were concerned with the preservation of the character of the neighborhood, primarily as it was affected by the entrance of "undesirables" into its housing and public schools, by the downgrading of zoning requirements, by plans to build unwanted facilities like low-income housing projects, jails, expressways, or by any noticeable decline in general housekeeping services. Such associations also funneled requests to the city government for improvements like installing new stop signs or traffic lights at particular spots.

In the last decade, and especially since the stimulation of community action programs by the 1964 Economic Opportunity (or Antipoverty) Act. neighborhood or community organizations have also emerged in lower-income, black areas. These poverty-area based organizations have run different programs like "consumer information centers," day-care centers, health centers, etc. But they also try to exert influence on city agencies: For example, the neighborhood organizations call for upgrading of city services like garbage removal and crime protection, taking care of "grievances" by welfare clients, getting desirable projects like parks and playgrounds built or repaired, or having abandoned apartment buildings boarded up or demolished so that they do not remain fire hazards or havens for drug pushers and users. In a very few cities, new community organizations have also been formed in neighborhoods heavy with Chicano, Puerto Rican, or newly-arrived white poor from Appalachia; an example of the latter is north side Chicago's JOIN (Jobs Or Income Now).

The advances secured by black groups have led to the establishment in some cities of protectionist, counter-organizations in white, working-class ethnic (i.e., eastern or southern European) neighborhoods. Their primary concern is usually fighting racial integration of their housing and schools.

"Good Government" Interests. Finally, almost every city has one or more good government groups with names like "Citizens Union," "Citizens League," "Municipal League," "City Club," as well as local chapters of the League of Women Voters. These groups have an interest in the reform or improvement of the structure, operation, methods, procedures, and efficiency of the city government and in the qualifications of candidates seeking election to city offices.

Membership and Organizational Form

City interest groups vary tremendously in the size of their membership, in the extent to which the enrolled membership encompasses all those in the city or neighborhood that share their nominal interest, in the state of their finances, and in the extent to which they are organized and staffed to give concentrated attention to governmental matters. What Sayre and Kaufman have written about New York City's interest groups applies more generally:

> . . . They vary in membership from a few score to many thousands. . . . Their operating budgets range from a few hundred to several hundred thousand dollars a year. The work of smaller, less well-financed groups is generally performed by part-time volunteer, and amateur workers. Some of the larger, or the more affluent, associations employ permanent, full-time, highly paid professional staffs and

> provide them with research and secretarial and clerical assistance. . . . Only a handful . . . are concerned primarily with government. The overwhelming majority are mobilized around other central interests, and active participation in the city's political process is merely one subsidiary phase of much broader sets of activities.[27]

Whatever the size of the rank-and-file membership, the influence of interest groups on city governmental decisions is normally exerted by their leaders. By "leaders" is meant the relatively small, often long-term and self-perpetuating inner core of activists—what David Truman has termed the "active minority"[28]—drawn from among the officers, the members of boards of directors, the chief financial contributors, and particularly the paid fulltime staff for groups affluent enough to have them. It is this active minority who shape and promulgate group policy and otherwise speak in the name of the organization.

Resources of Influence on City Decision-Making

The bases of influence of interest group leaders are many: their own greater than average readiness to become involved in the political process, including the on-going ties they establish with agencies, offices, or bureaus of special concern; the legitimacy accorded by city officials to spokesmen of organized groups; the combined group resources that they can draw on to support various political strategies and tactics; the information they possess about the technical or political consequences of particular decisions and their implementation; and, at times, the sanctions they can bring to bear on officials that prove unaccommodating.

Readiness for Activity and Involvement. Interest group leaders are more ready to become involved in the city policy process than the average member of the general public. This readiness for involvement has a number of facets: To the extent interest group leaders take their role seriously, one of its components is precisely to monitor and be attentive to the activities of the city government for decisions, policies, and programs that bear on their groups' interests and to take action to forestall unfavorable or promote favorable ones. Furthermore, individuals who select themselves to come forward and become interest group leaders probably have a greater than average attraction for politics and for the exercise of influence to begin with, and they become even more interested and skillful as a result of their experience. Finally, because of the normal great continuity in that role, the

[27]Sayre and Kaufman, *Governing New York City,* p. 77.

[28]See David B. Truman, *The Governmental Process* (New York: Knopf, 1951), p. 139.

leaders of interest groups, and especially those leaders who are full-time staff for the larger, more active groups, tend to have gained superior knowledge of the inner workings of the city government. They also are likely to have developed a wide range of acquaintances, contacts, allies, and sometimes friends both among individuals in the agencies and bureaus of greatest substantive concern to their interests and sometimes among elected officialdom. This understanding of the operation of the city government makes it easier for interest group leaders to go to the most appropriate agency or office in order to influence a particular kind of decision. Their having personal contacts in the bureaucracies, etc., helps insure that their requests will at least be given attention rather than just ignored.

Conceded Legitimacy of Numbers. When interest group leaders communicate their views to city officials and bureaucrats during public hearings, informal consultations and meetings, or through service on advisory boards or commissions, these views carry the legitimacy and prestige that come in our democracy from presumably being shared by numbers. And the larger the number of members that the interest group leader purportedly represents both in absolute terms and in proportion to the total population sharing the interest being spoken for, the greater the attention and consideration he is likely to receive. Of course, the higher the value that society attaches to the interest being represented, the greater the weight that officials will give to the view of its group spokesman. For example, an interest in delivering medical care is in all cities valued more than one in selling children's balloons. But normally organization leaders representing almost any interest that is not outright illegal are conceded the right to at least a minimal hearing.

Pooled Resources. Organization implies membership with some attentiveness, a means of communicating with the membership, and some predisposition on its part to take action to protect its interests. In attempting to exert influence on the city government, interest group leaders can normally draw on combined resources, including money provided by the membership, that is far greater than that normally available to any nonelite individual member of the general public. These resources can finance numerous activities such as staff efforts to expose flaws in a proposal or to develop a constructive alternative; lobbying and public relations campaigns; litigation; as well as making contributions and other assistance to candidates during city election campaigns.

Actually, only few interest group leaders—those perhaps of large unions, high-status professional groups, and very high income neighborhood associations—speak for a membership affluent or sizable enough to provide funds sufficient to mount extensive city-wide public relations campaigns through the mass media, billboards, or mailings to the general public. The rest, however, through skilled public relations can sometimes create the illusion, even if not the actual reality, of mass public support for their position.

Probably only the leaders of the labor unions and of some of the large black interest groups are in a position to provide significant help in elections beyond cash for campaign expenses. If provided, such help would involve endorsing candidates and circulating their records to the membership, providing forums with mass audiences to give candidates sympathetic exposure, and very occasionally conducting registration drives, house-to-house canvassing, and active efforts to get out the vote on election day.

Authoritative Information. Interest group leaders are in a position to have, and are conceded by city officials varying capacity to provide, authoritative information about the technical and political consequences of proposed policies. For the more complex the policy or program decision being considered, the less can city officials foresee on their own whether it will achieve its objective or how its implementation will impinge on different individual and group interests in the city. By providing technical forecasts, interest group leaders frequently can persuade city officials to change features by convincing them that those changes will improve the policy's or program's overall workability or will prevent unanticipated and undesired damage to the group's interests. As David Truman has put it:

> . . . the specialized information about industry conditions that a trade association can provide . . . is a major part of its stock-in-trade. . . . Where competing claims are not present, and where available knowledge of the likely political consequences suggests that the [decision-maker] will be little affected whatever decision he makes, technical information may control his decision. . . . Especially where official sources of information are deficient, command of technical knowledge may provide access for groups that can supply the deficiency. . . .[29]

City officials are also often uncertain as to how popular or unpopular a contemplated decision will turn out to be with various segments of the population. By providing this kind of political information showing that a certain policy or program would be widely applauded by their membership, interest group leaders can encourage officials to adopt it. By showing that it would be intensely disapproved of, the interest group leaders may cause the officials to hesitate and possibly even to drop at least the most objectionable features of a policy or program.

Still another type of information interest group leaders can use in attempts to exert influence is of the legal rights to services, benefits, or

[29] *Ibid.*, pp. 334–35.

protections their members are entitled to under existing policies, laws, and regulations. This kind of "program" information gives the interest group leader leverage to change actions or decisions of city officials and agencies that are violating their own regulations. According to Saul Alinsky, the professional organizer of neighborhood and other interest groups, one major "tactic" of influence is:

> *Make the enemy live up to their own book of rules. . . .* Use the power of the law by making the establishment obey its own rules.[30]

William Ellis tells of how Chicago's West Side Organization Welfare Union used knowledge of existing law to get satisfaction for its members:

> . . . All WSO Welfare Union workers have a firm mastery of the relevant welfare laws and the independence to recognize when city officials are violating them. . . . These skills have been mastered not through formal training but from daily work in the organization. . . . During its first two years, the Welfare Union handled more than a thousand grievances—all of them successfully. That is, they have handled only complaints that were justified, in which city officials were breaking administrative policy or public law, and have secured a redress of the grievances from the responsible officials. The initial grievance took more than six weeks to process; now no complaint requires more than a single day.[31]

Sanctions. Sometimes interest group leaders can influence officials because they are in a position to impose sanctions on those officials for non-cooperation. Actually, few interest group leaders speak for groups large enough to cause the defeat of an official elected from a city-wide constituency. And this is so even if the membership were perfectly cohesive and its votes deliverable by its leadership, which is almost never the case. On the other hand, to an official representing a constituency the size of a councilman's district, the threat of active opposition by an interest group leader with a large concentration of members living there can be weighty. And, when the interest group leader speaks for a membership of city government employees or of construction workers, taxidrivers, dock workers, newspapermen, etc., the threat of a strike, slowdown or feigned mass illness is a very powerful sanction.

Another sanction can be the instigation of a lawsuit. For if a particular city official is purportedly denying or violating a legal or constitutional

[30]Saul D. Alinsky, *Rules for Radicals* (New York: Random House, 1972), pp. 128, 138.

[31]William W. Ellis, *White Ethics and Black Power* (Chicago: Aldine, 1969), pp. 109–10.

right and attempts at persuasion prove unsuccessful, an interest group leader can institute litigation on behalf of the "class" represented by his membership or on behalf of some aggrieved individual group member. If successful, the litigation can compel compliance through court order.

The ability to make various kinds of other "trouble" for a city official operates as still one more sanction. Most city officials have neither the time nor energy for being constantly fought and harassed by those segments of the city population they have an obligation to serve or regulate. Nor do they want the possible adverse publicity that comes from such an encounter. An interest group leader who can make sustained trouble for a city official puts him under great pressure to at least give greater attention to the group's problems and demands and at times to work out some accommodation at least minimally satisfactory to that leader. The trouble can range from being subjected to the nuisance of repeated phone calls, letters, and requests for meetings to becoming a target of peaceful protest, picketing, demonstrations, and boycotts. Since the middle 1960s making trouble for officials has also included the possibility of more extreme confrontation tactics like disruptive demonstrations, "sit-ins," "stall-ins," and vandalism, variously coupled with implicit or explicit threats of mass violence. Leaders of groups of welfare clients, mothers, schoolteachers, black civil rights groups, anti-war demonstrators, "hard-hat" pro-war demonstrators, and civil service unions have all had their memberships participate in such disruptive direct action in recent years.

In the 1960s many "ghetto elites" generated considerable influence and capacity to extract money and other concessions from city agencies by their skills at convincing city officials that their "followers" would otherwise engage in violent acts. Tom Wolfe has called these tactics "mau-mauing" and described how they were developed to a refined art in the black ghettoes of San Francisco:

> Going downtown to mau-mau the bureaucrats got to be routine practice in San Francisco. The poverty program *encouraged* you to go in for mau-mauing. They wouldn't have known what to do without it. The bureaucrats at City Hall and in the Office of Economic Opportunity talked "ghetto" all the time, but they didn't know any more about what was going on in the Western Addition, Hunters Point, Potrero Hill, the Mission, Chinatown, or south of Market Street than they did about Zanzibar. They didn't know where to look. They didn't even know who to ask. So what could they do? Well . . . they used the Ethnic Catering Service . . . right . . . They sat back and waited for you to come rolling in with your certified angry militants, your guaranteed frustrated ghetto youth, looking like a bunch of wild men. Then you had your test confrontation. If you were outrageous enough, if you could shake up the bureaucrats so bad that their eyes

> froze up into iceballs and their mouths twisted up into smiles of sheer physical panic, into shit-eating grins, so to speak—then they knew you were the real goods. They knew you were the right studs to give the poverty grants and community organizing jobs to. Otherwise they wouldn't know.[32]

The leaders of some of the more extremist revolutionary groups have engaged occasionally in actual bombings, snipings, and shootouts, especially against city police. Presumably these groups are not interested in influencing specific city decisions, but in venting their anger at the political system as a whole.

Interest Groups and Pressure

The term "pressure group" is widely used as an equivalent for "interest group." Yet the contention here is that the influence of most interest group leaders most of the time is *not* based on "pressure," in the sense of the capacity to impose heavy negative sanctions. Rare indeed is the interest group leader who can pose a plausible threat to the reelection prospects of city-wide elected officials. David Greenstone has shown that the leaders of large labor unions like the United Auto Workers in Detroit have had very limited success in getting their membership to vote with any degree of solidarity for local candidates of their choice.[33] Even rarer is the interest group leader who can finance a large-scale, city-wide public relations campaign calculated to generate a public opinion that will demand that a particular official or agency do what the leader wants and retaliate electorally if that official or agency does not prove compliant. And, of course, the city commissioners and bureaucrats making decisions in the operating departments do not even stand for election.

True, interest group leaders often go through what has the external appearance of a pressure campaign: They stimulate their members to write or wire elected officials; they solicit the endorsement of other groups for their positions; they run full-page ads in the local press; they appear with large numbers of followers to testify and perhaps demonstrate at public hearings, especially if they are assured of receiving TV coverage; they gather signatures and petitions which they forward to key city officials; they hold meetings with and otherwise lobby officials to explain the intensity of support that purportedly exists among the general public for their position. But this kind of activity has become largely ritual by which interest group leaders occupy their time, gain the satisfaction of having engaged in

[32]Tom Wolfe, "Mau-Mauing the Flak Catchers," in *Radical Chic and Mau-Mauing the Flak Catchers* (New York: Farrar, Straus & Giroux, 1970), pp. 97–98.

[33]J. David Greenstone, *Labor in American Politics* (New York: Knopf, 1969), chap. 4.

missionary work for a cause they believe in, and seek to make themselves look good to their membership or boards of directors. These leaders normally have little serious expectation that this kind of pressure campaign will have major impact on the determination of final policy.

The normal day-in, day-out influence of most city interest group leaders rests on bases other than pressure. Group spokesmen seeking to veto a threatening policy take advantage of the norm apparently held by city officials that no legitimate interests should be unnecessarily injured and that in case of a conflict with other group interests, each one should get at least part of what it wants. The *extent* to which interest group leaders can influence the changing of decisions to reduce injury to their membership will depend primarily on the value conferred on that interest by the dominant "political culture" (shared by most officials) and the city officials' own personal standards.

In the long run, changing public values affect the influence exerted by an interest group more than does any short-run capacity to exert crude direct pressure: City groups attempting to block expressways that would destroy extensive housing enjoyed much more success in the late 1960s and in the 1970s than they had a decade earlier; groups trying to stop projects that would create pollution or otherwise damage natural resources have had increasing effectiveness. This was not the result of the groups themselves or their leaders developing the ability to impose some new heavy sanctions. Their increased influence was a reflection of changing values and priorities. Road-building lost the high priority it long enjoyed while the value of conserving housing and especially protecting the environment and natural areas sharply climbed in public esteem.

The influence of the leaders of the more continuously active "good government," "functional or program," and broad-based black groups is based on the implicit acknowledgement by city officials that they share the interest of the group's general purposes and values—"good" or "better" government, improved education, health, welfare, opportunities, and conditions for blacks, etc. The ideas, proposals, and positions that these group leaders generate, protect or advance goals that the city officials and group leaders hold in common. Consequently, city officials and bureaucrats encourage ongoing, and sometimes close, relationships with the leaders of those few groups whose interests are closely related to the officials' goals or the agency's activities. What develops then is a kind of standing alliance between interest group leaders and the relevant agency officials, based on their shared or parallel interests. City officials will, for example, see these group leaders when they request an appointment, take their telephone calls, read and answer their letters. They will alert them to impending policy and program changes. Their advice will be seriously considered and often incorporated into official decisions.

These ongoing relationships between interest group leaders and city officials are at times of benefit to the officials. Interest group leaders can conduct studies and develop the background data for city officials who do not have staffs. They can "sell" to their membership policy changes strongly desired by the officials without protesting, even though they, the group leaders, disagree with them; they can develop group and public support for their "allied" officials' efforts to expand their powers or appropriations; they can come to their aid if the particular city officials are subjected to attacks.

The extraction of concessions in the mid- and late 1960s by leaders of poor, black "community" or "neighborhood" groups, through the pressure they exerted on officials by their capacity to stimulate forcible disruptions and threaten violence, seems to go against the general pattern. The possible costs involved in interruption of governmental routine and damage to property plus the possibility of the disruption escalating into a large-scale riot were high. Most city officials were pressured at least into giving more attention to an issue than they otherwise would have. They were willing to grant a hearing to people with grievances in order not to incur those costs. Sometimes the desire to avoid these costs even "pressured" them into changing the content of a planned decision.

Yet, fundamentally, even this kind of pressure was effective only on sufferance by city officials and the general public.[34] For the protests and confrontations were more effective when they were new, when the demands were clear and specific enough to be feasibly given, and when what was demanded was so morally compelling in the light of widely accepted principles and its denial so clearly arbitrary and reprehensible, that the sympathy generated for the protestors' cause greatly outweighed whatever opprobrium was felt about their methods. Once protests and "mau-mauing" became routine and began to be used indiscriminately even for objectives which did not enjoy broad public support, their efficacy dropped sharply. Indeed, disruptive and violence-tinged tactics eventually generated increased hostility against the disruptive demonstrators and groups identified with them and thus damaged and reduced the overall support they enjoyed in public and official opinion and esteem, which is a basic factor in any group's long-term political power. As broad public opinion backlashed against violent confrontation tactics, city officials also developed greater experience and greater confidence in their capacity to use police action to contain the "confronters." These officials accordingly began to show greater determination to resist threats and bluffs.

[34]See Michael Lipsky, "Protest as a Political Resource," *American Political Science Review*, 62 (1968): 1144–58; and William A. Gamson, *The Strategy of Social Protest* (Homewood, Ill.: The Dorsey Press, 1975), esp. chap. 6.

Former New York City Welfare Commissioner Mitchell Ginsberg tells, for example, of how a dramatic shift of attitudes took place in the highest echelon of that city's government in the summer of 1967. One July day, members of the city's Neighborhood Youth Corps had demonstrated in front of City Hall for funds to provide more summer jobs for young people in poverty areas. The demonstration became violent, resulting in damage to cars and other property and in some bystanders being roughed up. There was firm evidence that the director of the Corps, a man named Willie Smith, had helped organize the demonstration. "It was clear to me," Ginsberg has recalled:

> that Smith had to be suspended. I had written evidence that he'd set up the demonstration. That night it happened I saw the Mayor. He asked me what I wanted to do, and I said I was going to suspend Smith. The [Mayor's] political tactician was there and several other advisers to the Mayor. They disagreed vehemently with me. "The black communities will blow up if you do that," one of them said. . . . I told the Mayor I didn't underestimate the dangers involved, but I couldn't let this pass by. If I did, there'd be more and more incidents like it. "If you stand by this decision," the Mayor told me, "there may be riots and burning and killing. Again, what do you want to do?" "I'm going to suspend him," I said. Then I had a sleepless night. It's one thing to know what you have to do, it's another thing to fear what the consequences will be. I suspended Smith the next morning. That was a Thursday.[35]

By the following Wednesday, Ginsberg decided to put Smith back in again. Smith had agreed that if the time came when he felt he had to engage in public action inconsistent with or contrary to city policy, he'd leave his job. Ginsberg felt that since "He'd been doing a good job with the Youth Corps, and now that he'd made that pledge, there was no reason not to reinstate him:

> But now there was trouble again. The very advisers to the Mayor who had most strongly urged that Smith not be suspended were now insisting that he not be unsuspended. It was too short a time, they said. Actually the Mayor gave the real reason. "We've gotten a tremendous positive response nationally as well as locally by being firm. A very good response politically."[36]

[35]Quoted in Nat Hentoff, *A Political Life: The Education of John V. Lindsay* (New York: Knopf, 1969), pp. 241–42.

[36]*Ibid.*

In any event, Ginsberg, with Mayor Lindsay's approval, reinstated Smith, who caused no further difficulties with demonstrations.

PRIVATE ELITES AND CITY POLICYMAKING

The private city elites discussed in this chapter—the social and economic notables and interest group leaders—probably do not constitute more than one percent of the population of any large city. Yet because of their greater attention to, knowledge of, and participation in the city's political process, and because of their superior strategic and tactical skills, it is these elites (as well as the special case of communications media elites which will be considered in the next chapter) who pretty much monopolize the direct "extragovernmental" influence exerted on the shaping of city governmental policies and programs.

The idea that such a large part of the extragovernmental influence over city governmental decisions normally is wielded by an extremely tiny minority of its members raises questions about how much reality there is to the operation of "democracy" and popular control in city politics. For clearly the elite stratum would constitute an unhealthy and undemocratic element if its influence were sufficiently great to control the actions of popularly elected city officials or if it were used to further some special interests of its own at the expense of the vast nonelite majority in the general public.

First, it should be clear that the resources at the command of any of these private elites are rarely sufficient to pressure officials to act against their own strongly felt convictions. Indeed, successful exertion of influence probably depends more on city officials happening to share the outlooks and objectives sought to be furthered by the elites than it does on any other single factor. And this in turn depends on the objectives being consistent with dominant social values. Second, it is difficult to think of any particular interests that are special to elites as elites. In truth, the private elites are highly diverse in background, interest, personal values, and ideologies. They consequently do not all support one set of policy positions. Many of them are often unmobilized or in contention among themselves. Officials frequently have to respond to conflicting elite claims and demands and thus are left with wide discretion on how to reconcile the conflict in those claims and demands. Furthermore, on the level of general city policy and programs, there are few decisions sought by private elites which would not also benefit some segment of the nonelite general public with similar interests. After all, much of the interest group leaders' influence comes from their speaking in a representative capacity for their memberships among the general public.

Finally, city officials, in deciding how to respond to the exertions of these elites, often themselves take into account in advance the interests and possible reactions of the general public. This gives the general public an important, albeit "indirect," form of influence on policymaking. For most city officials, particularly elected ones, believe that major governmental decisions should be consistent with mass opinion. These officials also know that if they do favor elite interests that are flagrantly at odds with those of the general public, there is the possibility of new elites emerging and calling attention to that fact in an effort to discredit them.

This argument does not deny that elites are likely to have an enormously greater chance than the average member of the general public of exerting influence on a city governmental decision. And the argument also does not deny that these private elites may have additional, indirect influence, in that anticipation of their opposition to certain proposals will keep them from being brought up, so that those proposals never become issues or questions for decisions.[37] And there are interests held by substantial numbers of citizens that have not enjoyed the degree of protection or enhancement of those interests provided by forceful elite spokesmen. For example, until they were organized in the last decade, primarily under the stimulus of the "community action" program of the Economic Opportunity Act, the interests of the lower-class, black poor were not asserted so that they could be forcefully impressed on the attention of city decision-makers on a day-to-day basis. Their erstwhile "surrogate" elites—church, settlement house, and other charity group leaders, as well as middle-class "professional reformers"—all were biased almost exclusively in favor of the "deserving poor" who aspired to middle-class standards.

The black poor now do have their own elite spokesmen both in indigenous "community group leaders" and in new surrogate elites like foundation people, "advocate planners," radical lawyers and professors, etc. But groups like the elderly white poor, Appalachian whites, or the white and black "struggling-to-break-even" blue collar workers still have no strong elite representation. Also, interests in such intangibles as architectural beauty or quiet or an overall high quality of city life are either not at all or only weakly represented among elite activists. Consequently, unless the city officials involved in a decision themselves happen to have an unusually strong attachment to such "underrepresented" interests, they are almost invariably sacrificed when competing with those that are more tangible and more powerfully organized and articulated.

[37]See Peter Bachrach and Morton S. Baratz, "Two Faces of Power," *American Political Science Review,* 56 (1962): 947–52 and "Decisions and Nondecisions: An Analytical Framework," *ibid.,* 57 (1963): 632–42.

14

City Communications Media Elites

A city's communications media elites have an impact on a city's policy-making process in four basic ways: by operating a communications channel which circulates information about city government and politics to all parts of a city's population; by playing a major role in shaping a city's "public action agenda"; by exerting short-run influence on attitudes toward the content of decisions and the outcome of elections; and by helping to create the long-term popular image held about certain key aspects of city government and politics. The term "media elites" refers to a city's newspaper publishers, broadcast station operators, and network presidents and vice-presidents who establish the basic policies governing the operation of their publications or stations. It also includes the city's newspaper editors, broadcast news directors, and newspaper and television reporters who control what is published or broadcast on a day-to-day basis.

The media that are most important in large cities are newspapers with city-wide circulation and television stations that regularly broadcast local news. The coverage of these newspapers and TV stations is by far more continuous and extensive and their reports and commentary fuller than other communications media that also circulate urban political news within a city. These are radio, various neighborhood and "ethnic" daily or weekly newspapers and national mass circulation news magazines, like *Time* or *Newsweek*. Some reference will, however, also be made to the distinctive impact of such limited circulation national journals of opinion with a heavy urban content like *The Public Interest,* and *The New Republic,* and individual big-city based, limited-circulation magazines like *New York, Philadelphia,* and *Chicago.*

FUNCTIONS OF THE CITY MEDIA ELITES

Operating a Neutral Communications Channel

The most fundamental and special impact that mass media have on the urban policy process is that they operate what is the primary, and often the exclusive, mass communications channel distributing information to members of the general public about city governmental decisions, policies, programs, and the activities of political actors. Except for the handful of persons who may have been direct participants or observers, governmental and political events not reported by the media have for all practical purposes simply not happened as far as a city's general population is concerned. By not knowing about these events, individuals in that population lose the opportunity to influence their future course and also are deprived of the possibility of rewarding or punishing city officials at election time for their roles in having shaped them. Prerequisites to using the vote as an instrument to affect policy are awareness of what city officials have been doing, knowledge about the possible alternatives, and an understanding of future developments. As the chief source of such information about what city officials are doing and what their opposition is saying about it, the mass media function as an intrinsic part of the mechanism of popular democratic control in American cities.

The mass media are also a supplementary communications channel for city officials and other elites. First, almost the only way for such officials and elites to beam a message to a wide audience among the public is through the reporting or live coverage of their statements and positions by the mass media. Second, officials and other elites use the mass media to talk to each other: News conference statements and answers to questions, press releases, planted stories, and letters to the editor are frequently directed not to their presumptive targets, the mass public, but to other activists. As V. O. Key has explained, the media thus provide "in a sense, an arena for the continuing discussion of politics among those principally concerned. . . . Men in political circles have to read these papers if they are to know what is going on and what is being said in the wider political world of which they are a part."[1] In this respect, the media supplement the direct, official lines of communication among city officials and other elites, those lines not having the media's capacity to carry a large volume of information to as many interested parties as quickly and simultaneously.

The city's mass media also provide a communications channel that is

[1]V. O. Key, Jr., *Public Opinion and American Democracy* (New York: Knopf, 1961), p. 405.

explicitly for hire: Through purchase of space in the newspapers for the printing of advertisements with political messages and through purchased time on television, any political activist who can afford the bill can communicate exactly what message he wants in an attempt to reach a mass audience.

Shaping the Urban Political Agenda

In operating the mass media as communications channels, the media elites do have opportunities themselves to exercise control over the flow of political intelligence that is transmitted. Of course, according to journalistic standards of "newsworthiness," the media have little discretion in whether or not to report activities and statements of key urban elites like mayors or events of intrinsic universal concern like major riots. But the media elites do have a choice in whether or not to report a wide range of other subjects and how much prominence to give to each of them.

For an almost infinite number of potentially "newsworthy" events occur every day in a large city: Newspaper editors, broadcast directors, and reporters are thus afforded opportunities for making decisions about which of these events to cover and write up. Furthermore, more stories are written up and filed than can possibly be printed (even in a newspaper with the massive coverage of *The New York Times,* let alone in smaller newspapers) or can be broadcast in the short span of a local TV news program. Newspaper and other media editors must therefore make further decisions as to which stories are to be printed or telecast and which must be left out. Then among those which are reported, they must also choose which stories should be "played up" and given greatest prominence and sustained treatment and which should be "played down" and quickly dropped. As the staff report on *Mass Media and Violence* of the National Commission on the Causes and Prevention of Violence put it:

> . . . A newsroom is inundated with a flood of competing information. Every news organization must select from the flood those driblets that will be allowed to surface for public view. A metropolitan newsroom, for instance, may have a half-dozen teletype machines, two newsphoto receivers, radio receivers on police and fire frequencies, dozens of press releases, hundreds of telephone tips from which to choose in a single day, and to these, add the product of the paper's own news staff. These galvanize the organization with an impending deadline. Compress the output into a finite amount of space column inches for a newspaper or minutes and seconds for a television news program—and the result is a package of information, selected, synthesized, honed. . . .[2]

[2]Robert K. Baker and Sandra J. Ball, *Mass Media and Violence: A Report to the National Commission on the Causes and Prevention of Violence,* Vol. IX (Washington, D.C.: U.S. Government Printing Office, 1969), p. 136.

And in addition to the choices already mentioned, the media elite have almost complete discretion in deciding whether to run features, exposés, or interpretative articles that are not part of the previous day's "spot news."

It is the stories to which the media decide to give the most sustained and prominent coverage (meaning for newspapers front-page coverage) that determine to a large extent what a city's "public action agenda" will be—i.e., what its governmental officials, private elites, and members of the general public will be thinking and talking about on a given day and what issues they will consider to be important ones that have to be dealt with. In part, these decisions of the media elites are not self-consciously calculated to shape the public agenda in a particular way. They simply reflect the supposedly neutral standards of newsworthiness held by reporters and editors. But in part these decisions do reflect the conscious desire of the media people to focus elite and public attention on particular topics. As Sayre and Kaufman have explained:

> A series of articles on any aspect of [city] government . . . if treated prominently or spectacularly, is likely to cause a good deal of comment and generate a good many questions in official circles and among the general citizenry. . . . A sensational exposure, a revelation of scandal, can set off a wave of popular indignation strong enough to compel remedial or symbolic action by officials. . . . A story that appears on the front pages of all the newspapers, even for a day, may have the same effect. By constant reiteration, by implication, by editorial comment, by feature items, as well as by straight news coverage, the press is sometimes able to instigate public outrage or to summon up popular enthusiasm. Even the major newspapers cannot do this at will; if there is no basis in fact for reports, or if minor occurrences are blown up out of all proportion by a reporter or his editor, the stories are apt to collapse fairly quickly or even to be laughed off. And if attempts to provoke the public are made too often, they lose their effectiveness. This is not something to be done every day.[3]

But even given those limits, it is the mass media, and most of all the newspapers, that have a greater ability than any other political actors, except possibly a large city's mayor, to force items to the city's public action agenda and to generate public expectations or demands that something be done about them.

[3]Wallace S. Sayre and Herbert Kaufman, *Governing New York City* (New York: Norton, 1965), pp. 491–92.

Influencing Short-Run Attitudes

The media also influence urban policymaking through the impact that their editorializing and reporting have on the specific content of governmental decisions and on the outcome of particular elections. To some extent simply placing particular issues or items on the public action agenda influences the nature of their disposition. Widely publicizing such things as corruption, dishonesty, or massive inefficiency by city officials and employers almost dictates that some kind of remedial action will have to be taken.

Editorializing. The most obvious way that the media elites attempt to influence the content of city politics is by editorializing. The underlying assumption is that the media's editorials will generate broad public opinion in agreement with their positions. This broad opinion will then purportedly translate itself into grass-roots pressure on officials or "correct" votes in the polling booth. Whatever evidence exists, however, suggests that the influence editorials have in changing the attitudes and behavior of the mass public is much less than media editors like to think.

One important reason that editorials have limited impact among the broad public is that few people read editorials. An old (and nonurban) example, reported by V. O. Key, demonstrates this point: In the summer of 1940 during the presidential election between Republican Wendell Willkie and Democrat Franklin D. Roosevelt, "the Cleveland *Plain Dealer,* the paper with the largest circulation in Erie County, Ohio, splashed on the front-page an announcement in support of Willkie; it followed up during the campaign with daily front-page editorials." Yet in September, "50 percent of a sample of Erie County did not know which candidate the *Plain Dealer* was supporting." And of the persons that the newspaper was presumably trying to reach in order to influence their likely vote—Democrats with a predisposition to vote for Roosevelt—almost six out of seven did not know the paper's editorial position.[4] This reflects the general pattern that readers, even when they pay attention to editorials, tend to pay attention to those items with which they agree, not to those that seek to convert them.[5]

The second obstacle to successful editorializing is that many persons do not trust mass media editorializing, particularly by the newspapers. These members of the public therefore react with skepticism or disbelief to what the media are advocating. In a study of the United Auto Workers in Detroit, Arthur Kornhauser found that only 23 percent of his sample placed a high

[4]V. O. Key, Jr., *Public Opinion,* pp. 352–53.
[5]*Ibid.*

degree of trust in what they read in the newspapers.[6] Another study, of the 1959 election for mayor in Boston, showed that one factor in the defeat of the highly favored candidate was the strong editorial support of the newspapers: Since many members of the Boston public perceived the newspapers as part of a local concentration of power that was not interested in the public's welfare, the papers' candidate was tarnished rather than helped by the newspapers' backing.[7]

Still a third obstacle is that media editorializing, even to the extent that it reaches its audience, reaches persons with preexisting standards, values, group identifications, and beliefs. This is especially so when the editorials concern elections to highly "visible" offices, like the mayoralty, where large amounts of information are available from sources besides editorials, like TV coverage and the news columns. It is also the case when the policies involved have clear and immediate implications for the reader's or viewer's own central interests, which he can readily perceive on his own. In this kind of context, the reader's or viewer's own attitudes operate to discount, rebut, and misinterpret the editorial message of the mass media when it calls for any action that is inconsistent with those attitudes.

On the other hand, when the editorializing concerns policy matters on which members of the public have only the vaguest kinds of internalized standards of judgment, its impact is bound to be heavier. Thus on various new issues—issues that have never come up before for the reader to have thought about—or on elections that are for "low visibility" posts—like alderman or councilman, where almost no information may be available about the candidates except that conveyed by the media's editorial position —the media have more significant influence through their editorials. This is especially true where, as in elections in de facto nonpartisan cities, there is an absence of competing cues like a candidate's known party affiliation. Similarly, an editorial may have relatively high impact when large numbers of persons already have strong underlying, latent feelings about the subject-matter of an editorial and the editorial simply makes conscious and crystallizes beliefs about the desirability or undesirability of a particular action.

All of this is not to say, however, that because media editorializing has slight direct influence on mass attitudes and behavior, it has only the same amount of limited influence on actual policymaking. Elected city officials and other elites not being in a position to have accurate gauges of mass opinion, sometimes treat media editorials as a functional equivalent. Thus editorial and other kinds of media support for controversial policies makes it easier for officials to put them into effect, while strong opposition may

[6]See Arthur Kornhauser, *When Labor Votes* (New York: University Books, 1966), pp. 89-90.

[7]See Murray B. Levin, *The Alienated Voter* (New York: Holt, Rinehart & Winston, 1960).

make them hesitate to act. Furthermore, some city officials and private elites place an independent value on being praised and not blamed on a newspaper's editorial page. Either because of the pleasure that praise or the pain that blame brings to their egos or the belief that it affects their own or their organization's popularity and therefore their power, these city officials and elites may therefore shape their decisions and actions so as to court praise and avoid blame. As Sayre and Kaufman have explained:

> Elected officials worry about newspaper treatment because it may have electoral repercussions, while appointed officers and employees fear it may affect their jurisdiction. Sympathetic, or even neutral coverage, may help them get ahead in their careers or achieve programs dear to them; negative treatment may do just the opposite. It may alienate their supporters or gain new ones for them. Governmental decisions of all kinds in the city are often profoundly influenced by anticipated or actual press reactions.[8]

Finally, although media editorializing directly influences the opinions of only a small proportion of the mass public directly, it may indirectly influence the opinions of a much larger proportion, through the so-called "two-step" flow of communication. The way this two-step flow works is that people who pay attention to political editorializing tend also to talk about city politics and give advice to their friends and acquaintances. Thus they radiate the media's editorial messages, with their own interpretations to be sure, to a wider public than immediately perceives them.[9]

Reporting of "Straight News." Unquestionably larger in its impact on a city's mass opinions and behavior are the biases contained in the media's "straight," day-to-day presentation of the news. For through such simple methods as their placement of stories, the headlines they assign to them, and the wording of their lead paragraphs, media elites can advance their own preferences in policy or candidates outside of the editorial columns. Also, by prominently reporting the views and positions of those officials and other political actors with whose policies they agree, media elites can give them greater visibility and the appearance of enjoying wide support. Conversely, by playing down or even suppressing the views of political activists to whom they are opposed, media elites can limit their audience and deny them any aura of mass support. And often the framework within which media elites choose to present events goes far toward determining whether the readers become sympathetic or hostile to a particular point of view.

[8]Sayre and Kaufman, *Governing New York City,* p. 492.

[9]See Paul Lazarsfeld, Bernard Berelson, and Helen Gaudet, *The People's Choice* (New York: Duell, Sloan, and Pearce, 1944), chap. 16; Key, *Public Opinion,* pp. 359–63.

Similarly, the media can use their regular news coverage to give prominence and provide flattering treatment for city officials or candidates whom they support. And they can also ignore, give less prominence to, or highlight negative aspects of officials and candidates whom they oppose. Indeed, it is the media that pretty much determine the public personality of leading candidates or officials. As one of Mayor Lindsay's aides complained,

> This whole business . . . of characterizing people in public life is so weird. All those who *know* Lindsay is this or is that. On what do they base their judgments? On interpretations by people who don't know a hell of a lot themselves. The so-called well-informed intellectuals interested in politics read the news analyses and the political coverage in the *Times*; they read the *New York Review of Books* and maybe *Newsweek* and such columnists as Evans and Novak. And on that basis, they come up with the most facile assumptions. . . . Did you ever realize that out of this way of "knowing" things from magazines and political columnists, there are five or six anecdotes about a guy which will be cited to you again and again as the core of a man. And all these people think they're informed![10]

Wallace Sayre has argued that the media essentially "type-cast" a city's leading political personages through the cumulative effects of their coverage, producing a roster of clowns, heroes, and villains:

> Only a fortunate few of the actors can ever escape from unfavorable initial type-casting, although it is apparently less difficult, especially for mayors, to fall from stardom as hero.[11]

Nicholas Pileggi has documented John Lindsay's falling from favor as a "hero" in *The New York Times* coverage during the last years of his mayoralty. When Lindsay was campaigning for the 1972 Democratic nomination for president, as Pileggi tells it, "no matter how sweet Lindsay's out-of-town conquests," every victory was questioned by *The Times* and every glory belittled:

> Where Long Island's *Newsday* recently reported, "LINDSAY WOWS THEM," the *Times'* version of the same story said, "1,500 students at the University of Buffalo greeted the mayoral message with almost sullen silence." When the *Tampa Tribune* headline read, "LINDSAY

[10]Nat Hentoff, *A Political Life: The Education of John V. Lindsay* (New York: Knopf, 1969), pp. 269–70.

[11]Wallace S. Sayre, "The Mayor," in Lyle C. Fitch and Annmarie Hauck Walsh, eds., *Agenda for a City* (Beverly Hills, Calif.: Sage, 1970), p. 584.

> DRAWS TAMPA THRONGS,'' the *Times* reporter in Tampa wrote . . . , ''The crowds at the parade shopping center were slim, by New York standards.'' ''Balanced reporting,'' is the way a number of *Times*men describe their coverage of Lindsay. . . . For every cheer a boo, for every Tampa throng, a slim New York crowd for comparison.
>
> Honolulu, Dec. 1—Mayor Lindsay's remarks were well received, but the convention was virtually over.
>
> Miami, Dec. 28—''I came here to get away from that guy,'' said one woman who identified herself as a former resident of Manhattan.
>
> Tallahassee, Jan. 21—The Mayor drew interested crowds wherever he went. When he walked into the state capitol to pay a call on Gov. Reuben Askew, secretaries lined the halls to shake hands with him (although one local newsman observed wryly that they had done the same for Governor Wallace a week or so before).[12]

A newspaper's capacity to mold public opinion on issues and candidates through the treatment it gives them in its regular news columns is obviously enhanced when there is no competitive coverage by other papers. In point of fact the number of cities with competitive daily newspapers has been steadily decreasing, so that currently only 3 percent of the nation's cities publish two or more newspapers under separate ownership.[13] In some of the vast majority of what are ''one newspaper'' towns, it may be extremely difficult, if not impossible, for the members of the public to learn of arguments, policy alternatives, or candidates not favored by those who control the city's single newspaper or newspaper chain.

Many media persons would deny that they allow their own personal political values and preferences to influence their treatment of ''straight news.'' But realistically, such influence is unavoidable. As Talese has written about *The New York Times,* a newspaper explicitly committed to keeping any bias out of its news columns:

> . . . *The Times* in principle tried to be objective in its news coverage, but in reality it could not always be. It was run by humans, flawed figures, men who saw things as they *could* see them, or sometimes *wished* to see them; interpreting principles to suit contemporary pressures, they wanted it both ways; it was the oldest story of all. Ideally, *The Times* desired no opinions within its news columns, restricting opinion to its editorial page. Realistically, this was not possible. The editor's opinions and tastes were imposed every day within the news—either by the space they allowed for a certain story,

[12]Nicholas Pileggi, ''John Lindsay and 'The New York Times': The End of the Affair,'' *New York Magazine,* March 20, 1972, p. 56.

[13]Baker and Ball, *Mass Media and Violence,* p. 201.

> or the position they assigned to it, or the headline they ordered for it, and also by the stories they did not print, or printed for only one edition, or edited heavily, or held out for a few days and then printed in the back of the thick Sunday edition between girdle advertisements and dozens of Bachrach photographs of pretty girls just engaged. The reporter's ego was also a factor in the news coverage—he wrote what he wrote best, he wrote what he understood, reflecting the total experience of his lifetime, shades of his pride and prejudice.[14]

And, of course, some newspapers don't even try very hard to be neutral in their straight news coverage.

Molding Long-term Evaluative Tones, Feelings, and Images

Perhaps even more important than the media elites' short-term impact on specific city governmental decisions and electoral outcomes, is their contribution to the creation of long-term popular images about key aspects of city politics. First, only a tiny fraction of the general public ever receives formal instruction about urban politics or participates directly. Consequently, it is the media that communicate the dominant image about the quality of the overall governmental process in large cities. Given prevailing journalistic standards, the image conveyed day after day and year after year is not one to inspire a citizen's confidence or pride in how his city is governed. For example, the media elites consider stories about wrongdoings, inadequacies, scandals, conflicts, controversies, and militant and extreme statements and actions much more newsworthy than stories about positive achievements, harmony, and cooperation, and statements or activities of moderate, orderly, accommodating political actors. Also, there is a strong tendency in the mass media to explain the motives of political activists, and especially of electoral or party politicians, in selfish terms. The media often ignore the activists' honest desire to solve public problems and their honest differences of opinion about the efficacy of different alternatives. The image about city politics conveyed by this kind of reporting no doubt discourages many persons from becoming involved themselves in the political arena and weakens their allegiance to the political system.

Second, the kind of long-term coverage and the positive or negative tone conveyed in media stories about particular social groups largely determines what the dominant feelings about them will be among the general public. If the coverage in the mass media is warmly supportive and sympathetic or

[14]Gay Talese, *The Kingdom and the Power* (New York: New American Library, 1969), pp. 59–60.

hostile and antagonistic, so will be the attitudes of the public. And although the actual behavior of these individuals and groups places limits on what kinds of images can be conveyed, most groups are sufficiently diversified to leave considerable leeway about communicating flattering, unflattering, or mixed pictures of what will be perceived as the typical pattern. Roy Wilkins of the NAACP and other nonextremist black leaders complained in the mid-1960s about the media's tendency to give prominent display to violence-laden and extremist black rhetoric and behavior, but not to statements and behavior by blacks indicating commitment to nonviolent, orderly procedures. The result, they argued, was to shrink the support previously enjoyed among whites for black political goals and aspirations.

The different, but still stereotyped, news coverage that blacks received until the late 1950s was equally unhelpful toward developing broad public support for alleviating the problems of ghetto poverty and achieving black equality. As the *Mass Media and Violence* report has stated:

> . . . most news coverage of blacks was limited to Negroes involved in crime, sports, or entertainment.
>
> Until recently, what most white Americans knew about blacks was that some of them were pretty good athletes, they had lots of rhythm, a lot of them were criminals—possibly by instinct—and they could be good entertainers. Many Americans, to be sure, had either met or heard of people like Ralph Bunche, but such Negroes were regarded as exceptions, of course. . . .
>
> Omitting the black press, no medium of communication was reporting for the Negro struggle for equality.[15]

And none was reporting on what it meant to live in a slum or be exposed to police brutality.

Third, big-city newspapers are themselves large businesses and their chief source of income is advertising revenues from other large businesses. As a consequence, their long-term news coverage is not such to create sympathetic attitudes among the public for proposals that advocate unorthodox schemes for redistribution of income or sharply attack major industries. William Allen White, former editor of the Kansas *Emporia Gazette,* once explained the feeling of identification that develops between publishers and big businessmen:

> If he is smart, and is an up-and-coming publisher in a town of 100,000 or 1,000,000 people, the publisher associates on terms of equality with the bankers, the merchant princes, the manufacturers

[15]Baker and Ball, *Mass Media and Violence,* p. 45.

> and the investment brokers. His friends unconsciously color his opinion. If he lives with them on any kind of social terms in the City Club, he must more or less merge his views into the common views of the other capitalists. The publisher is not bought like a chattel. . . . But he takes the color of his social environment.[16]

Finally, both television presentation of the news and television programming in general have had a powerful role over the years in creating attitudes supporting the use of force and violence. In the mid- to late 1960s, for example, television networks were prepared to cover almost any forcible demonstration or take-over of buildings or other facilities, thus giving the demonstrators a chance to be heard by a wide audience. This TV practice obviously gave great incentive for the use of confrontation tactics, especially by groups that lacked high enough status to be granted press conferences or to be given automatic coverage of their press releases. As Wallace Sayre has pointed out:

> Street demonstrations, the massing of demonstrators elsewhere, the threat or fact of violence, are each almost ideally "made" for the camera, and the managers of "confrontations" quickly perceived that the camera was, so to speak, "made" for them. When camera and commentator at the scene of confrontation are followed almost immediately on the television screen by camera and commentator demanding an instant declaration of action or intention from the official or other leader chosen by the media for that purpose . . . the impact of the electronic media . . . is magnified.[17]

An actual incident described in the report on *Mass Media and Violence* illustrates Sayre's point about demonstrations and the television camera being "made for each other":

> By now it was something after 8 p.m. and the television crews needed something to show on the 10 o'clock news. . . .
>
> Up came the three-man television crew: a camera man with a hand-held camera, a sound man, and a light man. Very discreet in the dark.
>
> "May as well get it."
>
> You could sense the disappointment in his voice, because pictorially it wasn't much of a demonstration.
>
> The light-man held up his 30-volt frezzi and laid a four-foot beam of light across one section of the picket line. Instantly the marcher's

[16]Quoted, *ibid.*, p. 77.

[17]Sayre, "The Mayor," pp. 584–85.

> heads snapped up, their eyes flashed. They threw up their arms in the clenched Communist fist. Some made a V with their fingers, and they held up their banners for the cameras. . . .[18]

Furthermore, there is some evidence that in its manner of covering the riots that took place in the 1960s, and especially the earliest ones, television news coverage contributed to increasing the size of the crowds involved and to escalating the violence. In some cases the presence of the camera led rioters or police to play to the television audience, thereby increasing tensions and aggressive behavior. But according to Morris Janowitz, the more important impact of the coverage was its effects on "potential rioters," who were not already involved, and on the public at large:

> Rioting is based on contagion, the process by which the mood and attitudes of those who are actually caught up in the riots are disseminated to a larger audience. . . . Television images served to spread the contagion pattern throughout urban areas and the nation. . . . Large audiences see the details of riots, the manner in which people participate in them, and especially the ferment associated with looting and obtaining commodities which was so much at the heart of riot behavior. Television presents detailed information about the tactics of participation and the gratifications that were derived. . . . The mass media serve to reinforce and spread a feeling of consciousness among those who participate or sympathize with extremist actions. . . .[19]

The Kerner Commission concluded in 1968 that although newspapers, radio, and television had "on the whole, made a real effort to give a balanced, factual account of the 1967 disorders," its portrayal of the violence "failed to reflect accurately its scale and character," with the overall effect being "an exaggeration of both mood and event."[20]

In the long run, perhaps the greatest impact of all in TV's shaping of public attitudes toward violence has been the tendency of its regular entertainment programs to depict violence and physical force as a normal way of settling conflict. As the *Mass Media and Violence* report explained:

> . . . films and television are profoundly educative for their viewers, teaching them that the world is a violent and untrustworthy place, and demonstrating to them a variety of violent techniques for coping with

[18]Baker and Ball, *Mass Media and Violence,* pp. 89–90.

[19]Quoted, *ibid.,* pp. 103–4.

[20]U.S. National Advisory Commission on Civil Disorders, *Report* (New York: Bantam, 1968), p. 363.

> this hostile environment. Whether this message is beamed as fact or fiction, it is accepted by young children. They incorporate in their own behavior patterns all the sequences of adult behavior they observe on television.
>
> . . . There was a murder every half hour during prime viewing time on 1968 network television. How many instances are there of constructive interventions to end disagreement? What other methods of resolving conflict are shown? How many instances of tact and decency could an avid television viewer chronicle during the same hours? How often is reconciliation dramatized?[21]

These questions were, of course, put rhetorically; standard TV fare only rarely portrays persuasion, accommodation, give-and-take, and self-sacrifice as useful or laudable tactics for bringing disagreements and conflicts to an end, whether in politics or private life.

UNFULFILLED PROMISE OF THE COMMUNICATIONS MEDIA

For a democratic political system with real popular control to operate effectively in large cities, broad segments of the public must have at least two fundamental kinds of information: One, they need general information about the processes by which city governmental decisions are made and how city governmental policy and programs attempt to cope with urban needs and problems. Two, they need specific information about what current policy issues are, what incumbent officials are doing about them, and, in times of elections, what different candidates stand for. Such specific information on issues would have to include an explanation of the proposals being disputed and the likely consequences of these proposals and of any alternatives also being considered for different sets of conditions and for different groups and individuals. The specific information on candidates should permit evaluation of their strengths and weaknesses and of what the effects are likely to be of one candidate or group of candidates gaining office rather than their opponents.

Only a tiny fraction of the public ever receives this kind of information through formal instruction in high school or college or can obtain this information through direct observation or participation. The newspapers and particularly television—with its huge, almost captive audience during the evening news programs[22]—do, however, have the capacity to transmit political information widely among the general public.

[21] Baker and Ball, *Mass Media and Violence*, p. 282.

[22] A majority of Americans apparently rely nowadays on television for their basic source of information about urban affairs. See *ibid.*, p. 35.

Unfortunately, in almost no city do either newspapers or television come close to utilizing this capacity. Most of the time, the media fail to communicate any fundamental understanding of the importance of city politics as a set of processes by which decisions are made and policies and programs implemented as a result of the competitive exertion of influence. Nor do they communicate any explanation of the social problems that such decisions and policies are trying to cope with. Rather, the dominant image the media convey is that politics is simply a personal struggle among opposed sets of politicians. It is, in sum, virtually impossible to gain an explanation of how politics operate as a vehicle either to preserve or change the existing distribution of such things as power, income, and social standing among broad groups and classes by reading the daily press or watching the nightly TV news programs.

Similarly, newspaper or television reporting of current policy controversies and election campaigns rarely goes much beyond "spot news" narration. The media reports are almost formulaic: On that or the previous day certain political activists said that they were for or against some named, but usually unexplained proposal. Or a candidate asserted that he possessed and his opponents lacked various kinds of desirable political and administrative ability.

This lack of in-depth analysis of urban political news is clearest in the case of television. Here deadlines for collecting and preparing stories are even shorter than for newspapers. The emphasis on providing pictures of action sequences is greater. And the need to tell about complex happenings in one- and two-minute presentations is more pressing. All these factors, plus an inherited show-business ethic in the medium, often lead TV news coverage to provide the most oversimplified and encapsulated explanations, indeed little more than headlines. These factors cause television to go farthest in sacrificing significance in selecting the stories they cover for the sake of those with the most theatrical or sensational qualities.

Another shortcoming of the media is that except in some exposés of corruption, they almost never report and analyze problems, conditions, or proposals unless particular activists are already talking about them. As Leon Sigal has put it, "most news is not what has happened, but what someone says has happened."[23] This is so even if such problems or conditions are in fact relevant to a story and to evaluating a situation and probably would be considered significant if attention were drawn to them. The media strongly prefer to report stories only after they have been "floated" by recognized public figures—city officials, prominent businessmen or civic groups leaders, or acknowledged experts. Newspapers and especially tele-

[23]Leon V. Sigal, *Reporters and Officials* (Lexington, Mass.: D.C. Heath Co., 1973), p. 69.

vision rarely cover new ideas or situations before they have been talked about by people of obvious newsworthy stature or become generally recognized crises. The media, for example, underreported or virtually ignored as "unnewsworthy" such conditions as slums, racial discrimination, or police brutality in northern urban areas before the riots of the 1960s erupted and made them certifiable crises.

There are some exceptions to the general low quality of media news coverage or urban affairs: A small handful of the top prestige papers, like *The New York Times, The Washington Post,* and *The Christian Science Monitor,* and occasional television documentaries or specials, do present background and interpretive analysis as part of their urban coverage. Such coverage provides at least a minimal explanation of who is really trying to do what to whom and of what the different possible or likely consequences of different measures are likely to be for different segments of the general public. Also, journals of opinion with heavy urban content such as *The Public Interest* and *The New Republic,* give background and interpretive reporting about various aspects of urban problems in depth and also initiate discussion of some new issues. Their editors and writers are, however, mostly centered in New York, so that the perspective they communicate is most helpful for understanding a particular city only to the extent that that city resembles the nation's largest. The New York- or Washington-centered media can and do, however, provide insightful analysis of the general dimensions of urban problems and do discuss the kinds of programs and funding that the federal government has or does not have available to help cities cope with their situations. Another relatively new source of in-depth analysis of urban news—and one that may grow in importance—is the noncommercial, so-called "educational" TV stations, most of which are affiliated with the Public Broadcasting Service (PBS). Particular big-city based weekly or monthly magazines, like *New York, Chicago,* and *Philadelphia,* are still another relatively new source of such analysis.

The readership or audience of these prestige papers, TV documentaries, PBS programs, and specialized journals and magazines is, of course, extremely limited. But that readership or audience usually includes heavy concentrations of various city political decision-makers and other activists, opinion-leaders, and politically attentive members of the public. Consequently, the influence of these smaller circulation, "quality" media on policymaking is disproportionately high, given the limited numbers who are direct recipients of their messages. And through the "two-step" flow, already explained, some of the ideas that are picked up and sponsored by their elite readership or audience are then also radiated through face-to-face conversations and the regular mass media to wider publics. Data exist to show that readers of magazines, for example, rank markedly higher than audiences of wider circulation media in willingness to express opinions to others.[24]

Causes of Shortcomings

This failure of the mass media to make its maximum contribution to the effective democratic functioning of city government and politics results from two basic causes. First, although the media already perform and are capable of performing even greater public functions, they are in fact not public service institutions supported by tax dollars. The media are private businesses. Consequently, their product must be one that has sufficient marketability to ensure them financial solvency. This, and not maximum transmission of political intelligence, must be their overriding objective. Given the apolitical nature of most of the general public (to be discussed in the next chapter), the actual "market" interest in or demand for serious analysis of urban political activity is small. Indeed, the amount of news on city political affairs already reported is probably more than the average member of the public is interested in receiving. It is certainly more than would be possible economically if the whole cost of assembling and transmitting it had to be paid for directly by the readers and viewers with high political orientation.

The major costs for both newspapers and TV are, of course, borne by their advertisers. In 1970, 83 percent of *The Washington Post's* and 75 percent of *The New York Times'* revenues came from advertising.[25] These advertisers use the media as a vehicle for transmitting appeals about their product; those transmissions are baited principally with entertainment and news of crimes, sex, sports, etc. It is only incidental that newspapers and TV collect and disseminate the two kinds of information essential to the workings of a democratic political system. As Key pointedly describes it:

> Unhappiness about the performance of the media as instruments of political education . . . arises from expectations that are quite unrealistic. . . . [N]ewspaper publishers are essentially people who sell white space on newsprint to advertisers. Many of them are beset by the continuing problem of how much to spend for what to fill the space around the ads to maintain enough paid circulation to make it unnecessary to convert the sheet into a shopping-news throwaway. . . .[26]

[24]See studies cited in Key, *Public Opinion,* p. 347.
[25]Calculated from data in Sigal, *Reporters and Officials,* p. 9.
[26]Key, *Public Opinion,* pp. 379–80.

Beside the limitations that these economic realities place on the volume of political news that is transmitted by newspapers and TV, they also discourage attempts at incisive interpretation. For such interpretation is likely to disturb and antagonize at least some readers, viewers, or potential buyers of the advertisers' products, and perhaps the advertisers themselves. This is particularly true in cities having only one paper or one TV station where publishers and owners seek to have the widest possible appeal. Of course a wealthy, highly successful newspaper with a huge volume of advertising like *The New York Times* can afford to take the attitude that "When *The New York Times* cares about what its advertisers think, . . . it will no longer be *The New York Times.*"[27] But the average big-city newspaper, worried about competition for the advertising dollar from suburban dailies, local radio and TV stations and national news magazines, is bound to be more sensitive about unnecessarily biting the advertising account that helps keep it solvent.

It is the high fixed costs of operating a newspaper or television station that generate such strong pressure not to offend and to maintain the maximum possible audience:

> For the print and electronic media, the cost of production has little correlation to circulation. If a newspaper or news magazine goes to the expense of gathering the news and selling and preparing the advertising messages to support it, the incremental cost of extra press runs is relatively low. . . . The pressure is greater for television. It costs no more to produce a program whether 30 or 30 million people watch. Yet, the single most important measure of revenues will be the projected cost per thousand television households delivered. If enough viewers are delivered for the network to break even, additional viewers produce additional revenues at no additional cost. It is for this reason that the pressures on the news media to attract and maintain audiences may seem quite out of proportion. . . . [T]he effect is for the media to present material of the broadest possible appeal, necessarily aiming at middle America. It is also true that the same high premium is placed on not offending any significant segment of the audience. It is this requirement that makes it more difficult for new ideas to gain access and limits reporting on those conditions which give rise to much of today's dissent.[28]

The second cause of the mass media's failure to fulfill their potential for educating the public politically is the lack of industry, competence, and

[27]Quoted in Talese, *The Kingdom and the Power,* p. 75.
[28]Baker and Ball, *Mass Media and Violence,* p. 81.

time of many reporters and editors of urban news. It is much easier for a reporter simply to write up a mimeographed news release that comes routinely from one of the standard "covered beats," like the mayor's office, the police department, some other major city agency, or city interest groups, than for him to find and develop a more significant story on his own. To get a story that explained background, motivation, and possible impact, a reporter would have to spend extra time and energy to probe and get behind the handout. He would have to make interpretive judgments about why different participants said or did various things, and to make predictions about the likely consequences of the events or decisions involved. Furthermore, to make a solid interpretation he has to have substantive understanding of broad social and political processes and of the details and impacts of various substantive programs. Finally, to provide this kind of insightful reporting, the reporter certainly would need more than the few hours between the particular newsworthy "happening" and the deadline for filing a story for that day's paper or the time of the scheduled TV news program.

In 1963 the new metropolitan editor of *The New York Times,* A. M. Rosenthal, insisted that his reporters no longer take facts at face value, but report on the significance of events, the motivations of different participants, and make judgments on the reliability of the information presented by city political activists. There was strong resistance by many old "Timesmen," who believed that Rosenthal's "hard, interpretive" reporting—as he called it—would necessarily be more partisan and less accurate than the "neutral" setting forth of the facts about a set of events in order of their descriptive importance and without interpretive commentary that was part of *The Times'* past tradition.[29]

Most reporters, like other human beings, are reluctant to spend any extra time and energy on their stories, if it can be avoided. They therefore tend to accept news handouts and to be content to provide the kind of descriptive, surface narrative that reflects readily observable facts rather than to search for additional ones. That is also the safest way of remaining on good terms with their sources, who might resent any independently-done critique of the "news," as those sources want it to get out. And since the press deadlines and the news show schedules go on relentlessly, even the reporters who happen to be industrious, knowledgeable, and competent typically lack the time to prepare a really serious report. The only exceptions are the rare occasions when a "quality" newspaper gives the reporter a chance to do a wrap-up of a story that has broken over the course of weeks or months or when a TV station chooses to present a "special" entirely devoted to a particular topic.

[29]See Paul H. Weaver, "Hard Reporting on *The New York Times,*" in Edward C. Banfield, ed., *Urban Government,* rev. ed. (New York: Free Press, 1969), pp. 480–86.

The failure of the media to give further "actionable" information about and interpretation of city government and politics is not one acutely felt by most of the general public, although more stimulating reporting might increase the number of city dwellers who would be attentive to or participate in large-city political processes. The media's unfilled promise is clearly most frustrating to that tiny fraction of the population who already have a strong interest in city politics. It is this segment of the public who cannot satisfy their desire for in-depth understanding of what is happening in their city's political process or of its significance through the fragmentary, surface accounts they normally receive from newspapers and television.

15

City General Publics

Members of the general public have essentially three avenues for trying to influence city governmental policies and decisions. They are (1) engaging in individual or group activity that either directly communicates their viewpoint to governmental officials or supports the influence efforts of elites with a similar outlook; (2) developing opinions and thus contributing to the make-up of overall "public opinion"; (3) voting and thus contributing to collective electoral decisions.

THE APOLITICAL NATURE OF THE GENERAL PUBLIC

The first proposition about how city general publics use these avenues of influence is that rank-and-file members of the general public are basically apolitical. They normally have little interest, concern, or informed judgment on policy issues. Accordingly they rarely participate in the city political arena except to vote. And in many instances, a majority of a city's enrolled voters or of its adult population does not even do that.[1] (See Table 15–1.)

[1]See also Sidney Verba and Norman Nie, *Participation in America: Political Democracy and Social Equality* (New York: Harper and Row, 1972), who report that only 47 percent of their sample claimed always to vote in local elections; Robert R. Alford and Eugene C. Lee, "Voting Turnout in American Cities," *American Political Science Review,* 62 (1968): Table 2–1, p. 31, 796–813, who on the basis of comparative examination of turnout in 282 cities found an average turnout of 47 percent of registered voters nationwide (Table 8, p. 808); Howard D. Hamilton, "The Municipal Voter: Voting and Nonvoting in City Elections," *American Political Science Review,* 65 (1971): 1135–40.

TABLE 15-1 Turnout in Mayoral and Presidential Elections, 1972–74, Selected Large Cities

City	Turnout As Percentage of Enrolled Voters	
	Mayoralty Election	*Presidential Election*
Philadelphia	77.2	77.5
San Francisco	74.1	71.4
Newark	69.0	78.9
Denver	68.9	80.0
Buffalo	67.2	81.3
Milwaukee	66.5	77.3
Indianapolis	64.8	68.5
Los Angeles	63.2	80.4
Boston	62.3	69.9
Seattle	58.5	72.2
Detroit	55.7	58.9
St. Louis	54.6	75.5
Atlanta	52.6	----
Cleveland	51.8	73.7
Minneapolis	49.6	73.6
Columbus	44.2	50.9
Baltimore	33.7	68.1
Pittsburgh	25.6	69.9

Source: Various boards of election

The lack of interest in politics on the part of the general public is supported by much data developed by sample surveys: Studies between 1952 and 1972 of national elections show that an average two-thirds of the voters in such elections were only "somewhat interested" or "not much interested" as opposed to "very much interested" in any particular campaign.[2]

In a survey of interest in "between-campaigns" political activity, some 65 percent of the sample allowed that they followed what was "going on in government and public affairs," only "some of the time," "now and then," or "hardly at all." A minority of 35 percent asserted that they paid attention "most of the time."[3]

Even during presidential campaigns, clear majorities of the public are willing to admit that they followed the campaign in the newspapers other

[2]Survey Research Center, The University of Michigan (Ann Arbor: Inter-University Consortium for Political Research). Data from election studies for 1952, 1956, 1958, 1960, 1962, 1964, 1966, 1968, 1970, and 1972.

[3]Survey Research Center, The University of Michigan, *The 1966 Election Study.*

than "regularly," or on television by watching fewer than "a good many" programs.[4]

These studies dealt with national and not local politics. There is good reason to believe, therefore, that they understate the apolitical nature of the general public with respect to local matters. The relative turnouts in local elections are substantially lower than in national ones.[5] The answers to explicit questions in various surveys also show that the general public is less interested in local governmental affairs than in nonlocal ones. The 1966 SRC survey, for example, specifically asked which kinds of "public affairs" the respondent followed "most closely." Only some 29 percent of those who followed public affairs with any degree of regularity and 24 percent of the total sample indicated that they followed "local affairs" most closely as opposed to "international affairs," "national affairs," or "state affairs." Another 19 percent of those following public affairs and 16 percent of the total sample indicated they followed local affairs second most closely. Another survey, conducted in 1965, of a national cross-section of high school seniors found that only 11 percent indicated that they followed local affairs most closely, as opposed to 39 percent for international, 44 percent for national, and 6 percent for state affairs.[6]

Large numbers of citizens are thus not sufficiently interested even to follow what is going on in government or public affairs with any degree of regularity or involved enough in local politics even to vote in elections for top city officials. But even larger proportions refrain from more burdensome kinds of participation. National surveys from 1952 to 1972 found that 95 to 98 percent of the general public reported not belonging to "any political club or organization," 88 to 96 percent reported not giving any money or buying tickets or anything else to help a particular party or candidate, 90 to 93 percent reported not having attended "any political meetings, rallies, dinners, or things like that," 93 to 97 percent reported not having performed any other work for a candidate or party, 79 to 91 percent reported that they had not worn a campaign button or put a campaign sticker on their car, 73 to 92 percent reported they had *never* written to "any public officials giving them their opinion about something that should be done," 67 to 83 percent reported that they had not even talked to other members of the public about the election to try to persuade them to vote a given way,

[4]Survey Research Center, cited in John P. Robinson, Gerrold G. Rusk, and Kendra B. Head, *Measures of Political Attitudes* (Ann Arbor: Survey Research Center, 1968), pp. 616–19.

[5]See Verba and Nie, *Participation in America,* who report that 72 percent of their sample claimed that they always voted in national elections as opposed to 47 percent in local one, Table 2-1, p. 31. Also see Table 15-1.

[6]Reported in Robinson et al., *Measures of Political Attitudes,* pp. 400–401.

and 93 to 98 percent reported they had never "written a letter to the editor of a newspaper, or a magazine giving any political opinions."[7]

Dahl, in his study of New Haven politics, found that 87 percent of his sample had not in the previous year done "anything actively in connection with some local problem—political or nonpolitical," 84 percent had not in the previous year had any contact with "political or governmental officials," 73 percent had not "ever contacted any local public official or politician" to let them know what they would like them to do, and 53 percent, when they and their friends got together, did not "ever talk about New Haven politics and local affairs."[8] The Kerner Commission *Supplemental Studies* found in their 1968 survey of fifteen large cities that 70 percent of their white sample and 71 percent of their Negro sample had *never* "called a city official with a complaint about poor service."[9]

Of course, because the vast bulk of the general public is apolitical does not mean that all of it is. Turning the percentages around reveals that varying percentages ranging up to one-quarter or one-third of the sample are "very interested" in politics, care "very much" about the outcome of elections, believe who wins would make "a good deal of difference," read political news "carefully" or "very carefully," discuss politics "regularly" and engage in some political activity in addition to voting. On the basis of his analysis of all the then existing survey data, V. O. Key estimated that 10 to 15 percent of the general public normally was "highly attentive and active"[10] in politics, with higher proportions focusing their attention on particular actions of government at times of crisis. Such a percentage in New York City would represent about a half-million adults who are fairly regularly attentive to or active in politics. And even in some of the smaller large cities like Cincinnati or Denver or Buffalo, those who are attentive and/or activists would number in the tens of thousands. An Urban Observatory Program survey of ten large cities found that proportions ranging from 6.2 percent in Kansas City, Kansas, to 19.1 percent in Atlanta, and averaging 14 percent for the entire sample claimed that they belonged to organizations "working on city problems in any way."[11]

Characteristics Associated with Political Interest and Activity

Those who are politically attentive and active are not a random sample of

[7]Survey Research Center, The University of Michigan. Data from election studies for 1952–72.

[8]Robert A. Dahl, *Who Governs?* (New Haven: Yale University Press, 1961), p. 279.

[9]Angus Campbell and Howard Schuman, "Racial Attitudes in Fifteen American Cities," *Supplemental Studies for the National Advisory Commission on Civil Disorders* (New York: Praeger, 1968), Table IV-c, p. 41.

[10]V.O. Key, Jr., *Public Opinion and American Democracy* (New York: Knopf, 1961), p. 546.

[11]Frank X. Steggert, *Community Action Groups and City Governments* (Cambridge, Mass.: Ballinger Publishing, 1975), pp. 11–13.

the entire general public: They include disproportionately large numbers of those with the most income, most prestigious occupations, and largest amount of formal education. Apparently these characteristics are associated with a heightened attention to political information and awareness of the relevance of political activity to one's own welfare; with greater sophistication in the use of analytical tools for understanding and judging some of the remote consequences of policies and decisions; with a stronger "sense of political efficacy"—i.e., a sense that what one does politically will matter—; with a stronger "sense of civic duty"—i.e., a sense that an act like voting is a duty to be performed regardless of how hopeless the cause; with greater verbal skills; and, in general, with a life-style which includes "keeping up" with politics and engaging in some kinds of political activity as simply part of the "thing to do."[12]

On the other hand, individuals with lower status occupations, having only grade school education, and low income are disproportionately underrepresented among those politically attentive and active. Apparently people with low status characteristics tend not to perceive the relevance of politics to the improvement or deterioration of their own immediate situation. They have less capacity to deal with abstract, remote issues. They do not learn norms requiring participation and knowledgeability about political matters, either because they lack a sense of civic responsibility or because of its simply not being expected among their friends and acquaintances. And perhaps most important overall, such persons have stronger feelings of futility and a general lack of self-confidence in their capacity to assert themselves successfully against the environment.[13] According to Angus Campbell, the surest single predictor of political involvement is the number of years of formal education:

> There are apathetic college graduates and highly involved people of very low educational level but the overall relationship of education and political interest is impressive. [14]

A notable exception is that blacks, and especially blacks who have developed self-consciousness as a deprived group, hold higher levels of interest and rates of participation than whites with similar statuses.[15] The Urban Observatory survey previously referred to found that 41 percent of the black as opposed to 24 percent of the white "upper class" sample

[12] Angus Campbell, Philip E. Converse, Warren E. Miller, and Donald E. Stokes, *The American Voter* (New York: Wiley, 1960), pp. 475–82; Verba and Nie, *Participation in America,* esp. chaps. 6 and 8; and Robert R. Alford and Harry M. Scoble, "Sources of Local Political Involvement," *American Political Science Review,* 62 (1968): 1192–1206.

[13] Robert E. Lane, *Political Life: Why People Get Involved in Politics* (New York: The Free Press of Glencoe, 1959), pp. 220–234.

[14] Angus Campbell, "The Passive Citizen," *Acta Sociologica,* 6 (1962): 20.

[15] Verba and Nie, *Participation in America,* chap. 10; Joel D. Aberbach and Jack L. Walker, *Race in the City* (Boston: Little, Brown, 1973), p. 34.

claimed membership in groups concerned with "city problems" and that at every class level, a higher percentage of blacks than whites claimed to be "very interested" in "city problems and city politics."[16]

Race by Social Class	Very Interested
White Upper Class	32.7%
Black Upper Class	45.3
White Middle Class	23.4
Black Middle Class	44.3
White Lower Class	18.7
Black Lower Class	35.5

In order for this general introductory discussion of the role of the general public in city politics not to be misunderstood, two further points need to be stressed. First, the proportional overrepresentation of persons with the highest education, income, and occupational status among the activist/attentive stratum tends to be mitigated by the fact that there are fewer of them in the overall population than persons with middle-to-low status characteristics. This means that in terms of sheer numbers, more of the working- and middle-class members of the general public may be interested and active in any large city's politics than upper-middle and upper-class persons despite the lower participation rates of individuals from the former, lower-status groups.

Second, those members of the general public who are normally apolitical are not that way irrevocably. Any of them can become attentive and even active if some politically-relevant development appears that clearly threatens central interests or values like their own jobs or homes or personal safety, the character of their neighborhood, or anything intertwined with their feelings of self-esteem and worth, and the ordered course of their existence.

VEHICLES OF RANK-AND-FILE INFLUENCE

Individual Political Activity

Through letters, telegrams, telephone, conversations in person, or testimony at public hearings, any rank-and-file urban-dweller can volunteer his wishes to city decision-makers, asking or demanding that they perform or refrain from some decision or action. The impact of such unsolicited communication on questions of general city policy is obviously likely to be limited. Even if staff members or secretaries do not screen out unsolicited

[16] Steggert, *Community Action Groups,* Table 2-2, p. 13, and Table 2-3, p. 15.

communications to save their superiors' time, the views of a single rank-and-file individual carry no special weight. Such individual views are not conceded the legitimacy of a position shared by large numbers nor are they likely to be backed by sanctions or inducements. Similarly, they normally neither reflect expert opinion on how best to achieve an official's own goals, nor carry the prestige of various elites of wealth or social standing.

If the individual communication has to do not with general policy, but with the handling by an administrator or bureaucrat of a specific case, it may have greater impact. A request for an exception from a general rule, or a reconsideration of an adverse decision, or a request to rectify a deficiency in some service can at times lead to favorable action. This would depend on how costly the granting is of the request in terms of resources or of upsetting ongoing routine, on how much time is available for rethinking the matter, and on how convincing are the "merits" of the case. If, for example, a city administrator or bureaucrat has control of a work force which must do a certain amount of work, he may be willing to install a stop sign at a particular corner or direct a garbage cleanup in a particular street since it costs him nothing to be accommodating. Verba and Nie call this kind of activity by the public "particularized contacting" and show that it takes place much more frequently than attempts to influence general policy.[17]

A person can also participate individually in city politics by discussing political issues in efforts to influence other members of the general public with respect to their opinions or votes. How much changing of views takes place in the course of these discussions is, however, open to question: For it is fairly clear that most political discussion takes place among people who already are in general agreement. The result is, as Robert Lane has put it, that the "most substantial 'theme'" of such discussion is "the reciprocal expression of agreed upon political cliches and stereotypes."[18]

Besides communicating his views directly to the city's decision-makers or to other members of the general public, the rank-and-file member of the public can try to influence city governmental policies less directly by supporting the efforts of interest group leaders or by campaigning for candidates who share his general position. By adding his name to an interest group's membership rolls, an individual increases the numbers the group leader can claim he is speaking for and hence, even if only in a very marginal way, the authority with which that group leader speaks. By paying his dues, making other cash contributions, performing needed services, writing letters to officials in conjunction with other like-minded individuals, an individual increases even more significantly the potential effectiveness of the group's leaders. If an organized group does not already exist that is protecting his interests in a pending or prospective policy dispute, an

[17]Verba and Nie, *Participation in America,* Pt. I.
[18]Lane, *Political Life,* p. 87.

individual can also try with others to form a new group that will stand for the policy he desires. Perhaps the classic example of the formation of a new, ad hoc interest group is the "Committee to Save the West Village," which succeeded through intensive lobbying and public relations campaigns in stopping an urban renewal project being planned in New York City by the Wagner administration. The "West Village" was a neighborhood in downtown Manhattan, adjoining Greenwich Village, consisting of a mixture of old factory buildings, a few tenements, and a substantial number of privately owned, renovated brownstone and brick town houses. These last were occupied largely by middle-class professionals who enjoyed living in a neighborhood of bohemian-intellectual, avant-garde atmosphere and reputation.

Within five days after the City announced its plans to conduct a survey and study the neighborhood in preparation for developing a specific urban renewal plan, a group of residents organized sufficient opposition (including from the local state assemblyman) to appear at a public hearing that it brought about the postponement for thirty days of any decision to proceed. The organization of this opposition was spearheaded by Mrs. Jane Jacobs, then an assistant editor of the magazine *Architectural Forum,* who was completing what later became her best-selling attack on city-planning, housing, and urban renewal practices, *The Life and Death of Great American Cities.* Two days after the hearing, at a meeting of about 300 people in the auditorium of a local school, the "Committee to Save the West Village" was formed. Fifty-four residents of the area volunteered to contribute time and effort in order to try to kill the project which they feared would lead to destroying the character of their neighborhood by bulldozing down and replacing existing structures with high-rise apartments.

The Committee, comprised mostly of housewives, conducted their own survey of the neighborhood in order to collect information proving that it was not considered "blighted" or a "slum." Mrs. Jacobs and a small group of other residents who included the editor of the Columbia University *Forum,* another editor for a major publishing house, a real estate attorney for a Wall Street firm, a physicist, a research expert for a leading advertising agency, and a professional public relations expert, operated as a high command. The Committee tried to make the city renewal plan and its official sponsors appear arbitrary and undemocratic, purportedly trying to "railroad" the project through, secretly, against the neighborhood's wishes and before it had a chance to say anything and in the face of evidence that it was not a blighted area. After their victory was won, chiefly by proving to Mayor Wagner that he had much to lose and little to gain in the midst of an election campaign by not dropping the project, the Committee voted to continue its existence, with a change of name, as the neighborhood's watchdog and "improvement" association. Mrs. Jacobs and a few of the other members even gave advice and aid to other neighborhoods on how to fight city urban renewal and other projects.[19]

This example is not meant to indicate that individual members of the public can always exert influence successfully by banding together in a new ad hoc interest group. In the West Village case individuals emerged who possessed the leadership skills required to take the actions necessary to contact other persons, hold meetings, and form a group. The threatened interests were sufficiently intense and central that large numbers of residents were willing to contribute time, energy, and money to protect them. From the beginning, some sympathetic city officials were found to "carry the ball" within the formal decision-making bodies and feed crucial inside information back to the group. The elected city officials who originally favored the project had no major personal stake in it and since popular support was lacking for the opposed project, they could easily be made to look "undemocratic" by going against the opinion of those who would be most affected. Finally, the conflict took place within months before a city election, when elected officials are maximally responsive to agitated, unified community opinion, particularly when heeding such opinion does not run the risk of losing votes elsewhere. In situations where even a single one of these factors is missing—and this is normally the case—rank-and-file individuals are highly unlikely to achieve this much success in influencing the decisions of their city government through group action.

Contributing to Mass Public Opinion

Another means that members of the general public have for influencing city policymaking is by contributing to mass public opinion. By public opinion is meant the aggregate of the opinions held by members of a city's public on politically relevant matters. Opinions are essentially beliefs or attitudes favoring or opposing some phenomenon. Public opinion is not used synonymously in this chapter with majority opinion. Public opinion exists when significant numbers hold opinions about a particular issue, whether or not those numbers are majority-sized. And public opinion need not be unanimous: Among those with opinions there may indeed be unanimity on some issues, but on the other issues there may be a majority and minority position or even three or more minority positions.

Students of public opinion approximate that certainly no more than about 10 to 15 percent of the general public regularly has opinions about the specifics of city policies, programs, and current issues.[20] This 10 to 15

[19]This account is based on J. Clarence Davies, III, Neighborhood Groups and Urban Renewal (New York: Columbia University Press, 1966), pp. 72–109.

[20]See Key, *Public Opinion,* p. 357.

percent can be defined as the "politically attentive" part of the public. Probably only a small fraction of even that small percentage has knowledge of what the city government is actually doing in various programmatic areas, and about the consequences and advantages and disadvantages of existing policies relative to possible alternatives. And without doubt, there are more members of a city's attentive public who follow only particular areas of city governmental activity or particular kinds of issues rather than everything the city government does across-the-board. Judging from the size of the "no-opinion" responses to various surveys, it can also be said with a reasonable amount of confidence that about one-fifth to one-quarter of the public have no politically relevant opinions at all.

Though unable to differentiate or explain the specifics of ongoing city governmental policies and programs and especially relative to possible alternatives, most city-dwellers do have a sense that certain problems or inadequacies exist—crime in the streets, poor schools, slums, poverty—or that taxes are too high. In a survey among Detroit's black and white population asking about satisfaction or dissatisfaction with five city services, Aberbach and Walker found, for example, that on the subject of police and garbage removal, an average of fully 96 percent of both the whites and blacks had opinions, although these averages dropped to 63 percent and 75 percent respectively when asked about public schools, parks, and teen centers. Similarly, the study of fifteen cities done for the Kerner Commission showed that at least 90 percent of samples of white and black men and women had opinions about their satisfaction with police protection and garbage collection; on the other hand, for services like sports and recreation centers for teenagers, parks and playgrounds for children, and quality of public schools, the percentages having an opinion dropped to an average of 78 percent for both whites and blacks.[21]

Furthermore, many members of the public have an awareness of what groupings in the population are causing or are most hurt by the problems or inadequacies they perceive and of whether the city government as a whole is or is not well-run, doing a good job, or giving adequate service for the local tax dollar.[22] And, finally, wide portions of the public have feelings, if not opinions, about whether the government can be trusted to look after broadly held interests or whether it is exploitative and unresponsive to mass needs.[23]

[21]Aberbach and Walker, *Race in the City,* Table 2–10, p. 51; Campbell and Schumann, "Racial Attitudes," Table IV–a, p. 40.

[22]See Floyd J. Fowler, Jr., *Citizen Attitudes Toward Local Government Services and Taxes* (Cambridge, Mass.: Ballinger Publishing, 1974), chaps. 5 and 10.

[23]See Aberbach and Walker, *Race in the City,* chap. 6; and Peter Rossi, Richard A. Berk, and Bettye K. Eidson, *The Roots of Urban Discontent* (New York: Wiley, 1974), chap. 12.

Linkage between Public Opinion and City Decision-Making

Obviously, a single individual's simply holding a politically relevant opinion cannot cause the city government to conform to that opinion. Opinions of individuals affect policy only in so far as they are not idiosyncratic, but are shared by numbers.

Directive Public Opinion.[24] Perhaps the clearest connection between public opinion and official decision-making is when that opinion is widespread, unified, and intense in its demand that certain action be taken. The occurrence, for example, in a city of a large-scale crisis like a massive riot or strike of some essential service like police or schools will almost certainly generate a large and almost unanimous opinion among a broad public that the city government do something to end the crisis. That opinion would probably target-in specifically on the mayor. In other words, when some happening, decision, or policy is immediately and visibly affecting central values of virtually the whole citizenry, public opinion can be compelling or directive, though even here the directive is likely to define the problem to be dealt with, but not how.

Negative or Forbidding Public Opinion. Similarly, there can be a clear connection between public opinion and official decision-making when that opinion is widespread, unified, and intense in its demand that some contemplated action *not* be taken. Sometimes, "trial balloons" are floated by city officials deliberately, when they cannot predict what public reaction is likely to be. This is done just so they can get a reading on whether this kind of negative or forbidding public opinion exists. If a plan were to be seriously advanced by incumbent officials to ban all motor vehicles, for example, from the central business district of any large city, an almost unanimous negative public opinion would no doubt be generated to stop it.

Permissive or Supportive Public Opinion. On most policy issues that come up, public opinion is neither directive nor forbidding and thus has a much more tenuous impact on the policies that city officials ultimately adopt. Sometimes, there is a complete absence of broad public opinion, as the issue is too technical or remote or new to catch on and attract significant attention. Other times, broad public opinion is internally divided about what should be done. Probably most of the time public opinion is simply supportive or permissive of the various general purposes or goals that the city government is already pursuing—fighting crime, collecting garbage,

[24]This analysis of the linkage between public opinion and city decision-making draws heavily on the work of V. O Key, Jr., who distinguished among supportive, permissive, decisive or directive, and negative public opinions. See *Public Opinion and American Democracy,* chap. 2.

eliminating slums—but silent on how these purposes or goals are to be achieved, including how any conflicting interests should be weighed or various costs allocated.

The absence of any significant public opinion, public opinion that is divided, or public opinion supportive or permissive of general purposes all leave city officials wide leeway within which to make specific policy and program decisions.

Establishing Public Opinion

Establishing what public opinion is on various issues that come up is a tricky business. Specially commissioned opinion polls are very expensive and not commonly used by city officials except at the time of running for reelection. The regular major polling organizations—Gallup or Harris—almost never publish opinion surveys of other than national or broad regional samples. City officials must therefore rely heavily on intuition, hunches, and impressions to arrive at their estimate of what public opinion "is" in their city. The flow of letters from the public to officials themselves or to the editor's columns of newspapers; conversations city officials or their aides or acquaintances have had with members of the public at chance encounters, meetings, parties, or public receptions; testimony presented at public hearings; newspaper commentary or interviews with the "man-in-the-street" on television news shows; the warmth of reaction of an audience to speeches delivered by officials, including the friendliness or hostility of questions; protest demonstrations—all these are taken as portents and auguries of how the public is likely to respond to a particular official action.

Obviously, almost all these avenues of communication are heavily weighted with the views and opinions of the minority of attentive, activist, opinion-molding, and opinion-expressing members of the general public.[25] But without any firm indication of what the mass of rank-and-file individuals is really thinking, this kind of elite or semi-elite public opinion is frequently accepted, sometimes consciously, sometimes unconsciously, as its equivalent.

The Sanctions of Public Opinion

The question arises as to what sanctions public opinion can apply to the acts of city officials? What could happen if these officials simply chose to disregard either "directive" or "negative" consensual opinion or chose to adopt policies that clearly fell outside the limits of existing permissive opinion?

[25]Verba and Nie, *Participation in America,* chap. 15.

The first and most immediate sanction is one that operates internally on most city elective officials and probably on many high appointive ones as well. For most such officials have learned that people outside the government have a right to be heard, their opinions deserve to be given some weight, and mass opinion when it exists and is unified should normally prevail. Flagrantly going against such opinion is likely to create guilt from violating their own principles.

The second sanction is that making governmental decisions contrary to mass opinion leads to expressions of disapproval for the city officials concerned. Normally, elective city officials do not relish the disapproval of others per se and especially do not relish the likely resulting loss of popularity. For loss of popularity may, in the shortrun, reduce their general ability to exert influence within the city's decision-making arenas and may, in the longrun, have negative repercussions electorally. High city appointive officials and even career bureaucrats also like to be regarded as competent, dedicated public servants doing a good job. Loss of popularity for appointive administrators may, if severe enough, necessitate their resignation or dismissal. Even in the case of civil service bureaucrats, loss of popularity may weaken their ability to protect or expand their agencies' programs or funds or to fight off jurisdictional attacks from other bureaucrats or direction from superior officers.

The third and most telling sanction of ignoring public opinion is that for elective officials, it may lead to defeat at the polls: For, to the extent that members of the public are issue-oriented in their voting, they will be motivated not to cast their ballot for a candidate who has acted counter to their general or specific policy concerns. And to the extent the voters also reward general likability, any severe loss of popularity means that the appeal of an incumbent's personality characteristics is reduced.

These potential sanctions of public opinion are not always successful in getting city officials to heed them for any single decision. Particular officials may not have much personal commitment to the principle of majority rule —they may instead adhere to the maxim "the public be damned"—or officials may sincerely believe that they know better what is in the public's own best interests and feel they have an obligation to put this "superior" policy into effect whatever the public thinks. Similarly, some officials have atypically weak needs for approval and, therefore, are prepared to "stand the flack" that will come from flouting public opinion and carrying out their own convictions and preferences. Also, an official may feel that it is more important to follow his own policy goals rather than public opinion and is thus willing to risk the possible loss of influence and electability.

Elective politicians who "bravely" make hard decisions without regard to how those decisions might affect their reelection prospects are normally praised by the mass media and by members of the general public. Elective city officials, on the other hand, who show greater sensitivity for changing currents of public opinion are typically damned as "mere politicians." Though no part of the argument of this book is that the supreme value of elective officials should be to get themselves reelected to office, it should be kept in mind that in a very real sense, democracy and popular control through public opinion can work only when elective officials do care about being reelected. For if our cities ever began to be widely staffed by electoral politicians who always were prepared to do what they thought was "right" and never to worry about how the consequences would affect their re-election prospects, the prevailing de facto form of government would become short-term, elective dictatorship.[26]

Voting

The vote is, of course, the chief resource of influence possessed by the citizenry. Every two or four years, the voter is given an opportunity to pass upon the continuation in office of any incumbent city officials running for reelection as well as to select from among fresh aspirants for city decision-making authority. At these times, the voter can, theoretically, compare the policy positions of all the available candidates on the different issues on which he feels strongly and then cast his ballot for the candidates whose policy views most coincide with his own.

Kinds of Issue-Oriented Voting. The actual way that the average voter makes up his mind about how to cast his ballot does not, however, coincide with this civics textbook theory of voting. All the voting studies available show that the average member of the general public does not differentiate the specific issues being discussed by the competing candidates very much and does not have sufficient information to make the connection between the candidate's stands and his, the voter's, own preferences.

There are, unfortunately, no comprehensive studies of local elections. The classic study of American national elections—*The American Voter*—show, however, that only a small segment of the voters (15 to 16 percent for the elections it analyzed) was sophisticated enough to test the policy stands of candidates on issues by comparing them to reasonably self-conscious, articulated ideological or quasi-ideological principles and standards that the voters held.

Voters can, however, be in some sense issue-oriented even without detailed knowledge of specific issues. A sizable segment of the voting

[26]Kenneth Prewitt has shown that the indifference to being reelected of many of the 400 city councilmen he interviewed in the cities of the San Francisco Bay area (other than San Francisco) seriously interfered with their being responsive to majority preferences among the public. See his "Political Ambitions, Volunteerism, and Electoral Accountability," *American Political Science Review,* 64 (1970): 5–17, and *The Recruitment of Public Leaders: A Study of Citizen-Politicians* (Indianapolis: Bobbs-Merrill, 1970).

public (22 percent)[27] apparently took into account some issue content in elections to the extent of having overall feelings of satisfaction or dissatisfaction with conditions and governmental performance in general.[28] Opinions such as these might take the form of "the city's a mess," or "they're just not doing enough to keep the streets safe," or "the streets are just filthy," or "things have gotten much better, they opened a new school (or park or swimming pool)." These feelings of satisfaction or dissatisfaction convert into credit or blame for incumbent officials, with dissatisfaction and blame because of past performance more often being brought to bear on the vote than satisfaction and credit. As the authors of *The American Voter* put it:

> There is no need to presume that [the voter] sees any specific way in which the administration has courted the current ills, or that he has a sense of what might have been done differently, or even that he knows what the opposition intends to do, save for its predictable promises that ills will be remedied. The salient fact is that the [person or] party in power has failed . . . and deserves to be turned out.[29]

A still larger segment of the voters (45 percent) apparently came to believe that the election of some particular candidate or party was, in general, better or worse for one or more social groupings in the city's population, such as the poor, the working man, Negro people, taxpayers, and the rich. These voters had either positive and empathetic or negative and hostile feelings about many of these groupings and especially the ones in which they felt they belonged. These perceptions of what groups would be benefited or harmed thus serve as a substitute for evaluation of specific issue positions in judging positions of candidates.

About one-fifth of the voters (17 to 18 percent) did not consider issues at all in deciding how to vote. These voters made their voting decision entirely as a result of the relative personal attractiveness of the candidates, the party they and the candidates belonged to, or other factors that were not closely related to current policy issues.

It should be noted these voting studies were based on presidential elections. A study of congressional elections found, for example, "not more than a chemical trace" of detailed information among the voters of policy issues

[27]The percentages in the parentheses will continue to be from *The American Voters.* They are meant to give only a sense of the general order of magnitude of voters engaging in different kinds of issue-voting. Besides their being based on national instead of city elections, there is some question whether the particular elections on which those percentages are based were not atypically low on issue-orientation.

[28]See Campbell et al., *The American Voter,* chap. 10.

[29]*Ibid.,* p. 260.

and stands of the candidates.[30] One could guess that in city elections for high visibility posts such as the mayoralty, the proportion of the population that perceives specific issue differences would be closer to that demonstrated in presidential than in congressional elections. In elections for councilmen, city clerks, comptrollers, and other lower visibility city posts, the issue content of the vote probably approaches zero.

Impediments to Issue-Oriented Voting

Even for those voters who do consider issues in deciding how to vote, a number of other factors enter into the voting decision: the cross-cutting nature of issue positions and the candidate's party affiliation, personality, and ethnicity.

Cross-cutting or Noncongruent Issue Positions. One impediment to policy-oriented voting is that in any actual city election, each candidate normally stands for more than a single policy position. Moreover, the candidate develops an image of being sympathetic or hostile to a variety of sometimes competing social groupings. Unless the voter happens to have exactly the same set of policy preferences and group biases as some particular candidate, he will find only some issue positions and professed group friendships and animosities appealing, but the rest unappealing. In short, even the voter who is issue-oriented can cast his vote only for that "market basket" of preferred policy positions, friendships toward liked groups, and kind of past performance that suits him more than any other "market basket" that happens to be available in that particular election. Only rarely can a voter use his vote to endorse a candidate who offers the precise "market basket" that the voter, himself, would have chosen if he could have selected all the items with which it is filled.

Party Affiliation. Another impediment to issue-oriented voting in a city that has de facto or de jure partisan elections is the psychological identification that the average voter feels for one or another of the country's two major political parties. Voting studies show that roughly two-thirds of the public have persistent, long-term emotional attachments to the Democratic or Republican party.[31] Some of this attachment is reflected in the large proportions of the public registering as Democrats or Republicans on the voting lists. These attachments to a party provide the voter with moti-

[30]Warren E. Miller and Donald E. Stokes, "Constituency Influence in Congress," in Angus Campbell et al., *Elections and the Political Order* (New York: Wiley, 1966), p. 367.

[31]See Campbell et al., *The American Voter,* chaps. 6 and 7; Angus Campbell, Gerald Gurin, and Warren E. Miller, *The Voter Decides* (Evanston, Ill.: Row, Peterson and Co., 1954), chap. 7, and SRC voting studies of more recent elections.

vating force of varying intensity to vote for candidates of the party with which he identifies.

Once again there is no survey evidence on the specific impact of party identification on elections for city officials. Probably, however, the impact of party identification varies inversely with the visibility of the office contested. That is, in election for mayor, where the mass media provide ample voting cues in the form of impressions of the opposed candidates' personalities and statements on issues, the voter has a base other than partisan feelings for deciding his vote. In elections for councilmen or lesser executive officials, on the other hand, the candidate's party as shown on the ballot may be the only information the voter ever has about him. Consequently, that factor is more likely to be determinative.

Of course, party voting need not be ineffective in promoting a voter's policy ends on the leading issues. If the parties in particular cities had clear, cohesive, and differentiated long-term sets of policy and programmatic principles that all of its candidates shared and if the voter acquired and subsequently held his party identification through conscious choice based on an evaluation of the respective party principles, then voting automatically for or against candidates because of party labels would be an economical, issue-relevant, mental shortcut. That shortcut would reduce the need to consider specifics and to make new judgments at every election and for every candidate.

But we know that not all candidates bearing a party label are guaranteed to share any particular policy position, since capturing the party nomination in a direct primary or a nominating convention or caucus does not depend on passing any party ideological test. Second, the policy images of the parties that most voters have—more willingness to use government action to solve social problems and more concern for the disadvantaged on the part of the Democrats and more resistance to government regulation and more concern for the welfare of the better-off on the part of the Republicans—are based on the performance of their candidates and elected officials in national office, most importantly the presidency. Party affiliation may be completely misleading with respect to providing guidance about the general policy and programmatic outlook of candidates and officials of that party in a particular city.

Also, we know that most people acquire their loyalties before they reach voting age by what is, in effect, "inheritance." That is, for most voters party identification is learned from their families as they are growing up—much like their religion—and is not consciously selected by the voter as an adult because he is most sympathetic to a particular party's policy position. Once formed these attachments become relatively stable. In normal times only very small numbers of voters change their party identifications to more closely correspond with their own adult policy preference as those preferences develop.[32]

Feelings Toward a Candidate's Personality. The way people vote is also greatly influenced by the personality characteristics and style of the candidates—their apparent sincerity, warmth, intelligence, commitment, speaking ability, good family life, religious convictions, polish, glamor, charisma and general likability.

In recent decades, Richard Lee of New Haven, John Lindsay of New York, Jerome Cavanaugh of Detroit, and Kevin White of Boston all projected an image of dedication and excitement that drew the support of many voters. On the other hand, the image projected by Mayor Richard Daley of Chicago—the not overly sensitive, not overly well-educated, domineering boss—caused him to lose support within certain segments of the electorate during the 1960s, though not enough to bring about his defeat. Fiorello LaGuardia, thrice elected to the mayoralty of New York City in the 1930s and early 1940s, was perhaps the most popular mayoral candidate in recent history. LaGuardia was a maverick Republican who was elected and re-elected on a combination of party tickets in a heavily Democratic town and for much of the same time that the city's voters were electing Democrats to the state house, to Congress, and to the presidency.

Television in recent decades has provided most people with the opportunity to view the candidates for the highest city offices like the mayoralty, and to develop impressions about the kind of person the candidate is. Television is thus probably increasing the weight that personality characteristics—both real ones and those manufactured by the ad agencies—have in shaping the average person's vote. A candidate's personality characteristics obviously have their greatest impact in de facto nonpartisan elections and in primary elections for party nominations, where a strong competing voting cue, like party affiliation, is absent.

Some aspects of the candidate's personality—competence, keeping his word, etc.—are indeed relevant and need to be taken into account even for an issue-oriented vote. For such characteristics bear on whether that candidate will have the ability or the commitment to implement the particular policy point of view that he espouses. But even these qualities must be evaluated in conjunction with policy stands. For when they are taken by

[32]Apparently occasional major "cataclysmic" events, the most recent of which has been the great depression of the late 1920s and early 1930s, do have the power to produce changes of party identification in large numbers of voters against the party perceived as responsible for the cataclysm and in favor of the party that provides effective remedies (see Campbell et al., *The American Voter,* pp. 149–67). Perhaps the "cataclysm" of Democratic national officials promoting and implementing policies aimed at guaranteeing civil rights such as desegregation for southern blacks has been changing the party identifications of large numbers of southerners from Democrat to Republican in recent years.

themselves—as when the voter reports he votes "for the best man"—neither characteristics like ability or integrity, nor totally irrelevant ones like a good speaking voice or movie star glamor will determine what the candidate will do on matters of policy as an official.

Ethnicity. Another factor that influences the way people cast their votes is the national origin or the racial or religious characteristics of the candidate, especially when those are other than northwestern European, white, and Protestant. The most common way that these "ethnic" factors influence voting—to use the term "ethnic" as shorthand for all three—is to provide an extra "pull" for the candidate whose ethnic background the voter is conscious of sharing. Thus, whatever other motivations may also operate, the candidate with the clearly Irish surname has had special appeal to many voters of Irish descent; the Italian name for many Italians; the Polish name for many Poles; the Jewish name for many Jews; and black skin for many blacks.

Ethnic characteristics can exert strong *negative* effects, as when voters cast their ballot against a candidate from an ethnic group they dislike. Voters of earlier waves of immigration like the Yankees of English descent or later the Irish, for example, attached negative weight to a candidate being from a more recently arrived, lower-status ethnic background, like an Italian or an Eastern European. Logically, ethnicity is only a special kind of nonpolicy-, nonparty-relevant personality characteristic. But because it is so important in local elections it is discussed here separately.

The strength of the ethnic appeal varies from voter to voter and from city election to city election. The salience of national origins and religion appear to be generally higher among the voters in the older cities of the Northeast and Middle West than in the newer cities of the Pacific Coast and the Southwest. And the positive appeal of the candidate being a fellow ethnic is normally strongest of all when his candidacy is a "first," especially for the office at the head of the ticket.[33] Being a "first" means that members of that ethnic group had never previously been able to attain a nomination for a particular office—being, for example, the first Italian to run for mayor. The gaining of that coveted nomination by a co-ethnic thus symbolizes the long-awaited recognition of the worth and dignity of the group by the wider society. And even if it doesn't do all that, it at least symbolizes the ending of that ethnic group's unacceptability and low evaluation as well as the recognition of its voting power.

[33]See Raymond E. Wolfinger, "Some Consequences of Ethnic Voting," in M. Kent Jennings and L. Harmon Zeigler, eds., *The Electoral Process* (Englewood Cliffs, N.J.: Prentice-Hall, 1966); Raymond E. Wolfinger, "The Development and Persistence of Ethnic Voting," *American Political Science Review,* 59 (1965): 896–908 and *The Politics of Progress* (Englewood Cliffs, N.J.: Prentice-Hall, 1974), chap. 3.

Only a small amount of immigration has taken place in recent decades and there has been an increasing assimilation of the descendents of previous immigrants—particularly those who took on middle-class occupations and life styles—into an overall, "core" American culture. Also, there has been a developing ecumenical religious spirit. The most salient "ethnic" characteristic in recent city elections has therefore not been candidates' national origins or religion, but their race: For example, some white voters—because of racism, anger generated by black rioting, the rhetoric of black extremists, or the threat they perceive of a black takeover of their neighborhoods—will vote against any candidate who is black. Similarly, many black voters—because of black racism, hostility toward and distrust of whites, or heightened feelings of pride in their own identities—will vote against any white candidate if a black is also running, particularly in constituencies where blacks constitute large percentages of the population.

During the late 1960s and early 1970s, there were mayoral elections in Atlanta, Cleveland, Detroit, Newark, and Los Angeles, where black and white mayoral candidates were running against one another. In many white "blue-collar" election districts, the black candidate received almost no votes, while in black ghetto districts the white candidate did equally as poorly. When, for example, Carl Stokes ran in 1965 and 1967 as the first black candidate for mayor in Cleveland's history, the percentage of the vote he won in the city's predominately solid black and white wards is shown in the following table:[34]

TABLE 15-2

	Percent of Stokes Votes		
	White wards	*Black wards*	*City Totals*
1965 General Election	3.0	85.4	35.8
1967 Primary Election	15.2	96.2	52.5
1967 General Election	19.3	95.0	50.5

A candidate's ethnic characteristics are likely to be especially influential when there are no salient competing cues for making a judgment, like party affiliation, differing issue positions, or important visible differences in personality traits. A study by Gerald Pomper of voting in Newark, New Jersey, shows the striking difference between nonpartisan and partisan elections in the effect of ethnic considerations on the voting decision: Pomper found that in the Newark municipal election he studied—which

[34]Adapted from J. K. Hadden, L. H. Masotti, and V. Thiessen, "The Making of the Negro Mayors, 1967," *Trans-Action,* January 1968, Table I.

was nonpartisan—"the only explanation of the vote which can be supported is that which emphasizes ethnic considerations."

> Regardless of party, slate, or policy positions, the votes for candidates of the same stock are closely related, especially in those wards populated by members of that stock. . . .
>
> Generally, candidates received disproportionately high support from areas populated by members of their own ethnic groups.[35]

On the other hand, one year earlier in a partisan election for the New Jersey State Assembly, the voting returns showed that:

> party voting [was] the more important factor. In every case, there are positive correlations of the votes for members of the same party, and these are high in all but one case. Conversely, correlations of votes for candidates of the same ethnic group but of different parties are always negative and generally highly negative. . . . In the partisan Assembly elections, the parties act to bridge ethnic differences and to achieve unified support of their candidates.[36]

It should be noted that as with party- and personality-oriented voting, ethnic-based voting is not always irrelevant to an individual's policy preferences on issues. When a particular ethnic group has been severely shortchanged or mistreated over the years by a succession of non-fellow-ethnic officeholders, it may not be unrealistic to believe that a fellow-ethnic may be more sensitive, responsive, and equipped in dealing with problems unique to that group and in providing fairer treatment. And where the issues are trivial or the difference in positions among the candidates insignificant, the value of the symbolic recognition or the gratification that will be received by a member of a low-status group by the election of a co-ethnic may well be more important than any other consideration.

In most cases, however, ethnic characteristics are irrelevant to policy or performance. Most often, the voter who takes them into account allow his feelings to interfere with using the vote to bring about governmental policies and programs that will be most beneficial to himself. Raymond Wolfinger argues that the turn-of-the-century immigrant poor might have used their energies and voting power to press for substantive programs. But, according to Wolfinger, the immigrants were diverted from this course by ethnic voting, which gained for the voter only the satisfaction of seeing fellow-ethnics appointed or elected to particular city offices. These fellow-ethnics,

[35]Gerald Pomper, "Ethnic and Group Voting in Nonpartisan Municipal Elections," *Public Opinion Quarterly,* 30 (1966): 87.

[36]*Ibid.,* pp. 92, 93.

once in office, were more interested in advancing their own careers and in individual self-enrichment than in pushing for any redistribution of income or power or for broad-scale expansion of social and economic opportunities for those co-ethnics who supported them.[37] Even currently, as Edgar Litt and others have pointed out, ethnic-based voting resulting from interethnic conflicts and animosities has retarded the aggregation of the voting strength of the "have-not" part of the population in demand of a greater share of political power and material benefits.[38]

Linkage Between the Vote and Public Policy.

The vote of any single individual almost never, of course, has an identifiable impact on public policy. The policy influence of the average voter depends upon his being part of the plurality or majority that controls the outcome of an election. But even a sought-after outcome in an election for elective city offices guarantees only that some particular individuals rather than some others will fill those offices. Such an outcome does not automatically convert itself into some predetermined set of policies and programs preferred by the voters who supported the winning side. Indeed, given the diverse array of motives—and especially non-issue-oriented motives—that influence the individual voting choice, can any mandate for future governmental policy validly be inferred from the outcome of any particular city election?

As the late brilliant student of American electoral behavior, V. O. Key, explained, at least in a few elections, the actions of the total electorate do constitute a kind of "collective decision" with relatively clear policy overtones.

"Votes of No Confidence" in Incumbents. The clearest policy meaning of an electoral decision is when the voters provide a decisive defeat for incumbent city officials running for reelection. Such an electoral outcome indicates disapproval or "lack of confidence" in past policy or general performance. This kind of decision "may not specify with minuteness the elements of policy or performance of which it disapproves and cannot indicate with precision the lines of policy that should be pursued," but it does make it obvious that some "changes should be made."[39] Indeed, "an election of this type may amount, if not to revolution, to its functional equivalent."[40] The victorious challengers, it can be presumed, will try to change those aspects of past policy and performance that they gauge were the leading causes of the mass dissatisfaction against the previous incumbents.

[37] Wolfinger, "Some Consequences of Ethnic Voting."

[38] Edgar Litt, *Ethnic Politics in America* (Glenview, Ill.: Scott, Foresman, 1970), p. 24.

[39] Key, *Public Opinion*, p. 473.

[40] V. O. Key, Jr., *Politics, Parties, and Pressure Groups*, 5th ed. (New York: Thomas Y. Crowell, 1964), p. 523.

It should be noted that the ease with which widespread dissatisfaction with performance can cause the defeat of incumbent officials varies in different cities. In a city like Chicago where the mayor has been in recent decades the boss of a strong party machine that can provide a large assured vote in a primary election, only extreme dissatisfaction—not yet evident—can lead to the defeat of the party's choice. Similarly in partisan cities where the underlying distribution of party loyalties is heavily lop-sided in favor of the party in power, even large-scale dissatisfaction may not cause the vote of majority party candidates to drop below a winning margin. A heavy erosion of support may, however, give the reelected officials a scare and motivate them to change some of their ways, lest on the next occasion that they are contested at the polls, their supporters turn out to have shrunk to a minority. Thus Mayor Lindsay of New York, after narrowly escaping defeat in his 1969 reelection attempt, instituted numerous changes calculated to appeal to those parts of the electorate whose support he had lost.

In the period since World War II, in almost every large city the voters have had occasion to make their dissatisfactions effective by at least turning out incumbent mayors. This has been done either by defeating them in a party primary or in a partisan or nonpartisan general election or by making the prospects of victory so dim that the incumbent mayor decided not to seek reelection. The voters have usually not been able, however, to turn out of office simultaneously with the mayor, a majority of the incumbents in the city's legislative body and replace them with a team committed to support the new policies of the winning mayoral candidate.

"Votes of Confidence" in Incumbents. Another fairly clear meaning of a collective electoral decision is when broad approval is given to newly instituted changes in policy, program, or basic approach by reelecting incumbent city officials, especially if the margin of victory significantly exceeds that of their previous election. Such a vote of confidence essentially ratifies those changes and largely relegates them to the body of settled questions. The smashing reelection victories gained by New Haven's Mayor Richard Lee in 1955 and 1957, for example, after a close initial win in 1953, were almost universally interpreted as widespread endorsements for moving ahead on his massive urban renewal program.[41]

Mixed Verdicts. Other kinds of electoral outcomes—and this constitutes the largest category of cases—can be considered "stand-offs" or "mixed verdicts." In such elections incumbents may be reelected or defeated, but the distribution of the vote will be much like that of the previous election, thus leaving no clear meaning about the collective judgment of the public on policy matters. Mixed verdict elections may indicate that one large segment of a city's public is satisfied, while another such segment is dissatisfied. Under these circumstances, city officials are

[41] See Allan R. Talbot, *The Mayor's Game* (New York: Harper & Row, 1967), chap. 4; Dahl, *Who Governs?* p. 121.

left with maximum leeway in resolving questions of policy and program as they come up.

Referendum-type Elections. Unlike national elections, voters have opportunity in regular or special city elections to vote directly on specific matters of substantive policy or program when presented by initiative and referendum procedures. Probably the most common items appearing on the ballot are bond issues, the size of school budgets, and charter amendments. Fewer voters normally take the opportunity for trying to influence policy on referendum and initiative proposals than vote in city candidate elections, with voters of low income, low-status occupations, and low education being especially unlikely to turn out.[42]

In deciding whether to vote for or against particular referendum proposals, probably only a tiny fraction of the public studies the nature of the proposals—some of which are extremely complicated in their phraseology—and casts its vote on the basis of real understanding of the "merits" of the case. As in candidate elections, individuals are more likely to vote on the basis of how they feel about the officials and private elites who are supporting or opposing the proposals and about the groups that appear to be in line for benefit or harm. From what little evidence that exists, for example, it appears that few people who voted in the New York City referendum that abolished the civilian police review board in 1966 understood either how that board operated or whether or not it interfered with the effectiveness of the police. In essence, most voters decided on the basis of whom they liked most or disliked least: the police, who wanted to remain free of any civilian evaluation of the propriety of their acts, or the black and Puerto Rican community, who saw the police review board as a symbolic protection against police brutality. The friends of the police won.

Apparently, there is a bloc of voters of varying, but always substantial, proportions who are predisposed to vote "no" on any referendum proposal, but particularly on those that add programs or authorize additional spending and borrowing. The predispositions underlying this "free floating" no vote are held disproportionately by lower-status voters. Many such voters feel a sense of powerlessness and alienation—of things being run by the "establishment," the "better-off" and "better-educated," who purportedly pay no attention to common folk like them nor take into account their interests. These alienated, normally inattentive members of the public then seize the opportunity of referenda and initiatives to assert themselves by frustrating the purposes of those who normally are beyond their control.[43]

[42]Howard D. Hamilton, "Direct Legislation: Some Implications of Open Housing Referenda," *American Political Science Review,* 64 (1970): 124–38.

[43]See Alvin Boskoff and Harmon Zeigler, *Voting Patterns in a Local Election* (Philadelphia: Lippincott, 1964); James S. Coleman, *Community Conflict* (New York: Free Press, 1957); and John E. Horton and Wayne E. Thompson, "Powerlessness and Political Negativism: A Study of Defeated Referendums," *American Journal of Sociology,* 67 (1962): 485–93.

APOLITICAL GENERAL PUBLICS AND URBAN DEMOCRACY

As has been seen, the direct influence of a city's general public is high on the question of who its elected officials are to be. For only this public, acting as an electorate, can confer legal, decision-making authority on particular individuals. On matters of policy and program, however, the general public mostly just sets broad limits that condition the kinds of purposes that officials can promote. To the extent that the general public influences the specifics of city decision-making at all, it is the opinions of the thin attentive stratum of that public that carry disproportionately high impact. At times the broader public can express at least a mood about the urgency or complacency with which particular problems or the demands and grievances of particular groups should be addressed. And on rare occasions, it can even be a directive that some particular thing be done. But on the specifics or details of day-to-day city governmental policies and programs, the general public is normally without direct influence, as city officials and other activists negotiate and bargain-out their settlements in virtual privacy.

On occasion, this privacy can be broken. For when the city activists are themselves in fundamental disagreement, at least one set may become sufficiently distressed with the likely outcome of these low-visibility maneuvers to appeal to the general populace for support of its own position. Concerning many issues, the broad public may still simply refuse to listen or become involved. But if the issue is one that happens to engage the interest and attention of significant portions of a city's general public and that part of the public also develops a clearly dominant point of view about what should be done, then this view may prevail even on the disposition of issues of specific policy or program. The choice can also be put more formally to the public, as when one set of activists forces a referendum on a particular issue. And at intervals, some candidate elections can, in effect, be turned into referenda on the general policy stand or performance of some incumbent.

Given the limited influence of the general public, how democratic is the operation of the city governmental process? The answer obviously depends on the concept that is held of a democratic political system. If that concept requires extensive attention to, and interest and participation in, a city's decision-making process by substantially all the adult citizenry, that all citizens have equal influence and receive equal benefits and that a city's policy decisions be made by the citizenry in some sort of continuing informal referendum process where in all cases the mass majority rules, then the political systems of our large cities fail the "democratic test" by wide margins.[44] If on the other hand, our concept of democracy requires only that no restrictions exist to, and that there be opportunity afforded for, widespread interest, attention, and participation in a city's politics to develop, including especially the opportunity to support challengers and displace incumbent city officials at decently short intervals if mass dissatisfaction forms over their conduct of governmental affairs, then the political systems of our large cities are found less wanting. Here, the major shortcoming is that because of various combinations of separation of powers in mayor-council cities and of nonpartisanship or weak party organization, elections for the most part can be used only to reward or penalize a mayor, but cannot replace an entire administration. As a consequence, only incremental changes are usually possible in city policymaking as a result of elections, however widespread the demands for more dramatic new departures. Another shortcoming, given this concept of democracy, is the absence from almost any large city of an organized opposition to the officials in power, which can beam critical messages to the public about official proposals and decisions and inform the public about constructive alternatives.

Which is the more valid conception of democracy is not a trivial question. The concept a member of the general public holds will determine in large part to what degree he feels shortchanged and alienated, and thus loses faith in and allegiance to the existing system or to what degree he feels satisfied that he is exerting the kind of influence that can realistically be open in a democracy to nonofficials. The first, "equality of influence" and "continuous public referendum" concept of democracy is so demanding that except possibly for a brief period of early Athenian democracy or for the town-meeting local governments of colonial times, no political system of even moderately large scale that we know about would pass the test. One must, therefore, accept the second concept of democracy, both because of the widely shared conviction that most political systems in the United States, in Western Europe, and in the British Commonwealth are in some true sense "democratic" and because this conception does not require any unrealistic expectations about the extent of "politicization" of, or the amount of influence that can be exerted by, the average person. As Robert Dahl has put it about urban Americans:

> At the focus of most men's lives are primary activities involving food, sex, love, family, work, play, shelter, comfort, friendship, social

[44] Writers like Parenti, Katznelson, and Kesselman, for example, would argue essentially that a political system cannot be called democratic unless it affords equal influence and equal benefits to everyone. See especially Michael Parenti, *Democracy for the Few* (New York: St. Martin's Press, 1974), pp. 38–39, and Ira Katznelson and Mark Kesselman, *The Politics of Power* (New York: Harcourt Brace Jovanovich, 1975), pp. vii, 32.

> esteem, and the like. Activities like these—not politics—are the primary concerns of most men and women. . . . [P]olitics is a remote, alien, and unrewarding activity. Instead of seeking to explain why [most] citizens are not interested, concerned, and active, the task is to explain why a few citizens *are* .[45]

Disincentives to Politicization

The reasons why most persons are not "interested, concerned, and active" are many. First, their own immediate, personal stake in city decision-making is usually small. The general psychological and material well-being of the majority of the citizenry who are not slum-ghetto-dwellers, is not centrally affected by what the city government does. Its day-to-day pursuits and goals are satisfied or frustrated through individually-pursued, private means. As one woman explained to an interviewer:

> I don't think politics or election results will or do affect my own life very much. Regardless of who is in power, I'll keep my job and my home. I realize that politics does affect me, but it still doesn't really seem to touch me.[46]

Furthermore, for most people politics as a subject-matter is simply too abstract, impersonal, and remote to make it intrinsically rewarding to follow regularly.

Second, giving attention to, gathering information about, and participating in a city's politics are all expensive in terms of time, energy, and sometimes money. Even the participation involved in merely keeping informed is for many people unacceptably or impossibly costly: For monitoring the press and television, let alone news magazines and journals of opinion, for political intelligence with sufficient thoroughness to permit any kind of understanding of the background and nature of an issue is very time-consuming. Furthermore, digesting the information, putting it into a frame of reference, and drawing from it implications about what decisions should be made is probably beyond the intellectual capacity of many people. Also, following politics regularly may result in being confronted with certain kinds of information that prove disturbing, if that information is unpleasant or if it conflicts with strongly felt biases.

Third, expressing opinions to other people in group discussions makes many people uncomfortable. For one thing it can expose their lack of understanding or rhetorical or logical skill. As one candid respondent put it

[45]Dahl, *Who Governs?,* p. 279.

[46]Quoted in Morris Rosenberg, "Some Determinants of Political Apathy," *Public Opinion Quarterly,* 18 (1954): 363.

to an interviewer asking her if she discussed politics, "No, since I don't understand too much about politics, I just keep my mouth closed. . . . I really don't understand too much about politics. People should know what they are talking about and this takes an education which goes beyond the high-school level."[47] Also, discussing politics can lead to disagreements and thus interfere with a need of many Americans to maintain superficial harmonious relationships with everyone and not to possibly alienate neighbors, acquaintances, employers, or customers.[48]

Finally, even if a person does care and is willing to spend the time and energy to become informed on political matters and developed considered judgments, these judgments normally would not be politically actionable. That is, there is little that the average person can do with them, in the sense of directly influencing the city government's actual decisions. The prospects must appear slim to an individual that his single letter, his monetary contribution, his attendance at a meeting, or his single vote is going to change city policy. For as the typical member of the general public is likely to perceive it, policy is determined much more by the imperatives of the situation, the needs, desires, and problems of city officials, and pressures from more powerful people than someone like himself.

The Insufficiency of Democracy

Even though most large city political systems operate democratically, sizable numbers of citizens still feel that they have insufficient influences to cause their city government to be responsive to their needs and grievances. Our existing system of democracy works most satisfyingly, after all, for those individuals whose stake in public policy is small and for those who have greater than average "slack" resources to direct to politics. It also works well for those whose stakes or interests are shared by majorities, so that if those stakes or interests become threatened, there is a good chance of successfully influencing officials to make policy or program changes. Those individuals who have a high stake in city governmental policy—slum-dwellers dependent on governmental programs for income, housing, education, antidiscrimination, etc.—but who have few slack resources to mobilize and who even in voting strength represent only a minority of any electorate or do not vote at all, may find their limited influence to be severely frustrating. Indeed, individuals who find themselves *always* on the losing side in elections or policy disputes may either cease accepting the principle of majority rule democracy and become apathetic or turn to using violence and terror in attempts to influence or destroy the system. Figure 15-1 shows the great

[47]*Ibid.,* pp. 353-54.

[48]Lane, *Political Life,* p. 109.

increase between 1964 and 1972—a period during which the problems of blacks, poor, and city-dwellers fell from being a high priority item to one subjected to "benign neglect"—of the proportion of blacks whose answers to survey questions testing their attitudes toward the political system placed them in the "opposed" or "cynical" as opposed to the "trustful" or "supporter" categories. A stable democracy requires that the majority, or the officials or other activists who speak for the majority, satisfy not only majority preferences but also accommodate to some extent the intensely felt needs of minorities.

The demand for "community," i.e. neighborhood-based, participation and "control" in city governmental operations reflects the desire to decentralize city governmental authority. The result would be that even groups who are minorities city-wide, would be able to exert majority control in the areas where they live. Apart from the resistance of city bureaucrats to

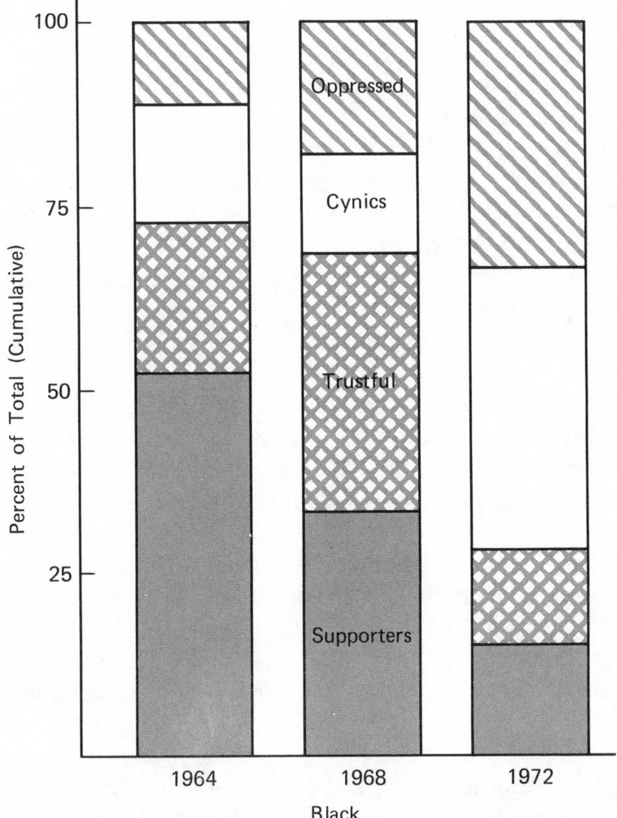

FIGURE 15-1 Black Voter Attitude Toward the Political System, 1964–72.

Source: Adapted from Gerald Pomper, *Voters' Choice* (New York: Dodd, Mead Co., 1975), p. 126, figure 6-1.

increased control over them by their clientele, the major obstacle to such community control achieving its objectives is that improved services and expanded programs inevitably require additional money being made available. That money cannot, however, be raised within the neighborhoods with the greatest need. Consequently, even if through "community control," city-wide minorities could dominate any decision-making machinery that were set up in their neighborhoods, the funds that would be available to run programs would still be determined by city-wide (or with respect to congressional grants, national) majorities. This does not mean that mechanisms giving neighborhood "councils" or other bodies greater influence over how available money, and especially available "new" money, is spent or shortages are absorbed among different programs might not have salutary effects. At least, neighborhood majorities would then have the power to impress their own priorities on what the city government does spend in their areas.

A Silver Lining?

Thus far the argument has been that "mass apolitics" it not inconsistent with the democratic operation of our large-city political systems. But, paradoxically, the apolitical nature of the general public may actually be conducive or even essential to two other valued aspects of city politics—the stability that comes from its being "low temperature" and the safeguarding of civil liberties and procedural due process guarantees. On the first point, if large cities had a general public that was constantly highly interested and attentive to political issues, city officials and other activists would not be as free as they are now to negotiate compromise agreements to bring policy conflicts to an end. Constant watchfulness and extensive emotional involvement by the public on every policy issue that came up would lead to city officials and other elites becoming captives of the inflexible emotions of their mass followings and thus fearful of coming to terms with their opponents lest they be accused of "selling out." As the usual case is now:

> given only peripheral popular focus on political issues, leadership must clamor for attention, and when attention is aroused it may be only fitful and transient. Rather than being anchored to their following, leadership blocks [are] under a compulsion to settle for what they can when they can as they negotiate from points of weakness.[49]

In the last decade, issues associated with race, such as desegregation of schools and neighborhoods, forced busing, and school decentralization, have aroused large proportions of normally quiescent segments of the general public in many cities. They have caused ugly confrontations, hardening of antagonisms, and emerging polarization between groups.

[49]Key, *Public Opinion,* p. 47.

If this degree of tension was concentrated on a continuing basis on every issue that came up in city policymaking, the consequences would be frightening: The resulting cleavages and hostilities among the citizenry might render impossible both civility in day-to-day interactions and peaceful reconcilability by particular segments of the public to governmental decisions that they did not favor. Once lines hardened so that segments of the public saw themselves not as only occasional opponents on policy questions, but as permanent enemies, the losing side in elections might begin to find it difficult to accept election returns peacefully.

On the second point, numerous studies have shown that the lower the economic, occupational, and educational characteristics of members of the general public, the less their support for specific applications of civil liberties and procedural due process.[50] Although almost everyone indicates approval of the central principles of civil liberties like freedom of speech and procedural due process in criminal trials when stated as general abstractions, broad segments including even majorities of the general public normally do not support certain specific applications of those principles to members of widely unpopular groups—in past decades Communists or atheists and more recently protestors, rioters, drug pushers, or Black Panthers. Yet large-city political systems operate with a high degree of protection for the civil liberties and procedural rights of even the most despised individuals and groups.

The primary reason why the political system of large cities can be more protective of civil liberties and procedural due process than is supported by their general publics is precisely the limited extent of their publics' knowledge about and influence over the detailed content and specific application of the political rules-of-the-game. This limited influence of the public allows city officials and other elites and activists, who as higher status individuals are much more strongly committed to the civil libertarian and procedural-due-process creed, to impose their norms on the operation of the system. As Dahl has explained:

> Ordinarily, . . . it is not difficult for a stable system of rights and privileges to exist that, at least in important details, does not have widespread public support and occasionally even lacks majority approval. As long as the matter is not a salient public issue . . . the question is substantially determined within the political stratum itself. When disagreements arise, these are adjudicated by officials who share the beliefs of the political stratum rather than those of the populace. . . .[51]

[50] *Ibid.*, pp. 135ff; Dahl, *Who Governs?*, p. 312; James W. Prothro and Charles M. Grigg, "Fundamental Principles of Democracy: Bases of Agreement and Disagreement," *Journal of Politics*, 22 (1960): 276–94; Fred I. Greenstein, *The American Party System and the American People*, 2nd ed. (Englewood Cliffs, N.J.: Prentice-Hall, 1970), chap. 2.

[51] Dahl, *Who Governs?*, p. 321.

16

General Characteristics of Urban Political Influence: An Overview

The preceding chapters have described and analyzed the characteristic ways in which different participants exercise influence over a city's policy process. This chapter attempts to integrate the findings in order to explain the dominant characteristics of the urban influence process in general, the most important kinds of resources on which such influence is based, and the determinants of success in attempts to influence city governmental decisions.

MULTIPLICITY OF POINTS OF POTENTIAL INFLUENCE

One crucial general characteristic of large-city governments is the multiplicity of decision-making points that they contain, through which political influence can be exercised. That is, "decisions" of city governments do not emanate from a single source which would then be the only target of attempted influence. Instead, decision-making powers in large cities are dispersed among a number of officials and agencies. Each of these officials and agencies has varying, but always substantial, amounts of autonomy and discretion for choice-making and each becomes a target for a variety of influence-seekers.

This multiplicity of decision-making centers is the result of a number of factors. First, with the exception of the minority of those that have council-manager systems, large-city governments are organized on the traditional American pattern of separation of powers and thus have executive, legislative, and judicial branches with independent decision-making authority.

Furthermore, all large cities have varying numbers of largely autonomous authorities, boards, and commissions, which operate in particular substantive areas like schools, housing, transportation, etc., without any direct lines of responsibility to the mayor or the city's legislative body. Also, city legislatures and the governing bodies of authorities, boards, and commissions are multi-membered, so that each member becomes an independent decision-maker in choosing whether to support or oppose particular proposals. Finally, political party leaders and party committees are invested by state law with certain independent powers of their own over aspects of the nominating and electoral process for city offices.

This amount of dispersion of decision-making powers reflects the fragmentation of legal authority in large cities. Additional amounts of dispersion of decision-making powers result, however, from the large measure of de facto autonomy enjoyed by such nominal subordinate officials as city managers, staff aides, city commissioners, and especially career bureaucrats in a city's different operating departments. Admittedly, all the decisions of these nominal subordinates theoretically can be overruled by their legal superiors. But in reality, these nominally subordinate officials and employees function as decision-makers with a high degree of autonomy and therefore become targets of influence in their own right.

KEY RESOURCES OF POLITICAL INFLUENCE IN CITIES

Political influence is the ability to affect in an intended way decisions issuing from any of a city's legally established or de facto decision-making points. Political influence can operate at any or all stages of the decision-making process: articulating the existence of a problem; formulating the content of a proposed decision for meeting the situation; forcing or blocking consideration by official decision makers of a desired outcome; amending or modifying a proposal or substituting a different proposal during consideration; promulgating the decision; and shaping a decision's detailed implementation. A resource of influence is anything that provides the capacity or leverage to intervene and affect the content of a contemplated or actual decision at any of these stages.

Obviously, holding an official position to which legal decision-making powers are attached is such a resource. But there are many other resources that are central to influencing the decision-making of large-city governments: information and ideas; time, energy, and persistence; prestige, popularity, and respect; money; strategically-placed friends and allies; numbers; and legal rights. All of these can be considered base resources, in that they provide the leverage for influence to be exerted. Other resources which affect the amount of influence that can be exerted are the strategic, tactical, and organizational skills with which the base resources are employed.

Official Position

Under provisions of city charters, city ordinances, or state laws, it is officials who hold elective and higher appointive offices who are granted the legal power to actually make decisions in specified matters. But appointive officials and employees who hold official positions lower in the governmental hierarchy usually also come to possess some decision-making powers, either by explicit delegation or as an inevitable concomitant of having to implement general policies and programs. If a decisional matter is within a particular official's own formal or de facto scope of authority and if that official is invulnerable to, does not care about retaliation by, and also does not need the cooperation of, other influentials including other city officials, he can influence the decision by promulgating it in the exact form he wishes.

The more common case is that a city official holds only a share of the legal power necessary to make a decision and is also subject to influence by others. Holding a share of the decision-making powers allows an official to participate in the consideration and deliberation of a contemplated decision as a matter of right. Furthermore, the official can use his share of powers for trading purposes, that is, he can bargain for concessions in the contemplated proposal in exchange for his vote. Or he can simply go along on a matter of indifference to him or against his own preferences in order to build up a store of favors to be owed to him by other city decision makers.

Official position often allows an individual to participate in the shaping of decisions that are not clearly within the scope of his legal powers. For a city official with a strong interest in a particular decision can simply become involved, fairly confident that other city officials will concede him the implicit right to be interested and have a say just because he is an official or because they may want to influence a decision under his control at some other time or both.

In short, holding official position is a powerful resource. This is because it is officials who control a city government's decision-promulgating machinery and because it is these officials who collectively have a monopoly of legal decision-making powers for stated periods of time, like two or four years. During that time all other potential influentials can influence a city's decision-making process only by succeeding first in influencing those holding official positions.

Information and Ideas

Even if knowledge is not always power in urban decision-making, the possession of relevant information and ideas can be a resource of influence, while total lack of information and ideas almost guarantees impotence. There are essentially three kinds of influential information and ideas: governmental, technical, and political.

Governmental knowledge consists of information and ideas about how the city's governmental process works and about the exact locus of de jure or de facto decision-making power on the kind of matter that is to be influenced. Without this kind of governmental knowledge, a would-be seeker of influence would not know whom to approach, or how otherwise to proceed. Technical knowledge consists of information and ideas about the substance of a problem that a city decision-maker is facing: its logic, the conditions causing it, possible ways to change those conditions, and the design of governmental policies and programs to achieve the desired changes. Technical knowledge gives leverage to its possessor to the extent that city officials do not themselves have the information and ideas necessary for deciding on a policy or program. Political knowledge consists of information and ideas about the identity and kinds of support and opposition that exist for various proposals. The leverage from this kind of knowledge comes from convicing a decision-maker that his own political power—including for those in elective office their popularity and consequent electability—will be enhanced or damaged by adopting a particular position.

Time and Energy

Direct influence can never be exercised without some expenditure of time and energy to persuade, coerce, or bargain with decision-makers or even to able to formulate a preferred position, develop supporting arguments, and draft supporting papers. It takes time and energy to attend meetings and mobilize allies, public opinion, or other resources. In short, it takes time and energy to persuade, coerce, or bargain with decision-makers or even to exercise one's own decision-making powers.

Since everyone possesses some time and energy, the resource that gives leverage is having them *available* to invest in trying to influence a particular decisional conflict. Most members of the general public will have the demands of their regular job, family, friends, hobbies, and relaxation capable of consuming all of their waking hours, leaving them little time and energy for trying to influence city governmental decisions. Most city officials and other regular activists, like interest group staff members, will obviously have the time and energy involved in their fulltime jobs available for governmental matters. But even they will normally be involved in more than a single decision-making issue at any one time. These officials must therefore not be fully invested as far as using their time and energy in order to have time available to concentrate on still another decision-making issue.

High Prestige, Respectability, and Popularity

An influential person's being accorded high prestige or respect means that he will normally be given a hearing and his position will receive more than token consideration. The prestige or respect of a person will enhance the impact of the ideas or information he is presenting in a persuasive argument, providing extra incentive to the decision-maker to accept the argument or otherwise comply with his wishes. "Even a nod from a person who is esteemed," Plutarch once wrote, "is of more force than a thousand arguments or studied sentences from others."[1]

Popularity is an important resource of influence in at least two respects. First, mass personal popularity is a central factor in winning public office. And public office in turn brings legal powers, some prestige, and other resources of influence. Second, popularity and general likability can also enhance influence in decision-making conflicts directly. Individual officials, for example, like most human beings, typically want to please people they like. Also, city officials prefer not to get involved in a visible policy conflict with another official who is highly popular or with some other popular activist or group because they are aware that such a conflict will tend to diminish their own public support.[2]

Money

Money is an important, though probably overrated resource of urban political influence. The major leverage of money is that it can buy other people's time and energy and their information and ideas for direct lobbying or public relations campaigns, the instigation of lawsuits, and the pursuit of other tactics that require sustained, and especially organized, effort. This is true both for city officials having control of public money and for private individuals or group activists. Money can also be used for election campaign purposes to help capture official position and the influence that derives from that resource either for one's own self or for other individuals who appear disposed to make favorable decisions.

Money can also be used to purchase certain decisions from corrupt city officials. The corrupt use of money usually involves the securing of special treatment for individual cases. Only very rarely can money be used to buy decisions on general policies or programs. Perhaps the closest equivalent is the promise to give or the threat to withhold a large campaign contribution to an incumbent official or a new candidate, contingent on his taking a particular position.

[1]Quoted in Harold D. Lasswell and Abraham Kaplan, *Power and Society: A Framework for Political Inquiry* (New Haven: Yale University Press, 1950), p. 135.

[2]See Robert E. Lane and David O. Sears, *Public Opinion* (Englewood Cliffs, N.J.: Prentice-Hall, 1964), chap. 5.

In the last analysis, money, except for its corrupt use, is more a necessary than a sufficient resource of influence: A lack of money can make it impossible to engage in the activities necessary to shape decisions in a certain direction or to compete for a certain office. But on the other hand, spending money—even in massive quantities—cannot guarantee the bringing about of the desired policy or election outcome sought. Indeed, under some conditions, too massive expenditures may backfire by alienating rather than influencing. Fortunately for those of us of only average affluence or less, most city officials and electorates do not consider themselves to be objects in an auction, bound to go to the highest monetary bid.

Strategically-Placed Allies and Friends

A frequently overlooked resource of influence is strategically-placed allies and friends. Strategically-placed means in this context being at or near key decision-making points. By allies is meant persons who are motivated to comply with the wishes of a would-be influential because they share goals. By friends is meant persons who are motivated to comply because of mutual affection and goodwill and the consequent desire to be accommodating if possible. Alliances and friendships are sometimes also based on one or both partners having done political favors for the other in the past.

A private activist's having a strategically-placed ally or friend gives him a crucial inside track to influence decision-making. Part of an "outsider" or private influential's efforts and resources must usually be directed to making contact with the relevant city official and gaining a hearing. Having a strategically-placed ally or friend means that there is within the formal structure of government a person who is already self-motivated to use his insider's legal powers, information, and time and energy to promote the policy goals or decisions that the outsider wants. Furthermore, a strategic ally or friend can feed back crucial inside information—governmental, technical, and political—that comes from access to city governmental private meetings, plans, or documents to help guide the outsider's strategy and tactics.

Strategically-placed allies or friends is a resource not only for private activists, but also for city officials. For key characteristics of large city governments are the fragmentation of their legal powers, the dispersion of decision-making points, and the difficulties of ensuring compliance merely by invoking superior legal authority. Accordingly, the adoption and effective implementation of many important policies and programs require the largely voluntary cooperation of numerous persons scattered in different branches and agencies and at different hierarchical levels. The mayor needs cooperative councilmen to vote for ordinances and budgets and cooperative commissioners and bureaucrats to implement his policies and programs without doing violence to them. The commissioners in turn may need the mayor's help in dealing with the council, their clientele, or with insubordinate lower-level bureaucrats. Councilmen too need cooperation from within the executive branch to gain the mayor's support for a policy they desire or to secure various administrative decisions of interest to themselves or their constituents. Much time, effort, and other resources are saved if the official whose cooperation another official needs is self-motivated to be accommodating because he shares the other's goals or has established ties of personal friendship.

Numbers

First, large numbers of people can pool individually meager resources of time and energy, knowledge, money, or allies to aggregate sizable quantities in furtherance of a cause they collectively support. Second, existence of support by large numbers gives legitimacy to demands for or against a certain decision. Third, it is the votes of large numbers that confer and can take away official position from a city government's highest decision-makers and that can approve or disapprove propositions incorporated in referenda. Finally, large numbers, even if they do not constitute majorities of electorates, have the capacity to disrupt the life of city decision-makers by obstructive demonstrations, lootings, and riots. This is a capacity that is taken into account, implicitly or explicitly, by city officials when deciding whether to heed demands.

Legal Rights

Having an established legal right to have a city government act in a particular way is still another important, and sometimes controlling, resource of influence. Of course, much decision-making involves precisely what rights and obligations different categories of individuals and groups should have as a matter of general policy. But sometimes an issue whose manner of disposition is being treated as an open question may in fact be controlled by some existing provision in a city charter, local ordinance, state law, or the state or federal constitution.

Becoming aware of having and then invoking a legal right to a certain action or decision gives a would-be urban influential two kinds of leverage: that of being able to enlist as an ally the judicial machinery of government and that produced by the fact that most city officials do not want to act illegally. This is powerful leverage and it can be exercised without supportive large numbers, strategic allies, high prestige, or other basic influence resources except the services of a lawyer.

Superior Strategic, Tactical, and Organizational Skills

This discussion thus far has concentrated on the base resources of influence—i.e., those that supply the leverage or underlying motivation for compliance on the part of city decision-makers. But all these base resources can be used with different degrees of skill. By superior skill is meant the ability to gain more influence with a given kind and amount of "base" resources than the average person.

Skills useful for exerting influence are essentially of three kinds: strategic, tactical, and organizational. Strategic skills consist of the ability to formulate an overall plan of action for using resources to achieve a certain impact on a city governmental decision. More specifically, strategic skills involve determining what resources to direct against different individuals, groups, or publics, including the substance of the arguments to be made and the nature and timing of specific tactical actions, what alliances or coalitions to enter into, how to shape proposals so as to attract allies and divide opponents, and what the resources and staying-power are of the opposition so as to calculate at what point any concessions should be made and compromises put forth or accepted.

Tactical skills refer to the specific techniques, acts, or tools that are used in carrying out a strategy for converting base resources into influence. Marshalling facts and presenting arguments orally or in writing so that they will be found forceful and appealing; being persistent so as to wear down or outstay opponents in meetings or more extended campaigns; conducting public relations campaigns; developing or countering effective lawsuits; electioneering; "mau-mauing" and other direct confrontation techniques—these are the kinds of tactical skills where superior ability can make a difference in the attempted exertion of influence on city governmental decisions.

Strategic and tactical skills are always applicable in influence campaigns, whether they are conducted by individuals or groups. Organizational skills become relevant when more than a single person is involved in an influence campaign and especially when the number participating is sizable and the nature of the campaign is complex. The organizational skills that then come into play include such things as greater-than-average ability in defining all the different tasks that have to be performed in maintaining the group as a formally or informally organized entity; recruiting people and assigning these different tasks to the persons best qualified to perform them; stimulating members of the group to actually provide the contribution that is required of them; and coordinating the activities being performed so that they become mutually reinforcing in promoting the group effort.

DETERMINANTS OF SUCCESS IN INFLUENCE CAMPAIGNS

The actual influence of a participant depends not only on possessing resources, but also on how much of those resources he commits to the particular influence campaign, on what resources are committed by other actors in opposition, on the degree to which any target city decision-maker's own personal preferences coincide with what the would-be influential wants, on the immediate costs that compliance with the sought-after decision poses to the city decision-maker, and on the future reaction that the decision-maker anticipates by making the decision in the way being proposed.

Weight of Proponent's Resources

The possession of resources normally constitutes only influence *potential*. For that potential to be actualized, the resources must be brought to bear on a city decision-maker through invocation of authority, persuasive argument, coercion, or bargaining in such a way that they generate an incentive to provide the decision or other act being sought. The greater the incentive they generate, the weightier those resources can be said to be.

Obviously, no one can mobilize greater resources than the total he has access to. But a person normally will not be committing even that total in order to influence one particular decision. First, he may already be using part or all of his resources trying to influence other decisions or for non-political purposes. Second, even if he has sufficient resources available, actually committing them represents a cost. The cost can be calculated in terms of the value of the resources actually consumed—the time, energy, money, goodwill, drawing on past favors or obligations, etc. Or the costs can be thought of as the value of the foregone alternative uses to which such resources could be put at that time or in the future. This latter represents so-called "opportunity costs." In short, attempts to influence a decision are almost never "free" for a would-be influential so that accordingly, he may decide to commit only a minor part of his available resources or pass up the opportunity at influence altogether as not being worth the cost. Of course, if the influence attempt is successful, one consequence may be the replenishing of the resources used or even their increase beyond their initial level. This latter is called "pyramiding" resources and fortunate is the influential who has the opportunity and skill to do so.[3]

Although normally resources have to be used in order to generate influence, occasionally they do not. This is because certain individuals or groups develop a reputation for influence, based on having possession of important resources which city officials believe might be used against them if they

[3]See Robert A. Dahl, *Who Governs?* (New Haven: Yale University Press, 1961), p. 308.

made or resisted a certain decision. This sometimes causes city decision-makers or private activists to shape their position in order to forestall those resources being put to use as sanctions against them. In such a case, resources would have influenced a city decision without actually being committed, but while they were at rest. This, according to Bachrach and Baratz, represents the "nondecisional" or other "face" of influence.[4]

Weight of Opponent's Resources

To the extent that a decisional issue is controversial, the proponents of a certain outcome normally will find that they have opponents who are also trying to influence the relevant city decision-maker, but in a different direction. Whether the resources mobilized by the proponents are large enough to be successful depends on whether those resources provide a stronger or weaker incentive for the city decision-maker to comply than do any resources being mobilized in opposition. Thus, limited resources used against little or no opposition may spell success for a would-be influential. On the other hand, even a large-scale campaign committing huge resources may result in failure if, all other things being equal, the opposition mobilizes larger and weightier resources still. For this reason, it is sometimes strategically useful for original proponents to deliberately make a lower-level commitment of resources than they are capable of. The reasoning behind such a strategy is that a low profile will be sufficient to achieve the desired outcome without attracting the attention of potential opponents—opponents who would be alerted and countermobilized by a noisier, higher-level effort.

Coincidence with Decision-Maker's Preferences

City decision-makers normally have views of their own on what is desirable or undesirable in different areas of city policy, and especially in those areas over which they have legal or organizational jurisdiction. They are, as David Truman once put it, "not equivalent to the steel ball in a pinball game, bumping passively from post to post down an inclined plane."[5] Therefore, to the extent that an influence-seeker is promoting a policy or decision that a city decision-maker already agrees with, and agrees with strongly, the greater that influential's chance of success, regardless of the weight of his own resources in absolute terms or relative to those of his opponents. To the extent, on the other hand, that an influence-seeker is advocating a policy or decision that conflicts with the city decision-maker's

[4]See Peter Bachrach and Morton S. Baratz, "Two Faces of Power," *American Political Science Review,* 56 (1962): 947–52, and "Decisions and Nondecisions: An Analytical Framework," *Ibid.,* 57 (1963): 632–42.

[5]David B. Truman, *The Governmental Process* (New York: Knopf, 1951), p. 332.

policy preferences, the less the would-be influential's chance of success. And if the decision-maker disagrees intensely, he may present such a hard target that success in influencing him to make the desired decision is impossible, however ponderous the weight of resources mobilized against him.

Low Costs of Compliance

A fourth factor that crucially affects the success of an influence campaign is the costs posed to a city decision-maker by complying with the demand, claim or proposed decision presented to him. Essentially two sets of costs are involved: pure decisional costs and implementational costs. Decisional costs are the costs in time, energy, staff resources, etc., that are necessary to process the proposed decision. Thus to the extent that what is requested of a decision-maker is relatively simple and can be disposed of by him without much or any staff investigation, expenditure of time, or the need to influence other decision-makers or officials to join in making it, the less the decision-maker will have any separate incentive to resist. To the extent that what is requested requires a complicated decision, such incentive to resist will exist.

For example, a request to a highway commissioner or an urban renewal director to reconsider certain carefully thought-out plans for the location of a major artery or a large-scale housing and shopping complex and to reject them in favor of alternatives presented to him would pose great decisional costs in new staff work, time, energy, negotiations, etc. This might determine his refusal to reopen the question regardless of whether "off the top of his head," he thought the alternatives being proposed might possibly be better than the adopted plan.

Implementational costs involve the money, manpower, physical facilities, and even technological know-how necessary for carrying out a decision to achieve a particular objective. To the extent that the implementational costs of a desired decision are low—ordering and erecting a stop sign consumes a few dollars and a few minutes' time of existing staff—the chances for successfully influencing a city decision-maker with a given amount of resources are good. However, if the implementational costs of a decision are high, its proponents may not be able to succeed in influencing a decision-maker to adopt it, whatever the weight of the resources brought to bear. City decision-makers very often find themselves being pressured to do something that they, themselves, already want to do, such as expanding programs to deal with slums or poverty or street crime. But because they do not have available the funds or manpower to implement any such decision, they cannot be influenced successfully.

Magnitude of Any Anticipated Negative Reaction

A city decision-maker's anticipation about what might happen after a certain decision is announced also functions to encourage or deter compliance. A city decision-maker who expects little or no negative reaction from making a proposed decision will not be deterred out of fear of future consequences. And a decision-maker who expects a net favorable reaction will be encouraged to comply.

The anticipated reaction factor is important because most city decision-makers, and especially elective city officials, know that not all resourceful individuals or groups who have potentially strong feelings about a particular issue are active at the time it is being debated. Some may have no means of becoming aware of the issue being decided before the decision is announced. Others may be too distracted or otherwise occupied to bother to mobilize. But their inactivity at the time of decision-making does not mean that they might not use their resources, including their vote, to help or hurt a decision-maker later, on the basis of what his decision was. In short, city decision-makers know that taking into account only those resources that are actually mobilized may be misleading about the total capacity that exists for gaining or losing support in the long run.

Further Complications

The preceding discussion makes the process of influencing city decisions appear mechanistic and almost susceptible to exact measurement with respect to who will win or lose in any particular attempt to exert influence. In actuality, the process is much more confused, vague, and unpredictable. First, all the factors that for purposes of analysis were discussed separately, operate in real life simultaneously. Furthermore, many city decision-makers are neither sophisticated enough nor unbusy enough to weigh all the different forces bearing on them and then act in the way that some outside observer might predict. For city decision-makers (and the higher in the city hierarchy the more so this is true) are acting and deciding "on the run." Often, they do not have the time even to become aware of all the resources mobilized for or against a particular position and to calculate exactly what benefit or harm those resources can produce. They normally have not even weighed the strength of their own preferences and figured how these will be affected by deciding one way or another. They typically do not know precisely what the decisional and implementational costs of compliance will be in order to make a rational, explicitly thought-out allocation of available resources in terms of some kind of overall view of their own long-term objective interests. And they seldom can predict with any degree of certainty the size, intensity, and direction of the reaction any decision of theirs will produce.

All this uncertainty and vagueness in the process results in city decision-makers being left with great capacity to resist attempts to influence them in directions in which they strongly do not want to go. For city decision-makers must be seen not as inert, "standing targets" whose positions are simply preordained resultants of externally and internally generated pressures. City decision-makers are very much "moving targets." They cannot be easily pinned down, made to listen to or accept particular arguments, or forced to take at face value threats or promises. City decision-making officials themselves decide what relative weights to assign to the different forces brought to bear on them. Some officials, for example, weight short-term opposition among public opinion or private activists very heavily while other officials severely discount such temporary fluctuations. Even the seemingly extreme sanction to an elective city official of a credible threat to his reelection fails to be controlling to an official if he determines that disposing of that particular issue in his own way is more important to him than whether he will be reelected.

Not only are city decision-makers "moving targets" when being "shot" at but they are also capable of "shooting back." City decision-makers can and frequently do mobilize their own resources against those who have sought to influence them, the objective being to stop their exertions. And city decision-makers are often in a favorable position to "shoot back," since they have various combinations of sanctions, inducements, and persuasive arguments at their command, including almost final say about whether or not a particular decision is technically feasible and whether or not the costs of implementing it can be borne by the city government or agency involved. That is, a proposal can be declared possible or impossible depending more or less on how the particular city decision-maker wants it to come out. In short, the process of decision-making in city government is much of the time one in which mutual attempts at influence are taking place between individuals who are both targets and advocates at the same time.

For simplicity, much of the preceding narrative discussed the influence process in city decision-making in terms of its being essentially a two-person game in which one individual attempts to influence another or in which two individuals engage in such efforts mutually and simultaneously. However, campaigns to influence decisions, and especially important decisions, are usually complex coalition efforts in which rival sets of elective city officials, bureaucrats, interest group leaders, private elites, and, occasionally, rival newspapers exert influence competitively in support of or in opposition to a particular position. In various specific areas of policy, and especially on the departmental or bureau level, particular standing coalitions may persist over time. At the higher levels of decision-making, however, the coalitions shift frequently, with today's coalition partner being tomorrow's opponent on another issue or even different officials and other activists being allies on some issues and opponents on other issues at the same time.

The discussion of determinants of successful influence should not be misunderstood to imply that in every policymaking conflict in large cities, there is a side that gains a complete victory and another side that suffers a complete defeat. Probably most decisions in large city governments are compromises in which each side gets some of what it wants, but no side gets all. This aspect of the influence process has implications for the coherence of city government policymaking: Given the rarity of clear-cut victories and defeats, policies are most often not established as "grand" decisions by which universally agreed-upon optimum means are adopted for reaching clearly defined goals. Overall policy is, instead, most often simply the pattern implicit in a series of discrete, limited decisions—and often compromise decisions—which were made without much conscious thought about their interrelations and general implications.

Occasionally, of course, there are showdowns where a city decisional outcome represents the pure preferences of the winning side. This can happen, for example, when a new, cohesive city administration that holds all the formal, key decision-making points decides to enact various parts of its platform, regardless of the opposition from different party leaders, defeated candidates, hold-over bureaucrats, private elites, or any other opponents who cannot break into the monopoly of decision-making powers that the new administration has in its hands. But most often, going for a clearcut showdown victory does not make sense for any of the participants in a conflict. For city activists involved simultaneously in a number of decision-making situations, the value to them of a pure victory over an at least satisfactory compromise may simply not be worth the prolongation of the conflict that would be necessary to get it. Not only must resources, especially of time and energy, be husbanded by city activists so that they will be available to influence other decisions besides the one immediately at hand, but also neither side in a conflict can be absolutely certain in advance about what degree of greater success a further expenditure of resources will bring. Indeed, there is always the risk that even "going for broke," so to speak, will lead not to an all-out victory but to a worse defeat, thus demonstrating weakness and reducing long-term reputation for power. And an additional factor working against showdown situations in influence campaigns is the kind of unwritten rule of reciprocity that operates as part of the political culture of the official and other activist stratum of large city governments. That rule goes something like, "I'll give in on the things that you feel very strongly about in the expectation that now or in future conflicts you'll give in on things about which I feel very strongly." In sum, there is operating in decision-making conflicts in city governments in addition to the "strain" toward conflict caused by the different participants' incompatible or conflicting stakes also a "strain" toward agreement. That is, most activists in city politics have an independent value in getting an issue settled—even if with only half-a-loaf rather than a whole—in order to get it off the active agenda, so that all of the parties can go on, with reduced distractions, to other things.

DISTRIBUTION OF INFLUENCE IN LARGE CITIES

The distribution of influence in large cities is obviously uneven. The bulk of the resources necessary for direct, day-to-day influence on city decision-making is in the hands of a tiny share of any city's population, including its activist stratum of elective and appointive city officials and employees, party leaders, and various private elites and attentive publics. The remaining vast majority of the population has only the slight influence potential represented by their vote and the possibility that various segments of them may mobilize, pool slack resources like information, money, and skills, and divert time and energy from nonpolitical to political ends. And this public has indirect influence insofar as its possible anticipated reaction shapes the positions of the immediate activists.

Within the stratum of activists, the single most important characteristic of the resources held by most city influentials is that they are what might be called "narrow-gauged" or "issue-bound." That is, the resources of most city officials and other activists permit them to be consistently influential only in particular narrow segments of governmental policy, but not across the entire spectrum of decisions that are promulgated in the name of a city government. A major reason is that a very large fraction of decision-making is parceled out among a city government's operating departments, with the influence of the leaders of those departments largely confined to matters within their immediate jurisdiction. Thus, police administrators and bureaucrats constitute what Sayre and Kaufman have termed the "core groups"[6] for decisions on police matters; welfare administrators and bureaucrats, for welfare matters; school administrators and bureaucrats, for school matters; housing administrators and bureaucrats, for housing matters; etc.

These functionally specialized appointive city officials and employees carry out ongoing routines and dispose of most issues that come up for decisions largely without regard to their elective, legal superiors. Another set of narrow-gauged influentials are most of a city's private elites, organized

[6]Wallace S. Sayre and Herbert Kaufman, *Governing New York City* (New York: W.W. Norton, 1965), p. 710.

groups, and attentive publics: These consist of spokesmen for the clientele served or regulated by the different city operating departments and agencies. They include professional associations and societies from whose professional ranks are drawn the leadership of particular government units. They involve labor unions whose membership provides the bulk of the departmental work-forces. And they also consist of interest group leaders and parts of the general public that may for still other reasons be interested in and attentive to the kinds of functions and programs that a particular agency is performing. These different constellations of functionally specialized influentials that surround a particular "core group" and invest time, energy, information, skill, etc. to influence its decisions can be thought of as its "satellite" influentials.

The overall consequence of most resources being narrow-gauged or issue-bound is that different sets of city officials and nonofficial activists have a high degree of influence, approaching control, over the content of policy within particular areas, as most decisions are worked out by an interplay among the specialized cores and their satellites. But those city officials and satellite activists have little or no influence in other unrelated functional areas. In other words, influence on city decision-making is in the hands not of a single set, but of a "plurality" of elites. Indeed, it is not too far from the truth to think of cities as not having a single city government, but a series of highly autonomous subgovernments, "each of which brings forth official programs and policies through the interactions of its own inhabitants."[7]

These subgovernments are not completely autonomous, however. For there are some city officials and private activists whose resources are broad-gauged, giving them capacity to influence policy and program decisions whatever their functional area. The most important city influentials with broad-gauged resources are a city's highest elective officials like the mayor and the leaders of the city's legislative body, the city government's overhead appointive officials like budget officers, city hall staff members, and, in council-manager cities, city managers. These officials have on their own or by delegation, legal powers that are wide-ranging with respect to approving proposed changes from any operating department's programs, jurisdiction, budget, and key appointments. And these broad-gauged city officials can also use their legal powers to intervene on their own initiative in order to influence a decision or change a policy within the immediate jurisdiction of the different functionally-specialized agency core groups. Thus, *theoretically,* a city's broad-gauged officials, especially the elective ones, are in a position to dominate a city's policymaking process. They can exercise their superior legal powers to bring the policies of the various subgovernment core groups

[7] *Ibid.,* p. 716.

into harmony and balance with each other. They can also impress upon those policies the viewpoint of broad interests and constituencies to counter the tendency of the city government's departmental core groups and their surrounding satellites to be concerned only about maximizing their own parochial, special interests.

Alas, *actuality* does not coincide with *theory*. For there is the "you-can't-have-your-cake-and-eat-it" rule of urban influence—i.e., that resources, most especially time and energy, are limited and that their use on some issues normally precludes the possibility of their use on others. Consequently, not even the highest city officials with broad-gauged resources can be involved in influencing key city decisions in all substantive areas simultaneously. What their broad-gauged resources gives these high-level city officials is the right to refuse to ratify officially, if such higher-level ratification is necessary, the agreements or accommodations reached by the different constellations of functional specialists. Their broad-gauged resources also give high city officials the opportunity to select from among two or more alternatives presented when the "core" appointed officials and "satellite" individuals and groups who constitute the functional specialists on the particular subject-matter have been unable to agree. But only rarely do the broad-gauged resources of high city officials allow them to concentrate time, energy, and staff resources for developing on their initiative a preferred policy of their own and for following up to see that the policy is adopted and also not sabotaged in the process of implementation.

Besides high city officials, a few private individuals and groups possess broad-gauged resources which give them the potential for exercising influence across different substantive boundaries. The leaders of a city's few "good government" interest groups and expecially the city's mass media elites have the resources to intervene, each in their characteristic fashion, on any substantive matter that becomes important to them and to try to shape its outcome. But civic groups and the mass media also are constrained by the inherent scarcity of certain key resources, like time and energy, and by the difficulty of maintaining interest and attention among their members or their audience on any wide range of issues simultaneously. Therefore, although they may range widely before doing so, they too pick and choose a limited number of issues from among all those upon which they may wish to impress their views.

Thus, there is a central paradox concerning the distribution of influence resources in large cities: On the one hand, there are influentials whose resources permit them to exert heavy influence on city governmental decisions in detail, but they can do so only on a narrow range of policy. On the other hand, there are other influentials whose resources permit them to exert influence along a wide spectrum. But, most often, these broad-gauged influentials can only set limits on the possible policies to be chosen by the functional specialists in the various fields or they can choose among alternatives sponsored by different ones of these specialists when on occasion they disagree. The individuals and groups whose resources would allow them to influence policies and programs *both* across the entire policy spectrum *and* in detail simply do not appear to exist in large cities. However, those who lack resources to directly influence city decisions *either* across the policy spectrum *or* in detail are plentiful.

IS THE LARGE CITY BECOMING UNGOVERNABLE?

Those who raise the question about the governability of large cities are not implying that large-city governments are in any imminent danger of actually "breaking down" in the sense of becoming incapable of continuing to guarantee the minimum physical and biological requirements essential for the survival of urban life. Nor, with the overwhelming coercive powers available to city governments from their parent states and the federal government, are they implying that these large-city governments are in any danger of being forcibly overthrown. But "governing" must mean more than simple success in averting complete breakdown or revolution. It must include some capacity to steer, direct, or guide the body politic toward some desirable goals or some desirable future. And it is this kind of capacity that appears increasingly to be lacking in large-city governments.

Part IV explains how present trends coupled with the existing incapacity of city governments to alter them are turning many large cities into slum ghettoes. The "slum ghetto" future for large cities is not inevitable. For if certain key obstacles—epistemological, fiscal, and, particularly, political—were to be overcome, the governing capacity of city governments could be strengthened so as to steer large cities varying distances toward "healthy, multiracial" futures.

17

Alternative Futures: "Slum Ghetto" vs. "Healthy, Multiracial" Cities

If the present level of inadequate performance of city governments continues, the most likely future for large cities, and especially for the older, larger ones of the East and Middle West, will be a drift into underserviced, crime-ridden, bankruptcy-skirting slum ghettoes.

DRIFTING INTO "SLUM GHETTO" FUTURES

First, given existing trends, the present quality of housekeeping services and amenities, crime protection, and antislum and poverty programs will continue to deteriorate. For the costs of financing them will be increasing, both because of inflation and other increased costs such as higher salaries and fringe benefits of civil service workers. Yet the number of tax dollars available at given rates will be increasing slowly or even declining as additional numbers of middle-income taxpayers continue to move to suburbia and as business volume and property values in the cities continue to drop relative to increased costs or even absolutely. City governments will thus be caught in a constantly tighter "fiscal crunch." If only the present level of aid from higher levels of government is forthcoming, city governments will have to both cut services and raise tax rates to close the revenue gap. And since such actions would aggravate even further the mismatch between taxes paid and services received, it would strengthen the stimulus to move to the suburbs for families and businesses wealthy enough to do so, thus leading to faster erosion of the tax base, larger revenue gaps, further cuts in services, and so on, in a continually accelerating vicious circle. And as their fiscal position weakens, city governments will find it increasingly difficult to borrow money, either for long-term capital projects or to cover short-term shortages in cash for meeting their bills. In 1975 New York City found itself incapable of selling bonds to refinance its existing debt and for other needs. Even after massive layoffs of personnel, freezing budgetary expenditures, and state intervention and help, the city for almost a year tottered on the brink of bankruptcy.

Second, none of the trends causing white flight from and the expansion of the black population in large cities has been reversed or even stopped. Admittedly, the 1970 to 1974 population changes suggest that black immigration to nonsouthern central cities has slowed.[1] But given the large black population in these central cities, the natural increase of the black population already there, rather than immigration from the South, has since 1960 been accounting for the larger share of the total black growth.[2] Furthermore, since 1960 it has been the white exodus from central cities that accounted for a larger share of the increase in the black *proportion* of central-city populations than black immigration and natural increase combined,[3] and that white exodus is not stopping.[4] In short, even if black immigration from the South to nonsouthern central cities should continue to slow (and indeed even if it should stop), that in itself would not reverse either the absolute or proportionate expansion of the black population of central cities but only dampen its rate of growth.

Third, with a continuation of past discriminatory renting and selling practices in housing, the bulk of the expanding black population will remain concentrated in the older, racially-segregated, all-black neighborhoods and in "changing" neighborhoods on their periphery. And if past patterns continue, as the changing neighborhoods inexorably shift toward heavier black occupancy, "massive racial transition" will take place and the ghetto will spread.

Fourth, under present conditions, as the ghetto spreads, so will the slum, though not as fast. At the present intensity of building code enforcement and renewal and rehabilitation of central-city housing, and with the present

[1] U.S. Bureau of the Census, *Current Population Surveys,* Series P–20, No. 273, "Mobility of the Population of the United States, March 1970 to March 1974" (Washington, D.C.: U.S. Government Printing Office, 1974) and No. 279, "Population Profile of the United States: 1974" (Washington, D.C.: U.S. Government Printing Office, 1975).

[2] U.S. National Advisory Commission on Civil Disorders, *Report* (New York: Bantam, 1968), p. 241 (hereinafter cited as *Kerner Commission Report*); U.S. Bureau of the Census, Census of Population and Housing: 1970, *General Demographic Trends for Metropolitan Areas, 1960–1970,* Final Report PHC(2)–1 (Washington, D.C.: U.S. Government Printing Office, 1971), Table 7, p. 1–31 (hereinafter cited as PHC(2)–1); U.S. Bureau of the Census, *The Social and Economic Status of the Black Population in the United States, 1973* (Washington, D.C.: U.S. Government Printing Office, 1974), p. 1.

[3] PHC(2)–1, Table E, p. 12.

[4] "Mobility of the Population," p. 1.

inability of large portions of the ghetto population to pay rents sufficient to enable landlords to keep their buildings in good repair, an increasing number of blocks of older residential properties will continue to deteriorate, and many will become abandoned. Large parts of the ghetto population will therefore live in or very near neighborhoods that will have the physical characteristics of slums.

Fifth, with only the present levels of effort to enrich schools in slum ghetto areas, improve job skills and motivation, and provide greater job opportunities, the size of the poverty population will be at least as large as and probably larger than in the past. The number of black males from fifteen to twenty-four years of age is, for example, growing at a very fast rate.[5] Yet this group is in large degree unskilled and experiences disproportionately high rates of unemployment and underemployment. The decline in job opportunities will be especially severe whenever the overall job market is contracted because of recession in the national economy. During the economic slowdown of the mid-1970s, the unemployment rate among all blacks climbed to 9.9 percent in 1974 (compared to 5.0 percent for white workers) and for black workers aged twenty to twenty-four, the unemployment rate soared to 16.5 percent.[6] Also, the evidence shows there has been no reversal of the steady increase in the number of black families with female heads.[7] Various projections indicate that there will probably continue to be sharp increases in "nonwhite households headed by women in U.S. central cities—especially the largest ones—in the next two decades."[8] And it is precisely persons in this group that suffer the highest incidence of poverty in central cities. According to Downs:

> In central cities . . . by 1985, . . . the number of nonwhite children will rise 3.4 million (91.8 percent). Since about one-third of nonwhite children in central cities lived in poverty in 1968, this rapid expansion will pose a very serious problem in any antipoverty program. It might add as many as 1.4 million poor nonwhite children to central cities by 1985. The addition of children from fifteen to eighteen might raise this total as high as 1.7 million. . . . To policy makers interested in eliminating poverty, . . . households [with these children] pose the most intractable of all problems.[9]

[5]*Kerner Commission Report,* p. 392.

[6]U.S. Bureau of the Census, *The Social and Economic Status of the Black Population in the United States,* 1974 (Washington, D.C.: U.S. Government Printing Office, 1975), p. 55.

[7]*Ibid.,* Table 72, p. 107.

[8]Anthony Downs, *Who Are the Urban Poor?,* rev. ed. (New York: Committee for Economic Development, 1970), p. 55.

[9]*Ibid.,* pp. 55–56.

Sixth, the propensity toward crime in cities with these conditions would obviously be very high. Nothing would be going on, as the Kerner Commission put it, "to raise the hopes, absorb the energies, or constructively challenge the talents of the rapidly growing number of young Negro men in central cities. . . . These young men have contributed disproportionately to crime and violence in the past, and there is danger, obviously, that they will continue to do so."[10] Unless there were to be some dramatic but at this point unforeseeable improvement in the efficiency of the total law enforcement system of police, prosecutors, courts, and prisons, large cities would almost necessarily encounter still higher crime rates.

The main victims of this increase in crime would obviously continue to be the slum-ghetto-dwellers themselves, since their physical proximity to the potential perpetrators would be the closest. But more of this crime would no doubt spill out into the city's mass transit systems, its downtowns and other shopping areas, and its middle- and upper-income residential areas. And as the actual risk of becoming a victim grew and the fear of victimization grew even faster, more and more middle-class patrons—both white and black—would increasingly shun the downtown areas and the public transportation that might conveniently take them there, especially at night, thus reducing the shopping at department and specialty stores and the use of restaurants, theaters, concert halls, museums, art galleries, etc. The increased crime in the downtowns would therefore add another stimulus for faster deterioration of the city's economy and contribute to the destruction of its attraction as a cultural center. Perhaps some of these big-city downtown facilities that traditionally have been deemed essential for pursuing an urban style of life might become dispersed to the suburbs, but others would probably completely disappear from the metropolitan scene. Greatly increased crime in middle- and upper-income residential areas would obviously provide strong stimulus to even the most committed devotees of big-city, apartment house living to join, even if only reluctantly, the ongoing exodus to the suburbs.

Acquiescence or Explosions?

The quality of life in these cities would obviously not be very attractive for anyone. But those for whom life would continue to be the most oppressive would be the concentrations of poor, black slum-dwellers. Their reaction to the burden of their oppressive conditions might take one of two forms: There might come to be a widespread apathetic acceptance of poverty and slum conditions as a permanent way of life. The failure of the hard-core poor to see clearly discernable improvement after declarations of "wars on poverty," promises of "model cities," and adoption of other

[10]*Kerner Commission Report,* p. 397.

highly advertised new programs might eventually lead to the belief that nothing really can be done. If that happened, there could take place a phenomenon of "falling" rather than of "rising" expectations. The bulk of the poverty- and slum-living black population might then adjust to the prospects of remaining a permanent "underclass" in an otherwise relatively prosperous American society, settling for the possibility that a certain limited number of especially resourceful or fortunate persons could "bootstrap" themselves into the "mainstream" through their own individual efforts.

Complete elimination of discriminatory barriers based on race that led to real equality of opportunity in jobs, housing, and education so that those with ability and motivation could escape the life of slum poverty would no doubt aid the development of acquiescent attitudes among the remainder who did not. (Ironically, such an elimination of discrimination would probably worsen the economic base of large cities. For to the extent that the suburbs became more open to blacks, it would no doubt be a disproportionately large number of the better-off black families that would join the white exodus to suburbia while a disproportionately large number of black poor stayed behind.) Also helping to develop acquiescent attitudes among blacks in large cities would be the pattern of increasing black control of city governments. For not only are blacks likely to be elected to large-city elective positions, including the mayoralty, as they already were in Cleveland in 1967 and 1969, in Newark in 1970 and 1974, and in Los Angeles, Atlanta, and Detroit in 1973, but larger and larger numbers of blacks will no doubt also come to staff the city civil service bureaucracies, including such crucial ones as those of the school teachers, welfare workers, and the police. As city officialdoms with strong black representation responded to any precipitating incidents of violence in black neighborhoods, and with what by then could be more heavily black police, the interracial character of the confrontations could be blurred and the possibility of escalations reduced.

There might develop, on the other hand, not an apathetic acceptance of conditions by the black slum poor, but an increase in resentment and bitterness because improvement was not taking place on a mass scale. Especially among the young, there could be intensifying hostility both toward "white society" and toward those successful middle-class blacks who found opportunities and exercised their option to live at a distance from central-city slums. Such bitterness and hatred, if widespread, would provide fuel for multiday riots such as those of the 1960s.

The combustibility of cities where large segments of their black slum populations seethed with anger at the wide gap between their own life in the slums and what they would see depicted by the mass media as the "normal American" style of life would obviously be very high. Providing further fuel for combustion in this kind of black "tinderbox" cities would probably be those lower-middle- and working-class whites not affluent or mobile enough to become suburbanites themselves. These whites would in all likelihood feel increasingly alienated and deserted in what was becoming or had become predominantly black cities, perceiving themselves to be "penned-in" and "de-classed" as blacks moved closer or into their neighborhoods and also feeling increased danger of losing their jobs to black competitors. And they would probably come to feel oppressed and discriminated against by their city's increasingly black officialdom. Already there is evidence that low-income whites have been even more alienated than comparable low-income blacks, in the sense of believing that what they think "doesn't count much" (60 percent as compared to 40 percent for low-income blacks), that "people in power don't care about us" (50 percent as compared to 32 percent), and that "nobody understands problems I have" (40 percent to 32 percent).[11]

How often large-scale combustions of the "slum ghetto" cities actually take place will no doubt vary. This will depend on the amount of generalized hostility or goodwill felt by slum-dwellers toward high officials and the police in particular large cities, on the occurrence of chance precipitating events or situations, and on the effectiveness of such control forces as the police, the national guard, and the army. Despite the tightness of budgets and the need for compensating contractions, the resources allocated by city governments to police forces will almost certainly be kept at levels to sustain the capacity to respond, with assistance if necessary from the national guard, to outbreaks of violence quickly and with sufficient manpower to be able to head off any recurrence of the frequent, prolonged multiday riots of the 1960s. On the other hand, probably no amount of increase in police capacity will be sufficient to prevent sudden "flash-fire" types of burnings, lootings, and vandalism confined to small areas, nor is it likely to prevent periodic sniping at and ambushing of the police themselves.

Whether augmented police power, including an increase in the amount and quality of infiltration and undercover work, would be able to prevent serious outbreaks of terroristic violence or guerrilla warfare directed against the white community remains an open question. Such violence could probably be sustained at a highly disruptive level by even small numbers of determined nihilistic revolutionaries or gunmen who were not concerned about their own eventual safety or apprehension. The National Commission on the Causes and Prevention of Violence projected the following scenario for large cities if terrorism and guerrilla warfare were to break out:

> Central business districts in the heart of the city, surrounded by mixed areas of accelerating deterioration, will be partially protected by large numbers of people shopping or working in commercial buildings

[11]William Brink and Louis Harris, *Black and White* (New York: Simon and Schuster, 1969), p. 135.

during daytime hours, plus a substantial police presence, [but] will be largely deserted except for police patrols during night-time hours.

High-rise apartment buildings and residential compounds protected by private guards and security devices will be fortified cells for upper-middle and high-income populations living at prime locations in the city.

Suburban neighborhoods, geographically far removed from the city, will be protected mainly by economic homogeneity and by distance from population groups with the highest propensities to commit crimes. . . .

High-speed, patrolled expressways will be sanitized corridors connecting safe areas, and private automobiles, taxicabs, and commercial vehicles will be routinely equipped with unbreakable glass, light armor, and other security features. Inside garages or valet parking will be available at safe buildings in or near the central city, armed guards will "ride shotgun" on all forms of public transportation.

Streets and residential neighborhoods in the central city will be unsafe in differing degrees, and the ghetto slum neighborhoods will be places of terror with widespread crime, perhaps entirely out of police control during the night-time hours. Armed guards will protect all public facilities such as schools, libraries, and playgrounds in these areas.

Between the unsafe, deteriorating central city on the one hand and the network of safe, prosperous areas . . . there will be, not unnaturally, intensifying hatred and deepening division.[12]

Obviously, if this violent parade of horrors were to come to pass, the nine-to-one white majority in the population would most likely retaliate massively and indiscriminately against all blacks, both through vigilantism and the use of official governmental force. Among the measures that might be resorted to by an angered majoritarian democracy (or by the right-wing dictatorship that could conceivably emerge if democratically elected politicians failed to act repressively enough) are a formalization of the urban apartheid alluded to by the Kerner Commission (through the imposition, for example, of strict restrictions on the residence and movement of dark-skinned persons in white areas) and the drastic curtailment of civil liberties and procedural due process for all Americans, but particularly for blacks.

GOVERNING TOWARD "HEALTHY, MULTIRACIAL" FUTURES

It is not inevitable that large cities drift into slum ghettoes, whether of the quiescent or explosive tinderbox variety. Admittedly city governments with

[12]U.S. National Commission on the Causes and Prevention of Violence, *To Establish Justice, To Insure Domestic Tranquility: Final Report* (New York: Bantam, 1968), pp. 38-39.

only their own tax resources and present level of financial assistance from the states and the federal government cannot improve their housekeeping services or amenities or develop the capacity to deal with the most serious unresolved problems within their jurisdictions. This is particularly true of the tangle of pathology associated with slum poverty. Also, some of the major causes of city problems—e.g., suburbanization, black migration to cities, a changing economy having ever-fewer jobs for the unskilled, recession and/or inflation in the economy, the high cost of new housing, and the loosening inhibitions on the use of violence—are national in scope or origin and are thus beyond any particular city's legal reach.

But it can certainly be argued that the American political system as a whole—that is, city governments in conjunction with the states and especially the revenue-raising machinery of the federal government—has the capacity to brake the adverse trends currently affecting large cities and improve the ability of their governments to govern them toward healthy, multiracial futures. These futures postulate large cities with across-the-board upgraded housekeeping services and amenities. The level of unemployment, underemployment, and poverty would be sharply lower. Deteriorating neighborhoods would be rehabilitated and new housing constructed at a rate sufficiently rapid to cut down sharply the proportion of the population living under the physical aspects of slum conditions.

More highly effective public schools and preschool enrichment efforts would be developed to enable large proportions of the next generation of slum-ghetto children to break out of the culture of poverty and become self-sustaining and fully participating members of the overall society. The quality of the police and other parts of the law enforcement system would be improved, so as both to protect the residents of slum ghettos better against the jungle atmosphere of violence to which they are now subjected and to reduce street crime throughout the city and to be able to deal with riots and disruption if they were to recur. The downtown areas of these cities would be clean, safe, and otherwise attractive. Thus, they would be able to retain a large share of the offices of top national firms, serve as the shopping area within their metropolitan areas with the greatest range and diversity of products and services, and function as the metropolitan area's high-style cultural and recreational hub.

Even these healthy, multiracial cities would have a disproportionately high percentage of blacks, and especially working-class blacks, in their populations relative to their surrounding suburbs or to the country as a whole. But that percentage would hold steady or perhaps even decrease. Instead of an increasing ghettoization of neighborhoods, there could be an expanded number of multiracial residential areas.

Large cities could have their performance improved if massively larger sums of money were fed into them in the form of grants or revenue-sharing for upgrading housekeeping services and amenities, for expanded job-creation and job-training including the guarantee of jobs by some level of government as "employer of last resort," for a concentrated attack on the physical conditions of slums, and for sharply strengthened law-enforcement efforts. In addition there would probably have to be a federal take-over of the complete cost of welfare programs, both to release state and local funds now being spent on welfare for other purposes and to equalize benefits throughout the country so that no artificial stimulus was provided for the poor to migrate to or stay in large cities because of relatively high benefits available there. Finally, strong measures would have to be implemented for stopping increased ghettoization. This slowing down or stopping of black ghettoization would not be easy. It would require some combination of a reduction of black immigration from the South to large central cities, a large-scale increase in movement of blacks from cities to suburbs, deliberate "managed integration" of central-city neighborhoods, and a slowing down of mass white flight to the suburbs.

The healthy, multiracial future for large cities does not assume a reversal of basic trends towards suburbanization of population and jobs or a re-emergence of the central city as the overwhelmingly dominant force in the metropolis. Whether the energy crisis, the trend toward smaller families, and the very high cost of housing in suburbia might yet affect even those basic trends must be an open question. But this healthy future does assume that even within the limits set by those trends, the possibility exists for large cities to be viable enough to be the preferred choice for work or residence or leisure for a substantial portion of the metropolitan population, whether white or black, or with low-, middle-, or high-income. This future also concedes that the bulk of the black population might still be concentrated in all-black neighborhoods. But that situation would be in some real sense the result of preference by blacks for living in neighborhoods where *they* would be culturally dominant. For blacks would in fact be coming to have the same kinds of choices in housing and schools and in careers as whites of similar ability, incomes, and education.

THE SLUM GHETTO—HEALTHY, MULTIRACIAL CONTINUUM

The "slum ghetto" and "healthy, multiracial" futures can most usefully be conceived as poles on a continuum. The slum ghetto future essentially represents cities experiencing existing urban problems, but in greatly aggravated form. The healthy, multiracial future is in effect a description of cities without these problems or at least with their present severity much reduced. In the future, large cities will no doubt fall, as they do now, at different points of the continuum between the two poles. What is being contended is that most large cities, especially in the East and Middle West, are well on their way to the continuum's slum ghetto end, with a city like Newark, almost already there. This is not to deny that there are still some large cities, particularly in the "sunbelt" of the South and Far West, that are relatively problem-free and thus remain closer to the continuum's healthy, multiracial end of the continuum.

18

Epistemological Obstacles

The epistemological obstacle to governing large cities toward more healthy futures refers to the fact that we do not always have sufficient knowledge to design or improve existing policies and programs so that they will remedy existing failings of city governments. Shortage of knowledge is not a serious obstacle to upgrading the quality of tangible housekeeping services and amenities. In these so-called "hardware" areas, more money, more men, and more and newer equipment would certainly produce more frequent garbage collections and cleaner streets, more parks, cultural and recreational events, better fire protection, better staffed and equipped hospitals, better repaired school buildings, cleaner and more reliable transportation, streets more frequently patrolled by police (which would reduce fear of crime if not necessarily its actual incidence) and more trial judges, prosecutors, and courtrooms to provide speedier trials. How important such an upgrading in standard services and amenities would be in improving the quality and attractiveness of city life for its entire population and also in raising the morale of those living in slum ghettoes should not be underestimated. It has become fashionable to question the efficacy of spending additional sums of money on existing programs because we do not know if they are working. But in order to bring about improvements in housekeeping services and amenities, there is no knowledge gap, just a money gap.

GAPS IN KNOWLEDGE

It is in the "software" areas of complex social programs that the knowledge gap presents real difficulties. That is, even if vast sums of additional money were to become available to city governments to attack complicated social problems like poverty, welfare dependency, the causes of juvenile delinquency and crime, hard-core unemployment, failure to learn in school, etc., it is not clear how to spend that money so it would have the greatest impact (or in some cases any impact) on improving undesirable conditions. For in these software areas, only the most meager data exist about the actual consequences of ongoing programs, such as exactly whom they are reaching and with what effect. And there is even less data for predicting with any confidence what the consequences would be of new, untried programs. To give specific examples, although both systematic studies and simple observation show that crime, family disorganization, low achievement in school, welfare dependency, etc., are in general associated with slum neighborhoods, probably no city (or federal) decision-maker could give conclusive answers supported by firm evidence on the level of specificity required for shaping programs to questions such as:

> What are the specific effects of housing on family life? Are crowded living conditions in themselves seriously detrimental? (Census data list as "substandard," housing units with more than one person per room, yet much of the population in many advanced foreign countries and substantial percentages even of American families with middle and upper incomes live in this degree of overcrowding without having their health or social organization adversely affected.) Do crowded neighborhoods have adverse consequences on living conditions?
>
> How can crime rates be reduced? Given existing social conditions, is street crime reduced by increasing the concentration of foot patrolmen? What forms of treatment or punishment—imprisonment, probation, remedial education, work training, psychotherapy—can most reduce convicted criminals from becoming repeaters?
>
> How is drug addiction cured or prevented?
>
> How can the teaching of disadvantaged children be improved? What is the effect on learning of smaller classes, more attractive buildings, integrated classes, long-distance busing, use of "para-professionals," raising teachers' salaries? Are special compensatory programs for small children more effective than those for teenagers? How can the overall environments of disadvantaged school children be enriched, given their existing home life?
>
> How can delinquent behavior be reduced or prevented?
>
> How can motivation to learn skills and reliable work habits be

instilled in the chronically unemployed? How can opportunities for nondead-end jobs for slum-dwellers be expanded?

Would increasing the income of poor slum-dwellers to some guaranteed minimum through family allowances, negative income taxes, or other grants have a major beneficial impact on upgrading their home life and solvency, reducing family breakups, and helping the educational achievements of their children? Would a guaranteed income have a deleterious effect on the incentive to work, especially of those holding low-paying, dead-end, "dirty" jobs? Would a guaranteed income based on family size increase birthrates among the poor? What are the effects on children of welfare-supported mothers having to work?

How can benefactory programs for the poor be designed so as not to stigmatize recipients as degraded or foster dependency?

Would providing scattered-site housing for slum-dwellers in non-slum areas of central cities (or in the suburbs) upgrade their living conditions without adversely affecting the new neighborhoods or would it spread slum conditions to more parts of metropolitan areas?

What accounts for individuals and families living in slum neighborhoods that manage to *escape* getting caught up in the slum's "tangle of pathology"?

INCREASING KNOWLEDGE

Obviously, a first step for increasing knowledge to answer questions such as these simply involves collecting much better information about the operation of existing programs. Such information would allow evaluation of whether those programs are achieving their objectives, whether any failure to achieve objectives is due to improper design or to inadequate level of financial effort or inefficiency, and what changes might improve the accomplishments and reduce any defects of the programs. This information might also permit the development of more reliable causal theories about various slum conditions and the means for their elimination.

City governmental programs are not currently organized so as to automatically generate information about their effectiveness. Consequently, a special effort must be made and probably even special staff units organized to perform this evaluative function. Expansion of the mayor's or city manager's staff or that of the heads of major departments to include units with primary responsibility for program analysis and evaluation could begin to institutionalize this process and way of thinking within city governments.[1] The greater use of Planning-Programming-Budgeting-Systems (PPBS) in city government decision-making would also make available an improved tool for generating information, by forcing the explicit identification and articulation of the objectives of particular programs, the development and presentation of data about the contribution the program makes toward meeting those and other objectives, and about the full range of costs associated with the program. That kind of analysis or evaluational thinking may also contribute to making habitual in city agencies the consideration of alternative means of meeting existing objectives and the systematic comparison of ongoing programs and various alternatives in terms of their contributions and costs.[2] Thus decisions to continue, enlarge, reduce, or drop particular programs could begin to be made with firmer evidence on how successful those programs have been, on whether there might be modifications that would increase their desired benefits or decrease their undesired costs, and on whether the commitment of certain funds and personnel to other programs would have a higher payoff in terms of overall priorities or objectives the city government might have.

A second step for increasing the knowledge needed for improving the performance of city governments would involve undertaking new research aimed specifically at answering questions immediately relevant to program and policy development. Possibly some parts of these questions could be answered with armchair, library, or laboratory research. But since our knowledge of social and psychological processes is so incomplete, for the most part it will be necessary to actually try various alternative new program designs and thus test experimentally whether or not they work in practice.

Many pilot projects have already been conducted in recent years by city governments, academicians, and community and other organizations, primarily under grants from HUD, HEW, OEO, and some private foundations, on what Alice Rivlin has called a "random innovation" basis.[3] Some of these projects have already added and will continue to add to our store of knowledge about urban problems and processes. The shortcoming of this approach thus far has been that the results of such pilot projects have not been carefully enough evaluated and the findings consolidated, disseminated, and thus made available to improve city decision-making generally. Further-

[1]For a specific set of recommendations on how this could be done, see Demetrios Caraley, *New York City's Deputy Mayor—City Administrator* (New York: Citizens Budget Commission, 1966), esp. chap. 5.

[2]See U.S. Senate, *Criteria for Evaluation in Planning State and Local Programs.* Subcommittee on Intergovernmental Relations of the Committee on Governmental Operations, Print. 90th Cong., 1st sess., (1967).

[3]Alice M. Rivlin, *Systematic Thinking for Social Action* (Washington, D.C.: Brookings Institution, 1971), pp. 87ff.

more, few really "far-out" ideas have been tried because of the reluctance to risk failure and the funds concentrated on any particular project have almost never been sufficient to reach what Anthony Downs has called the "critical mass" point necessary for even a well-designed project to have any realistic chance of making major impact in changing undesired conditions and trends.[4] Finally, even with respect to projects that appear to be successful, it is never clear how dependent the success was on the unique conditions surrounding that particular project or whether similar successes could be achieved with the same approach under a variety of conditions.

It is primarily because of this last difficulty that Rivlin has strongly advocated an additional research strategy of "systematic experimentation." Under systematic experimentation, an innovative project or program would be:

> . . . tried in enough places to establish its capacity to make a difference and the conditions under which it works best. There should be controls to make the new method comparable with the old method or with no action at all. In other words, the conditions of scientific experiments should be realized as nearly as possible.
>
> Systematic experimentation involves enormous problems of organization and execution, for it inherently involves different people in different places—groups of schools or health centers or towns or community organizations—working within a careful overall plan. Furthermore, individual project leaders have to agree to follow the plan and to use common measures of what is done and what is accomplished so that the results can be compared.[5]

Rivlin argues that the federal government is in the best position to "take the leadership in organizing, funding, and evaluating systematic experiments" because it can do it on a large enough scale, in the largest variety of places, and under the greatest diversity of conditions. But she also points out that many city governments themselves run large enough operations to

[4]For an analysis of the barriers to innovation in urban decision-making, see Anthony Downs, "The Future of American Ghettos," in U.S. Senate, *Federal Role in Urban Affairs,* Hearings before the Subcommittee on Executive Reorganization of the Committee on Governmental Operations, 89th and 90th Cong. (1966–67), pp. 3483–3500.

[5]Rivlin, *Systematic Thinking,* p. 91. For another assessment of the need for social experimentation plus summaries of the findings of a number of completed experiments such as the "New Jersey Negative Income Tax" and the "Manhattan Bail Bond," see Henry W. Riecken and Robert F. Boruch, eds., *Social Experimentation: A Method for Planning and Evaluating Social Intervention* (New York: Academic Press, 1974). For evaluations of specific social experiments, see Joseph A. Pechman and P. Michael Timpane, eds., *Work Incentives and Income Guarantees: The New Jersey Negative Income Tax Experiment* (Washington, D.C.: Brookings Institution, 1975; and Alice M. Rivlin and P. Michael Timpane, eds., *Planned Variation in Education: Should We Give Up or Try Harder?* (Washington, D.C.: Brookings Institution, 1975).

carry out systematic experimentation on a major scale with suitable controls:

> . . . A [large-city] school superintendent, eager to do a better job, would, it would seem, engage in systematic innovation without any prodding. He would track down the best new ideas in curriculum and approaches and mixes of students and resources, turning for help to literature on experimental projects and results of random innovation in his own and other communities. He would then map out a plan for trying the most promising ideas in a systematic way in his own system, using one approach in several different types of schools and another approach in another set of schools and keeping careful records of the results so that he could extend the productive approaches and phase out the others.[6]

Of course, if the funds necessary to make a single experimental or demonstration project succeed are very large, the city's budgetary constraints may prevent the tested techniques from being spread throughout the city, however successful and adaptable the systematic experiment shows them to be. For, while adequate knowledge is a necessary prerequisite to undertaking new programs that will better remedy existing urban ills, it is clearly not a sufficient one.

BENEFITS OF INCREASED KNOWLEDGE

The benefits of closing the "knowledge gap" about the causes of the most intractable urban problems and about the full effects of both ongoing and new, untried programs would be great: More precise knowledge in the hands of city decision-makers would enable them to concentrate their limited funds on programs that have a demonstrable positive impact and, if faced with a choice, on those programs that have the greatest impact per dollar spent. It would also help city officials (as well as state and federal officials with urban-oriented responsibilities) to design new programs or re-design existing programs so that in the process of reaching desired objectives, they would not also produce unanticipated, undesired side-effects. An important example of such side-effects has been the breakup of families and the "cycle of dependency" that in a perverse way has been fostered by certain aspects of the present welfare system.

Such increased knowledge would also have political consequences: It would increase the morale of those committed to solving urban problems by giving them programs that they know would produce results if tried, and it would weaken the opponents of increased urban spending by taking away

[6]Rivlin, *Systematic Thinking,* p. 92.

the plausibility of the argument that making available additional money would not accomplish anything anyway.

Additional knowledge could also lead to new technological discoveries and breakthroughs. This could improve "efficiency" or "productivity" by creating less expensive means—either in terms of money or of changes of behavior required—for accomplishing particular objectives.[7] Improved managerial techniques have a high potentiality for improving productivity. Further technological innovations in mass transit facilities or sewage treatment plants or the conversion of salt water to potable water or teaching machines could also conceivably produce a higher level of performance at the present level of expenditure or maintain the present level of performance with reduced expenditures.

Recent examples of technological breakthroughs that have already proved beneficial are new contraceptive devices (like the birth control pill and intrauterine device) and methadone. Both of these innovations have been able to decrease problem-causing effects—like unwanted pregnancies in poor families already without adequate income or the disorganized, crime-prone, and potentially lethal life-pattern of a heroin addict—without first having to bring about difficult-to-achieve changes in certain kinds of slum styles of behavior. Probably the single most productive technological breakthrough that could take place would be discovery of new construction methods or materials that would reduce the cost of new, standard housing in cities. Such a breakthrough could provide more housing within the financial means of the poor and near poor, and it would also bring down the cost of new housing deemed acceptable by current middle-class standards so that it could be easily within the financial means of middle-income families.

[7]See Emmanuel G. Mesthene, "How Technology Will Shape the Future," *Science*, 161 (1968): 135–43.

19

Fiscal Obstacles

"Everybody knows" that a severe obstacle to improving the performance of large-city governments is their shortage of money. Obviously all problems that exist in cities will not be solved simply by the expenditure of larger sums of money. But without the expenditure of additional money, it is certain that they will not be solved at all. For it takes money to pay for salaries, equipment, and facilities to deliver expanded services and amenities. It takes money to change the physical environment of slums and raise the income of the poor. It takes money to expand the crime prevention efforts of the city through the deployment of additional police, the purchase of more sophisticated equipment, the provision of more courtrooms, judges, and prosecutors, and the upgrading of corrective institutions and other services provided to convicted defendants in order to increase the chances of their rehabilitation or to keep them incarcerated.

Large-city governments already spend huge sums of money, both in absolute terms and relative to other kinds of local governmental jurisdictions. For the fiscal year 1973-74, cities of over 300,000 in population (excluding Washington, D.C.) spent some $21.6 billion or $547 per capita.[1] The level of per capita spending by large cities is typically higher than city governments in general and also higher than the per capita spending in their surrounding

[1]U.S. Bureau of the Census, *City Government Finances in 1973–74* (Washington, D.C.: U.S. Government Printing Office, 1974).

suburban rings.[2] Yet even with this high level of expenditure, city services and programs are seriously underfinanced for the purposes of giving high quality housekeeping services and amenities, eliminating slum poverty, and reducing crime.

THE HIGH COST OF CITY GOVERNMENTAL PERFORMANCE

The major reasons that high quality performance by city governments is very expensive are (1) cities contain disproportionately high concentrations of persons—like the poor and the aged—who are dependent on expensive governmental programs for assistance, (2) large cities provide a wider array of services than other kinds of local governments, and (3) the cost of delivering a given unit of service tends to be higher in large cities than elsewhere.

The changing nature of the population that large cities have had to service is obviously a primary cause of the high cost of operating their governments. Although the overall size of large-city populations has remained stable or even declined, what has increased is the proportion of the population who are high-cost citizens: school age children from disadvantaged backgrounds, families with below-average incomes, and the elderly. In other words, there has been an expansion in that part of the populace who are direct consumers of expensive services and cash benefits like welfare payments, subsidized housing, etc., but who have little or no capacity to pay taxes for the city governments' support.

The second major cause for high levels of spending by city governments not resulting in high quality performance is that large-city spending is spread over a wider range of programs than in other local governmental jurisdictions. Big cities have traditionally provided a richer array of services and facilities than small town, rural, or suburban areas where a number of services have either been provided by the private sector or simply go unprovided. And even in this period of city penury, city governments have continued to add to their programs, e.g., pollution control, consumer protection, drug rehabilitation, family planning, day care, community colleges, compensatory education, expanded hospital and clinic care, community action, etc. All these programs have been added in the past ten to fifteen years, stimulated in large part by federal grants, as expectations of the role of city governments have expanded and as poverty-oriented programs have been used in part to try to "buy" good behavior from the slum poor during the period of urban rioting.

[2]The generalization about suburban rings held true in 1970 in all but three cases. See Advisory Commission on Intergovernmental Relations, *City Financial Emergencies: The Intergovernmental Dimension* (Washington, D.C.: U.S. Government Printing Office, 1973), Table B-14, p. 123.

The third major cause of the high cost of operating large-city governments is that it has become very expensive to produce a given level of service. Part of the high expense of delivering services in large cities is the result of their having to be performed under crowded, congested conditions which both waste time and wear facilities out fast. But the larger part of the high expense is the high wages and fringe benefits that large city municipal workers have been able to extract over the past decade. As a Brookings Institution study explains:

> By any measure, the recent rise in the compensation of local government employees has been spectacular. . . . Through the mid-1960s, municipal wages roughly kept pace with those in manufacturing, but beginning in about 1966 the rate of increase appears to have been much greater for municipal workers. Along with wage increases, liberalized pension benefits and health plans also contributed to the rising cost of labor. Reductions in the length of the average workday and more generous provisions regarding sick leave, lunch breaks, vacations, and paid holidays further pushed up the hourly cost of labor in the public sector. The importance of such fringe benefits should not be underestimated. For example, the city administrator of New York reported that although the number of policemen increased from 16,000 to 24,000 between 1940 and 1965, the total number of hours worked by the entire force was less in 1965 then it had been a quarter of a century earlier.[3]

The decline in man-hours bought with each dollar spent has itself been the result of a number of interrelated factors—public acceptance of greater-than-average wage increases for city employees because they were regarded as long having been "underpaid," and increased unionization of city employees combined with aggressive tactics including the threat and use of job actions or strikes. The Brookings study points out that the sudden acceleration of public employee strikes beginning in 1966 coincided dramatically with the sharp upsurge in relative wages of municipal employees.[4] (See Fig. 19–1.)

The final, and more recent, contribution to the high cost of producing services is the rapid rate of inflation that has been taking place since the late 1960s and most sharply since 1973. This has meant that given the spiralling cost of labor, standard products, construction, interest on borrowing, etc., city governments have had to find very large sums of additional dollars each year simply to maintain an existing or even declining level of services.

[3]Charles L. Schultze, Edward R. Fried, Alice M. Rivlin, and Nancy H. Teeters, *Setting National Priorities: The 1973 Budget* (Washington, D.C.: Brookings Institution, 1973), p. 296.

[4]*Ibid.*, p. 298.

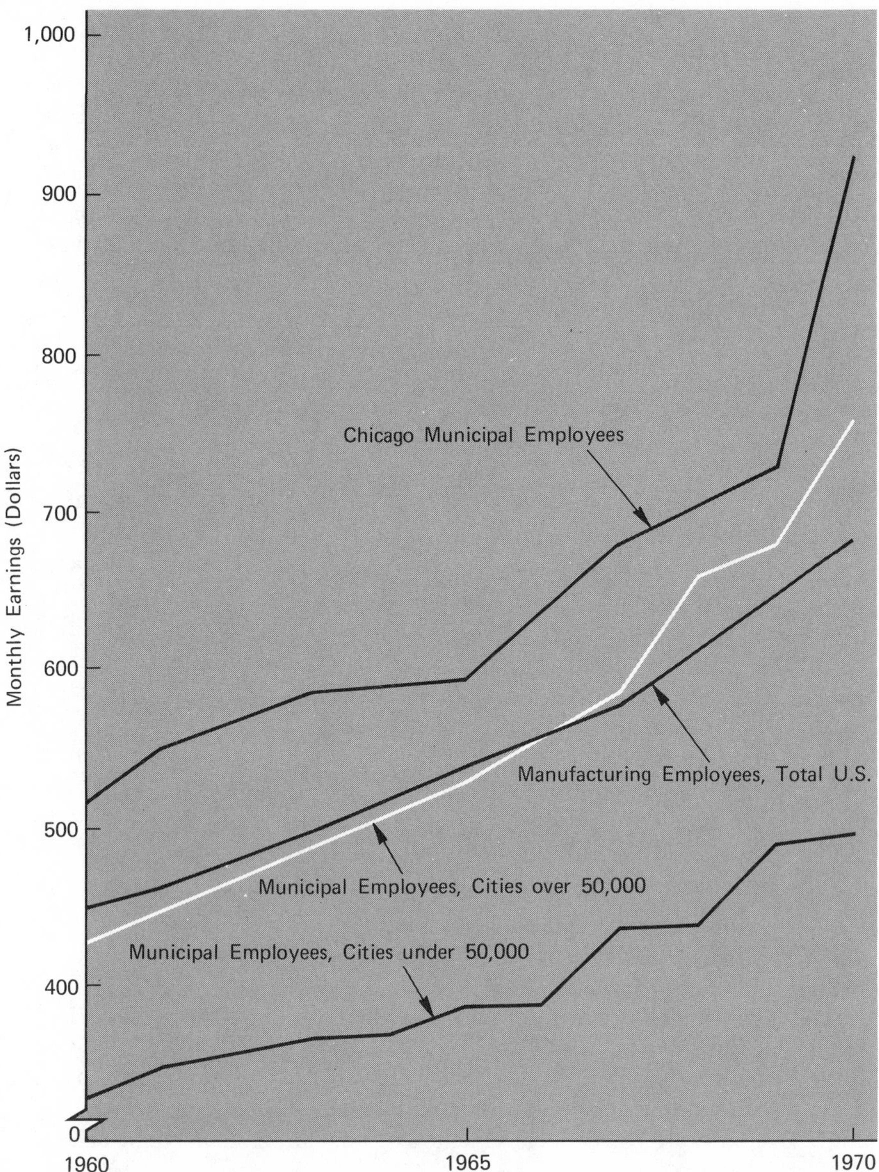

FIGURE 19-1 Average Monthly Earnings of All U.S. Manufacturing Employees and of Municipal Employees in Chicago and in Cities Over and under 50,000, 1960–1970.

Source: Charles L. Schultze, *et al, Setting National Priorities: The 1973 Budget* (Washington, D.C.: Brookings Institution, 1973), p. 297.

DIFFICULTIES OF INCREASING REVENUES

The high cost of operating large-city governments would not in itself be an obstacle to improving performance if it were easy to increase revenues as fast as or faster than the needed increase in expenditures. As was explained in Chapter 1, large cities in the past could generate such revenues without great difficulty because their economies were more vigorous than those of any other kind of local jurisdiction. The advantageous position of large cities was derived from the fact that expensive commercial and residential properties, high volumes of retail sales, new construction, and high-income-producing jobs were disproportionately concentrated and growing in such cities. When these sources of revenues were growing vigorously, large additional amounts of taxes would be generated each year automatically, without having to raise rates. And even if rates had to be raised, the cities' growing economic base could easily afford the new extractions for the tax collector.

But in recent decades the automatic increases in the revenues of large city governments at given rates have not been able to keep up with the mounting costs of maintaining existing programs, let alone provide the massive funds needed for their across-the-board upgrading or for any intensive attack on slum conditions. One reason for this is that most cities still rely heavily on property taxes, which are not highly "growth-responsive," meaning that they do not have the capacity to generate additional revenues faster than the growth of the economy or than increases in the cost of living. The other reason is that the comparative advantage large cities have had in the strength of their economies has been steadily eroding as property values, retail sales, and well-paying jobs have either been growing only very slowly or actually declining. And this weakening of large city economies has also made it much more difficult for them to absorb greater taxation.

New or increased taxes, excises, fees, and user charges have had to be steadily imposed, however, even though city governments have also obtained larger amounts of federal and state aid and have gone further into debt. But these tax increases and additions almost always have been hesitant and incremental, calculated to raise just the amount of extra money necessary to balance the next year's budget. City governments have never raised their taxes sharply enough to give themselves real "fiscal elbow-room" in the sense of providing a substantial, uncommitted pool of money which they could then allocate for deliberately chosen innovations that might dramatically alleviate some high-priority problems.[5]

It should be noted that the economies of some large cities are still strong enough to raise more of the money they need by sharply increasing their own taxes. In his survey of state and local fiscal systems, George F. Break concluded that it was doubtful:

[5]See Arnold J. Meltsner, *The Politics of City Revenue* (Berkeley: University of California Press, 1971).

> . . . that any city has yet come very close to the limit of its ability to finance its own public services. Property taxes could be improved [i.e., increased] in many ways, local sales and income taxes could be used more effectively and intensively than they now are, and a revamping of municipal service charges could convert them into a more equitable and productive source of general revenue.[6]

More recently Arnold Meltsner has argued that "[a]lthough there may be some . . . poor cities . . . , there is no long-run scarcity of resources."[7] Meltsner urged city officials to be more aggressive in using various strategies and tactics to extract greater revenues from the public, concluding that, "Without committing political suicide, local leaders can do something about the fiscal condition of their cities."[8]

That some cities can make a greater tax effort is apparent from the fact that as late as fiscal 1973-74, twenty-one cities of over 300,000 still did not impose a sales tax, thirty-two did not impose a payroll or income tax, and eleven imposed neither.[9] Furthermore, over the years various studies have shown that some large cities raise five times the taxes per capita and over three times the taxes in proportion to average personal income of their residents than do other cities. This indicates that Break and Meltsner are certainly correct about the abilities of city governments to extract greater revenues, at least with respect to the low-tax, low-effort cities. A study conducted by the Advisory Commission on Intergovernmental Relations (ACIR) shows, for example, that in 1970 San Francisco, New York City, Boston, and Newark were taxing their citizens $436, $384, $369, and $352 per capita respectively, while the per capita taxes raised in San Antonio, New Orleans, and Houston were only $102, $148, and $170. Calculated as percentages of personal income, Cleveland, Boston, San Francisco, and Newark were taking 14.1 percent, 11.6 percent, 10.5 percent, and 10.2 percent in taxes while San Antonio, New Orleans, Houston, and Seattle were extracting only 4 percent, 4.8 percent, 5.1 percent, and 5.2 percent.[10]

[6]George F. Break, *Intergovernmental Fiscal Relations in the United States* (Washington, D.C.: Brookings Institution, 1967), p. 223.

[7]Meltsner, *The Politics of City Revenue,* pp. 248–49.

[8]*Ibid.,* p. 284.

[9]U.S. Bureau of the Census, *City Government Finances in 1973–74.*

[10]Advisory Commission on Intergovernmental Relations, *City Financial Emergencies,* calculated from Tables B-7 and B-18. See also Alan K. Campbell and Seymour Sacks, *Metropolitan America: Fiscal Patterns and Governmental Systems* (New York: Free Press, 1967), esp. Appendix B. It should be noted that intercity comparisons are not perfect indicators of the respective efforts being made because different city governments have different sets of responsibilities, especially with respect to whether they or a county government or independent school district are responsible for financing the welfare function or the schools.

TABLE 19-1 Measures of Local Government Revenue-Effort for 14 Selected Cities

City	Local Government Revenue Effort (% of capacity)
New York	131
Baltimore	118
Los Angeles	117
Philadelphia	115
Boston	113
San Diego	112
Seattle	110
St. Louis	108
Pittsburgh	103
Memphis	96
Cleveland	91
Columbus	88
Chicago	85
New Orleans	75
Washington, D.C.	70

Source: Adapted from Advisory Commission on Intergovernmental Relations, *Measuring the Fiscal Capacity and Effort of State and Local Areas,* (Washington, D.C.: U.S. Government Printing Office, 1971), Table A-4, as revised in "An Information Report Revision," January 1972.

Another recent study by the ACIR which tried to establish the theoretical revenue-capacity of sixty-nine selected cities of over 100,000 in population and the relative revenue-effort such cities were making (calculated as the proportion of their capacity that they were using) found that among major cities such "efforts" ranged from highs of 131 percent, 118 percent, and 117 percent for New York City, Baltimore, and Los Angeles to lows of 75 percent, 85 percent, and 88 percent for New Orleans, Chicago, and Columbus. This means that the cities on the high end of the scale were making an effort of between one-and-one-half to two times those on the low end.[11] (See Table 19-1.)

Despite the theoretical capacity for raising larger revenues, there are constraints preventing large-city governments from actually making greater tax efforts: City governments may lack the legal authority to raise existing taxes or to impose new ones; their key decision-making officials are aware that increasing taxes may have unfavorable electoral repercussions; city officials typically believe that sharply increasing taxes will accelerate the ongoing flight of middle- and upper-income families and of businesses to the suburbs. Per capita expenditures and per capita taxes are already higher

[11]Advisory Commission on Intergovernmental Relations, *Measuring the Fiscal Capacity and Effort of State and Local Areas* (Washington, D.C.: U.S. Government Printing Office, 1971), Table A-4, as revised in "An Information Report Revision," January, 1972.

in almost all central cities than the average in their surrounding suburban rings. And since almost all large cities have lower average-family-incomes than their surrounding suburbs,[12] residents of large cities are paying higher taxes both in absolute terms and in proportion to their lower incomes.

FISCAL REMEDIES FOR CITIES

What can be done to remedy the fiscal crunch in which large cities are caught? This crunch is caused by their having to provide constantly more expensive services and benefits to what has been a sizable and expanding high-service and benefit-consuming minority of their populations while being able to draw revenues from only an ever decreasing number of individuals and businesses with moderate to high tax-paying ability that remain in the city.

Extending the City's Tax Reach

One expedient for relieving the cities' fiscal plight would be to extend the central city's tax reach to the purportedly more affluent tax base of the suburbs: Central-city decision-makers have long argued that suburbanites going to the city to work or shop or to visit such facilities as parks and museums impose costs in the need for greater police and fire protection, sanitation, and traffic control and transit facilities far in excess of the taxes recovered on their business property or purchases. However, clear evidence in support of this point is lacking. Indeed, a 1974 study by David Bradford and Wallace Oates argues that "suburban commuters may more than pay for the extra costs of the public services that the city must provide:

> In particular, it is clear that suburban commuters do make some positive contributions to the fiscal well-being of the city. Many cities such as Philadelphia, Detroit, and New York, have local income or wage taxes levied on income earned in the city. In addition, most cities levy sales taxes and, in some cases, a variety of user charges, including such things as tolls on bridges and tunnels leading into the city. Less directly, but perhaps at least as important, the use of city facilities by a greater number of suburban residents may increase the level of economic activity in the city and thereby enhance city property values with a corresponding stimulus to city receipts from property taxation. In fact, residential suburbs have been known to claim that the cities take advantage of them by reaping the tax benefits from a high concentration of commercial-industrial property, whereas the suburbs

[12]Advisory Commission on Intergovernmental Relations, *City Financial Emergencies,* Table B–8.

> must service the population (particularly the heavy expense of providing public education). The existence of a positive correlation between central-city expenditures per capita and the fraction of the population living in the suburbs is not convincing evidence for the exploitation thesis.[13]

Central-city decision-makers also argue, and here the evidence is clearer, that suburbanites certainly profit from the concentrations of black poor in the central cities and in part have caused those concentrations through racially discriminatory selling and renting practices and through "large lot" and other zoning policies that have prevented the construction of inexpensive new housing in suburbia. Dick Netzer has explained the impact of this kind of deliberate exclusion of the nonwhite and the impecunious from suburban jurisdictions:

> Locally financed services [in cities with populations over 300,000] which are fairly directly linked to poverty absorbed nearly one-fourth of the big-city property tax revenues in 1964, or one-sixth of their collections of taxes of all types. In a number of the larger metropolitan areas, if the local tax drain due to central city financing of social services were equalized over the entire area, central city tax loads would be well below those elsewhere in the metropolitan areas, rather than above, which is the more usual case.[14]

Some dozen large central cities have, under authority of their state legislatures, imposed local income or wage taxes on commuting suburbanites employed in the city. These include Baltimore, Detroit, St. Louis, New York City, Cleveland, and Philadelphia.[15] But thus far the rates have been too low—the most common rate is 1 percent—to spread to the suburbs in a significant way the central city's burden of servicing the poor and otherwise disadvantaged. Furthermore, each year a decreasing proportion of suburbanites is being employed in central cities as a result of the decentralization of jobs in metropolitan areas.[16] A payroll or income tax on

[13]David F. Bradford and Wallace E. Oates, "Suburban Exploitation of Central Cities," in Harold M. Hochman and George F. Peterson, eds., *Redistribution Through Public Choice* (New York: Columbia University Press, 1974), p. 46.

[14]Dick Netzer, "Financing Urban Government," in James Q. Wilson, ed., *The Metropolitan Enigma* (Cambridge, Mass.: Harvard University Press, 1967), p. 68. See also Dick Netzer, *Economics of the Property Tax* (Washington, D.C.: Brookings Institution, 1973).

[15]Advisory Commission on Intergovernmental Relations, *Federal-State-Local Finances: Significant Features of Fiscal Federalism,* 1973–74 edition (Washington, D.C.: U.S. Government Printing Office, 1974), Table 150, pp. 291–94 and *The Commuter and the Municipal Income Tax* (Washington, D.C.: U.S. Government Printing Office, 1970).

[16]The 1970 census showed that only a 24 percent minority of the working residents of Westchester County, normally considered the epitome of a bedroom commuters' haven, were employed within New York City.

commuters therefore still does not reach all the suburban beneficiaries of the central city's fiscal squeeze while it does provide further incentives for shifting employment out of the central city.

Other devices that would enable the central city to reach the tax resources of the suburbs are (1) expanding city boundaries through annexation or city-county consolidation and (2) establishing a metropolitan taxing district that would collect taxes throughout both the central city and the suburbs and then distribute the revenues according to some formula, presumably based in part on the need of each jurisdiction. The major city-county consolidations in Jacksonville, Nashville, and Indianapolis have been discussed in Chapter 5. Some extensive annexation by central cities has also taken place since 1950, especially in the South and Southwest (e.g., Oklahoma City, Houston, Phoenix, Dallas). But annexation requires either special action by the state legislature or, more typically, the approval in a referendum by the areas to be annexed if they are already incorporated as suburban municipalities. Consequently it has been almost impossible to accomplish by the older cities that are in the most serious economic plight. This is because the older cities in the East and Midwest lack extensive tracts of unincorporated land adjacent to their boundaries and because suburban legislators and voters strenuously object to giving up (by special legislation or by referendum) the small-scale jurisdictional autonomy that is so prized in the suburbs both for its own sake and for any tax advantages it confers. And, in the past decade, black and other minority residents in central cities, who because of their large numbers have achieved or are about to achieve electoral control, have also opposed annexation because of the obvious dilution in their voting power that would result.

Metropolitan taxing districts have usually been favored by central-city decision-makers as a means of redistributing wealth from the "richer" suburbs to the "poorer" central city. But the whole premise of the superior wealth of the suburbs is based on the Census Bureau's practice of comparing the central city with the entire "outside central city" (OCC) part of the metropolitan area. In point of fact, this OCC is never a single governmental jurisdiction. It consists of from one or more counties and scores to hundreds of independent villages, satellite cities, school districts, and other special districts. Some of these jurisdictions are obviously as favorably as or more favorably situated than the OCC median or average figures reported by the Census Bureau and thus would lose in any metropolitan-wide tax that took need into account. Some suburban jurisdictions are, however, in even worse condition than their central city in terms of the mismatch between their service needs and tax base. These jurisdictions would, therefore, have revenues redistributed *to* them by any formula based on need.

A metropolitan taxing district was established recently in the Minneapolis-St. Paul area. Each governmental jurisdiction contributes 40 percent of its property tax receipts attributable to increases of commercial and industrial property within its boundaries. The revenues collected are then redistributed according to a formula based on population and per capita property wealth.[17] The distribution formula has provided the central cities of Minneapolis and St. Paul with only an average share of the metropolitan-wide taxes.

The Bradford and Oates study previously quoted concludes that imposing a metropolitan area-wide, single-rate property tax to finance services for both the central city and suburban area would primarily redistribute income:

> . . . in the short run away from property owners in the suburbs as a group to owners of property in the cities with some longer-run effects probably filtering down to renters in the city. In addition, the shift . . . would generate a considerable redistribution of income among residents of the suburbs, ranging from changes in tax payments for a typical resident . . . from +$226 to −$226. . . . These redistribution effects among suburbs would seem at best to be only very weakly income related. It thus appears that, at least in the short run, the introduction of a metropolitan-wide tax on real property would redistribute income in nontrivial sums but in a rather haphazard way.[18]

Of course, greater and more systematic wealth-related redistributions could take place if the metropolitan area-tax was not based exclusively on property but was, for example, related to income in a progressive manner. Still the redistributions would not all be in favor of the central cities (which is not to say that such area-wide redistributions should not be instituted), since wide disparities also exist among different suburbs. And to the extent that any formula could be developed to simply redistribute revenues from the suburbs to the central city, the same suburban opposition that exists toward annexation would no doubt arise to block that formula's adoption and implementation.

Increasing State and Federal Aid

A second and much more powerful expedient for easing the fiscal bind of large cities is to shift a larger share of the cost of providing services and benefits for the big-city poor to the states and federal government. And, indeed, both the states and the federal government have increased their grants to large cities over the past two decades, both in absolute terms and as a proportion of those cities' general expenditures (See Figure 19–2). These

[17] Schultze et al., *Setting National Priorities: The 1973 Budget,* p. 309.

[18] Bradford and Oates, "Suburban Exploitation," pp. 77–78.

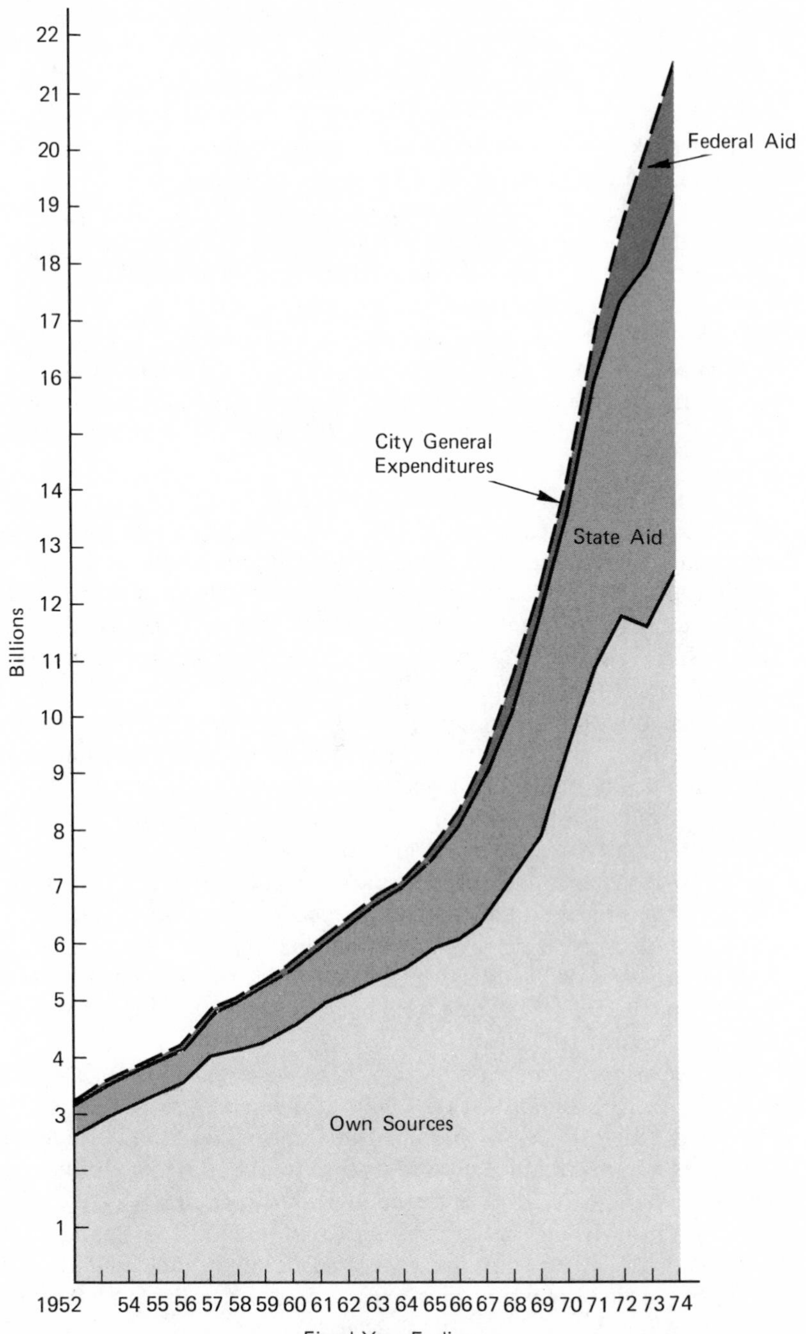

FIGURE 19-2 General Expenditures of Large-City Governments from Own Sources, State Aid, and Federal Aid, 1952–1974 (Cities of Over 300,000 in Population, Excluding Washington, D.C.).

Source: Calculated from U.S. Bureau of the Census, *City Government Finances,* 1951–52 to 1973–74.

higher levels of government can spread the burden of combating urban poverty and slums more widely by using their broader-reaching tax powers to gather funds throughout an entire state or throughout the nation and then redistributing those funds to aid large-city (and other local) governments in the form of grants and shared taxes. And the higher levels of government can directly operate or completely finance welfare and other programs that provide benefits to the poor, such as nonpoverty-related but highly expensive services as education. Throughout the mid- to late 1960s, for example, the Advisory Commission on Intergovernmental Relations advocated that the federal government assume all the costs of public welfare and medicaid and that the state governments assume substantially all the costs of elementary and secondary school education, to be financed in part by state funds thus released.[19]

If higher levels of government expanded their roles as direct deliverers or as "financiers" of some expensive services now provided by cities, the governments of large cities would have additional funds freed for improving nonpoverty-related programs. They would thus be relieved from having to raise local taxes further toward counter-productive levels that would stimulate the move of more affluent families and businesses from central cities to the suburbs.

As between the states and the federal government, it is the federal government that is in the strongest position to raise the large sums required for dramatically improving urban conditions. This is because its revenue system, heavily based on progressive income taxes, is much more highly growth-responsive—producing greater revenues at given rates as the economy expands—than those of most states. Another reason is that the federal government's reach is geographically all-inclusive, so that, unlike the states or cities, it need not fear that tax increases would erode its tax base by driving individuals and businesses to other lower-taxing jurisdictions. Finally, the federal government need not balance its budget each year but can choose to resort to deficit financing.

The federal government did, in fact, increase spending for poverty- and urban-oriented programs in the 1960s at a rapid rate. Further, in 1972 it instituted general revenue-sharing. But the original level of federal assistance was minimal relative both to its own total outlays and to the spending of city governments. And since the increased spending was never concentrated exclusively on the largest cities but extended to smaller cities, to suburbs, and even to rural areas, that spending did not ease the financial plight of the cities in any dramatic way. Direct federal aid to large cities still constituted under 1 percent of total federal outlays in fiscal 1973–74, up from .03 percent in 1951–52. (See Table 19–2.)

[19]See, e.g., Advisory Commission on Intergovernmental Relations, *Urban America and the Federal System* (Washington, D.C.: U.S. Government Printing Office, 1969).

TABLE 19-2 Effort of Federal Government in Direct Grants to Large-City Governments, 1952–1974 (Cities of over 300,000 in Population, Excluding Washington, D.C.)

Fiscal Year Ending	Federal Payments to Cities (thousands of dollars)	Total Federal Outlays (billions of dollars)	Federal Payments As Percent of Outlays
1952	23,147	66.6	.03
1953	27,185	76.2	.04
1956	30,596	69.5	.04
1957	43,422	76.5	.06
1958	47,771	82.8	.06
1959	68,386	90.3	.08
1960	108,816	92.2	.12
1961	123,528	97.8	.13
1962	135,631	106.2	.13
1963	141,512	112.3	.13
1964	152,487	118.6	.13
1965	208,245	118.4	.18
1966	258,830	134.7	.19
1967	386,507	158.3	.24
1968	466,481	178.8	.26
1969	532,635	184.6	.29
1970	606,643	196.6	.31
1971	914,295	211.4	.43
1972	1,244,605	231.9	.54
1973	2,041,957	246.5	.83
1974	2,293,944	268.4	.85

Sources: Calculated from U.S. Bureau of the Census, *City Government Finances,* 1951–52 to 1973–74; and *Statistical Abstract of the United States,* 1952–1975.

There was a time that "massive infusion" into cities of additional federal funds was seen as a feasible and short-term prospect because of the availability of so-called "fiscal dividends." After the federal income tax cut of 1964, Walter W. Heller, then chairman of the Council of Economic Advisors, postulated that with a continuing rapidly-growing economy, the then existing rates of the federal tax system would produce built-in average increases of $7 to $8 billion a year in revenues in excess of those needed to meet rising federal expenditures. This excess of revenues over expenditures constituted a fiscal dividend that would have been available for direct spending or grants. Indeed, this excess revenue would have become an undesirable "drag" on the economy if it were not spent or returned to the taxpayers in further tax cuts.[20] There was at that time considerable discus-

[20]See Walter W. Heller, *New Dimensions of Political Economy* (New York: W.W. Norton, 1967).

sion concerning the possibility that sizable portions of these fiscal dividends could be devoted to alleviating poverty and other urban problems.

Unfortunately for the fiscal state of large cities, the escalation of the war in Vietnam beginning in 1965 absorbed all the expanded revenues that became available. It also caused huge deficits and necessitated the 1968 tax surcharge to raise still greater sums to pay for that war and thus put a heavy damper on any greatly expanded federal spending for urban problems. Even as expenses for the Vietnam war stabilized and began to contract between 1969 and 1972 with the reduction of the American ground force commitment, no fiscal dividends became available to be diverted to urban needs. There are three reasons for this: First, the entire amount of the reduced military expenditures was smaller than the federal deficit. Thus the reduction in defense spending of some $15 billion between fiscal 1970 and fiscal 1973 was not available as a surplus to be spent on urban or poverty programs, but simply kept down what would have been an even more enormous deficit in what was no longer an expanding but a recessionary economy.

Second, the ending of the tax surcharge and the general reduction in personal and corporate income taxes that had been legislated in 1964, 1969, and again in 1971 seriously weakened the previous capacity of the federal revenue-raising system to generate large amounts of new revenues year after year. The Brookings Institution's study of the 1973 budget calculated that as a result of these tax cuts, total federal revenues in 1973 were $26 billion below what they would have been if the 1963 tax rates and provisions had remained in effect. The federal revenue loss would have been substantially greater except that there had also been imposed substantial increases in social security taxes to pay for expanded social security benefits and medicare. The loss in tax collections by 1973 caused by the cuts since 1964 in individual and corporate income taxes and in excise taxes actually came to about $44.6 billion—an amount more than twice as large as the general expenditures of the city government of all forty-eight large cities of over 300,000 in population combined.

Third, just as federal tax collections were showing a substantially smaller automatic annual growth, expenditures for civilian programs, of which urban-oriented and income maintenance "Great Society" grant programs were a big chunk, began in 1965 to increase much more sharply than in the past and than the growth in the nation's economy (measured by its gross national product or GNP). The implication of all these trends for the financial needs of cities was simply that with the existing federal tax structure and even a non-recessionary economy, the projected automatic growth in civilian expenditures alone had begun to exceed the projected annual gain in revenues yielded by economic growth. This meant that any

[21]See Schultze et al., *Setting National Priorities: The 1973 Budget,* "What Happened to the Fiscal Dividend," esp. chap. 12.

new or expanded urban categorical grant programs or increased revenue-sharing could not be funded by the federal government "painlessly" out of fiscal dividends but had to come at the expense of other programs or from a tax increase. There was also a third alternative for the federal government which, unlike city governments, is not required by law to have a balanced budget, and that was financing new and expanded programs through continuous and large budgeted deficits. But that alternative too was not "painless," as it normally caried the possibility of serious inflationary effects.[22]

The 1974 budget reflected the federal government's predicament. There was no "new money" available for increasing urban programs "painlessly" out of fiscal dividends. And even without such new increases, the built-in increases for existing programs seemed likely to produce a large budgetary deficit that would have further fueled that year's already inflationary economy. "This situation left the President with three major options: (1) he could propose a budget that implied a substantial deficit on a full employment basis; (2) he could propose a tax increase; (3) he could cut expenditures."[23] President Nixon chose the third option. Moreover, he imposed the heaviest reductions—about half of his total budget cuts—on the newer urban-oriented programs like manpower-training, education, health care, housing, urban development, social services, and environmental pollution.[24] The 1975 budget reflected the same predicament and the same choices.[25]

President Ford's proposed budget for fiscal 1976, though premised on a planned deficit of about $60 billion because of the severe recession that began in 1974, also did not provide spending increases for poverty- and urban-oriented programs but sought to reduce expenditures in these areas by cutting the federal share of funding for public assistance (welfare) and medicaid and by tightening eligibility for food stamps.[26] The most pessimistic long-term implication for cities in President Ford's fiscal 1976 budget was that it carried long-term commitments both to cut the federal government's overall spending when measured as a proportion of the nation's GNP and to increase the share of federal spending committed to defense. If these two proposed commitments were carried out, federal

[22]See *ibid.*, pp. 411, 423.

[23]Edward R. Fried, Alice M. Rivlin, Charles L. Schultze, and Nancy H. Teeters, *Setting National Priorities: The 1974 Budget* (Washington, D.C.: Brookings Institution, 1974), pp. 11–12.

[24]*Ibid.*, p. 19.

[25]Barry M. Blechman, Edward M. Gramlich, and Robert W. Hartman, *Setting National Priorities: The 1975 Budget* (Washington, D.C.: Brookings Institution, 1975), pp. 34–42.

[26]See Barry M. Blechman, Edward M. Gramlich, and Robert W. Hartman, *Setting National Priorities: The 1976 Budget* (Washington, D.C.: Brookings Institution, 1975), chaps. 1–3.

funding for urban- and poverty-oriented programs would be coming out of a very slowly growing- or constantly shrinking-sized tax pie.

The Brookings study of the 1976 budget projected that if by 1980 the nation reached a full-employment economy with medium growth, a margin of only $21–25 billion would be available by that year for new or expanded programs without deficit spending, though of course much larger amounts would be available if the economy reached full employment and deficit spending were continued.[27] Even if the assumptions on which these projections were based—the most important one being a full-employment economy—held true, there would certainly be competing claims for any margin of uncommitted revenues from a variety of sources, such as the military, possible new energy research-and-development programs, a new national health insurance system, and a variety of other existing or new nonurban-oriented programs. Undoubtedly there would also be demands for making permanent the "temporary" tax cut that was imposed in 1975 to boost the economy and for further general tax reduction, as inflation was forcing people to pay taxes at steadily higher effective rates. The political "clout" of the protax cut forces has been demonstrated in the past to be greater than that of those who urged retaining the old tax rates and the larger fiscal dividends they produced in order to finance new domestic programs. The "clout" of those opposed to tax increases or reforms has been shown to be even stronger. And, of course, the "clout" of those committed to increased expenditures for certain nonurban programs like military spending has also been demonstrated. What part, if any, of the "margins" or fiscal dividends that might be generated would be targeted to help the fiscal plight of large cities and not be given away in tax cuts or diverted to other areas of governmental activity is an open question. For even if the federal tax system did begin again to generate new uncommitted revenues painlessly, the political obstacles that would have to be overcome before those revenues could be diverted to urban programs are many and powerful.

[27] *Ibid.*, Tables 7–9, p. 218.

20

Political Obstacles and Prospects

The most intractable obstacles to improving large-city governmental performance are not epistemological or even fiscal ones. For it is reasonable to assume that a country whose advanced technology can place men on and return them from the moon and design equipment to intercept in mid-air missiles traveling some twenty times the speed of sound can assemble or develop sufficient knowledge to deal successfully with at least the most oppressive symptoms of urban problems, even if not immediately with their underlying causes. And if there were a committed decision to do so, sufficient additional revenues could be extracted from an overall economy of some 1.6 to 1.7 trillion dollars in gross national product to pay for the cost of moving large cities a considerable way toward healthy, multiracial futures. For even if large sums of "free" money did not again become available in the near future through fiscal dividends, reform of or increases in federal taxes that would shift even one or two percent more of the gross national product from private to public spending would make very substantial sums available that could be spent on urban- and poverty-oriented programs.

The most intractable obstacles to improving conditions of large cities are obviously the political ones. That is, those who oppose the courses of action necessary to alleviate city problems have greater political influence than those who support them. This political opposition is directed at three separable aspects of the governmental action required: increasing spending for upgrading housekeeping services and amenities and for eliminating poverty and slums; increasing integration; and reducing crime.

OPPOSITION TO INCREASED SPENDING

Opposition to increased spending for across-the-board upgrading of housekeeping services and amenities comes in the first instance from city officials (like mayors, managers, budget directors, legislators) responsible for approving budgets and raising revenues. Their opposition reflects their perception of the widespread reluctance of city electorates to pay any but the most unavoidable increases in taxes and their fear of causing an even faster erosion of the city's tax base. A survey of ten large cities conducted in 1970 by the Urban Observatory Program found that 87 percent of the respondents felt that the level of their local taxes was "about right" or "too high"; indeed, in four of the cities—Baltimore, Boston, Kansas City, and Milwaukee—majorities of 68, 67, 53, and 67 percent respectively thought that their local taxes were "too high" already.[1] At the height of New York City's summer 1975 budget crisis in the midst of threatened mass layoffs and cutbacks in services, a *New York Times* survey asked whether the city should increase taxes to keep services at the highest possible level or keep taxes as low as possible, even though this might require reductions in services. A clear majority (60.7 percent) favored keeping taxes low and only 17.1 percent favored increasing taxes.[2]

Since all city residents would benefit from improved housekeeping services and amenities, it might appear paradoxical that large segments of that residential population do oppose the increased spending necessary for such improvements. But most city-dwellers seem to have accepted the declining quality of city services in general, however critical they may be of a deficiency in some service of central interest to them, like police protection or schools. The fifteen-city attitude survey conducted by the Survey Research Center for the Kerner Commission found, for example, that when asked about their satisfaction with certain specified housekeeping services and amenities (public schools, parks and playgrounds for children, sports and recreation centers for teenagers, police protection, garbage collection) the proportion of both whites and blacks who were "generally satisfied" and only "somewhat dissatisfied" was larger than those who were "very dissatisfied." Indeed, except for blacks asked about "sports and recreation centers for teenagers," the proportion of those who were generally satisfied exceeded those who were very dissatisfied.[3] Similarly, a survey of police, public school teachers and administrators, social workers, park workers, public and private personnel officers, and retail merchants

[1]Floyd Fowler, Jr., *Citizen Attitudes Toward Local Government Services and Taxes* (Cambridge: Ballinger, 1974), Table 5-1, p. 58.

[2]*New York Times*, July 21, 1975.

[3]Angus Campbell and Howard Schuman, "Racial Attitudes in Fifteen American Cities," in *Supplemental Studies of the National Advisory Commission on Civil Disorders* (New York: Praeger, 1968), Table IV-a, p. 40.

found that in only one city—Newark—did a majority of the sample regard a list of selected problems as being "very serious." The list included problems directly related to city services—i.e., control of crime, air pollution, providing quality education, finding tax funds for municipal services, traffic and highways, preventing violence and other civil disorders, and lack of recreational facilities—and problems with a broader societal base like unemployment, race relations, and corruption of public officials.[4]

The Urban Observatory Program's ten-city survey found that an average of 61 percent responded that their city was "run" in an "excellent" or "very good" or a "good enough" way, while an average of only 35 percent answered that the way it was run was "not so good" or not "good at all." In two cities of the ten surveyed, however, majorities did indicate that the way their city was run was "not so good" or "not good at all"—Boston by 58 percent and Kansas City, Missouri, by 55 percent.[5] Yet, even there, majorities of 89 percent and 83 percent, respectively, maintained that their taxes were "too high" or "about right" and presumably were opposed to higher taxes for better services. Such a position could be reasonably maintained since 70 percent and 62 percent of the respondents in those two cities did not believe they were getting their money's worth for the taxes they were already paying.[6]

In short, when the average large-city-dweller comes to balancing his interest in receiving better quality services and amenities against his other interest in not paying out a sharply larger share of his income in increased taxes, the latter interest normally wins out and thus makes him, on net, an opponent of increased spending. Reaching this "antispending" posture is abetted by his realization that even paying increased taxes probably would not lead to improvements in his neighborhood or in services that he otherwise regards as most important. And it is further buttressed by the assumption that if services become intolerable, he can move to the suburbs where overall services appear to be better and tax dollars seem to have a clearer link to those services he uses.

Opposition to increased spending for any radical improvement of slum conditions and poverty also comes from city officials who have budgetary responsibilities. Once again this reflects their reluctance to risk faster erosion of the tax base and their perception of widespread reluctance among the public to paying increased taxes. The resistance is especially strong when, as in this case, the amount of extra taxes needed would be large and the benefits of slum-and poverty-directed spending would not in any direct tangible sense be broadly shared.

[4]Peter H. Rossi, Richard A. Berk, and Bettye K. Eidson, *The Roots of Urban Discontent: Public Policy, Municipal Institutions, and the Ghetto* (New York: Wiley, 1974), Table 4.4, p. 89.

[5]Computed from Fowler, *Citizen Attitudes,* Table 10–11, p. 213.

[6]*Ibid.,* Tables 5–1, p. 58 and 5–10, p. 69.

Admittedly, the dissatisfaction with conditions among the poor, mostly black residents of big-city slums has been high. But this poor, slum-dwelling population is a minority in every large city and its needs and demands for better city services and facilities are not backed up by a capacity to pay increased taxes for their support. Therefore, these needs and demands can be satisfied only if the broader public is willing to redistribute a larger share of its income for the amelioration of slum conditions. And this the broad publics of large cities have been unwilling to do. The funds for increased spending can come from state-wide or nation-wide publics through the mechanism of state and federal grants and different forms of revenue-sharing. The advantages of providing increased funds to cities from the state and especially from the federal government have already been discussed. But both state and federal officials and state and federal publics have—except in the rare periods discussed in Chapter 6—also been opposed to transferring increasingly larger amounts of tax dollars to the increasingly smaller minority of the American population that lives within large cities and to the minority of that minority which is poor and black. For it is important to recognize that despite much talk of ours being an increasingly urban nation, in reality it is "urban" only in the sense of being "metropolitan-area living," but not in the sense of being "big-city living." While, according to the 1970 census, 69 percent of all Americans lived in metropolitan areas, only 31 percent lived in the central city portions while 38 percent lived in the "outside central city" or suburban portions. The 31 percent included all those living in cities of 50,000 and larger and represented a decline from 33 percent in 1960 and 35 percent in 1950.[7] (See Figure 20–1.)

When one looks at how many Americans in 1970 lived in really large cities, one finds that only 21 percent lived in cities of one-quarter million and larger, 16 percent resided in cities of half-million and larger, and a mere 9 percent in the cities with populations of a million or over.[8] Furthermore, the census figures show that of the white population only 24 percent lived in cities of 50,000 and larger, and only 17 percent in the central cities of metropolitan areas of 500,000 and up.[9] Finally, national surveys show that only a small and decreasing minority of the population—22 percent in 1966, 17 percent in 1971, and 13 percent in 1972—express a preference for living in a city as opposed to a suburb, small town, or farm.[10]

[7]U.S. Bureau of the Census, *Statistical Abstract of the United States, 1973,* (Washington, D.C.: U.S. Government Printing Office, 1973). Tables 16 and 22.

[8]*Ibid.*

[9]U.S. Bureau of the Census, Census of Population and Housing: 1970, *General Demographic Trends for Metropolitan Areas, 1960–1970,* Final Report PHC(2)-1 (Washington, D.C.: U.S. Government Printing Office, 1971), Tables 1, 9.

[10]*Gallup Opinion Index,* March 1966, August 1971, and December 1972.

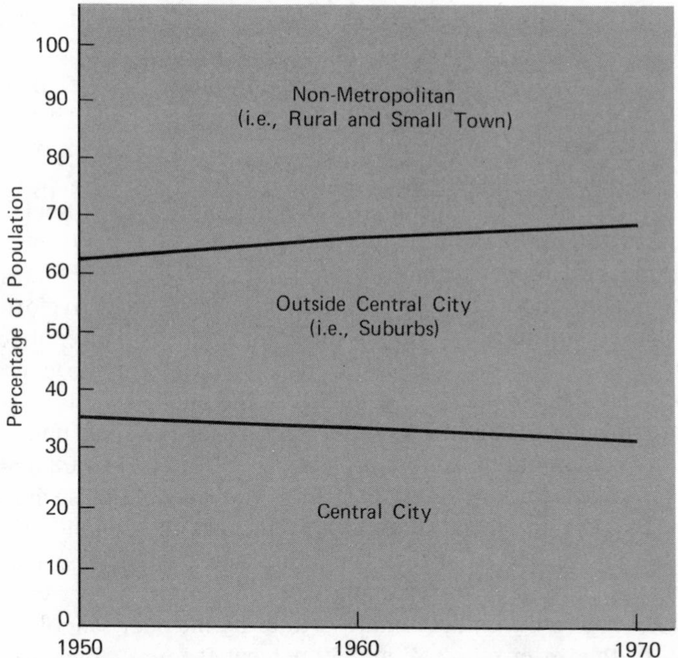

FIGURE 20-1 Distribution of Population by Place of Residence: Central City, Outside Central City, and Nonmetropolitan, 1950–1970.

Source: Calculated from U.S. Bureau of the Census, *Statistical Abstract of the United States, 1973,* Tables 16 and 22.

Since, if fiscal dividends were ever to reappear, federal spending for cities could expand without any tax increases, it is important to establish whether political opposition to such spending is based on factors other than money cost. Nation-wide, such nonmonetary opposition to increased federal spending for cities appears to result from the "optimistic denial" by most Americans of the seriousness of the urban situation and from the failure to recognize the consequences of present trends. Such optimistic denial was found to be widespread even in the late 1960s when riots were occurring in the ghettoes of large cities.[11] Since that time it has become even easier to pursue "optimistic denial"; as large-scale riots have ceased an eminent urban scholar can write that "the plain fact is that the overwhelming majority of city dwellers live more comfortably and conveniently than ever

[11]Peter H. Rossi, Richard A. Berk, David P. Boesel, Bettye K. Eidson, and W. Eugene Groves, "Between White and Black: The Faces of American Institutions in the Ghetto," in *Supplemental Studies for the National Advisory Commission on Civil Disorders,* (New York: Praeger, 1968), p. 73.

before, and that by any conceivable measure of material welfare, the present generation of urban Americans is, on the whole, better off than any other large group of people has ever been anywhere;''[12] a key presidential advisor can express a policy toward slum-dwellers of ''benign neglect,''[13] and two presidents can simply declare that the ''urban crisis'' is over.[14]

The opinion data suggest that there is probably little ideological opposition, i. e., opposition in principle, to spending more money for improving the minimal *physical* conditions of slum ghettoes, providing jobs for the unemployed, and improving basic services like schools.[15] There does appear to be ideological opposition, however, among federal executive officials in Republican administrations, among the great majority of Republican and southern Democratic members of Congress who form the conservative coalition, and also among large segments of the public to federal spending for improving the social and political standing of the slum poor by such measures as community action programs, increased welfare payments, negative income taxes, or rent supplements. Many people see such measures as giving the poor too much of an improvement in their quality of life and social standing beyond what they earn with their own efforts. The Survey Research Center found, for example, that 78 percent of a white sample favored government providing money ''to bring the poor schools up to the standard of the better schools'' and 59 percent favored money to provide extra jobs needed to help improve the housing in rundown and overcrowded areas. But the same SRC survey found that only 17 percent believed the ''antipoverty program'' was ''doing a good job''[16] and only 19 percent believed that ''on the average,'' blacks had ''worse jobs, education and housing than white people'' mainly because of ''discrimination.''[17] Similarly, 1972 Harris polls found that 89 percent of the public supported the proposition that the federal government ''provide jobs for the unemployed'' and 70 percent agreed that ''low income people will never have adequate housing unless the federal government pays some of the cost. . .''—questions that went more to tangible benefits. On the other hand, the Harris organization also found that 88 percent favored ''making people on welfare go to work,''[18] 57 percent thought ''blacks were asking far more than they were ready for,''

[12]Edward C. Banfield, *The Unheavenly City Revisited* (Boston: Little, Brown, 1974), pp. 1-2.

[13]That term was used by President Nixon's advisor, Daniel P. Moynihan, in 1970. For a copy of his memorandum, see *Congressional Quarterly Weekly Report,* March 6, 1970, pp. 672–73.

[14]See ''President [Nixon] Finds End of City Crisis,'' *New York Times,* March 4, 1973, and ''Urban Crisis of the 1960s Is Over, Ford Aides Say,'' *New York Times,* March 23, 1975.

[15]See Campbell and Schuman, ''Racial Attitudes,'' Tables III–s, III–t, III–u, pp. 36–37; Louis Harris, *The Anguish of Change* (New York: W. W. Norton, 1973), esp. chap. 8.

[16]Campbell and Schuman, ''Racial Attitudes,'' Table IV–e, p. 41.

[17]*Ibid.,* Table III–d, p. 30.

[18]Harris, *Anguish,* p. 120.

and 52 percent believed "blacks were trying to move too fast in their push for equality,"[19] thus still indicating the existence of substantial opposition to benefiting the poor and blacks when the improvements suggested were vague and could be interpreted as connoting social equality. As could be expected, this opposition is strongest among those segments of the population closest in income, education, and status to those who would receive the benefits of these latter measures.

OPPOSITION TO INCREASED INTEGRATION

Discrimination and segregation in housing or schools is, of course, already illegal. Moreover, opinion polls in 1972 found that 68 percent of all whites felt that "one of my fondest hopes is that housing be desegregated in America," and 71 percent said, "one of my fondest hopes is that the public schools all over the country be desegregated."[20] The political opposition that exists concerning increased integration is directed against such implementational measures as rigorous enforcement of open housing laws to permit blacks to have an equal chance to obtain vacancies in white, nonslum central-city or suburban neighborhoods; the construction of "scattered-site" housing projects that are expected to have a black clientele in or adjoining such white neighborhoods; and pairing of schools, using busing or other plans for exchanging black and white children from all-white and all-black neighborhoods in such a way as to produce integrated schools.

Part of the opposition to this kind of intergration measures may be the result of white racism—the desire to avoid contact with blacks because of hostility or the belief that they are inherently inferior beings. Various opinion surveys still pick up what appears to be an irreducible hard core of whites who are willing to tell interviewers that they agree that "whites have a right to keep Negroes out of their neighborhoods" (30 percent),[21] they would "mind a lot" "if a Negro family with about the same income and education . . . moved next door" (19 percent);[22] they are opposed to "laws to prevent discrimination against Negroes in job hiring and promotion" (19 percent);[23] and they would prefer that their small children "had only white friends" (33 percent).[24] But the proportion that espouses such attitudes decreases with age,[25] and all organizations which have repeated similar surveys over time have found that the percentage of Americans that subscribes

[19]*Ibid.*, pp. 234–35.
[20]*Ibid.*, p. 231.
[21]Campbell and Schuman, "Racial Attitudes," Table III-h, p. 32.
[22]*Ibid.*, Table III-k, p. 33.
[23]*Ibid.*, Table III-l, p. 33.
[24]*Ibid.*, Table III-o, p. 34.
[25]See *ibid.*, pp. 34–35.

to a racist view is a constantly shrinking minority.[26] Aberbach and Walker have summed up the evidence:

> . . . the "respectability" of prejudice has declined since World War II and people (especially the educated) are often embarrassed to give illiberal answers to questions about race. Even if not deep seated, these feelings are important since people tend to behave in accordance with them. Related to this are the effects of the Supreme Court decisions, Executive Orders, and statutes which have steadily eroded legal discrimination. Changes in the law have required changes in behavior in many areas, and these eventually have led to changes in attitude. . . . Intertwined with the other factors cited, is the impact of age and education. "Younger and better educated whites [are generally] more tolerant and favorable to integration [than] the older and less educated." Since the young are better educated than their parents, the long-term trend toward liberal racial attitudes should remain as the general level of educational attainment increases.[27]

Most political opposition to residential integration comes not from those whites who are racist but from that much larger group who incorrectly attribute to all blacks the life style of lower-class slum-dwellers. "Integration" to these whites consequently means an increase in street crime, a deterioration in the learning atmosphere in their neighborhood schools, and, in general, a reduction in their ability to remain "culturally dominant" where they live. There is also the fear that even a small amount of integration will inevitably result in a complete black takeover of a neighborhood. This opposition to integration is strongest in those central-city neighborhoods closest to the ghettoes,[28] where class differences between whites and blacks are minimal, status anxieties among whites are maximum, and the fear is most widespread that complete black takeovers might necessitate moving out of neighborhoods in which the whites have deep roots and long-term social ties.

The pressure of blacks to move into all-white central-city neighborhoods would be reduced if the black population were "suburbanizing" at the same rate as whites. But there is also opposition to measures that would promote

[26]See Harris, *Anguish,* pp. 236–37; Hazel Erskine, "The Polls: Negro Housing," *Public Opinion Quarterly,* 31 (1967):485; Herbert Hyman and Paul Sheatsley, "Attitudes Toward Desegregation," *Scientific American,* July 1964, pp. 2–9; Joel D. Aberbach and Jack L. Walker, *Race in the City* (Boston: Little, Brown, 1973), esp. chap. 5.

[27]Aberbach and Walker, *Race in the City,* p. 150, footnote references omitted.

[28]A late 1966 Harris survey found, for example, that while 52 percent of a white national sample would be "upset" by Negroes moving into their neighborhood, this percentage rose to 76 percent among whites living in areas where Negroes would actually like to move. William Brink and Louis Harris, *Black and White* (New York: Simon and Schuster, 1966), p. 109.

such suburbanization. Although some of the opposition is based on racism, the larger part is probably based on fear that large-scale suburbanization of blacks would simply transfer the problems of large cities to the suburbs. For it would take a five- to ten-fold increase in the current growth rate of the black suburban population to slow down or stop further ghettoization of central cities.

It should be noted that some well-educated and higher-income blacks living in large cities also oppose various integration measures.[29] This opposition appears to be based on a positive desire to have large cities become black ghettoes. Some of this desire is motivated by black racism or a commitment to separatism. Another part is based on the expectation of greater opportunities for blacks to capture top political offices and take over other major institutions in central cities that are heavily black. It is this kind of thinking that causes most black spokesmen to oppose plans for metropolitan consolidation, since such consolidation would effectively dilute the heavy electoral impact the concentrated black vote now enjoys in many central cities.

Given the reality of mostly all-white or all-black neighborhoods both in central cities and suburbs, the inevitable result is all-white or all-black neighborhood public schools. Those committed to integrated schools either on ideological grounds or because they believe such schools will provide a better learning environment for children have therefore turned to busing as a means of promoting integrated schools while residential patterns remain nonintegrated. Busing allows children to go to schools outside of their immediate neighborhoods, and busing plans calculated to promote integration essentially consist of some combination of transferring children from previously heavily- or all-white schools to previously heavily- or all-black schools and vice versa. These transfers across nonintegrated residential neighborhoods can be used to create racially mixed student bodies.

Intense political opposition exists among whites against any busing of their children away from their neighborhoods to heavily black schools. A national Harris survey in 1972 found that 82 percent of all whites "opposed busing school children to achieve racial balance." According to Harris:

> The reasons for the opposition were twofold:
>
> (1) White parents were worried that their children would be shipped considerable distances and with a loss of time to inner city areas where their physical safety might be in jeopardy;
>
> (2) Whites were also worried their children would wind up going to inferior black schools.[30]

[29]Thirteen percent of the SRC sample expressed a preference to live in a neighborhood of all Negroes or mostly Negroes. Campbell and Schuman, "Racial Attitudes," Table II–a, p. 15.

[30]Harris, *Anguish,* p. 244.

Substantial opposition to busing was also found among blacks, as "no more than 50 percent . . . favored busing to achieve desegregation."[31] Some black parents worried about the safety of their children as a token minority in previously all-white schools[32], while others apparently thought such busing antithetical to their growing "concern with black culture, black solidarity, and the improvement of the facilities and institutions in the areas now inhabited by blacks."[33]

The opposition to busing among whites was considerably less—only 46 percent—when that busing was one-way, bringing black children to white schools without transporting any white children elsewhere.[34]

OPPOSITION TO REDUCTION OF CRIME

There is obviously no significant political opposition to the principle of reducing crime. But there are constellations of attitudes that constitute political obstacles to bringing about such a reduction, and these obstacles come from three diverse sources: the "antispenders," the police, and the slum-ghetto population.

Slum conditions are not, of course, a sufficient cause for engaging in street crime or mass violence like rioting. Some slum-ridden cities experienced no major riots even in the 1960s, and majorities of slum populations probably never have engaged in street crime. Yet, whatever the exact connection, living in slums within the "culture of poverty" is highly conducive to criminal activity and generates an underlying reservoir of grievances that has provided fuel for mass disorders.[35] Thus those who oppose spending for drastic amelioration of slums and poverty are preventing the removal of one basic cause of street crime and mass violence. Opposition to spending also blocks efforts to reduce crime in much more direct ways: It prevents the expenditure of the large additional sums of money necessary for strengthening the law enforcement system through the expansion of police forces, the addition of more prosecutors and judges to cut down court congestion and various forms of undesirable plea-bargaining, and the expansion and improvement of correctional institutions to give them the capacity not only to incarcerate but also to rehabilitate convicted criminals.[36]

[31] *Ibid.*
[32] *Ibid.*
[33] Aberbach and Walker, *Race in the City,* p. 151.
[34] Harris, *Anguish,* p. 244.
[35] See U.S. National Advisory Commission on Civil Disorders, *Report* (New York: Bantam, 1968), esp. chap. 4.
[36] See President's Commission on Law Enforcement and the Administration of Justice, *The Challenge of Crime in a Free Society* (Washington D.C.: U.S. Government Printing Office, 1967), esp. chaps. 4–6.

The police themselves provide an obstacle to the reduction of crime by the generalized hostility many feel toward slum-ghetto-dwellers,[37] especially those who defy or sometimes even question police authority. Some policemen act out their hostility against black slum-dwellers by using insulting or abusive language or unnecessary force during routine police contact and chance encounters. Some have lost self-control when faced with rioting or nonviolent protest demonstrations and have employed excessive gunfire that injured or killed innocent parties, and some, on occasion, have engaged in what essentially were "police riots" against demonstrators.

Unauthorized verbal and physical abuses and excesses by police are no less illegal than violence engaged in by regular criminals. Furthermore, the resentments and hatreds generated by police brutality stimulate retaliatory sniping and other violence against police, and interferes with the kind of cooperation from the community that could help the police reduce street crime.

A political obstacle to the reduction of crime that is closely related to the hostility police feel toward slum ghetto-dwellers is the hostility that the slum ghetto community feels toward the police. A part of this hostility is generated by the low level of protection against victimization afforded to ghetto residents and by police abuses.[38] However, a larger part of the ghetto community's hostility is misdirected. The police become the target for grievances felt against the city government's failure to improve conditions, simply because police officers in the slums are the city's most visible and continuously available representatives. And there is evidence to indicate that the more police use vigorous techniques, such as "aggressive patrolling," in order to offer better protection, the more the noncriminal residents feel they are being abused.[39] As a result of the hostility felt against them, even when police are engaged in perfectly proper actions in black neighborhoods such as stopping a speeding motorist or raiding an illegal business or intervening to stop a fight, bystanders will frequently treat the police officer as an enemy. They may verbally taunt him, throw rocks, or even physically interfere to prevent his carrying out a valid arrest.

This kind of lack of support of, indiscriminate hostility toward, and sometimes actual interference with the police when performing their legal duties has in the past served as a precipitating factor to mass disorders. But more importantly, it predictably increases the sense of threat police feel in the ghetto and strengthens their belief that slum-dwellers are not really interested in better police protection. These feelings in turn further

[37]See Rossi et al., "Between White and Black," chaps. 5 and 6.

[38]See Campbell and Schuman, "Racial Attitudes," Tables IV–f, g, h, and i, pp. 42–43; and Fowler, *Citizen Attitudes,* p. 165.

[39]See Rossi et al., *The Roots of Urban Discontent,* pp. 193ff.

stimulate the hostility of the police toward the black community as a whole and make the police less likely to act in a restrained manner—all of which adversely affect both the incentive and capacity of the police to control street crime in the ghetto.

PROSPECTS FOR OVERCOMING POLITICAL OBSTACLES

In the America of the 1970s is there any possibility for overcoming the political opposition that currently exists to spending massively larger amounts of money on the problems of cities, to racially integrating central-city neighborhoods and schools while stimulating large numbers of central-city blacks to resettle in almost exclusively white suburbia, and to reducing crime by attacking both its causes and symptoms and without simultaneously curtailing nonviolent dissent, civil liberties, and procedural due process? Realistically speaking, the answer is "no." And it will remain "no" unless there develops a conscious and deliberate long-term national commitment to help large cities much like the long-term commitments made to rebuild the European economy after World War II through the Marshall Plan, to build a massive system of interstate highways, and to develop a space program and place a man on the moon. And in order to succeed, it is probably necessary that an expanded national commitment to aid cities be part of a still larger one aimed at eliminating poverty and improving the quality of life of the entire less-affluent third of the population, whether urban or rural, black or white.

The supportive constituency for a commitment to the package of policies and programs needed to move large cities toward healthy, multiracial futures is potentially broad. In terms of individuals and groups who stand to gain specific, tangible benefits, such a constituency would include:

Black slum-dwellers looking to improved incomes and better living conditions.

Other urban and rural poor, currently largely ignored, who would benefit from any general upgrading of incomes and quality of life for the nonaffluent.

Local and state elective and appointive officeholders, whose fiscal capacity to cope with demands and problems in their jurisdictions would be enhanced by federal absorption of more or all of the cost of welfare and poverty programs.

Large-city downtown retailers, bankers, utility and newspaper owners, restaurant, hotel, and theater operators, and other similar businessmen whose enterprises are largely "locked in" the central-city downtown areas and whose economic success and survival depend on a healthy central city.

White upper-middle and upper-income devotees of apartment or townhouse big-city living, whose enjoyment would be increased by greater safety on the streets and by greater assurance that slum sights would not be spilling over into their neighborhoods.

Middle-income blacks who would experience a much wider choice of housing in middle-income neighborhoods safely distant from slum ghettoes.

Middle-income white suburbanites who prefer big-city living and who, with improved safety and quality of public schools, might again indulge these preferences.

White blue-collar and white-collar workers, who could see increased long-term security through "managed integration" against massive transition of their neighborhoods and could also expect improved city housekeeping services, once poverty-related costs were absorbed by the federal government.

White or black suburbanites who commute to or want to patronize the stores and the recreational or cultural facilities of the large city and whose safety and enjoyment would be better protected by "healthy, multiracial," central-city conditions.

Persons who are highly disturbed by crime, forcible demonstrations, riots, and lootings, and would thus approve of the strengthened law enforcement parts of the "healthy city" strategy.

Incumbent national politicians of high visibility and from competitive constituencies, particularly the President, but also House members of the President's party, who know that their reputations and reelection prospects will suffer if large-scale outbreaks of violence were to take place during their own or their party's administration.

On a higher level of generality, support for the package of policies and programs conducive to progress toward healthy, multiracial cities would come also from all whites and blacks who, regardless of actual place of residence, are ideologically or emotionally attached to large cities. These are the people who regard large cities as the nation's traditional centers of population, business, and culture and oppose their becoming deteriorating slum ghettoes.

Finally, on the highest level of generality, a supportive constituency for healthy, multiracial cities may be found in the great mass of middle-class Americans whose feelings of humanitarianism, justice, and fairness make them want to help the underprivileged and guarantee a minimally decent standard of living for everybody. These Americans would not feel comfortable with the prospects of an increasingly racially-segregated society. They may have a positive ideological commitment to racial equality and feel moral guilt over the inequality that would be inherent in such separation. Or they may simply recognize that allowing large cities to drift into "slum ghettoes" and improving public order exclusively through strengthened law enforcement do not solve the problems of cities or race, but merely postpone their solution until some time when their dimensions are still larger. Certainly the findings that two-to-one and three-to-one nationwide and big-city majorities have favored "large-scale governmental work projects to give jobs to *all* the umemployed;" "federal programs to tear down ghettoes in cities;" "money (from the government) to bring the poorer schools up to the standard of the better schools;" "government money to help improve housing where the housing is rundown and over-crowded;" "a program of spending more money for jobs, schools, and housing for Negroes . . . to prevent riots;"—all these findings give grounds for optimism that such underlying feelings and recognition exist.[40] Perhaps the single most optimistic survey finding is that even at the height of the major riots, white majorities by five-to-one expressed the view that "thinking about the next five to ten years . . . the best thing to do about the problem of riots" was *not* simply to "build up tighter police control in the Negro areas," but to "try harder to improve the condition of the Negroes" or to "do both."[41]

To say that this kind of generalized support for the "healthy, multiracial city" future is potentially forthcoming assumes that most white Americans, particularly younger, middle-class, and college-educated white Americans, are not unmitigated racists. Admittedly, they are limited in the extent to which they are enthusiastic about converting their humanitarian feelings into actual sacrifices of cash for the benefit of the black poor and downtrodden. And a few might still harbor irrational prejudices against certain kinds of very close social contacts with blacks. But there is no evidence to show that most white Americans are strongly hostile to black people per se and firmly committed to keeping them in a position of permanent economic and social separation and inferiority, while there is much evidence to the contrary. In this respect it was probably a mistake for the Kerner Commission to refer to the racial prejudice interfering with black advancement by the term "white racism," with its strong connotation that prejudice is an inherent characteristic of all whites, all-encompassing in the relationships to which it attaches, and somehow fundamental and unchanging.

Whether or not the broad array of individuals, groups, and publics with tangible, ideological, and moral stakes in a healthy, multiracial city future can be mobilized and their combined resources be brought to bear in support of the strategy necessary to bring it about is an open question. The

[40]See Harris polls reported in Erskine, "The Polls," and Campbell and Schuman, "Racial Attitudes."

[41]Campbell and Schuman, "Racial Attitudes," Table III–w, p. 37.

answer will depend in great part on what kind of leadership is forthcoming, especially from national political officials, but also from large-city mayoralties, from universities, from the mass media, and from business leaders. Such leadership would have to capture the attention and sympathetic understanding of the American public so as to dispel its optimistic denial and benign neglect, by educating it about the harsh realities of the current urban situation and about the even harsher likely consequences of allowing existing trends to continue. It would also have to restore confidence in the efficacy of governmental action by explaining that strategies, policies, and programs do exist that when managed effectively and funded at a sufficiently high level can ameliorate current conditions and shift adverse trends.[42]

Probably only the President is capable of this kind of instructional role. For only he can command the widespread and sustained attention that is necessary for developing broad support for a complex and expensive set of policies and programs. The most important targets of his instruction must be that small stratum of politically active or attentive individuals who have disproportionately large influence over governmental decisions. This includes enough of the 435 members of the House of Representatives and the 100 members of the Senate to constitute solid working majorities in Congress for authorization of necessary programs and the appropriation of sufficient funds.

The answer to whether the supportive coalition for a healthy, multiracial city future can develop also depends on the presence of strong, responsible, and courageous black leadership that will explain to the black community other harsh realities of the situation: that black time perspectives need to be lengthened as dramatic short-term improvements in the most oppressive physical conditions of slums are technically impossible to bring about regardless of the sincerity and magnitude of the effort made; that any reemergence of widespread extremist antiwhite rhetoric or outbursts of large-scale mass riots or guerrilla-type violence are almost certain to produce a counterproductive white backlash. For such rhetoric and violence by blacks breed anxiety and hostility among whites, inevitably contract support for ameliorative urban policies, and provide backing for political leadership that is oriented toward responding to urban problems solely by imposing order through repressive force. The Harris organization concluded that the reactions of most whites to the rioting of the 1960s was "high fury and indignation" and that the feeling evoked by the rioting was that:

[42]For evidence that within the limits of its expenditures, the Johnson Administration's "Great Society" programs did produce significant benefits for the poor and for cities, see Sar. A. Levitan and Robert Taggart, *The Promise of Greatness* (Cambridge: Harvard University Press, 1976).

> Negroes are not stable in character, want black power to the exclusion of white power, and have an avaricious tendency to want something for nothing. It is hard to conceive of a set of episodes better designed to bring forth from white people all their worst possible prejudices about Negroes than riots.[43]

How receptive white or black publics would be if the correct kind of leadership emerged depends on a number of factors: If national and city officials were making clear that they regarded the problems of cities as urgent even if no mass guerrilla violence was taking place; if reasonable demands of responsible, nonviolent, nonseparatist black leaders were being met; and if ameliorative change—especially toward the complete elimination of discrimination in housing, employment, and elections to political Offices—were taking place, the vast majority of the urban black community may well accede to pleas for patience. More importantly, if the national economy was experiencing rapid economic growth and the nation was not engaged in large-scale military operations, the dominant majority of the public might well provide support for or at least tolerate decisions by officials in the White House, in Congress, in various city halls, and in state houses to engage in an overall national commitment to achieve a healthy future for large cities. Under these circumstances the real income of almost all people would—as in the 1960s—be rising, thus helping them to feel generous. In addition the monetary costs of the new programs could be borne painlessly out of the fiscal dividends that would again be generated be the federal tax system. Finally the expanding number of jobs in a growth economy would reduce the numbers of unemployed and underemployed and thus decrease the magnitude of the governmental effort required to deal with urban poverty.

But if the national economy should be less prosperous so that because of inflation or recession or a combination of the two, real incomes were not rising, or fiscal dividends were unavailable or being consumed by major new weapons procurement programs or by expansion of nonurban and nonpoverty-related domestic programs, the costs of achieving the healthy, multiracial future for large cities would fall more painfully on its potential supportive constituency. Increased taxes might then be required to finance that healthy future and, depending on how fast personal incomes were rising relative to inflation, cuts in existing standards of living might even be necessary. Sustained support for any national commitment to improve the conditions of large cities would then depend on how successful political and other leaders were in convincing the more affluent two-thirds of the American public to sacrifice some personal income for a society whose cities would be healthy and multiracial and whose poor no longer had to live under conditions that might nauseate the average member of the middle class. And

[43]Brink and Harris, *Black and White,* pp. 122–23.

success in that task would depend ultimately on how receptive most Americans were to the idea that in such a society, a somewhat smaller income could actually lead to a more enjoyable life than a larger income in a society whose poor continued to live in degrading circumstances and where its large cities has become slum ghettoes, whether of the quiescent or explosive tinderbox variety. While it is far from certain, it is not inconceiveable that enough Americans might prove receptive.

Index